BRINGING
THE WAR HOME

by

William Thomas

ISBN 1-890693-24-3

Cover Art Design and Layout by: Jennifer Long

Maps and illustrations by:

William Thomas and Paul Grignon

First Printing

Printed in the United States of America

Anchorage, Alaska

Earthpulse Press Incorporated
P. O. Box 201393
Anchorage, Alaska   99520

for Angela, who took me in from the storm

TABLE OF CONTENTS

Title Page

Biography

Dedication

Maps

PART III: MICRO-HUNTERS

MAPS

Euphrates R.

Iran

Tigris R.

As Samawah

Iraq

An Nasiriyah

Khamisiyah

Rumayah

Wadi al Batin

Kuwait City

fallout

Saudi Arabia

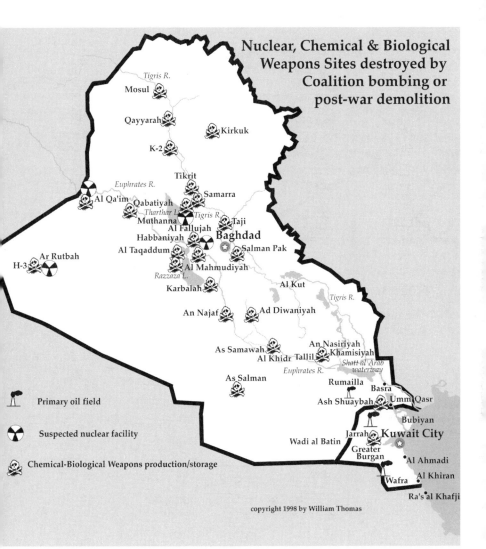

Nuclear, Chemical & Biological Weapons Sites destroyed by Coalition bombing or post-war demolition

Tigris R.

Mosul

Qayyarah

Kirkuk

K-2

Tikrit

Euphrates R.

Al Qa'im

Samarra

Qabatiyah

Tharthar L.

Tigris R.

Muthanna

Taji

Al Fallujah

Habbaniyah

Baghdad

Al Taqaddum

Salman Pak

H-3

Ar Rutbah

Al Mahmudiyah

Razzaza L.

Karbalah

Al Kut

An Najaf

Ad Diwaniyah

Tigris R.

As Samawah

Al Khidr

Tallil

An Nasiriyah

Khamisiyah

Euphrates R.

Shatt al Arab waterway

As Salman

Rumailla

Basra

Primary oil field

Ash Shuaybah

Umm Qasr

Suspected nuclear facility

Bubiyan

Jarrah

Kuwait City

Wadi al Batin

Greater Burgan

Chemical-Biological Weapons production/storage

Al Ahmadi

Wafra

Al Khiran

Ra's al Khafji

copyright 1998 by William Thomas

SYRIA

Baghdad

IRAN

JORDAN

IRAQ

Kuwait City

KUWAIT

Hafar al Batin

Safaniya

Karan

SAUDI ARABIA

Al Jubayl

Damman
Manama

Dhahran

Qatar

Riyadh

SCUD missile attacks,
Kuwait Theater Operations

AUTHOR'S BIOGRAPHY

William Thomas was born in Grand Rapids, Michigan in 1948. He is an independent journalist who learned his craft on the streets of Milwaukee and Chicago in the mid-1960s. Mr. Thomas is also the author of *SCORCHED EARTH: The Military's War Against the Environment,* published by New Society Publishers in December, 1994. Mr. Thomas' writing and photography have appeared in more than 55 publications with translations into French, Dutch and Japanese. Specializing in environmental reporting, he is a regular contributor to *Monday* and *Ecodecision* magazines.

William Thomas won the 1989 Western Canada Magazine Award for "Best Feature", the 1990 Canadian Weekly Periodicals "Best Feature Award" and the 1997 British Columbia and Yukon Community Newspaper Award for "Excellence in Outdoor Writing." His 30-minute Gulf war documentary – "Eco War," won the United States Environmental Film Festival Award for "Best Documentary Short" in 1991.

William Thomas is a Canadian citizen currently residing and working in the Gulf Islands of British Columbia, Canada.

William Thomas may be reached at:
www.islandnet.com/~wilco.html

A special thanks to the veterans,
doctors, researchers and journalists who
contributed to this book – a book intended to
give them a voice which will always be heard.

PART I

THE WAR THAT
WOUNDED THE WORLD

CHAPTER 1.

THE GENERAL

It begins like a storm at sea. Out of a stillness deeper than held breath, dust-devils awaken and begin dancing across an ocean of dunes. Appearing suddenly, only to die away, the spouts of swirling sand spook the great raptors who break off their thermal soaring and flee. The rapidly darkening horizon advances so swiftly, any human trespasser caught in the open has time only to hunker within the lee of a camel or truck as the first probing gusts become a shriek that flings sand like spindrift across the face of the sky. Blowing sand, fine as talcum, replaces air. Heaping in drifts, it quickly smothers uniformed men and their hulking war machines.

No stranger to the Middle East, the general commanding his own Desert Storm knew that the desert winds belonged to Allah. Battle tanks heavy as small houses, with uranium armor capable of shrugging off exploding shells while surfing over the crests of dunes, could be brought to a grinding halt as transmissions and turrets clogged with grains of sand. Advanced tactical aircraft made nearly sentient with infrared, laser and radar sensors would be blinded, then grounded by the same but coarser silicon that formed their circuitry. While his troops cursed the blowing sands and lightning armored thrusts disintegrated in breakdowns and phantom contacts, soldiers more accustomed to the desert and less dependent on electronics would be waiting to extract their vengeance like the cruel Caliph conquerors of ancient Baghdad.

The shamal winds were more worrying than his Iraqi counterpart. Saddam Hussein was no more a general than a man who bought his badges of rank at an army surplus store. "As far as Saddam Hussein being a great military strategist," the general enjoyed telling reporters, "he is neither a strategist, nor is he schooled in the operational art, nor is he a tactician, nor is he a general, nor is he a soldier. Other than that, he's a great military man."

It was true that Iraq boasted the world's fourth largest army. But it was a Third World army, locked in a bygone era, unable even to defeat barefoot boys waving sticks as Iranian Imams urged them into martyrdom by clearing minefields with their feet. During the decisive al Fao campaign, Iraqi armor had maneuvered and fought well. The T-72s were good tanks. And the Soviet doctrine that went with them had defeated Hitler's Panzers.

But it was the profligate use of chemical weapons that finally turned that eight year bloodletting in Iraq's favor. A UN Special Commission report put it best: "During the latter stages of the war, Iraq apparently used chemical weapons whenever it was considered tactically appropriate. Iraq was not at all constrained in its use of chemical weapons."

No, it was not Saddam the generalissimo who worried him. It was Saddam the thug, armed with the dirtiest weapons ever devised, and the willingness to throw them in the faces of his former friends that haunted the coalition commander's dreams.

He would have to wind up this waiting war soon. Before the shamal blew in earnest. Before the Islamic fasting period of Ramadan further tested the resolve of his shaky Arab allies. Political pressure was also mounting back home. Faced with their president's sudden call-up of hundreds of thousands of reservists, a patriotic populace had rallied behind its own. Yellow ribbons had blossomed like bright fall flowers on porches and church steeples across the country.

But congress might not wait for either Ramadan or the shamal to pull the plug on an impending war whose necessity and cost so sharply divided senators, representatives and their constituents. Only a last-minute publicity stunt by the world's biggest PR firm had persuaded lawmakers and taxpayers to spill American blood and treasure in a country most could not find on a map.

Kuwait's royal family had gotten their $11 million worth. In one of the slickest public relations coups ever perpetrated, Hill & Knowlton arranged the testimony of a mysterious teenager named "Nayirah" before the Congressional Human Rights Caucus. The sight of a sobbing 15 year old tearfully telling how she had watched Iraqi soldiers pull infants from their incubators in a Kuwait City hospital and leave them screaming on a cold floor had shocked the world – and enraged a nation. The president repeatedly referred to this reprehensible incident during his own carefully coached television appearances.

Only later, after so many had died and so many others had been wounded in ways that were not always apparent, would it be revealed that Nayirah was the daughter of the Kuwait ambassador. Her tall tale – which never happened – would prove pivotal in the US Senate's decision to ratify the presence of American forces even then cursing Arabian sand.

But it was still touch-and-go. A veteran of Vietnam and Grenada, the general had seen how quickly public opinion could swing against an incomprehensible conflict that sent their children home in body bags. If Americans knew half of what his intelligence officers were telling him about the horrors waiting in the warheads of artillery shells and ballistic missiles arrayed against his forces, he probably wouldn't be standing in the Saudi desert testing the winds for the coming assault. Even now the doubters who had lost an earlier Asian war were pushing hard for further negotiations, more time for sanctions to bite.

The five month old economic blockade had nearly exhausted Iraq's six month reserves of food and raw materials. Half of that nation's gross domestic earnings had been erased. Fresh milk, poultry, and eggs were available only on the black market at wildly inflated prices: sugar was going for more than $60 a pound. Spare parts for cars and trucks quickly eroded by the desert's relentless entropy were nearly nonexistent. But delay would prove more quickly fatal to his mission than haste. Nearly a million troops from 28 nations could not be kept in a monotonous sandscape indefinitely. A sign posted outside a US Air Force gate on a Saudi air base mirrored sentiments he was hearing at every camp he visited: SEND US IN TO KICK SOME, OR SEND US HOME TO GET SOME. It was time to grant the first wish in hopes of soon providing the second. After an unprecedented long-distance deployment, the man responsible for wielding its nation-crushing force was about to send in the same Seventh Cavalry whose predecessors had followed another general in a hurry to attack an "inferior" enemy.

The desert was as quiet today as the long grass of the Dakotas after the buffalo and warriors had gone. Taking no notice of his four bodyguards and their AR-15s, or the massive mechanized storm gathering at his back, the silent implacable dunes marched away with their burden of centuries into Kuwait. Staring through field glasses into this sand-swept Indian country, he remarked to an aide on how peaceful the desert was.

"General?"

Sweeping an arm in a gesture Patton would have recognized, General Norman Schwarzkopf pronounced: "It's perfect for tank warfare."

* * *

Even before attending the Bordentown Military Institute near his Trenton, New Jersey, birthplace, young Schwarzkopf had toured Teheran. As a career-Army officer, his father was a seasoned desert hand. During the recently concluded Second World War, he had commanded 30,000 US troops sent to protect Saudi Arabia's vast oil deposits beneath the "Dammam Dome." The real threat was not a canny German "Desert Fox," but the British expeditionary forces pursuing him who might end up with an even richer prize instead.

After finishing a tour as Provost Marshall in conquered Germany, Schwarzkopf Sr. had been ordered to Teheran. With son in hand, he made contact with Bruce Odell, a CIA operative whose task was to keep Iran's oil wealth in the hands of its richest families. The year was 1951. When a popular candidate named Mosodek won the 1953 election, Washington feared that Iran's new president would move to nationalize American oil interests.

It had happened before. Tired of watching foreign oil companies siphon prodigious profits along with Iranian oil, Teheran had seized a British oil company. Washington and London had reacted swiftly, arranging a boycott of Iranian oil that nearly brought down the country. After a CIA-instigated coup installed a more compliant Shah, nearly half of that nationalized British company had been transferred into American hands.

As Mosodek moved to undo that Shah's treachery, he was quickly deposed in another coup arranged by Odell, Schwarzkopf Sr., and the future head of Standard Oil. The Shah was returned to the throne. Opposed by his own people, who had elected Mosodek in his place, the ruler requested American assistance in training his SAVAK secret police. President Roosevelt asked Norman Schwarzkopf Sr. to lend the Shah a hand in fashioning a force strong enough to keep an unhappy citizenry in hand. The senior Schwarzkopf was not unfamiliar with police work. As the former head of the New Jersey State Police, the senior Schwarzkopf had led headlined investigations into the "Lindbergh kidnapping" that had quickly convicted an apparently innocent carpenter.

While father and son toured Teheran, Washington worked to secure the immense oil deposits just coming onstream in Saudi Arabia. As Secretary of the Navy James Forrestal told Secretary of State Byrnes: "I don't care which American company or companies develop the Arabian reserves, but I think most emphatically that it should be American."

Jockeying for ascendancy in a region that fed their growing oil dependence, the US and the UK become increasingly allied in a common strategic interest centered on Kuwait. Settled since the early 1700s by nomadic tribes following gently rising ground water eastward out of the Najd region of north-central Saudi Arabia, Kuwait afforded fresh water just 15 feet below the desert sands. Its location on the shores of the Arabian Sea also proved an ideal trading nexus for caravans and the swift sailing dhows that ranged the Gulf and beyond. Before the end of the 18th century, the Sabahs emerged as the family who would rule Kuwait for the next 200 years.

But their power was provisional. Long considered part of Iraq's Basra Province, Kuwait had been declared a British colony in 1899. When the provinces of Baghdad and Basra became League of Nations mandates in the early 1920s, Kuwait continued to be a British-held protectorate. In 1922, in a move to restrict Iraq's access to the sea, Britain's proconsul in the Gulf, Sir Percy Cox, set the present-day boundaries between Kuwait, Saudi Arabia and Iraq.

In the late 1930s, and again in 1961 when Kuwait won independence, Iraq twice tried to "restore" Kuwait to its rule. Baghdad also never dropped its claims on two uninhabited border islands – Bubiyan and Warba – which it considered vital gateways to the Gulf.

In 1958, following a US Marine landing in Lebanon and president Eisenhower's threat to use nuclear weapons "to prevent any unfriendly forces from moving into Kuwait," Britain first considered granting an "independence" to Kuwait that would provide, in Foreign Secretary Selwyn Lloyd's words, for "the need, if things go wrong, ruthlessly to intervene."

Lloyd emphasized "the complete United States solidarity with us over the Gulf," even if that meant taking "firm action to maintain our position in Kuwait." Referring to the oil boom just getting underway in Saudi Arabia, Bahrain, Kuwait and Qatar, Lloyd affirmed that London and Washington "agree that at all costs these oil fields must be kept in Western hands," on favorable terms for sterling.

Even as it set on the British Empire, a shamal-shrouded sun rose on American claims to the Gulf. By 1960, five of the 12 biggest US corporations were oil monopolies. While the Baathist Party machine-gunned its way to power in Iraq, American oil companies were counting their profits from Persian Gulf concessions held over just a dozen years; that $13 billion represented half of the return on all overseas investment made by US companies between 1948 and 1960. By 1979, US control had been so firmly established through its influence over the sheiks of Saudi Arabia and the Shah of Iran, this region flowing with black gold could have been renamed "Amerabia."

* * *

Behind the rhetoric of "freeing Kuwait," Norman Schwarzkopf Jr. understood that the real stakes extended far beyond its borders. A West Point graduate like his father, he also knew the hazards of war. During two tours in Vietnam, he had served as a paratroops adviser to the South Vietnamese, and commanded a US infantry battalion. Back in 1965, Norman Schwarzkopf had been a 30 year old major when a journalist the same age had entered his still-smoking firebase in the Highlands. Peter Arnett had come to photograph the commander who had held out under siege.

Arnett was famous for the quote he had picked up from an American adviser in the Mekong who declared it "necessary to destroy the village in order to save it." The Kiwi correspondent would go on to win a Pulitzer for covering a war that would award the general two wounds and three Silver Stars – once for entering a minefield to rescue a wounded soldier. Neither man suspected that they would clash decades later in a distant desert war.

* * *

General Norman Schwarzkopf Jr. had always believed the big fight would come in the Middle East. But as he returned to the reassuring routines of his command bunker 40 feet underground, he must have wondered at the kismet that had thrust him into the center of the Middle East arena his father had done so much to shape.

The US had continued to support the Shah of Iran for 25 years, selling him billions of dollars in sophisticated arms and sending thousands of advisers to help train his expanding army

and secret police. In 1972, Henry Kissinger met with the Shah to punish Baghdad's Baathist regime for providing refuge to an exiled Ayatollah Khomeini. Hoping to maintain a pro-American power balance in the Gulf, President Nixon elected to assist Iran by supporting the Kurds in their revolt in northern Iraq. Kissinger, Nixon and the Shah wanted the Kurds to distract and bleed Iraq without upsetting the status quo by winning a homeland for themselves.

Washington did not fear rising oil prices as a result of these adventures. "The rise in the price of energy would affect primarily Europe and Japan and probably improve America's competitive position," Kissinger explained.

When Arab oil producers slashed output and sent petroleum prices spiraling upwards in late 1973 in retaliation over steadfast American support for Israel, oil-dependent Japan declared a national emergency.

But in the USA at least, "the Arab embargo was a symbolic gesture of limited practical impact," Kissinger later admitted. International oil corporations were able to pool their oil, making up most of the Saudi shortfall in the US. In Japan, the "Oil Shocku" convinced the nation to adopt energy efficiencies that would give it a commanding competitive edge, while stashing about two million barrels of oil in secret reserve.

By 1975, the *New York Times* was praising Saddam Hussein's "personal strength," calling his administration "pragmatic, cooperative" even as that regime gassed Kurdish families, and tortured and executed political rivals. Acknowledging a growing addiction, Secretary of State Henry Kissinger warned that the US would intervene with military force to prevent any Arab nation from cutting off "our oil lifeline."

Just two years later, the newly inaugurated Jimmy Carter endorsed an idea first proposed during the Vietnam era. Dubbed the "Rapid Deployment Force," this concept reduced standing armies abroad in exchange for a military force capable of being quickly dispatched to the Persian Gulf or any other trouble spot.

In 1979, when the Shah of Iran was overthrown by popular outrage, the jolt to US interests was worse than the Arab oil embargo five years before. The issue was not vital oil supplies. Former CIA analyst Major General Edward Atkeson calculated that if all Gulf oil was curtailed, simply stopping the recreational driving which then accounted for 10 percent of all US oil consumption would reduce Western petroleum needs to a level easily replaceable from non-Gulf sources.

The real crisis of '79 was the sudden loss of a vital US front-man in a critical and volatile region. In the first month of the new year, President Carter proclaimed the "Carter Doctrine." Calling the "protection of the oil flow from the Middle East... clearly part of our vital interest," Secretary of Defense Harold Brown warned that "we'll take any action that's appropriate, including the use of military force."

Washington's Mideast policy did not play well in sheik-doms seen as being dependent on American arms to fend off fellow Arabs. Frequent references by Washington about "taking over the oil fields" in response to another embargo – and a Congressional feasibility study to accomplish that objective – made the Gulf states increasingly nervous.

But it was the Soviet invasion of Afghanistan that kept lights burning late on Capitol Hill. As Carter pushed for rapidly deployed combat capability, his best military analysts insisted that the Soviet's own Vietnam would keep their troops out of the Gulf indefinitely. But the president continued speaking gravely about the Soviet threat to Mideast oil.

Iran turned out to be a bigger worry. The resurgence of Khomeini-fueled fundamentalism and the seizing of US Embassy staff caused Washington to tilt toward Iran's arch-rival. Direct links with Iraq had been broken during Israel's lightning "Six Day War" in 1967. But once again, observed *Harper's* Christopher Huchens, the think tanks were thinking tanks.

* * *

Washington was not alone in supporting a country it had previously helped destabilize. France followed substantial financial investment in Iraq to become Baghdad's principle source of high-tech weaponry. Moscow became Iraq's biggest conventional arms supplier. Israel sold weapons to Iran, hoping to see both of its enemies batter each other. At least 10 nations profited from selling arms to both sides of the next Mideast conflict.

The Iran-Iraq War began with an all-out surprise invasion by Iraqi forces on September 22, 1980. The Iranians fell back before a torrent of armor. But Iraq's bid for a quick victory was frustrated when the desperate Iranians rallied and counter-attacked. By mid-1982, the Iranians had pushed the invaders out. By June of that year, Iraq was fighting on its own soil.

Iraq was not following its script. In 1983, as Washington worried about fundamentalist Iranian fanaticism in the wake of the Shah's sudden departure, the Pentagon transformed its Rapid Deployment Force into a separate military command called Central Command, or CENTCOM. Seventeen ships loaded with supplies for an intervention force steamed for an Indian Ocean stronghold called Diego Garcia.

The following year, as Iranian battlefield victories mounted, the US government appealed to its allies to stop selling arms to Teheran. But "Operation Staunch" was undercut by Washington's continuing weapons deliveries to Iran. In 1986, a direct Washington-to-Baghdad link was opened to provide the Iraqi military command with rapid intelligence updates from steerable US spy satellites. Falsified photos showing fake Iraqi troop concentrations were supplied to Teheran.

Intelligence photos were not the only gifts sent to the beleaguered Iraqis. Lethal botulism and other virulent cell cultures sent to Baghdad from six NATO countries enabled a desperate despot to build what the CIA termed one of the world's "biggest and most aggressive" bio-warfare production facilities. By 1986, Saddam's scientists were annually producing thousands of tons of mustard and sarin agents. Dried into talc-like powders, these invisible weapons could be sprayed from aircraft or loaded into a variety of munitions and dispersed invisibly on the wind. As Iran's child-army advanced through Iraq's swamp-ridden eastern flank, the Iraqi dictator was quick to exploit photographs that unroofed his opponent from a keyhole in space.

* * *

Tried and tested mustard agent was the Iraqi Chemical Corps' immediate weapon of choice. Termed "a higher form of killing" by Nobel Prize winner and poison gas pioneer, Fritz Haber, "mustard" had first been used by the German army against the British during World War One. Flanders' terrible lesson was not lost on Britain's Secretary of State for the Royal Air Force. In a memo signed in 1919, Winston Churchill argued: "I do not understand this squeamishness about the use of gas. It is sheer affectation to lacerate a man with the poisonous fragment of a bursting shell and then to boggle at making his eyes water by means of a lachrymatory gas. I am strongly in favor of using poisonous gas against uncivilized tribes [where it could] spread a lively terror."

At the second battle of Ypres, 5,000 British soldiers died in lively terror after 170 tons of mustard gas was loosed on the wind by the Kaiser's army. Britain responded in kind. By war's end, nearly a hundred thousand young men had died and another million no longer young boys were blinded or crippled by the searing cough and shriveled lungs left by a single encounter with "gas".

Warmakers soon turned to more potent chemistries. Unlike mustard agents which burn skin, mucus membranes and nerve endings, the unholy trinity of sarin, tabun and soman nerve agents developed by Dr. Gerhard Schrader in 1936, kill by disrupting the electrical impulses transmitted from the brain to the muscles. Once researchers realized that a chemical called choline neutralizes the acetylcholine messages lighting up the central nervous switchboard, it was a relatively simple matter to block choline's inhibiting action. Then the runaway acetylcholine would keep firing nerve impulses without pause. Victims would begin vomiting and twitching uncontrollably until irreversible nerve damage or death finally shut them down.

Germany's chemical warfare research received fresh impetus under the Nazis, whose death camps provided an unlimited stream of test subjects. Medical "doctors" as perverted as

Joseph Mengele were soon injecting lethal germs into Jews spared one horror for another. One survivor recalls how the shots "shriveled the body or caused great sores that would not close." But Germany's growing stockpiles of newly developed nerve agents were never used; perhaps because Hitler was himself a victim of the Flanders gas attacks.

The Japanese preferred plague. During the war in the Pacific, a scientist named Ishii built the world's biggest biological weapons complex at Pingfan, north of Beijing. Every month, the bubbling vats of Unit 731 bred another eight tons of germs. The diary of one Unit 731 participant describes how allied prisoners were exposed to anthrax, typhoid, tetanus, beriberi, dysentery, plague and numerous other germs too small to be seen with the unaided eye.

As many as 12,000 American and British POWs died after being infected by Ishii's diabolical weapons. At least eight Chinese cities were attacked with virulent rice and wheat grains and plague-infected fleas. Within weeks, days or hours of these bio-attacks, plague broke out in Ch'u-hsien, Ningpo and Ch'ang-te.

Following the emperor's unthinkable capitulation, Ishii was repatriated to the US and put to work developing chemical biological weapons (CBW). He was not alone. Hundreds of former Nazi rocket and chemical warfare scientists were also granted a secret amnesty dubbed "Project Paperclip" in return for their terrible expertise. In March, 1952, when the waves of seemingly inexhaustible Chinese cannon-fodder threatened to undo American valor on a lonely peninsula, a lone F-86 circled the city of Mukden dropping small objects that broke gently instead of exploding against the budding ground.

Ishii would have recognized the ceramic containers tumbling from the Saber jet's wings as his favorite infectious delivery devices. An American missionary in Mukden emarked on a massive public health campaign that stopped and sprayed southbound trains, quarantined entire districts and inoculated the city populations for cholera, typhoid and other plagues. After US aircraft were seen over Pyonyang, other American observers found clumps of non-native insects in the wrong habitat and the wrong season for hatching.

But these early experiments with spreading death on the wind would soon be eclipsed by a tyrant with big ambitions. According to a top level Soviet defector, during the mid-1960s Iraq was very concerned that its arch-enemy Israel was "going nuclear." When Moscow refused Iraq's request for atomic arms, Baghdad opted for a much cheaper, less spectacular but even more effective equalizer. In late 1967, just after Israel's stunning defeat of its Arab attackers in the Six Day War, the Soviets providing Saddam with chemical and biological agents in their raw, "non-weaponized" form.

* * *

The Iraqi dictator quickly demonstrated an affinity for the "poor man's atom bomb." Aided by American satellites and cell cultures, the world's first nation became the first country to deploy nerve agents on the battlefield. That initial CBW attack came in August, 1983, when Soviet Su-22 Fitters wearing Iraqi markings and carrying chemical spray tanks hit Iranian troops in the northern battle sector. Over the next five years, at least 10 major chemical warfare attacks involving more than 100 sorties were carried out by Iraqi forces, including SCUD ballistic missile strikes against civilian cities.

Human wave attacks by young imam sluzbah (conscripts) were repeatedly broken up by chemical weapons. Iraq's battlefield commanders quickly found that wind, rain and range are the only factors limiting the use of chemical warfare. Their leader provided another innovation by giving his corps commanders autonomous release authority. The freedom of field headquarters to issue their own chemical attack orders to the divisions, brigades, battalions and companies under their command without waiting for approval from Baghdad greatly facilitated the army's flexibility in initiating their own CW response to fast-changing battlefield conditions.

It also led to more frequent use of sarin and mustard blister agents against Iranian troops who had captured Iraqi terrain, or appeared to be readying a major thrust. Employing mortars, artillery, helicopters and prop-driven spray planes or Su-22 ground-attack aircraft, Iraqi forces saturated the killing ground with chemical agents. Following this toxic softening up, Iraqi forces would wait just 30 minutes or an hour before launching their ground assault. Saddam's expendable soldiers were also equipped with excellent protective masks and hooded overgarments.

Iraq also continued to harass shipping in its "Tanker War." In May, 1984, Iran finally responded to three years of sporadic Iraqi shipping raids with several attacks by patrol boat on Iraq-bound ships.

Washington continued to play both sides. Realpolitik – the notion that nations have no permanent friends and no permanent principles – was still the watchword governing world affairs. Entries in Oliver North's journal show scheduled meetings for May 15, 1986, with nearly every major Middle East gun runner, including "Sarkis/Cunningham/Sarkis/Secord." As North noted in his abbreviated entries: "Cunningham running guns to Baghdad for CIA then weps. to Teheran. Secord running guns to Iran."

In September, 1986, as Iranian battlefield successes mounted, tankers loaded with Kuwait crude came under fire from Iranian gunboats. The emir's emissaries asked Washington and Moscow to "reflag" Kuwait vessels under their respective ensigns. Doing so would require both flag-of-convenience nations to protect their adopted vessels. The following July, after learning that the Soviet Union had offered to reflag 11 tankers, the Reagan administration offered to reflag the same ships. The Kuwaitis chose the American offer. Within weeks, US warships were patrolling the Persian Gulf and Indian Ocean approaches.

By August, 1987, a fleet the US Congress called "the largest single naval armada deployed since the height of the Vietnam war" was patrolling the Gulf. Flexing a carrier, a battleship and 10 destroyers and frigates, President Reagan warned of "dire consequences" if tankers were interdicted in the narrow Strait of Hormuz.

The former Hollywood war-actor must have forgotten that two-thirds of the oil sent from the Gulf is carried by pipeline, not tankers. As oil prices *fell* by 50 percent during the Iran-Iraq War, Congress learned that even the unlikely strangulation of Gulf shipping would have minimal impact on US oil supplies and prices. Gary Sick, former National Security Council head on Iran, warned that American naval units were being "deployed aggressively and provocatively in the hottest parts of the Persian Gulf." This aggressive patrolling strategy, Sick pointed out, "tends to start fights, not to end them."

Other Gulf states shared the analyst's concerns. After a US ship fired at a nighttime "attacker," killing one fisherman and wounding three others aboard a United Arab Emirates fishing boat, the UAE newspaper *Al Ittihad* criticized the US attacks for adding "fuel to the gulf tension."

Less than two in 100 ships transiting the Strait of Hormuz were being attacked by Iranian gunboats; only a tenth of those attacks caused real damage. A more serious threat turned out to be a rogue US guided-missile cruiser. Dubbed "Robo-Cruiser" by navy hands for her commander's aggressive flouting of operational orders, a frustrated and unbloodied *USS Vincennes* finally sent out a helicopter to provoke a response from an Iranian patrol boat operating in its own waters.

When the pestered patrol craft fired on the intruding infidels, *Vincennes* charged into Iranian inshore waters. Turning tightly to engage several darting patrol craft, the main gun jammed. An officer sang out: they were under attack by a diving fighter-jet! The captain ordered "missiles free." Seconds later, a rocket leaped from the cruiser's rails. One lookout nearly vomited when he watched a wing too big to belong to a fighter splash into the sea. Robo-Cruiser's final tally was 291 women, men and children aboard the Iranian Airbus, which radar tapes later showed to be climbing away from the cruiser. As admirals scurried to alter logbooks and radar records, every crewmember aboard *Vincennes* received a medal for their bravery.

* * *

By 1988, CBW had become a cornerstone of Iraq's tactical doctrine. After a March 17, 1988, attack against Halabja killed as many as 5,000 rebellious Iraqi citizens within an hour, news magazine photos showed entire families crumpled as if asleep in the Kurdish village streets. Despite finding evidence of mustard agent, which the Iraqis called khardel, and other chemical weapons, a subsequent UN investigation was unable to rule on who carried out the attack. Other investigators insisted that Iraq used "mixed agent" weapons combining thickened sarin, blister (mustard) agent and tabun against the Kurds.

What really happened at Halabja? Using advanced analytical techniques, Physicians for Human Rights and Human Rights Watch later proved the presence of mustard gas and sarin in the attack against the Kurdish village. Reportedly dropped by aircraft on August 25, 1988, the CBW bombs killed another four people in Birjinni as survivors watched the writhing victims cough blood. Soil samples subsequently gathered and delivered to the British chemical biological warfare laboratory at Porton Down confirmed the killers as mustard agent and sarin.

Mixing biological spores in a "cocktail" with dried chemical agents followed the military doctrine of Baghdad's Soviet advisers. The resulting mix makes these invisible munitions much more difficult to detect and defend against. In April, 1988, a barrage of artillery rounds filled with a sarin-mustard mixture led to the recapture of Iraq's al Faw peninsula in less than 36 hours. As the eight-year war drew to an end, Iraq may have also tested T-2 and DAS "mixed agent" tricothecene mycotoxins against Majnoon Island.

When the firing stopped on August 20, 1988, a slaughter profiting only arms dealers had cost more than a million deaths. Many more civilians and young conscripts were wounded or displaced. The resources squandered on a war which returned to its original boundaries exceeded the entire developing world's public health expenditures during that decade.

On September 8, a relieved Iraqi Foreign Minister Sa'dun Hammadi looked forward to discussing renewed trade links with US Secretary of State George Schulz. Two hours before their scheduled meeting, State Department spokesman Charles Redman called a press conference to charge Iraq with using chemical weapons against the Kurds. "We don't know the extent to which chemical weapons have been used," Redman declared, "but any use in this context is abhorrent and unjustifiable."

Neglecting to mention that Washington had never discouraged the use of US-supplied pathogens against Iran, Redman explained that his country had made the Iraqi government "well aware of our position that the use of chemical weapons is totally unjustifiable and unacceptable." Within 24 hours, the US Senate voted unanimously to impose economic sanctions on Iraq, including an embargo on all sales of food and technology.

* * *

Intelligence summaries of Iraq's growing chemical-biological warfare capabilities did not make for pleasant bedtime reading. CENTCOM's best guess was that 50,000 Iranian soldiers had been killed by weaponry whose insidious lethality only emboldened the "Butcher of Baghdad."

Saddam Hussein emerged from a ruinous eight-year war still speaking loudly and often of fulfilling his personal destiny to assume the ancient mantle of Sumerian rule over the entire Middle East. A ruthless and paranoid dictator, Saddam had purportedly handed machines guns to his cabinet ministers while ordering accused party plotters brought forward with their hands bound and mouths taped shut. According to a cabinet member who took part in that ordeal, every cabinet member was forced to start firing. At least 21 prisoners disintegrated under a storm of bullets.

Executing those closest to him had become the tyrant's trademark. Saddam Hussein also instituted many public works, thrilled many Arabs with his tough talk, and instituted state-controlled learning throughout his country. A Muslim fatalist who believed that his destiny lay in Allah's hands, Saddam Hussein also saw himself as an updated Nasser. In 1967, that former Egyptian leader had emerged from his crushing defeat by Israel an authentic Arabian hero for daring to attack their Zionist foe. Twelve years after coming to power, Saddam Hussein was prepared to lose again, in the words of Strobe Talbot, "on a heroic, even mythic scale."

Within a year of the Iraq-Iran cease-fire, the Soviet Union's steepening economic decline and humiliating defeat in Afghanistan had led Washington to once again shift its Mideast military focus. The US could count few friends among Arab governments who condemned the United States for its often sole support of a Jewish state that continued to defy scores of UN resolutions. Surrounded by ancient enmity, Israel felt it had no choice but to act decisively or be overrun. But to Arab eyes, the trampling of Palestinian rights, the invasion of Lebanon which took tens of thousands of Arab lives, and Israel's ongoing occupation of south Lebanon, the Golan Heights, the West Bank and Gaza were provocations that never could have taken place without the support of its American ally.

In 1989, CIA Director William Webster informed Congress that a slowdown in American oil production had doubled Gulf petroleum imports to fully 10 percent of US needs. By the turn of the century, Webster predicted, a quarter of the country's oil consumption would come from that region.

On December 20 of that year, the failure of another former ally to follow US directives regarding traffic in another addiction saw President Bush order a full-scale military assault on Panama. Employing massive firepower against a few frightened resisters, at least 2,000 Panamanians were killed during the apprehension of Manuel Noriega. Between 15,000 and 30,000 people were made homeless as el Chorillo and other slum districts were flattened by artillery, helicopter gunships and the new Stealth bombers. Panama's economy was wrecked.

Unmoved by world opinion, Washington vetoed two UN Security Council resolutions condemning the invasion. During the council's debate, UN Ambassador Thomas Pickering told member nations that Article 51 of the Charter, which restricts the use of force to self-defense against armed attack, meant that the US could use "armed force...to defend our interests." As US foreign policy expert Noam Chomsky later uncharitably pointed out, "The US invasion of Panama was just as much a violation of national sovereignty as Hussein's invasion of Kuwait."

* * *

The Panamanian adventure was followed by the "rescue" of students from equally surprised Cuban airport contractors. But Grenada was a sideshow. Early in 1990, General Norman Schwarzkopf informed the Senate Armed Services Committee of a new US military strategy aimed at protecting US access to Arab oil in the event of regional conflicts.

Despite the specter of Baghdad's unpredictable bagman rubbing a lamp filled with nuclear, chemical and biological jinns, another unprovoked unilateral attack against a sovereign nation would be as tough to sell internationally as it would be at home. The increasingly urgent question before Whitehall and the White House was how to disarm a Middle East monster largely of their own devising.

The key was Kuwait. Within a year of Iran's defeat, that oil-soaked sheikdom had followed Washington's wishes by refusing Saddam's appeal to annul his country's crippling war loans. Instead, the Sabahs broke OPEC's oil production guidelines by pumping more oil. The resulting oil glut saw the price of petroleum plummet as Iraq looked to oil revenues to recover from a war it had fought partly on Kuwait's behalf. Already reeling from a $70 billion war debt, Saddam protested that Kuwait's new oil policy was costing Iraq an additional $14 billion a year in lost revenue. Iraq's leader was also stung by Kuwait's refusal to arrange Iraqi access to the Persian Gulf.

But it was Kuwait's theft of Iraqi oil by "slant drilling" across a disputed border into the Iraqi side of the Rumayah oil field that pushed Saddam too far – as it was intended to. The Iraqi president might have known that the mobile slant-drilling rigs were owned by the US-based Harken oil company. But he probably never guessed that one of Harken's principal shareholders was George Bush. Or that the little Texas company had gained access to the Gulf after winning a coveted contract to drill in Bahrainian waters, despite having never drilled either offshore or overseas.

Saddam was being set up. Throughout much of 1990, US representatives to Baghdad "sympathized" with Iraq's leader in his dispute over the Rumayah oil reserves. But in March, despite President Bush's surprisingly vigorous support for the Iraqi dictator, congress voted to impose further sanctions against Iraq as punishment for its leader's long record of human rights abuses.

The following month, Saddam Hussein offered to destroy his chemical and biological weapons if Israel agreed to destroy the nuclear bombs waiting in its desert bunkers. The State Department praised Baghdad's offer, but rejected all links "to other issues or weapons systems."

In May, during an emergency meeting of the Arab League, Saddam Hussein bitterly denounced Kuwait's policy of "economic warfare" against his country. Hinting strongly that if Kuwait did not cease its price-fixing, Iraq would take military action, he called on fellow Arabs to present a united front against aggression by "pooling resources" and "matching rhetoric with deeds."

If Saddam stirred some Arabs to nervously exult in his fantasies of humbling the Great Satan, the "spoiled kingdom" of the Gulf elicited mostly contempt. As a Cairo resident named Mohammed Fawzy explained, "People do not like Kuwaitis. The Kuwaitis are always in the nightclub and casino. All they think about is money. They think they can buy anything."

With so few friends and so much to lose, why was tiny Kuwait taunting the bully next door? As Mideast analyst Brian Becker asks: "How could such a "tiny, undemocratic little sheikdom, which had in the past tread lightly when it came to its relations with Iraq...remain so defiant against a country ten times larger than Kuwait?"

It could not, of course, unless its ruling family had received assurances of protection from a much stronger power.

* * *

General Norman Schwarzkopf was already moving to meet Saddam's threat. In June, just two months before Iraq's invasion, the American Gulf commander commenced a month-long war game. "Air Land Battle Plan 90-1002" pitted at least a hundred thousand US troops against Iraq's best armored divisions. The elaborate computer simulation showed that Saudi Arabia could only be held against Iraqi invaders at the cost of many American lives.

The Saudis had been set up too – but as a Mideast base, not bait. For the past decade, Saudi Arabia had poured almost $50 billion into erecting a Gulf-wide air defense system to US and NATO specifications. By 1988, the US Army Corps of Engineers had also constructed a $14 billion network of military facilities across Saudi Arabia, including military cantonments at Khamis Mushayat, Tabuk and King Khalid Military City. Military port facilities were also expanded at Ras al Mishlab, Jidda and al Jubayl. In August, as Iraqi troops massed on Kuwait's border, the Corps of Engineers returned to construct additional buildings and facilities at al Jubayl in anticipation of a large deployment of American ground forces.

"As the build-up was going along the border, we really weren't quite sure what we were seeing," Schwarzkopf later told BBC's Radio 5. "We knew that the area to the west of Basra was a traditional maneuver area for the Iraqi military forces and particularly for their armored forces. So initially, when we saw the armored divisions moving down to that area, we weren't sure whether there was a build-up along the border to threaten Kuwait or whether it was just maneuvers we were seeing and because it was the same time that they normally conduct their maneuvers."

In late July, Egypt's Hosri Mubarak traveled to Baghdad to demand an explanation of Iraq's intentions. Swearing Mubarak to secrecy, Saddam assured him that the armed build-up was meant only to pressure the Sabahs into settling with Iraq.

Secretary of State James Baker was already warning his Soviet counterpart, Eduard Shevardnadze, that Iraq was about to invade Kuwait. "As time went on a pattern started to emerge," Schwarzkopf explained. "We saw, for instance Marine units side by side with the amphibious transport, we saw Special Forces units side by side with the helicopter units. What I think finally convinced us was we saw logistical supplies being brought up and delivered to these units and, of course, the units were camped in the fashion that showed that they weren't really going on maneuvers. And then finally as they started moving down towards the border, I think we became convinced that there was going to be some kind of an invasion."

On the last day of July, General Schwarzkopf briefed the Joint Chiefs of Staff on an impending Iraqi attack. Just the day before, Washington's ambassador to Iraq had given the green light to a dictator furious over what he termed Kuwait's theft of Iraqi oil and land. Saddam also claimed that Kuwait was opening settlements 60 kilometers inside Iraq's borders.

In addition to these provocations, Saddam was outraged by Kuwait's continued undercutting of OPEC oil prices on world markets. "Military wars kill people," Saddam told ambassador April Glaspie, "but economic wars kill their humanity by depriving them of the chance to have a good standard of living. Iraqis have a right to live proudly. We do not accept that anyone could injure Iraqi pride or the Iraqi right to have a high standard of living."

Ominously, Saddam added: "We want others to know that our patience is running out" regarding Kuwait policies which deny "even the milk our children drink, and the pensions of the widow who lost her husband during the war." Insisting that his people were not aggressors, Saddam declared, "we do not accept aggression either."

His warning included Iraq's former ally. "You can come to Iraq with aircraft and missiles, but do not push us to the point we cease to care," he told the American ambassador. "And when we feel that you want to injure our pride and take away the Iraqi's chance of a high standard of living, then we will cease to care and death will be the choice for us. Then we would not care if you fired 100 missiles for each missile we fired because without pride, life would have no value."

Thanking the dictator for his frankness, Glaspie assured him that she clearly understood his message. "We studied history at school and were taught to say, 'freedom or death,'" Glaspie soothed Saddam. "I believe that you know well that we as a nation have our own experience with colonialism." Washington's emissary also reminded the dictator that the president of the United States had "absolutely and constantly" rejected Congressionally-mandated trade sanctions against Iraq. "I have direct instructions from the president himself," she said, "to expand and enhance relations with Iraq."

"But how can we achieve this?" an exasperated Hussein burst out. "We too have the same desire, but the way things are going is not compatible with that desire!"

Glaspie reassured him, saying that "President Bush seeks better and deeper relations with Iraq." Then came the go-ahead: "We know you need funds. We are of the opinion that you should have the opportunity to rebuild your country. But what we hold no opinion about are inter-Arab disputes, such as your border disagreement with Kuwait."

Referring to the instructions she'd received while serving in the American embassy in Kuwait during the late 1960s, Glaspie said her directive had been that "we should have nothing to do with this issue and that the issue was not connected with US concerns. James Baker has directed our official spokesman to emphasize his instruction."

Even as the assistant Secretary of State was informing Congress that "the United States historically takes no position on the border disputes in the area, nor on matters pertaining to internal OPEC deliberations," April Glaspie told Saddam that she had been worried before the meeting. But now, the ambassador said, she was relieved enough to go on holiday. The signal could not have been clearer if she had handed Saddam an engraved invitation to invade Kuwait.

* * *

Printed invitations for a last-ditch Arab summit to reconcile Iraq's grievances had already been sent from Saudi Arabia's King Fahd to the ruler of Kuwait. The note twice reminded the emir of "what you had agreed upon" in previous meetings regarding negotiations with Iraq.

Those previous agreements had led to the scheduled July 31 working session intended to iron out final details of a deal that would see the Saudis and Kuwaitis each pledge an initial $10-billion to assist the war-weary Iraqis. This $20 billion would act as down payment on the $30 billion Saddam had demanded the previous May in reparations for his proxy war against the common threat posed by Khomeini. Iraq's western neighbors could afford such largess. The Saudis controlled more than 40-percent of the world's oil reserves; Kuwait a bit over nine percent.

Just before the Iraqi leader's meeting with the US ambassador, Jordan's King Hussein and his entourage flew into Baghdad. "I honestly didn't think he would invade," King Hussein later said. "But I really got quite uncomfortable. Saddam was talking about how when the Kuwait emir was subjected to the 1985 assassination attempt, he decided to retaliate against the Iranians and sustained 1,500 casualties. He said, 'We took all that much, and now they are doing this to us.' I sensed an anger I hadn't seen before."

As Saddam received Glaspie's assurances that her country would not intervene if Iraq decided to invade Kuwait, an "extremely worried" Jordanian leader met with Kuwait's foreign minister in Kuwait City. The king was not reassured when Sheik Sabeh Ahmed Jaber Sabah opened discussions by ridiculing the Iraqi border buildup. Hussein rebuked him, reminding the foreign minister of the deal already worked out releasing Iraq from war loans made by Saudi Arabia and Kuwait, and resolving Iraq's long-standing border dispute with Kuwait.

The agreement was to be signed the next day in Jeddah. But the Kuwait foreign minister stunned the Jordanian delegation by declaring: "We are not going to respond to Iraq. If they don't like it, let them occupy our territory. We are going to bring in the Americans."

* * *

As he passed the emir's honor guard lined up at attention on the ramp of Kuwait's modern international airport, King Hussein sensed tension in the eyes of the young soldiers. He did not know that earlier in the week the Kuwait crown prince had called senior military officers together to inform them that in the event of an invasion they must hold off the Iraqis for 24 hours. By then, the crown prince assured them, "American and foreign forces would land in Kuwait and expel them."

The Jordanian peacemaker would have been even more upset had he seen the note scribbled across the emir's invitation to the Jeddah summit. The message instructed Kuwait's foreign minister to ignore Iraqi threats on the advice "of our friends in London, Washington and Egypt." The Iraqis, the emir wrote, are extortionists, while the Saudis wanted to deal Kuwait out of its share of a rich oil discovery made several years before in the diamond-shaped neutral zone just west of the emir's southern border. The oil in the al Waira field was shared by the Kuwait Oil Co. and Texaco. The American oil corporation in turn maintained a profit-sharing agreement with the Saudis. The hand-written note from the Kuwait ruler ended with a final encouragement: "We are stronger than they think."

Iraqi vice-president Izzat Ibrahim attended the July 31 summit in Jeddah expecting to sign a long-sought agreement with his Saudi hosts and Kuwait. To Ibrahim's astonishment, the Kuwaitis put just $500,000 instead of billions on the table. The meeting broke up "in anger and confusion" over the insult, without even discussing Iraq's oil production and border complaints.

By then, George Bush had sold two-thirds of his Harken oil shares for a hefty profit. The CIA's Webster reassured the president that Iraq's impending invasion would probably stop less than 30 kilometers inside the disputed border with Kuwait.

On August 2, 1990, a tyrant provoked beyond endurance overplayed his hand. Instead of reclaiming the Rumayah oil field, Saddam's mechanized army continued rolling rapidly south along Kuwait's splendid superhighway. As April Glaspie later told the *New York Times*, "We never expected they'd take all of Kuwait." A Kuwait academic put it even better when he told me by the light of his burning city: "One evening the newspaper was saying that everything was going to be all right. And the next morning there was an Iraqi soldier in my garden."

CHAPTER 2

FACE

It was around five on a Thursday morning, the second of August, 1990, when King Hussein was roused by an urgent call from King Fahd. The distraught "Protector of Mecca" announced that Kuwait's defenses had crumbled. Iraqi troops were racing toward Kuwait City.

As his country burned, the emir who had earlier contained his political opponents by dissolving parliament was easing his shaken nerves in what *People* magazine called "an artificial oasis of green grass and pink gardenias in Taif, the posh resort town favored by Saudi royalty." In their haste to reach this Saudi sanctuary, Kuwait's royal rulers had left splendors behind. Among the discards, journalist Michael Emery later counted "an irreplaceable collection of ancient Islamic art, fleets of luxury automobiles, thousands of top-secret documents," and 26 of the emir's wives.

Saudi Arabia's monarch was not worried about expendable females. "It's all the Kuwaiti's fault," the king blurted to Hussein. "Please tell Saddam to stop where he is."

King Hussein immediately called Baghdad. It was around 10 in the morning before he heard Saddam Hussein's voice on the line "What did you do?" King Hussein asked.

"Well, you heard," said Saddam.

"Please, tell me, don't stay there!"

"Well, I will withdraw. It is a matter of days, perhaps weeks," Saddam assured the head of Jordan.

"No. Don't talk about weeks, only a matter of days," King Hussein implored.

"Yes," Saddam answered, "but I have learned that the ministers are meeting in Cairo and they want to condemn us. If they do I am afraid that will not help."

As mutual rivals for the mantle of Arab leadership bequeathed by Nasser, the presidents of Iraq and Egypt were not pals. "Let them look at it seriously," Saddam continued, "and not take it that way, because if they do, we will not take it lightly and they will not like our reaction."

Realizing that all chances of striking a deal for an immediate pullout would evaporate if Egypt denounced Iraq, the king of Jordan mounted his royal jet and flew immediately to Alexandria. Around four that afternoon, he met with President Mubarak. Agreeing with the king's call for discretion, Egypt's president promised to restrain himself until King Hussein could see Saddam and try to talk him into withdrawing. Mubarak also offered to carry an invitation to the Iraqi president, asking him to attend a mini-summit to be hosted by the Saudis in Jeddah the following Sunday, just three days away.

Hussein replied that he preferred flying first to Cairo to head off condemnation by the Arab League already meeting there. After offering the use of his personal helicopter, Egypt's president excused himself to take a call from George Bush. When he returned, Mubarak told King Hussein that the American president wished to speak with him.

Bush was preoccupied by two urgent matters. He was worried about Americans in Kuwait and he wanted Iraq to withdraw. Hussein assured Bush that he was flying immediately to Baghdad to seek an Arab solution which could be ratified at the upcoming summit on Sunday.

As Michael Emery later revealed in the *Village Voice*, "King Hussein then tried to call King Fahd in Saudi Arabia to get approval of the mini-summit. But he couldn't get through." Mubarak finally phoned Fahd and asked the Saudi monarch to talk to Jordan's king. King Fahd said he would return the call.

He never did. As night fell on the first day of the Iraqi invasion, British Prime Minister Margaret Thatcher was winding up day-long meetings with George Bush in Aspen, Colorado. The "Iron Lady's" determination and uncanny timing would prove pivotal in reinforcing the American president's resolve.

Before Baghdad announced its annexation of Kuwait, the US and British governments invoked a total economic blockade against Iraq. "America stands where it always has, against aggression, against those who would use force to replace the rule of law," the US president declared.

This was an interesting stance, commented Canada's national newspaper, the *Globe and Mail*. "When the French invaded Algeria and occupied it until 1962, killing more than a million people, where were the Americans, where was the world? When the Soviets sent their forces into Afghanistan in 1979, where were the Americans, where was the world? When Israel invaded Lebanon in 1982, where were those Arab forces now pouring in to 'defend' Saudi Arabia?"

Washington continued to reject any "linkage" with regional issues. Expressing its "moral revulsion" at the notion of "rewarding an aggressor" by examining such longstanding regional irritants as arms, security, and human rights, the American administration instead favored war.

Support for the US stand was muted in Jordan, Algeria, Yemen, and Tunisia, where the baiting of a fellow Arab was immediately understood.

But the West had found a new Hitler. Echoing Bush's blast at Iraq's "unprovoked aggression," Australia's Prime Minister Hawke declared that "big countries cannot invade small neighbors and get away with it." Hawke's hawkish sentiment contrasted sharply with his own Foreign Minister, who had earlier explained his country's acquiescence to an Indonesian dictator's forcible annexation of East Timor and extermination of 200,000 East

Timorese by explaining that "the world is a pretty unfair place, littered with examples of acquisition by force."

* * *

Surprised by the forces so quickly arrayed against him, Saddam Hussein was already looking for a face-saving solution. The day after the invasion, he received Jordan's king in Baghdad. Agreeing that he or his representative would attend next Sunday's summit, Saddam told Hussein that he would begin withdrawing his troops even as that meeting began.

The jubilant Jordanian tried phoning Mubarak with the welcome news. But Egypt's leader did not return the call. Instead, moving quickly in what diplomats attending the Cairo talks later called a "heavy atmosphere" of dread and outside pressure, the Egyptian president sabotaged the peace bids of both Husseins by breaking his hours-old pledge not to condemn Iraq. Following the direction of Mubarak's denunciation, Arab League foreign ministers also slammed Saddam.

"Oh my God," exclaimed the Jordanian king on hearing of Mubarak's treachery, "the conspiracy is complete."

But it was still unclear whether Saudi sheiks would allow American infidels on Islam's most sacred soil. Jordan's Hussein considered an Iraqi invasion of Saudi Arabia, "preposterous." King Fahd agreed. If the Saudi king held firm, the US plan to disarm Iraq would be stalled before it even began.

"There was absolutely no way in the world we could rapidly deploy our air forces if we couldn't go in and use the Saudi military airfields that were in place. There was no way we could possibly deploy the Marine Corps and bring in the Marine pre-positioned ships and equipment, without using the Saudi ports," Schwarzkopf later told the BBC's radio audience.

* * *

High over the Atlantic Ocean, en route to meet with King Fahd, Secretary of Defense Dick Cheney drew Schwarzkopf aside and asked the general: "You've been working in this area for a couple of years now and you know these people, what do you think will happen?"

Schwarzkopf replied with the candor characteristic of military minds: "I think what will happen is we'll make our presentation and they'll listen very carefully and then they'll say, 'Thank you very much, we'll let you know' and we will get back on the airplane and fly back to Washington with no decision."

At first, it seemed Schwarzkopf was right. Meeting with the Americans in Riyadh on the night of August 6, King Fahd argued that if Saddam had wanted to invade Saudi Arabia, he would have swept on virtually unopposed. The Americans countered by saying that Iraq was following standard Soviet military doctrine, which always consolidated initial advances by stopping to refuel, rearm and regroup before pressing further.

The king was then handed a sheaf of satellite photos, compliments of the CIA. When Schwarzkopf showed King Fahd pictures of Iraqi tanks massing along and inside Saudi territory the king grew more infuriated than intimidated. The general quickly explained how many troops, ships and fighter squadrons would soon be arriving "to defend Saudi Arabia against what looked like to be a very possible invasion from the north."

As if awaiting his cue, Secretary Cheney then stepped forward to assure the Saudi monarch that while Washington was prepared to commit its forces for as long as necessary to defend Saudi interests, when the time came to leave, all US forces would be withdrawn from the Kingdom.

A heated discussion ensued between the King and members of the Royal Family. Ambassador Freeman, who understood Arabic, later told Schwarzkopf that the argument centered around not being hasty – and remembering what the Kuwaitis had done to invite Iraq's attack. King Hussein later observed that the Saudi king "pressed the panic button" when he turned to the American general and said, "OK!"

Schwarzkopf reports that he nearly fell out of his chair. Did "OK" mean thanks for the information or... Cheney quickly interjected, "So, you agree?"

The King replied, "Yes, I agree."

Making some comment about how many Kuwaitis were living in Saudi hotels because they weren't willing to make a decision, the Saudi ruler added, "I'm not going to have that happen."

Schwarzkopf still believes that the satellite photographs of Iraqi tanks on the Saudi border forced the king's hand. The next morning, Saudi Minister of Defense Prince Sultan was stunned when Schwarzkopf answered his query regarding the arrival of the first planes by saying, "Within 12 hours." As the prince struggled to digest the rapidity of the American response, Schwarzkopf added, "They're...they're on the way, as we speak."

* * *

As Chuck Horner's first flight of F-16s refueled over the Atlantic, Jordan's King Hussein was landing in London after conferring with President Bush in Washington. Prime Minister Margaret Thatcher was waiting. "It was one of the rowdiest discussions that I ever had with anybody," the Jordanian king later recalled. "Thatcher used language I wasn't used to from anybody."

The Muslim king was unused to hearing a woman curse. "She was very strong on her side and so was I – very strong language. She said troops were halfway to their destination before the request came for them to come."

In fact, advance elements of the US Rapid Deployment Force had begun landing in Saudi Arabia within 30 minutes of the Saudi-American meeting. Assuring the world his acts were "wholly defensive," the US president ordered 40,000 military personnel into Saudi Arabia without consulting congress. As for the short-lived but widely hailed "Peace Dividend," a Pentagon official explained to puzzled journalists: "If you're looking for it, it just left for Saudi Arabia."

Were the Americans rushing into a trap of their own devising? Six days after the Iraqi invasion of Kuwait, as the first US Air Force fighter planes began touching down at Dhahran, an urgent message was flashed from the Armed Forces Medical Intelligence Command at Fort Detrick, Maryland. The classified communiqué warned US commanders of Iraq's "mature" arsenal of biological weapons that might be unleashed in a campaign just announced by their Commander-In-Chief. The message further noted that Iraq had succeeded in "weaponizing" a number of biological agents. Kuwait's jailers had also acquired "aerosol generators" that could be mounted on trucks or small boats to launch biological agents.

Follow-up reports explained that Iraq had acquired at least 40 and possibly 52 Italian-built pesticide sprayers in the spring of 1990. Loaded from 55-gallon drums, the agricultural sprayers had been custom built to deliver liquid or dry material at rates approaching 800 gallons per hour through nozzles adjustable to 10 different particle sizes. The handy nozzles could be rotated 180 degrees, enabling dissemination of BW agents either along the ground, or upwards into prevailing winds.

A subsequent bulletin from the Defense Intelligence Agency's "Iraq Regional Task Force" noted that the portable foggers could fit into the back of a pickup truck, a small boat or aircraft. The known Iraqi BW agents named in the message – powdered anthrax and botulinum toxin – "are easily mixed with fillers, pose a considerably greater threat through inhalation, and are better able to withstand the shear forces experienced when disseminated through nozzles with a relatively small orifice."

This home-grown threat was considerable. Though it would not be pleasant work for its operators, according to a bio-war expert at the Army Chemical School at Fort McClellan, Alabama, pickup trucks or small boats equipped with a sprayer and favorable winds could contaminate hundreds of square miles of terrain. Added Colonel Gerry Schumacher: "CIA computer models had indicated to us that if just one of the sprayers were turned on, we could run a risk of contaminating over 100,000 US troops."

Schumacher was in charge of the Pentagon's crash program to develop a germ warfare detector. But as Schwarzkopf prepared to attack an acknowledged master of bio-warfare, no workable bio-agent detectors were available. The M8A1 automatic chemical agent alarm deployed by US forces could not detect mycotoxins. Nor was it sufficiently sensitive to pick up low concentrations of chemical nerve agents. The minimum amount of sarin required to activate the M8A1 exceeded the official US Army "hazardous" threshold by a factor of 1,000.

* * *

As dire warnings filtered through the US command, Saddam was offering a way out. On August 12, the Iraqi leader proposed linking Iraq's immediate withdrawal from Kuwait to Syria and Israel's withdrawal from Lebanon – plus an Israeli pullback from the territories it conquered in 1967.

Bush ignored Saddam's sally. Instead, just three days later, the US president declared that "the sanctions are working." With 95 percent of Iraq's export earnings dependent on oil sales, Saddam's regime was losing more than $1.75 billion a month in national revenues.

Why not negotiate? The *New York Times'* chief diplomatic correspondent Thomas Friedman provided the State Department's rationale on August 22 when he wrote that the administration's rejection of "a diplomatic track" was tied to its concern that fruitful negotiations might "defuse the crisis" at the cost of "a few token gains in Kuwait" for the Iraqi dictator; perhaps "a Kuwait island or minor border adjustments." The crisis could not be resolved, Friedman declared, until Iraq's dictator was forcibly disarmed.

One week later, a similar Iraqi peace offer was leaked to New York's *Newsday*. Delivered to National Security Adviser Brent Scowcroft by a former high-ranking US official on August 23, the Iraqi initiative called for its withdrawal from Kuwait in return for the lifting of sanctions and full Iraqi control of the Rumayah oil field, extending about two miles into disputed Kuwait territory. Baghdad also wanted guaranteed access to the Gulf through the two uninhabited islands assigned by Britain to Kuwait in an old imperial settlement that had left Iraq virtually landlocked.

In return, Iraq offered to augment its pullout by negotiating an oil agreement "satisfactory to both nations," as well as mutually satisfactory national security options "on the stability of the gulf." There was no mention of US troop withdrawal or other preconditions. An Administration official specializing in Mideast affairs described the proposal as "serious" and "negotiable."

The offer was discarded by the White House. On September 9, the *Chicago Tribune's* financial editor, William Nelkirk, explained to Americans that having "cornered the West's security market," the US must become "the world's rent-a-cops... as a lever to gain funds and economic concessions" from the twin economic powerhouses, Germany and Japan. Whatever naysayers may say, Nelkirk argued, "we should be able to pound our fists on a few desks" in Japan and Europe, and "extract a fair price for our considerable services" in protecting their oil. The US could abandon the role of enforcer, Nelkirk concluded. But to do so would sacrifice "much of our control over the world economic system."

There was something wrong with this picture. Or at least the pictures shown to King Fahd. Soviet satellite photos taken five weeks after the Iraqi invasion of Kuwait still showed empty desert where the CIA's photographs had shown tanks. Two American satellite imaging experts who examined the Soviet photos ruled them authentic. But they could find no evidence of a massive Iraqi presence in Kuwait. "The Pentagon keeps saying the bad guys were there, but we don't see anything to indicate an Iraqi force in Kuwait of even 20 percent the size the administration claimed," Peter Zimmerman reported.

Follow-up shots snapped by a Soviet commercial "bird" on September 11 also failed to find the 250,000 Iraqis and 1,500 tanks Washington claimed had massed in Kuwait. Zimmerman, a former US Arms Control and Disarmament Agency expert for the Reagan administration, as well as another former image specialist for the Defense Intelligence Agency (who asked not to be named because of the classified nature of his work), could see no Iraqi encampments or vehicle parks in Kuwait. But the much smaller American military presence at the Dhahran airport in Saudi Arabia stood out clearly in the photos.

"We could see five C-140s, one C-5A, and four smaller transport aircraft, probably C-130s. There is also a long line of fighters on the ground. We didn't find anything of that sort anywhere in Kuwait," Zimmerman explained. "We don't see any tent cities. We don't seen any congregations of tanks. We don't see any troop concentrations, and the main Kuwait airbase appears deserted." The Soviet satellite's camera resolution was 18 feet.

Five days later, Washington's agenda became clearer when Air Force Chief of Staff General Michael Dougan told the press of his service's plans to "destroy the Iraqi civilian economy." General Dougan was removed from his staff office that same day.

On September 18, two days after Dougan's abrupt departure, Schwarzkopf ordered four Army planners to begin work on a ground offensive. This might have seemed an innovative interpretation of Bush's "defensive" pledge, but by then, Washington was claiming that Iraqi forces in Kuwait had mushroomed to 360,000 troops and 2,800 tanks.

Such a massive movement of troops and vehicles would have left telltale tracks all over the desert. But repeated sweeps by independent commercial satellites could find no signs of such an overpowering threat. Unlike the Saudi roads, which had been swept clean, all of the roads on Kuwait's side of the border were drifted high with undisturbed sand. "There's no sign that tanks have used those roads," satellite-photo experts confirmed.

Would a government that had once fed "doctored" satellite photos to confuse Iranian leaders resort to the same tactic to assure Saudi Arabia's acquiescence to a huge buildup of foreign troops within its borders? Zimmerman made another point: "The Kuwait border with Saudi Arabia isn't very long. It wouldn't take more than 10,000 Iraqi soldiers to cover the border area to the point that people fleeing would run into them all over the place."

The former defense analyst added that 2,000 "nasty military police would have been enough to terrorize" Kuwait City, and that two US Marine divisions could have driven them back to Iraq, "relatively quickly and with relatively little bloodshed." At the time the photos were taken, there were already more than 100,000 American troops in Saudi Arabia.

* * *

Among them was US Army specialist Jim Brown. His alert notification to deploy to Saudi Arabia had come three days before Operation Desert Shield officially began. Over the following two weeks, as Brown and the other members of the 514th Maintenance Company, 10th Mountain Division prepared to move out, more than two billion pounds of weapons, food, medical supplies and ammunition would be trucked from around the United States and transported more than 7,000 miles to Saudi air and sea ports at Dhahran and al Jubayl.

On August 20, Brown's unit reported for their initial briefing and vaccinations at Fort Drum, New York. Trained to fight Soviet aggressors in the Arctic, the cold weather specialists learned they were going somewhere hot.

Because of the large number of personnel present, Brown recalls that this first round of shots saw 5 cc's of immune gamma globulin injected into each trooper in less than a minute. "In every medical journal I have read on the subject, there is a clear warning not to exceed 1 cc per minute," Brown says. But no one questioned the urgency of a process that gave the 514th their meningococcal vaccinations that same day.

The germ-laden shots shocked immune systems already mobilizing for combat in an alien arena. Brown believes that rest and avoidance of further such insults would have helped heal their bodies. But "there was no way for this to happen." On September 12, shortly after receiving anthrax and the botulinum toxoid shots, many of the soldiers in Brown's battalion fell ill with flu-like symptoms. Two weeks later, they flew to Frankfurt, Germany, staying overnight before alighting in Dhahran the following day.

As a generator and computer maintenance technician, Brown was placed in charge of an M88 recovery vehicle. With three other crewmen, he set out recovering broken-down tanks. His team was also responsible for repairing the huge tank transporters that were to cause many more casualties on the Saudi's narrow border roads than combat with the Iraqis. Their particular tasks involved repairing the 63 ton Abrams tanks' complicated hydraulic and depleted uranium fire-control systems. Over the following months of nonstop stress, missile alerts, caffeine jolts and deadlines, Brown's travels would take him from the Saudi ports of Dammam and al Jubayl to Kuwait City, Khafji, and Hafir al Batin.

* * *

Even before Brown boarded his airlift to Dhahran, Sergeant Tom Hare was camped at the Saudi border town of Sufla, about 65 miles west of Khafji. A stinging sandstorm made Hare rethink the rigors of his deployment. But it wasn't the sand, he says. It was the corpses his platoon found buried beneath their position. "There were hundreds of dead camels and goats on and around the hill we occupied," Hare relates. "They're desert animals. They have to deal with sandstorms all the time." Even spookier, all of the flies and insects that had been feeding on the desert-mummified flesh had died.

Another American soldier had never seen animals lay down at night in groups of five, 10, 20 or more and die. But the six "sleeping" camels he saw a few days after arriving in the country, "were dead as doornails." Venturing closer, the startled trooper saw that "even the insects on and around them were dead." Maybe, he decided, "they all thought that it was the end of the world, and died of fright." Or maybe someone didn't like infidels on sacred Saudi soil.

Sergeant Hare and his company had ample time to consider their predicament as they remained in the area, eating and sleeping on the hill of camel carcasses. Cuts would no longer heal, Hare recalls. and the lymph nodes on his neck swelled until he "looked like a bullfrog." Fine sand infiltrated everything. In November, as their long deployment dragged on, Hare and his companions learned of two dead goats floating in their water source. How the animals got there was never determined.

* * *

Hare couldn't know it, but his country's former Cold War enemy was working overtime to bring him and his buddies safely home. On October 5, 1990, President Mikhail Gorbachev's personal adviser met with Saddam at his Presidential Palace. Yevgeny Primakov delivered a "strong" note from the Soviet president telling him to get out of Kuwait.

"The atmosphere was tense," Primakov recalls, which was undoubtedly understated after handing Saddam such an ultimatum. After agreeing that 1,000 Soviet specialists could leave Iraq within a month, Saddam Hussein emphasized that Kuwait "historically belonged" to Iraq. With the price of oil down sharply from $21 to $12 a barrel, Saddam noted that Kuwait's machinations "spelled economic ruin" for Iraq. "If I have to fall

to my knees and surrender or fight, I will choose the latter,"
Iraq's president told Gorbachev's top aide.

The following day, Primakov briefed his boss in Moscow
on his meeting with the proud Iraqi leader. Gorbachev ordered
Primakov and his staff to draw up a peace proposal. Within two
days, Primakov was back with an offer that hinged, he said, on
finding the line between "rewarding aggression" and "saving
face" for Saddam.

Primakov then flew to Washington on October 18 to
discuss the Soviet initiative with US officials. Gorbachev's representative found "genuine interest" among the Americans, who
wanted to know more about his meetings with an opponent they
had not directly contacted since the crisis began. Primakov
explained to Dennis Ross, head of the president's policy planning
staff and the State Department's top Middle East expert, that the
main thrust of the Soviet plan was to make Saddam understand
that once his troops left Kuwait, "we would be ready to discuss the
Arab-Israeli issue in order to resolve the Palestinian problem."

"Israel won't go for that," Ross replied. Bush's Mideast
policy adviser was also skeptical about drawing any distinctions
between "rewarding" Saddam and "saving his face."

Primakov's party was received at the White House the next
day. According to the Soviet aide, the US president expressed
"extreme interest" in Saddam's psychological makeup. Did the
dictator's assurance that he was "realist" mean that he was ready
to withdraw from Kuwait?

Bush seemed to be hesitating, Primakov thought, over
whether or not to attack Iraq. The president said he favored a
second meeting between the Soviets and Saddam "to inform
Saddam about the uncompromising position of the US." Bush
added: "If a positive signal should come from Saddam, it will be
heard by us."

On his way home, the jet-lagged Primakov stopped to
meet with Margaret Thatcher in her country residence at
Chequers. For a good hour, the British Prime Minister lectured the
Soviet envoy without interruption, outlining a position that she
insisted was gaining favor with other allied governments.

Thatcher told Primakov that the object was "not to limit
things" to the withdrawal of Iraqi troops from Kuwait, but to
deliver a devastating blow to Iraq that would "break the back" of
Saddam and destroy the entire military, and perhaps industrial,
potential of that country. "No one should try to interfere with the
objective. No one should even try to ward off the blow against the
Saddam regime," Thatcher ranted. Bush would later present "the
Iron Lady" with the Medal of Freedom.

* * *

On October 24, Primakov again left Moscow, this time
bound for Cairo, Damascus, Riyadh and Baghdad. For his second

meeting with Saddam and his staff, everyone present was wearing military uniforms. Later, in a one-on-one, Primakov told Saddam: "You have known me for a long time, and apparently you have become convinced that I try to tell you the truth. At stake, moreover, a powerful strike against Iraq is unavoidable if you do not announce your withdrawal from Kuwait and carry out this withdrawal in practice."

Saddam wanted to know when US troops would be leaving Saudi Arabia. "Will the UN sanctions against Iraq be lifted, or will they remain in place? How will my country's interest concerning an outlet to the sea be ensured? Will there be some kind of linkage between the Iraq troop pullout from Kuwait and a solution to the Palestinian problem?"

Would America stay the course? A poll taken on November 1, 1991, showed that only 49 percent of Americans thought Kuwait was worth fighting for. The next day, Amnesty International reported that Saudi security forces were torturing and abusing hundreds of Yemeni "guest workers" and expelling 750,000 of them, "for no apparent reason other than their nationality or their suspected opposition to the Saudi Arabian government's position in the Gulf crisis."

On the 15th, Primakov arrived back in Washington as the UN Security Council opened debate on a resolution establishing a deadline for Iraq's pullout from Kuwait. The Soviet advisor feared that if the resolution passed, Saddam would feel trapped, "narrowing the field for political remedies."

With the US elections behind him, a reelected George Bush now made public his earlier order sending an additional 200,000 American troops to "defend Saudi Arabia." Congress was not advised of the reserves' mobilization. But the bogus "incubator" story plucked a resounding public chord. A new poll done on November 27 found that 59 percent of Americans now favored intervention on the emirate's behalf.

Bush had also scored photo-op points while visiting American troops grousing about a sandy Thanksgiving. During a private session with Schwarzkopf, the president asked his top general to assess "the best-case and worst-case scenario" for the upcoming ground war.

Schwarzkopf replied bluntly: "The best case would be about three days, which assumes that the Iraqis quickly fold and surrender en masse. The worst case would be a situation in which we fight to a stalemate. That could go on for months."

This prognosis did not please the president. "Isn't there some scenario in between?" Bush demanded.

"I can imagine a campaign lasting three to four weeks where we encounter tough resistance, but we're able to seize all our objectives and destroy the Republican Guard," General Schwarzkopf replied.

On November 29, UN Resolution 678 called on the US and its allies to "use all necessary means" to liberate Kuwait if Iraq did not withdraw by January 15, 1991.

There would be no "white Christmas" for US forces. As American troops began the most difficult month away from home, Iraq offered to "scrap chemical and mass destruction weapons if Israel was prepared to do so." In reply, the first cargo ship carrying VII Corps's armor docked at al Jubayl.

On December 5, CIA director William Webster appeared before the US Armed Services committee. America's top spook forecast that lack of spare parts and lubricating oil would shut down Iraqi aircraft and armor, as well as its military industries, by summer. Admiral William Crowe and General David Jones, both former chairmen of the Joint Chiefs of Staff concurred with Webster's assessment. The brass urged Bush to give sanctions at least a year to work.

By December 13, 1990, American "Intel" was reporting that the Republican Guard had moved multiple rocket launchers to two large field ammunition depots in the Rumayah area along the Kuwait border. During the last week of December, US intelligence also detected greatly increased activity at Iraq's main chemical plant at Samarra.

The British Ministry of Defense believed that Iraq "may have as many as 100,000 artillery shells filled with chemicals and several tons [of bulk chemical agent] stored near the front line." The *London Times* reported that Saddam Hussein had given front-line commanders permission to use these weapons at their discretion, and that "it was no longer a question of if, but when."

Except for the elite Republican Guard being held back in reserve, most of Iraq's armed forces were now in Kuwait. As the Iraqi Army scrambled to disperse its SCUD missiles and CBW stockpiles, deserters told their British captors that substantial supplies of chemical weapons were being cached along the entire front. Another Iraqi defector reported that "each brigade of the 20th Infantry Division has eight mustard and binary chemical rounds."

A captured Iraqi Army document gave orders from Saddam Hussein to Iraqi II Corps elements in Kuwait ordering them to "prepare the chemical ammunition." Intercepted radio messages also confirmed that Saddam had ordered his commanders to launch their "unconventional" weapons as soon as the allies' forces crossed the border into Iraq.

* * *

Schwarzkopf's soldiers were unprepared to counter this threat. The reassurances given to Congress and the American people by the head of the Joint Chiefs of Staff, General Colin

Powell, and Secretary of Defense Dick Cheney that their troops were properly equipped for possible NBC warfare were deemed necessary falsehoods. CENTCOM knew that the marines tasked with breaching the Iraqi's main defensive lines in Kuwait faced their chemically armed adversary with leaky gas masks and few replacement filters.

Nearly five months' deployment in the desert, constant NBC drills and the need to carry their masks at all times had greatly reduced the serviceability of American gas masks. According to Captain Manly's "NBC Material and Logistics" report, some marine reservists "were lacking in NBC equipment, many of their protective masks were obsolete, and they were deficient in NBC survival skills training." Manly also pointed to "the M17A2 Protective Mask and OG-84 Protective Suit, both of which were in critically short supply throughout the war."

As early as November 1, 1990, the US Marine Corps Logistics Base in Albany, Georgia was reporting up the chain-of-command that many Marines hastily deployed in Saudi Arabia were being forced to fix worn-out gas masks with duct tape. Faced with an at-home 26 to 40 percent failure rate, the Albany technicians feared that few masks and hoods could survive intact after being clogged and chafed by sand sifting into Marine mask carriers.

The previous month, Defense Intelligence Agency analysts warned General Powell that "tests indicate that dusty agents can penetrate US chemical and biological warfare overgarments...First battlefield use will most likely be detected by the onset of symptoms among exposed personnel."

The "dusty agent" referred to was liquid mustard gas absorbed onto a talc-like carrier medium. As CIA analyst Patrick Eddington explained in his heavily annotated Gassed In The Gulf: "We were in no position to deal with a real chemical threat on the battlefield. We had no way to defend effectively against [dusty agent] and DoD knew it."

While Schwarzkopf opened his Christmas package of sugar cookies, peanut butter fudge and shortbread sent by his wife Brenda, the Iraqis celebrated the Christian season of rejoicing with successful flight tests of al Hussein missiles filled with sarin nerve powder. On December 20, the first test firings of the new, improved SCUD saw two and possibly four al Husseins impact near Wadi Amij in western Iraq. Quoting unidentified intelligence sources, the New York Times claimed the new missiles were testing simulated chemical warheads. Another successful test was launched the day after Christmas.

Schwarzkopf's only consolation came from listening to "relaxation tapes" of wildlife sounds and ocean waves. Despite the latest developments, the general was sure that one desert Christmas was all that his soldiers could take.

Eager for adventure, David Prestwich had showed up at the recruiter's office when he was just 16. Told to come back, he reappeared on his next birthday saying, "take me." Two days later he was in boot camp and his life belonged to the Department of National Defense.

Trained as a medic, the young Canadian traveled the world from exotic Moose Jaw, Saskatchewan, to Germany, where he served for five years. Prestwich met and married Leanne during an eight-year posting to Esquimalt, British Columbia on Canada's "wet" coast.

Right up until the first day of 1991, the Prestwichs' matching military careers seemed ideal. Then, with an abruptness that characterizes military life, David's unit was ordered to stow their hangovers and start packing. Everyone guessed it was the Gulf. But no one figured that 1 Canadian Field Hospital would become the closest Canadians to a tempest called Desert Storm.

On January 2, as the Prestwichs prepared to assist Canada's contribution to what the UN Secretary General was already calling "a US war," Washington disclosed another Iraqi offer. This time, Saddam Hussein agreed "to withdraw from Kuwait if the United States pledges not to attack as soldiers are pulled out, if foreign troops leave the region, and if there is agreement on the Palestinian problem and on the banning of all weapons of mass destruction in the region."

Washington officials described the offer as "interesting" because it dropped all claims to the two disputed Gulf islands, as well as the Rumayah oil field. The new initiative "signals Iraqi interest in a negotiated settlement," the State Department believed. One of its Mideast experts described the proposal as a "serious pre-negotiation position." Bush immediately dismissed Iraq's offer.

While it failed to report the latest Iraqi proposal, the *New York Times* did note that after meeting with Saddam, neither Yasser Arafat nor the Iraqi president "insisted that the Palestinian problem be solved before Iraqi troops get out of Kuwait." According to Arafat, "Mr. Hussein's statement August 12, linking an Iraqi withdrawal to an Israeli withdrawal from the West Bank and Gaza Strip, was no longer operative as a negotiating demand." All that is necessary to achieve Iraq's withdrawal from Kuwait, the Palestinian leader went on, is a commitment by the UN Security Council to solve major regional problems.

But Bush was not interested in averting a war that would leave Iraq armed with unconventional weapons, including a program bent on producing nuclear bombs. Instead of poring over peace proposals, the US president was engrossed in Martin Gilbert's biography of Churchill at war.

* * *

Iraq's military command was already preparing for the inevitable. On January 7, American intelligence informed General Schwarzkopf that chemical weapons were being removed from the Samarra Chemical and Biological Warfare Research, Production, and Storage facility. Orbiting "Keyhole" satellites photographed similar activity at Iraq's top chemical weapons research and development center, the nearby Muthanna State Establishment. Located near Samarra, about 65 miles northwest of Baghdad, this sprawling desert complex was estimated by American intelligence to be producing more than 2,000 tons of mustard and sarin agents a year. UN on-site inspectors would later confirm this assessment.

On January 9, Bush was still insisting he had the constitutional authority to attack Iraq without congressional approval. But the world was holding its collective CNN breath as James Baker met Iraq's Tariq Aziz in a last-ditch, face-to-face effort to avert war. Meeting outside the conference room at Geneva's Intercontinental Hotel, Aziz assured reporters, "I have come, in good faith. I am open-minded, and I am ready to conduct positive, constructive talks with Secretary Baker, if he shows the same intention."

Inside the room, both sides took their places, pulling back seven or eight seats on each side of a long table. The American delegation had finally worked out what to do if the Iraqi representative offered to shake hands. When Aziz extended his hand, Baker shook it in a businesslike manner. As both men sat down, Baker handed Aziz a copy of a letter from the American president. The original message, addressed to Saddam Hussein, remained sealed in a brown manila envelope in the middle of the table.

Assistant Secretary of State John Kelly remembers that Tariq Aziz took 10 or 15 minutes to read the letter. As he stopped occasionally to underline passages, a thin bead of sweat ran down the temple of Saddam's closest adviser.

"We stand today at the brink of war between Iraq and the world," Bush had written. Urging Iraq to comply with the UN resolution and depart Kuwait, the president continued: "Iraq will regain the opportunity to rejoin the international community. More immediately, the Iraqi military and establishment will escape destruction." Alluding to the use of chemical biological weapons: "You and your country will pay a terrible price if you order unconscionable acts of that sort."

Aziz finished the note and looked at Baker. "Look, Mr. Secretary, this is not the kind of correspondence between two heads of state. This is a letter of threat, and I cannot receive from you a letter of threat to my president." Aziz returned the letter.

The language is strong, Baker responded, but it is not impolite. "It conveys an important message to your president, and I urge you to take this letter back to Baghdad and to give it to your president."

Again Aziz refused. "No, I won't do that, I can't do that. It's not appropriate language."

Baker said, "Well, minister, it seems to me you've taken a rather large burden on your shoulders since you're the only person on your side of the table, who has read the letter." Several Americans thought the Iraqi diplomat's hands trembled slightly at this sally.

Downstairs in the hotel lobby, rumors were already circulating among hundreds of reporters starved for hard news. Progress toward a settlement was being made!

"Mr. Secretary," Aziz continued. "Iraq is a very ancient nation. We lived for six thousand years, I have no doubt that you are a very powerful nation. I have no doubt that you have a very strong military machine and you will inflict on us, heavy losses. But Iraq will survive. And this leadership will decide the future of Iraq."

Baker corrected Aziz, saying that another leadership was going to decide Iraq's fate.

"You are wrong," Aziz shot back. "In this region, in our region, when a leadership fights against Americans, it politically survives. And remember what happened to Nasser when he was defeated in 1967, he resigned and then the people, the masses returned him to power."

The US Secretary of State tried to explain that the coalition's overwhelming military and technological superiority meant that, if it came to a war, Iraq would lose.

"We are very well aware of the situation. We have been very well aware of the situation from the very beginning. And I don't ..."

"I am trying not to threaten. I just want you to understand the consequences," Baker broke in. But Aziz insisted that American soldiers had never fought in the desert. They did not know desert conditions, and would not be able to fight. Although the war would be long and difficult for Iraq, he assured Baker that in the end Iraq would prevail.

At one point, when Aziz claimed that Iraq had to invade Kuwait because that country was threatening them. Baker brusquely replied: "That's ridiculous."

After more than six hours of discussion, it was clear that Saddam Hussein preferred the defeat of his armies – and possibly the ruin of his country – to losing face by backing down.

"Minister, I don't want to cut his off prematurely," Baker concluded. "But I have said everything that, er, that I have to say and everything that er, I think is important to say. And if you have anything further to offer, then we'll, I'll stay here as long as you want to."

Aziz replied, "We don't have anything. I don't have anything further to say." The meeting was adjourned. Aziz had told the American delegation that the people of his region believed in fatality. "They believe that when there is fate, you have to face it." As the meeting broke up, James Baker felt that his Iraqi counterpart was resigned to what was about to happen. The sealed envelope containing Bush's letter had remained on the table between Tariq Aziz and James Baker all day. Now the American Secretary of State half-turned toward Aziz. "Are you certain you wouldn't like to take the letter with you?" he asked. "No, I, I won't take it," said a man who knew very well his boss's reaction to such a note. James Baker picked up the envelope and brought it back to his room.

"We shook hands at the end," Baker recalls. "Each delegation shook hands and, and I was certain at the time, that we would be going to war. And going to war very, very, soon."

Down in the hotel lobby, excited conversations hushed as expectant reporters turned to hear James Baker: "The message that I conveyed from President Bush and our coalition partners was that Iraq must either comply with the will of the international community and withdraw peacefully from Kuwait, or be expelled by force. Regrettably ladies and gentlemen, I heard nothing today that, in over six hours, I heard nothing that suggested to me, any Iraqi flexibility whatsoever."

Baker's use of the word "regrettably,"with its implication of imminent conflict, sent world money and stock markets reeling. In a Saudi hotel, a sign shot up: "Iraq has won the toss and elected to receive."

In Riyadh, General Norman Schwarzkopf was checking the final details of his plans to send six hundred thousand troops into battle as he watched Tariq Aziz step to the hotel microphone.

"Well it was very late at night in, in, in Riyadh,' the general later recounted to the BBC. "And then Tariq Aziz came out and talked for, it seemed like for ever, and never mentioned one word about Kuwait. At that point, I realized we were going to war. So, so you have this, this, you know, you're torn by two ends. Number one you are going through detailed preparations to make sure you do, do it right and you do prevail. And at the same time, another part of you is saying, you know, gosh, it would really be nice if somehow this could all be brought about to a necessary conclusion without the need to go to war. It, it meant plain and simply, that we were going to war. That people were going to die."

* * *

Tariq Aziz also felt that war was inevitable. But for different reasons. "We were expecting an Israeli aggression or an American aggression, or both, during that period, regardless of what we do," he later told a BBC "Voices in the Storm" radio announcer. "Margaret Thatcher and George Bush spoke about dismantling Iraq's military power, even if Iraq withdraws from Kuwait. So what does that mean? It means some sort of a war. With or without Kuwait. Damned if you do it, damned if you don't."

Iraq's military leaders felt they could not back down. But they knew what would happen to their forces once they lost control of the skies. Between January 10 and 15, the Iraqi army transferred 2,160 sarin-tipped rockets from al Muthanna to an vast ammunition storage area at Khamisiyah, far to the south. Intended to be fired in barrages close above the ground, the rockets were placed in a Wal-Mart size bunker 73.

Some 200 unmarked aerial mustard bombs were also taken to al Taqqadum Air base near Khamisiyah. The touchy munitions did not enjoy rough treatment. At Khamisiyah and al Taqqadum, unhappy handlers quickly discovered that some of the bombs and rockets were already leaking toxins.

* * *

On Friday, January 11, a divided US congress began debating its decision to go to war. France and Algeria were lobbying hard for a peace plan that promised a Mideast peace conference if Iraq withdrew from Kuwait.

The next day, despite vehement pleas from some Representatives that the sanctions be given more time to work, Congress authorized the use of force by a 56 vote margin in the House. The Senate ratified the president's use of force in the Persian Gulf by just five votes.

Writing on "The Gulf Crisis and a New World Order" in the *Middle East International*, Khaill Barhoun voiced what many Arabs were thinking: "The US is conveying the dangerously cynical message that the only Arabs it cares about are those who are rich and have oil. The US seems intent on maintaining the Arab status quo and defending the excesses of the privileged few in the Arab Gulf."

How savvy was the American public? A poll reported in the January 13th edition of the *Boston Globe* showed that 50 percent of Americans believed that control over oil is the "key reason" for the US troop presence, 28 percent thought the buildup was for the "liberation of Kuwait from Iraqi occupation," and 14 percent figured the main reason for the adventure was "neutralization of Iraq's weapons capabilities."

As the clock ticked toward war, the French made a last-ditch effort to avoid a cataclysm. On January 14, the day before its pullout deadline, the UN Security Council once again called for "a rapid and massive withdrawal" from Kuwait. The demand was coupled with France's conciliatory promise that Council members would pool their "active contribution" to settle other problems in the region, "in particular to the Arab-Israeli conflict and in particular to the Palestinian problem by convening, at an appropriate moment, an international conference." The French initiative was backed by Belgium, as well as Germany, Spain, Italy, Algeria, Morocco, Tunisia, and several non-aligned nations.

The US and Britain rejected the French proposal. During an emergency meeting of the Iraqi legislature that day, Saddam referred to Kuwait as Iraq's 19th province.

* * *

Back in Petawawa, Ontario, the Canadian Forces sped up its preparations for providing battlefield medical care. Both Prestwichs worked 16 hour shifts to "pull in equipment" from military clinics around the country. Among the notations filling two pages of David's yellow immunization book were shots for cholera and plague. The vaccinations, he remembers, "seemed to go on forever." After a 46 hour flight in an overloaded Hercules, Prestwich adds that he "was exhausted by the time I got to the Gulf."

The PB tablets he was ordered to start taking at a refueling stop in Germany didn't help. As a practicing military pharmacist, Leanne Prestwich had questioned the safety of Pyridostigmine Bromide. The controversial treatment for muscular degeneration had never been tested against soman nerve agent for which it was now being prescribed.

For hundreds of thousands of British, American, Australian, Canadian, Czech and Norwegian troops, a new hazard of war was just beginning. On January 14, as French diplomats tried frantically to avert war, Jim Brown's commanding officer stepped into his platoon's tent with the unit's Nuclear, Biological, Chemical warfare officer in tow. "I'm here to hand out a new pill," the captain announced. "Keep it quiet." If the Iraqis found out the Americans were taking nerve agent pretreatment pills, the officer explained, they could change their warloads to agents not protected by the drug called PB.

The NBC sergeant handed each soldier a packet of pyridostigmine bromide tablets. Told to take only one, the captain watched as the men complied. "He said he would tell us if we needed another one," Hare remembers. "He also said this was in preparation for an attack by Saddam in response to the deadline the next day."

Brown sat on his bunk, waiting for some sign of effects. After what felt like 10 minutes had passed, his driver came up and shook his shoulder, asking what was wrong. "Nothing, why?" Brown asked. The driver told him that he had been sitting in the same position for over an hour without moving and that they had to leave on their next mission." Brown was shocked. Only later would he learn that blackouts were common after taking the PB pills.

. * * *

Tom Hare also began taking PB pills as ordered. The tiny tablets made him and others vomit. Hare was given at least 10 different vaccinations for Anthrax, Botulism, Gamma Globulin and other threats, in a single sitting. As they continued taking PB three times a day, half of the men in his platoons became sick with illness medics began referring to as "the illness" or the "Saudi flu."

The Pentagon estimates that two-thirds of the 695,000 US troops in Kuwait Theater of Operations (KTO) took PB for varying periods of time. Steve Hudspeth of the 1454th Transportation Company was one of many sickened by the experimental nerve agent. His debilitating diarrhea and nausea did not abate until he stopped taking the pills after two days, thinking; "If I'm going to feel like this I might as well be dead."

When it came time to take PB, rank held no privileges. After Lt. Col. Neil Tetzlaff started taking pyridostigmine bromide on the plane ride over to Saudi, his nausea and vomiting became so severe, emergency surgery was required to repair a hole in his stomach. The military doctor who told him to continue to take the pills acted, according to Tetzlaff, "as if the pyridostigmine was as safe as a cough drop."

* * *

Schwarzkopf's hard-nosed officers were simply doing their duty. Though the full extent of Iraq's CBW threat was never disclosed to the troops, their superiors were desperate for any remedy against the chemical and biological horrors their own governments had sold to Saddam Hussein.

Even without knowing the details of the Iraqi leader's enthusiasm for chemical/biological warfare, everyone serving in the Gulf was terrified of germ warfare. You could take cover from explosions or gunfire. But US Army manuals warned that if a speck of odorless and tasteless sarin landed on exposed skin, its instantaneous absorption would propel victims into a whole new world of hurt.

Within 60 seconds of direct exposure, pupils contract to a pinpoint. Vision blurs and becomes painfully sensitive to light. Chests burn with the effort to breathe. If the dose of sarin or tabun is high enough, the disruption of key neurotransmitters can quickly lead to vomiting, confusion, convulsions and death.

Even if they lived long enough to swallow the atrophine tablet needed to unbind the nerve agent from cholinesterase, convulsions from that heart stimulant would kill anyone who did not immediately take a dose of Valium, too. While a single milligram of sarin could kill if injected, in its vaporous form, a lethal concentration required at least 100 milligrams of sarin per cubic meter of still or gently moving air.

Sarin sounded bad enough. But Schwarzkopf and his advisers also worried that Iraq could have acquired some of the Soviet's Novichok (no-wee-shok) chemical agents. Several of these binary compounds, whose twin components must be combined just prior to release to achieve lethality, were reported to have long lasting effects. Even at microdose levels of exposure, vomiting, memory loss, twitching and internal organ dysfunction were ascribed to these "newcomer" weapons which Moscow may have presented to Iraq in place of nuclear arms. Russian scientists who had worked on the program told the Americans that the "time-release" of Novichok poisons absorbed into fatty tissues produced long-term birth and mutagenic effects. There were no known antidotes. Injuries from the "newcomer" chemical weapon were said to be practically incurable; test subjects affected by Novichok have remained disabled for the rest of their lives.

But a top Soviet CBW scientist told reporter Howard Uhal that the USSR never sent Novichok to Iraq. "I'm sure about that," Vil Mirzayanov said after the war. "But they could send a chemical agent named Substance 33 – an analog of VX gas." Mirzayanov claimed that Substance 33 could have been mixed with sand particles and transported on the wind while remaining undetected by American chemical detectors calibrated for much weaker VX. "If Iraq used 33, I'm sure that American chemical troops would have been unable to detect it," Mirzayanov concluded.

Even without the Novichok nemesis, the threat of Iraq's known biological warfare capabilities was worrying enough. As early as April 10, a memo from Tank Battalion Headquarters, 55 Republican Guards to an elite chemical company of the Tawakalna Ala Allah Forces Command indicated that the Iraqi Chemical Corps had prepared an entire manual devoted to the use of tricothecene mycotoxins.

Written on the back of a form 102 receipt for chemical weapons equipment, the space designated for remarks on weapons characteristics and quantities read: "In reference to your letter... dated April 2, 1990, we are sending you our commissioner Warrant Officer Ghanem Nohad Jamell, who has 4 Forms 102. Please give him the yellow rain manual (fungal toxins) number/894 delivered to our unit pursuant to delivery plan number 17. Please review and respond."

"Yellow Rain" includes the T-2 toxin and DAS believed by some US intelligence experts to have been released over Majnoon during the Iran-Iraq War. The most potent fungal toxins known, T-2 and DAS cause severe ailments in humans and animals. With an estimated lethal dose in humans of three to 35 thousandths of a gram, these mycotoxins are moderately toxic compared to chemical nerve agents such as sarin. But even microgram doses of T-2 and DAS can cause prolonged nausea and vomiting, as well as skin and eye irritation.

A significant military advantage of tricothecene mycotoxins is their extreme stability when air-dried to a powder form. These active bioagents can be stored for years at room temperature with no loss of activity, while retaining their full potency even after being boiled in water for an hour. Tricothecene (tri-co-thee-seen) toxins are difficult to decontaminate from clothing and equipment, and are highly persistent in the desert environment before eventually being broken down by bacteria in the soil. After its dispersal, the volatile DMSO evaporates, leaving a dry powder on exposed surfaces. Yellow residue is the telltale for Fusarium fungus, which contains a yellow pigment in addition to potent tricothecene toxins. The use of the solvent dimethyl-sulfoxide (DMSO) to speed absorption of tricothecenes through the skin produces a characteristic "metallic taste" sometimes described as tasting like "copper pennies."

Initial symptoms of tricothecene poisoning are burning and irritation of the mucous membranes, lungs and eyes. Shortness of breath, chest pain, lassitude and coughing accompany nausea and persistent vomiting. Bloody diarrhea is also common. Unlike mustard agents, which produce painful blisters three to eight hours after exposure, tricothecenes cause an immediate burning sensation on the skin. Damage to exposed skin can range from inflammation to the formation of small, hard, fluid-filled pustules.

Mycotoxins are "live" biological weapons. Because they inhibit protein manufacture, mycotoxin germs reproducing within their human targets can harm several organs simultaneously. They are especially damaging to rapidly dividing cells in the gastro-intestinal tract, bone marrow and the lymph nodes, where they produce symptoms similar to radiation poisoning.

* * *

On the eve of the air war, the best intelligence "guesstimates" reaching Schwarzkopf's desk concluded that intense research at Salman Pak had provided Iraq with at least one ton of anthrax, botulinum toxin and clostridium perfringens. CIA director William Woolsey estimated that Iraq possessed another 1,000 tons of chemical nerve agents capable of being delivered by thousands of 81mm mortars; 152mm, 130mm, and 122mm artillery rounds; hundreds of aerial bombs and possibly land mines.

Worst of all were scenarios involving CBW-tipped aerial weapons. Back in November, 1989, and again in May and August, 1990, Iraq had conducted trials of aflatoxin-tipped 122mm artillery rockets and R400 aerial bombs. By early January, 1991, Iraq had put three different biological agents in 191 bombs and missiles; at least 25 al Hussein warheads were tipped with botulinum toxin, anthrax and or aflatoxin and deployed to four locations.

Bombs filled with biological agents were also dispersed to three remote airfields, where they were placed in open pits, covered with canvas, and buried with dirt to shield them from attack. Biological warheads for the al Hussein missiles were reportedly hidden in a railroad tunnel and in earth-covered pits near the

Tigris canal. Developing the world's first biological warheads capable of withstanding the high G-loadings and heat generated by ballistic missiles had presented a formidable challenge. But UN officials later found that Iraq might have succeeded in developing as many as 16 BW, as well as dozens of CW al Hussein warheads before the war commenced.

By the time their invasion of Kuwait commenced, Iraqi forces could field up to 450 SCUD-type surface-to-surface missiles. While the original Soviet SCUDs had a flight radius of 300 kilometers, German know-how derived from the Nazi's V-2 missile programs helped Iraq reduce weight and warhead size to double that range. The reconfigured warheads of each al Hussein could carry five gallons of sarin nerve agent in aerosol form. Development of the 950 kilometer-range al Abbas missile was dropped after in-flight stability glitches proved uncorrectable.

Schwarzkopf also worried about FROGs. During the Iran-Iraq war, Iraqi forces had employed multiple launchers firing scores of chemically-tipped Free Rocket Over Ground against their Iranian opponents.

On January 15, 1991, General Norman Schwarzkopf received the UN's blessings to launch all-out war against Iraq. But the general was busy chewing out the Air Force for ignoring orders to include Saddam's elite Republican Guard in their initial bombing sorties, scheduled to commence early the next morning. An Iraqi lieutenant posted with a tank division to defend an air base at as Salman wrote in his war diary: "Leave was suspended today for officers and men because of the end of the period, (granted) by the (international) Security Council for Iraq to withdraw from Kuwait. We are there and it is a historic right that was stolen from us when we could do nothing."

As clocks ticked past midnight in Washington, alert Domino's Pizza operatives tallied a record number of pizza orders from the White House and Pentagon the previous night. At 0500 DC time, Domino's declared that war was imminent.

~ 43 ~

CHAPTER 3

THE ROCKETS' RED GLARE

Just after two in the morning, Baghdad time, Peter Arnett, John Hollman and Bernard Shaw were preparing to broadcast from the al Rasheed hotel. Months of pestering had finally pried permission from state censors to use a "four-wire." The two-way overseas telephone link would work without an operator, outside switching or even the local power grid. Such technological independence was about to prove invaluable. At 0244 on January 16, 1991, the city around the CNN news team erupted in bomb blasts and tracer fire.

At least 71 million households tuned into Ted Turner's upstart news service as Baghdad reeled under the opening salvos of the coalition air assault. Bright green flashes strobed the city skyline as 300 US jets stationed on four aircraft carriers in the Persian Gulf and another 700 coalition planes based in Bahrain and Saudi Arabia "went downtown" with a vengeance. Deadly robots were also on the wing as the first of 137 cruise missiles slammed into command centers, power plants and other targets centered primarily on Baghdad.

A British TV reporter standing on the hotel's sixth floor balcony watched incredulously as a cruise missile motored past at eye level, turned the corner, and slammed into the Defense Ministry building. The explosion brought Shaw to his knees. As he crawled across the hotel room to report "from the center of hell," his colleague continued narrating the most exclusive war commentary since Edward R. Morrow described the London blitz.

* * *

High over the city, Captain Steven Tait weaved his escorting F-16 Strike Eagle above the first wave of bomber aircraft. The first American to shoot down an Iraqi plane had an Eagle-eye view of Baghdad during the first hour of allied bombardment: "Flames rising up from the city, some neighborhoods lit up like a huge Christmas tree. The entire city was just sparkling at us."

With its air defense radars and telecommunications links either blown up, short-circuited or jammed, the city fought back with a frantic flak barrage so intense that incoming F-15s and F-16s were forced to bomb from as high as 20,000 feet. Accuracy evaporated. The Pentagon later admitted that less than seven percent of all bombs dropped on Iraq were guided "smart" bombs; at least 70 percent of those guided munitions missed their intended targets in the center of the city.

As a cascade of "dumb" bombs drenched Baghdad in explosions and fire, a hundred jubilant students marched through the Ohio State University campus chanting, "Mess with the best, die like the rest." Thousands of their opponents took to nearby streets waving placards saying "No Bodies For Barrels" and "A Kinder, Gentler War." Late polls showed that 79 percent of Americans had favored negotiations past the UN deadline.

* * *

But the aerial attacks were not one-way. As Baghdad burned, Staff Sergeant Willie Hicks was fast asleep in a Saudi encampment known as Cement City. Without warning, a tremendous blast shook the entire area. As Hicks roused himself and ran for his bunker, chemical alarms began shrieking. "Our faces were burning," Hicks remembers. "Some guy just dropped." When the first sergeant arrived and ordered everyone to go to MOPP-4, the frightened troopers struggled into the bulky rubber suits, masks, boots and gloves. They remained at Mission Oriented Protective Posture 4, the highest level of chemical warfare alert, for the next 24 hours.

As Hicks and his company dealt with stress-filled darkness, Iraqi personnel at CBW storage, research and production sites at Ubaydah Bin, al Jarrah Airfield, Habbaniyah-1, Habbaniyah-2, and the uncompleted Habbaniyah-3 were ducking avalanches of high explosives hurtling out of the night skies.

At Iraq's Multhanna State Establishment, some 65 miles northwest of Baghdad, underground pilot plants intended to produce the chemical warfare precursors dimethyl methylphosphonate and dimethyl hydrogen phosphite sustained little damage. But the main production facilities at Iraq's biggest chemical warfare production site were destroyed as 17 tons of sarin nerve agent rose skyward on superheated air. Soviet chemical weapons expert I. Yevstafyev issued a national warning, stating that the "strikes on chemical and biological weapons facilities on Iraq's territory could rebound on us and cause damage to the population of our country." But the desert wind was blowing the other way.

During the night, and the week that followed, a low pressure system over Iraq and a high pressure center over the Indian Ocean stalled the characteristic low clouds of a stationary front over the war zone. Stable night air might be expected to trap pollutants close to the surface. But the massive fires and explosions from incessant coalition air strikes lofted chemical agents into nocturnal, south-flowing jet streams that reached speeds of between 20 and 55 knots.

At 0500 on the 17th, Saddam Hussein took the biggest gamble of his nation's life by exploding a nerve agent in the darkness over the city of Tel Aviv. Marine Corps General R. I. Neal authenticated the cyclosarin (thickened sarin) attack in a military log. Israeli police also confirmed that three Israeli civilians were killed in the January 17 attack.

"There goes Baghdad!" some viewers decided as a gas-masked CNN camera crew reported the first chemical casualties arriving at a Tel Aviv hospital. The Israeli government had promised "unconventional" retaliation if Iraq attacked its cities with chemical or biological weapons. Despite sharp losses among US Navy pilots attacking SCUD sites, Schwarzkopf's worst fears were apparently coming to pass. Within 40 minutes, someone got through to Atlanta. CNN recanted its "mistaken" coverage.

Meanwhile, not all Iraqi pilots fled to Iran. As the sun rose on the second day of the air war, an Iraqi MiG-25 bagged an American F-18, 29 nautical miles southeast of Baghdad. Five more allied aircraft would be lost that day and 11 others damaged as a "mixing layer" of warming air spread sarin and other toxins from the first bombing raids in a widening pall before carrying them south.

By mid-afternoon on the 17th, low clouds still covered much of west and central Iraq as patchy ground fog gave way to 20 knot southerly winds. The lieutenant stationed in central Iraq was not having a good day. "Afterwards, the enemy planes began their intensive bombing on the airfield that we have been assigned to defend, at as Salman," he wrote in his diary. "Time drags. We wait and watch. Iraq on one side and 29 countries on the other. That is just not fair."

* * *

Six hours after the cyclosarin missile attack on Tel Aviv, at a US ammunition depot designated Log Base Alpha in the Saudi desert, NCO William Brady was jerked awake by the soul-shaking detonation of a SCUD being intercepted by a Patriot air-defense missile directly overhead. The deafening explosion was followed a flash of light. "Everything shook," Brady later told US Senate investigators. "Chemical alarms were going off everywhere, and there was sheer panic." Brady smelled and tasted sulfur. Then his nose began streaming mucus.

Brady reached for his litmus paper. While the M8A1 automatic alarms could not detect blister agent, the special "detection paper" could distinguish between mustard gas and two other nerve agents. While water gave no litmus reaction, drops of solvent, oil, fats or fuel could give false readings. None of those things were present as Brady watched the paper turn red. Nerve agent was yellow. Red meant that a mustard agent was present.

A more complicated and compelling confirmation came from his M-256 chemical detection kit. Though less sensitive than the M-256A kit which replaced it, the kit's horse enzyme could determine if it was safe to unmask. After spending some minutes manipulating the M-256, Brady was convinced that an invisible nerve agent drifted on the air around him.

* * *

Radioman Tommy Harper had just left the command post bunker to get some sleep when the two ground-shaking blasts which had so rudely woken Brady sent him hurrying back to the CP with numb lips and burning skin. He arrived in the bunker in time to hear an incoming message over the radio net: "Alpha Bravo Six, Alpha Bravo Six, we have a confirmed chemical agent." Then Harper's own camp net broadcast an urgent alert: "MOPP level four. This is not a drill."

Just as Schwarzkopf feared, Iraqi ground forces in southeastern Kuwait were also firing salvos of FROG rockets across the border into the area where the 644th Ordinance Company was trying to catch some sleep. Rocket-firing Apache gunships destroyed some of those FROG batteries soon after their first salvos.

Harper recalls more people running into the CP to report that "a fine mist had fallen over the camp." Some soldiers "were complaining of numbness in their lips and fingers. One man even pulled off his mask, complaining of not being able to breathe."

The radio net was jammed with frantic messages requesting orders and a decontamination team, or relaying messages "downwind." Harper kept busy donning his bulky MOPP gear while taking messages and trying to "keep from panicking."

Brady and Harper's 644th Ordnance Company remained at MOPP level 4 for five or six hours. When 16th Support Group Headquarters gave the "all clear," the shaken soldiers were informed that they had heard a "sonic boom." Brady's M9 litmus paper signified exposure to "diesel fumes." Later that morning, an officer trailed by the unit's NBC man came into the bunker and told Harper: "Not a fucking thing happened last night – is that clear? No MiG bombed us, and it's not lying belly up in the Gulf. No decon teams. Not a fucking thing happened."

But people who had been told to expect chemical attack weren't buying it. Other units had also reported being hit; the 644th suffered 85 severely sick casualties out of 110 active duty personnel. Though they took off their stifling NBC suits, no one unmasked. Brady accompanied a lieutenant named Bryant to deliver gas masks and nerve agent pretreatment pills to the 344th Maintenance Company. When they arrived back at their unit, everyone was once again dressed in their full chemical suits at MOPP 4. Brady and Bryant were told that while they were out driving around without a radio, another attack had come in.

Later that day, the official government newspaper in Baghdad announced that Iraq would unleash a secret weapon, "which will astonish our enemies and fascinate our friends," while unleashing "an unusual force."

On the third day of the air war, thousands of Americans demonstrated against the war in Washington, DC. In San Francisco, at least 20,000 people took to the streets to protest the bombing. Major American news networks failed to mention the size of the protests. But Andy Ach, a baker in the city of the Golden Gate, complained that the "sanitized news" gave no sense of casualties or destruction.

By January 19th, heavy allied air attacks had severely damaged the chemical weapons storage area at an Nasiriyah, near a place called Khamisiyah. Forward deployed field depots like Nasiriyah's placed munitions in open-air squares surrounded by earthen berms. The exposed weapons could be quickly accessed by Iraqi troops, as well as allied aircraft. When "lit off" by cruise missiles or bombs, adjacent ammunition was likely to be touched off in an explosive chain reaction.

The first of a month-long series of bombing raids against Muhammadiyat also commenced on the 19th in the teeth of northerly winds. At least three tons of nerve agents were lofted into the air at this chemical warfare production complex, situated about 410 kilometers from forward-deployed US troops stationed at Rafa.

Earlier that morning, coalition aircraft attacking CW storage facilities at Qabatiyah had again been hampered by very low cloud cover as frontal winds continued to blow toward the south-southeast. Several hours before dawn on the 18th, a NOAA satellite snapped infrared images of an intense thermal "point source" directly over the Muthanna State Establishment, where 2,500 chemical rockets had been blown up by fierce coalition air attacks.

The plume reached south, pointing like a finger toward an even larger area of thermal activity covering other bombed pesticide, chemical precursor and CW storage and manufacturing facilities. The plumes blended into a single toxic cloud streaming south. Four to six times heavier than air, the chemical agents began dropping to the ground over Saudi Arabia and Kuwait.

At a little past 0330 on the 19th, Mike Tidd of the Naval Mobile Construction Battalion 24 was standing security in Tower 6. From his post about 20 feet above the port of al Jubayl, Tidd heard a sudden, percussive *boom! boom!* off to the northwest. The double explosion was followed by a brilliant flash of light reflected against the overcast. Minutes later, general quarters sounded. Approximately 750 Seabees donned gas masks and ponchos. Minutes later, when the call for a chemical attack came through, they went to MOPP level 4.

The construction specialists of the 24th Naval Mobile Construction Battalion were housed in two camps. Camp 13 was situated about seven miles west of the commercial port, while a smaller Air Detachment was located south of the Saudi harbor at

King Abdul Aziz Naval Air Station. The double-explosion that followed the red flash delivered a shockwave powerful enough to collapse tents at Camp 13. At least one soldier was thrown to his knees.

As Tidd watched the light show from tower 6, shipmate Sterling Symms witnessed a "real bad explosion" overhead. The alarms went off. Petty Officer Symms joined everybody else running toward their bunkers. As Roy Butler later related: "All of my exposed skin was like it was on fire. It was burning like crazy. I couldn't breathe. I had to take my mask off and clear my nose. I immediately thought we got gassed."

As he sprinted for shelter, Symms smelled a sharp odor of ammonia. His eyes burned and his skin stung. Like the other Seabees around him, Symms donned full chemical gear for nearly two hours until the "all clear" was given.

Mike Moore was also in Symms' unit. Around 0300 he too was awakened by a loud double explosion. Before the sound of the bangs had faded, the alarms went off. "Go to MOPP level 4," a voice ordered over the unit intercom. Everyone inside Moore's tent donned their gas gear. Garbed like deep-sea divers in the desert heat, the men proceeded quickly to the bunker, where they stayed at MOPP-4 chemical alert until about 0700.

When the all-clear sounded, the Seabees emerged from the bunkers and ran to storage tanks dubbed "water buffaloes" to wash their reddened, burning skin. Though many men were convinced they had been exposed to a chemical attack, their commanding officer told them the explosion had been a "sonic boom" from a passing jet fighter. He ordered them to stop discussing the incident and return to barracks. Radio operators were later ordered to burn their log pages covering the incident.

Symm's unit was also told that they had heard a sonic boom. They too were ordered not to discuss the incident. But many of the Seabees were skeptical. Shortness of breath, and the instant numbing and burning felt by many of the Seabees were symptomatic of nerve, blister agent and mycotoxin exposure. Such symptoms were not indicative of the extremely corrosive red fuming nitric acid of SCUD missile propellants, said by their superiors to be the cause of their complaints.

* * *

At least one Iraqi chemical attack on the 19th could have been delivered by an aircraft. CENTCOM logs record explosions believed to be a sonic boom at 0339. At 0345, an aircraft was reported "overhead at time of explosion traveling at high rate of speed." Eighteen minutes later, someone asked if a nearby Patriot battery had picked up an in-bound SCUD. The answer was negative for the SCUD. But positive for a " liquid chemical alarm going off at grid 652832."

At 0440, CENTCOM's NBC desk log recorded that a British liaison officer near al Jubayl heard "a propeller driven aircraft in the area" at 0440 local. Several Iraqi Air Force Pilatus prop-planes were based at Umm Qasr airbase near Basra in southern Iraq. The Swiss-made turboprops had been used to deliver chemical weapons during the Iran-Iraq War. US intelligence also reported that "chemical bombs" were stored at Umm Qasr.

Plans for the airborne delivery of a biological warfare agent had been drawn up by the Iraqi Army on the orders of Saddam Hussein the previous year. Three MiG 21s armed with high-explosives were to attempt penetration of coalition air defenses. If they successfully bombed their target, a second mission was to launch a few days later and fly the same ingress route. This second gaggle of three MiGs were to serve as a decoy for a single Su-22 Fitter fighter-bomber flying between 50 and 100 meters altitude at an optimal delivery speed of 700 kilometers an hour.

Shortly after the air war commenced, three MiGs took off from Tallil Airfield in southern Iraq, where American troops later photographed an SU-22 outfitted with what intelligence sources identified as a "dry agent spray tank" – designed to spray up to 2,000 liters of anthrax on a target. All three Iraqi jets were shot down early in the mission, and the BW mission to be flown by the Sukhoi ground attack jet was apparently scrubbed.

Was it rescheduled? Under the cover of exploding SCUDS, it remains a strong possibility that a spray-tank equipped Pilatus or much faster Su-22 managed to penetrate coalition air defenses before being shot down by two Patriot air defense missiles fired over the port of al Jubayl on the night of the 19th.

* * *

Something was happening on the night of January 19th. At least four SCUDs impacted near al Jubayl. Two of the missiles hit about 35 miles away. The other two landed about 58 miles away.

Between 0300 and 0440, at least one and perhaps two loud explosions split the sky directly over the King Abdul Aziz Naval Air Station, three miles south of the port of al Jubayl. Near-panic broke out as Seabees from the Naval Mobile Construction Battalion's Air Detachment struggled to pull on their masks and rubberized suits. As the troops emerged from their tents and ran to the bunkers, the men who failed to mask in time or achieve a tight seal smelled a sharp, acrid odor. Many saw a dense yellowish mist floating over the camp. Some Seabees began to choke. Others experienced such profuse nasal secretions, mucus fouled their masks.

Seabee Fred Willoughby of Columbus, Georgia, was "hanging out" outside his tent when he heard a prolonged, loud explosion. He dashed inside to get his gas mask. When he came back outside, pandemonium had gripped the camp. People were yelling, "MOPP-4, MOPP-4, not a drill!" A siren sounded. Willoughby thought the numbing of his mouth, lips and face felt just like the novocaine at his dentist's office. Shipmate Nick Roberts felt his exposed skin burn. A strange metallic taste felt "like sucking on a penny."

At Camp 13, Seabee Terry Avery of Salem, Alabama, also heard the double explosion, followed by the wail of the alert siren. He put on his gas mask and went to the bunker, where he received the order to go to MOPP-4 over the camp loudspeaker. He was almost completely garbed in the bulky chemical suit when the "all clear" was announced. Scuttlebutt whispered around the camp claimed that an enemy plane had been shot down over the desert.

Theodore Myers remembers an ear-splitting bang as two Patriot missiles launched right outside his tent. The marine was asleep at Fleet Hospital 5 outside al Jubayl when his bunk "shook so hard it moved at least a foot." As Myers jumped up, startled, US marines patrolling the perimeter shouted into the tents for everyone to go to the bunkers. "We went to the bunkers without putting on any protection, as there were no alarm sirens going off," Myers recalls. "We were there about 10 or 15 minutes when our security people told us to go back to the tents, that everything was all-clear."

When Myers returned to his tent, the sirens sounded and everyone went to MOPP-4 instead. "Too late though," Myers recounts, "since we had just spent at least 10 minutes standing outside unprotected. I never did get all my gear on, nor did many others."

Larry Perry, a North Carolina naval construction worker stationed at King Abdul Aziz Naval Air Station remembers emerging from a bomb shelter wearing his gas mask and being enveloped by a mist.

William Larry Kay, an electrician also assigned to Construction Battalion 24, had fallen asleep at Camp 13's Recreation Center when two loud "booms" shook the entire building. As the sirens sounded, the camp intercom announced: "Confirmed mustard gas – go to MOPP-4." Like so many others, Kay went outside before putting his gas mask on. The mask immediately filled with fumes that smelled like ammonia.

Harold Jerome Edwards, the NCO in charge of the Nuclear/Biological/Chemical team for the 24th Seabees' Air Detachment at the King Abdul Aziz Naval Air Station was already conducting the first of three M-256 tests for chemical agents. A negative test was made between a rows of tents. But the other two tests turned out positive for blister agent. Even more convincing was the blister welling under shipmate Tom Muse's watch.

Witnesses later confirmed that Edwards had immediately reported the detections. But CENTCOM never recorded the event. Two British M9 and CAM detections were reported in CENTCOM's CCJ3-X NBC log during this time.

* * *

Just west of Log Base Echo, military police Staff Sergeant Dale Glover was awakened at 0330 by his Battalion NBC officer with the unwelcome news that they were under chemical attack. An M-256 kit registered a positive reading for a chemical agent as Glover's battalion went to MOPP level 4 for four hours. After taking off their chemical protection suits, everyone had a runny nose. "Most people were already sick from the pyridostigmine bromide pills," Glover later related. "Three or four had to be medevaced out."

Log Base Echo may have also been hit by fallout from allied bombing. Photos taken by a US weather satellite show a mass of warm air – most likely generated by heat from exploding bombs – moving south from Iraq's biggest CBW complex at Samarra, just northwest of Baghdad, into Saudi Arabia.

* * *

Later that day, an urgent message was sent to Rock Island Arsenal's Commandant of the Marine Corps demanding more CBW protection. "Review of chemical-biological mask-hood posture needed for protection against chemical or biological attack has reached a critical point," the official Marine communiqué read. "Request immediate procurement and shipment of [gas mask filters and hoods]."

At 1030 that morning, a log entry made by the ARCENT G-2 intelligence arm of Central Command, stated that an "IZ [Iraqi] chem plant" had been bombed. The message noted that "The IZ chem plant ...had its smoke blowing across border, Saudis in MOPP 3. CZ [Czech] chem tm [team] from KKMC [King Khalid Military City] detected minute traces of chem agent."

Around this date, a soldier located about 40 miles due east of King Khalid Military City heard every M-8 alarm go off – over 30 at once. His NBC officer radioed in that a nerve agent plant had been bombed about 150 miles away and to take no action.

At 1330, a British Major named Bobby Harris reported from the Iraq border that their Saudi companions were "masking" after reporting a smoke cloud coming their way from chemical/biological targets bombed earlier in the day. Ruling that the toxic plume was "not a likely hazard," CENTCOM killed the report.

At 1710, as allied warplanes continued their nonstop 72 hours bombardment of Iraqi power and chemical warfare plants, Czech chemical specialists at Hafir al Batin about 25 miles from the Iraqi border heard the ominous *whoop-whoop* of their chemical detectors going off. Attached to the Saudi Army, the Czechoslovak Federative Republic military chemical decontamination unit boasted the most sophisticated NBC detection and classification equipment in the Gulf.

While training with the Czech detection team, a platoon from the 371st Chemical Company found the Czech equipment to be even more reliable than their own. After the American unit's first sergeant recorded the ballistic missile attack, and the Czech chemical detection, he was ordered to send the logs to Washington for "historical purposes." The US platoon was then deployed on several occasions to decontaminate buses and other vehicles used to transport Iraqi EPWs to detention camps.

At 2000, a young American soldier began a letter home:

Dear Mom,
    I just talked to you on the phone. I really didn't want to call you and tell you about the SCUD missile/gas attack so you wouldn't worry, but I really needed to hear a familiar voice...I'm trying like hell to keep my mind off the fact that it's night time again, and we could get hit again.

    Mom, I can deal with getting shot at, because I can fight back and even if I got hit, I can be put back together, a missile, on the other hand, doesn't work like that, but I can even accept that. But gas scares the hell out of me. I know how to put on the protective suits and gear, but it's the thought. Once the missile hit (without warning!) we were so busy getting dressed in our chemical suits we never had time for it to sink in and be scared. I was proud of all of us because no one froze up – we all responded like we'd been trained to, but after we got suited up, we had to sit there and force ourselves to breathe slow and try and cool down – the suits are very hot. It's hard to slow your breathing when your heart's beating a million times a minute...[a] fire team [went] out and... patrolled the camp and checked all of the towers.

    The rest of the camp were in their bunkers except security and the chemical detection teams. I know they detected a cloud of dusty mustard gas because I was there with them, but today everyone denies it. I was there when they radioed the other camps north of us and warned them of the cloud...I talked to the look-outs that saw the air burst and cloud and had to stay with them for a few minutes to try and calm them down even though I was just as scared (probably more!). Jubail is South East of us, and that's where the SCUD hit that was confirmed, but the air burst my guys saw was only 200+ yards west of us. I don't know what that was, but that's where most of the

~ 53 ~

gas came from I think. But the wind was almost blowing due North. I probably won't sleep much tonight, but at least I'll be able to respond faster.."

At 2246 the ever vigilant Czechs again detected sarin, as well as sulfur mustard agent. CENTCOM dutifully recorded that the Czech chemical contingent had "Detected GA/GB, and that hazard is flowing down from factory storage bombed in Iraq. Predictably, this has become/is going to be a problem."

* * *

The predawn hours of January 20 continued to be busy ones for Iraqi missile crews and their intended targets. Seabee Roy Morrow of Phoenix City, Alabama, had been sleeping in the King Abdul Aziz stadium when he heard two explosions between 0300-0330. He ran to the bunker, and went to MOPP level 2 for about a half-hour before the "all clear" was given. When he took off his mask and exited the bunker, marines came running up screaming "MOPP-4!"

The siren sounded again, Morrow felt a burning sensation spread along his arms, legs and the back of his neck, as well as across his ears and face. His lips went numb. His unit went to full MOPP-4. As he headed back to the bunker, Morrow saw a strobe-like flash illuminate the sky above the commercial port of al Jubayl. The radio in the bunker began calling for the decontamination teams to respond. That meant Edwards. As the head of the unit's decontamination team, he was called later that day to decontaminate incoming personnel. Because the Mark 12 decontamination unit assigned to his team was inoperative, Edwards was assigned to take out a 500 gallon water truck and stand by. His team did not decontaminate anyone. But Edwards told Morrow that mustard gas and lewisite had been detected. When the Seabees questioned their commanding officer about the incident, he ordered them not to discuss it.

* * *

From his position near King Fahd International Airport, Rocky Gallegos, a Lance Corporal with Bravo Battery, 2nd Light Anti-aircraft Missile Battalion, watched what appeared to be a SCUD missile being shot out of the sky by a Patriot missile almost directly over his head. The explosion "blossomed like a flower."

The missile tumbled. Spitting flames, it exploded again when it struck the ground. Almost immediately Gallegos experienced a "very strong raunchy taste, like very bitter burnt toast" in his mouth. A sudden headache assailed him, and he felt like throwing up. About 10 minutes later, when the alert finally sounded and they were ordered to put on their masks, Gallegos found it painful to look at bright lights.

By the time he was assigned to drive his NBC officer to check the chemical detection units, the thoroughly miserable Gallegos was afflicted with diarrhea. At the fourth or fifth unit they visited, the NBC noncom came back with a written note. Shoving the paper into his pocket, the sergeant abruptly ordered Gallegos, "Get me back to camp. Now!"

* * *

At 0550, General Schwarzkopf's Central Command logged two British units "reporting positive H [mustard] readings, using M-9 detection paper." The incident was especially troubling because there was a shortage of American MOPP-4 gear throughout the Theater of Operations.

Five FROGs also hopped over the southern Kuwait border into Saudi Arabia. Four fell into the desert near US Marine positions. Another rocket landed across the street from a Saudi naval base. A US marine stationed nearby claimed that there had been as many as five "gas attack" alerts in a single day.

As dawn's first light percolated through an oily sky, navy reservist Nick Roberts noticed a thin yellow powder coating tents and vehicles. Other Seabees were already avoiding an area near the port's commercial entrance cordoned off with yellow "chemical-hazard" tape. They were encouraged to give the place a wide birth by the sight of fenced-in animals. Though apparently unmarked, the entire herd was dead.

Later that day, as Saddam Hussein made a radio address promising that Iraq would soon be fighting back with "all the means and potential God has given us," Seabee Mike Moore remembers everyone's chemical suits and masks being collected and replaced by the battalion's chemical officers. As CIA analyst Patrick Eddington later pointed out, such exchanges of MOPP gear were "an extremely rare occurrence because of suit shortages which persisted throughout the Gulf War."

Despite the unusual suit swap, Moore was told by his superior officers that the explosion was a sonic boom, to quit worrying about it, and to get back to work. When members of the unit continued to question the unit commanders about what had occurred, they were ordered not to discuss the incident.

* * *

Far from "neutralizing" deadly nerve agents, coalition aircrews were inadvertently dispersing chemical warfare toxins in quantities Saddam Hussein would have handed out decorations for.

As Jim Brown later described, the formula was simple: Blow up CBW storage and production facilities in the middle of a desert filled with aluminum silicate as fine as talcum and presto! – you have concocted a "dusty agent" capable of penetrating the best protective gear. Brown later found industry standards stating that at least 30% of any liquid will be immediately absorbed by "this type of particulate matter without the use of additional procedures."

Contaminate a third or more of the sand thrown high into the atmosphere with sarin, tabun or mycotoxins, Brown points out, and you have created a CBW agent able to travel long distances, penetrate protective gear and remain relatively stable in a desert environment, instead of dissipating quickly. This toxic fallout would also arrive over allied positions in low enough concentrations not to cause immediate casualties.

As high-altitude winds continued to blow from Iraq into Saudi Arabia and Kuwait, the Czech Federation soldiers continued to identify "borderline life-threatening concentrations of the chemical agents yperite and sarin" in King Khalid Military City. The official Czech report said the mustard and nerve agents were "probably the result of the Allies' air attacks on the storage facilities of chemical ammunition in the territory of Iraq assigned to an area near the Saudi-Iraqi border at Hafir al Batin." The Czechs believed that the detections were caused by the weather inversion which occurred that day as the weather front moved southward.

* * *

Miles away, in the north of the Saudi emirate, a driver/mechanic with the 601st Transportation Company was trying to ignore the war. Michael Kingsbury had taken leave to visit Riyadh for six hours' "rest and relaxation" when the first missile attack on that city took place. Three SCUDs came roaring in to explode almost simultaneously overhead. Kingsbury saw prismatic rainbow colors glisten in the sky as the chemical alarms sounded and everybody went to MOPP-4. By the time he had his suit on, Kingsbury was feeling nauseous. His nose began to run, his eyes burned a little, his skin felt prickly, and he had a sore throat.

In Dhahran that day, Staff Sergeant Patricia Browning was at the Khobar Towers when she observed a Patriot missile intercept a SCUD directly overhead.

Later that night, a sergeant with another Transportation Company – the 1113th – was outside the "Expo" building just north of Dhahran with about fifteen other troops, preparing to redeploy to Tent City. Suddenly the unit heard two or three loud explosions close enough to feel the concussion.

As Randall Vallee and his buddies ran for cover in school buses parked nearby, their officers began yelling for everyone to get back inside the Expo center and go to MOPP-4. Vallee dashed back to the building. Alarms were going off in the distance; nearby air raid sirens sounded after he had entered the building.

Vallee struggled into his chemical gear and sat down heavily, feeling nauseous and weak. His head throbbed and swam.

His vision blurred and he began sweating profusely. He felt so thirsty he feared he was dangerously dehydrated. The headache and nausea lasted about 20 minutes. About 45 minutes after the attack, Vallee started to recover from his swoon. The "all clear" sounded, and Vallee ventured back into the perilous desert night. There still didn't seem to be enough air to breathe. He noticed a "very suffocating smell...kind of like ammonia, but very strong." Other soldiers around him commented on the smell, which soon dissipated on the night breeze. Vallee popped a PB nerve agent pretreatment pill and boarded a bus for Tent City.

Several more attacks accompanied by the aroma of ammonia would visit Vallee there as fragments from intercepted missiles rained between the tents. As the days went by, the Seabee says his chest "started getting tight." He felt like he was getting bad flu as intermittent bouts of nausea, fatigue, headaches and breathing difficulty sometimes made him too dizzy to walk. Diagnosed with an ear infection, Vallee was sent home on January 28th.

William Brady, the Log Base Alpha NCO who had come under attack on the 18th, was by now coughing up blood. Staff Sergeant Willie Hicks, whose unit had been hit at Cement City the day before Brady's, was also feeling ill. There was blood in his urine, and "a couple of guys started getting sick. Some guys had a problem with their rectums." Despite orders from their CO not to discuss their distress, "We were discussing it anyway," Hicks recalls, "because I was in charge of ammunition movements and the guys there, they knew it had to be chemical."

CHAPTER 4

"YOU WILL LOSE"

The Americans were not alone in their experience or surmises. Corporal Richard Turnbull, a Royal Air Force NBC specialist who makes his home just outside Liverpool, was responsible for 27 NAIAD chemical alarms on the perimeter of the British sector of the al Jubayl airbase on the night of the 19th to 20th. "Within seconds of the warhead landing, every chemical-agent monitoring device in the area was blasting the alarm," Turnbull recalls.

The Brits went to Condition Black. "We were put into the highest alert for twenty minutes, and then we were told it was a false alarm caused by the fuel from aircraft taking off." But Turnbull had already carried out two residual-vapor detection tests for chemical and biological agents. Both were positive. His superiors dismissed the test results, claiming that jet fuel had triggered the indicators.

But Turnbull saw people getting sick in the chest and eyes. "They got infections and skin rashes," he recalls. "One lad had his whole body covered with spots from head to toe."

The British NBC expert was convinced the exploding SCUD carried a chemical warhead. "We tried on umpteen occasions, when aircraft were taking off in mass numbers," to fool the alarms he says. "We stood on the side of the runway closer to the area where the aircraft were taking off. We carried out tests, and we got no readings." Turnbull was finally warned to drop the case or find himself facing imprisonment under Britain's strict secrecy laws. "I've had a very, very senior officer friend of mine ring me up and say, 'Richie, back off, you're kicking over a can of worms.'"

* * *

Corporal Terry Walker was at the docks at al Jubayl around 0230. "There was a couple of mighty bangs above our heads and suddenly all the chemical alarms went off and there were soldiers just running around in sheer panic, running around trying to get on their chemical suits," recounted this British First Armored Division driver. The sirens went off, and an "ammonia-like smell" filled the air.

Walker had trouble getting his gas mask on. Soon after the SCUDs hit, he says, "I was feeling the burning sensation under the chin, around the back of the head as well." Many of the people around him also fell sick after the attack. "It was obvious that there was a chemical attack, but our superiors told us it was the jet fighters flying over with the sonic booms, and that it was also the fumes from the jets that set the alarms off. The thing is," Walker adds, "they never went off before. The planes were flying day in and day out, and the alarms never went off at all, and on January 20, for about a 10-mile, 15-mile radius, these alarms went off." The US Marines at al Jubayl were not worried about jet exhaust.

When Ken Allison of the 174th Marine Wing Support Squadron went to deliver supplies to al Jubayl airfield, the Lance Corporal was dismayed to see a sign posted on a guard shack at the airfield's southern gate warning that the area had tested positive for chemicals, to make sure that MOPP gear was ready, and that when the alarms go off it is for real.

At 1540 on the 20th, the Czech chemical detection specialists reported tabun, soman and sulfur-mustard agents at King Khalid Military City. Less than two hours later, David Pena, a mechanic attached to the 3rd Armor Division at KKMC, heard an explosion and saw a cloud form overhead. While his unit went to MOPP-4 for nearly two hours, Pena was stricken by nausea, blurred vision, aching lungs and rashes. Just outside al Jubayl, thousands of dead sheep, goats and dogs littered the highways. Blue bags, standard UN equipment for victims of chemical or biological attack, covered their heads.

* * *

The following day, Lance Corporal Rocky Gallegos was back out patrolling the area around King Fahd International Airport, where the previous day's explosion occurred. Gallegos and his team saw at least half a dozen dead sheep and a couple of camels that appeared to be very sick. Gallegos himself wasn't feeling so good. His headaches, nausea, diarrhea, and sensitivity to light would get worse before he finally departed Saudi Arabia.

By now, the Seabees who had experienced burning skin, facial numbness, and choking following the unexplained double explosion on the 19th were beginning to suffer from extreme flulike symptoms. Fever, sweating, diarrhea and muscle spasms were common among the 24th Construction Battalion. Exposed skin also broke out in rashes, welts and small pustules. When the blisters burst, they turned into ulcerating sores that scabbed over and appeared to heal, but later reopened. Some Seabees began complaining of aching joints. As the pain became progressively worse, several sailors developed painfully swollen lymph nodes.

Michael Adcock, a four-year high school football letterman who worked out daily and broke a unit weight lifting record while stationed in Germany, was also sick on the 21st after experiencing three attacks on al Jubayl the previous night. Four days later, Adcock reported to the Battalion Evacuation hospital. He was told he probably had hemorrhoids, and was given the drug Motrin for his symptoms.

Brian Martin, of Niles, Michigan, was serving with the 37th Airborne Combat Engineer Battalion between Rafha and Naryian about six miles south of the Iraqi border when he recorded in his journal that chemical alarms were going off almost every day. At first, Martin and his buddies were told that the "false alarms" were being caused by oil vapors coming off the sand. But when the alarms kept going off, the increasingly skeptical engineers were informed by both their battalion commander and the top NBC officer that the alarms were sounding because of "minute" quantities of nerve agent released by the coalition bombing of Iraqi chemical weapons facilities. The troops were assured that there was no danger. But Martin, who later watched what looked like a Patriot interception of an incoming SCUD over the desert between al Khafji and Wadi al Batin, was already feeling jittery from taking pyridostigmine bromide. The anti-nerve agent also made his vision "jiggle."

Troy Albuck, a former anti-tank platoon leader with the 82nd Airborne Division, was told that the chemical alarms were going off because of fallout from the Coalition bombings. He was also informed that non-lethal exposure was not harmful and would be counteracted by fresh air.

Jim Brown's camp hadn't been hit yet. But the 514th Maintenance Company specialist was growing tired of the chemical alarms sounding every night. The battalion NBC officer finally instructed his company's NBC personnel to remove batteries from the MA81 detectors. "This was due," says Brown, "to the frustration of having an alarm go off at 0200, and after responding, finding either nothing, or nothing that made sense."

But the Egyptians stationed just three to four kilometers away from the 514th continued firing Red Star clusters, the allied signal for chemical attack. Brown now says that if the 514th "had been fully informed as to the types of agents available, I believe that these false-positives would have met more serious concern, rather than being dismissed." Instead, he and the others in his company were told by their officers to ignore the "malfunctioning" alarms.

* * *

Sergeant House never heard any alarms. The US Air Force technician was tasked with decontaminating F-111s as they returned from bombing raids against Iraqi chemical and biological warfare facilities. During the early part of the air war, his unit's swing-wing bombers hit 32 chemical targets, 113 bunkers and 11 SCUD Missile sites. Despite regulations calling for chemical decontamination solutions to be applied while wearing special suits, House and several other Air Force techs had worn their MOPP suits without masks – and used water to decontaminate the aircraft. On the evening of the 21st, after decontaminating several returning aircraft reeking with a pungent odor, House's face began to burn and swell. A splitting headache, prolonged coughing, nausea, vomiting and diarrhea quickly followed.

At 2115 that same evening, the Czechs came back on the net to report a trace quantity of tabun, soman and yperite, which they claimed to be fallout from heavy bombing raids against Iraqi chemical storage and weapons sites. As the Czechs warned of chemicals in the air, demonstrators shouting, "No blood for oil!" and waving signs warning that the world had been "amBushed," were being arrested by Washington, DC cops. *Newsweek* had just hit the stands, asking, "No Way Out?" The news magazine helpfully supplied a map showing Schwarzkopf's secret strategy: a possible flanking attack led by his VII and VIII Corps when the ground war got underway.

Rival *Time* magazine later explained to its readers that "The US intends to smash Iraq's offensive military capability so that it is no longer a menace to its neighbors. Yet Washington wishes to leave enough of the Iraq army intact to keep the defeated nation from being riven by internal strife or carved up by Iran, Syria and Turkey." The editors added that US military strategists "were worried that the allies would win too quickly, inducing Saddam to pull out of Kuwait with his personal power and most of his military machine intact."

* * *

For now, all of the action was in the air. At 0040 Saudi time on January 21st, Army Lieutenant Phoebe Jeter was watching a green radar scope when she heard "Okay folks, we have a SCUD alert" in her headphones. A sudden blip showed a tactical missile coming in. The heart of the only woman to launch Patriot missiles during the war began to race. "All around I could hear the *Boom! Boom! Boom! Boom!* of other Patriot batteries starting to fire," Jeter recalls. "The van began to rock." For five interminable minutes, SCUDs, Patriots and debris filled her screen like popcorn. She put her gas mask on. Outside the radar van, soldiers were commenting excitedly about a sky that looked like Star Wars. The Patriots had downed four SCUDs.

Later that night, John Sewart, a road master in the US Marine Reserves, watched a SCUD penetrate a Patriot air defense battery and explode over the Port of al Jubayl. A siren sounded, and the Marines donned their protective gear. After some time passed, someone supposedly gave the "all clear." The Marine reservists removed their gas masks only to discover a strange odor lingering on the air. The smell soon dissipated. But people began heading over to the port's American Hospital for cough medicine and headache tablets.

* * *

Every Iraqi schoolboy understood that Saddam's pledge to "burn the ground under their feet" referred to a battle immortalized in the Koran, when Arabs drove back an infidel army by hurtling huge fiery stones from on high. As burning warheads continued to fall on Israeli cities, threatening to pull that country into the war, frantic coalition targeters were finding that locating and destroying 35-foot long missiles that took nearly five hours to fuel was much more difficult than they had anticipated.

As coalition jets flying up to 3,000 sorties a day tried in vain to neutralize mobile SCUD launchers disguised by wood-and-fiberglass decoys or hidden under highway overpasses, a US Navy air attack against a Norwegian oil tanker earned a threat of court martial from Schwarzkopf for polluting the Gulf.

Attacks against the Iraqi lieutenant's air base were also unremitting. An attack on the 22nd deposited four unexploded bombs in soft sand outside his bunker. "The situation was very difficult, because we had to pass close by them. But God protects," the officer wrote. "What an awful sight: one of the soldiers (disturbed) one of the bombs and suddenly it exploded and the soldier disappeared and I saw (two pieces) of his flesh on the second story of the bunker. Allah akbar. What a horrible thing to see."

* * *

Despite flying round-the-clock sorties at the rate of one flight every 1.8 minutes, the allied air forces had so far lost only 22 planes – most of them American carrier jets – early in the "missile war." Another 15, including a giant B-52, had been damaged. For most pilots, it was a cakewalk. As US Air Force pilot Captain Genther Drummond remarked: "It was as if we had no adversary."

British pilots flying at jet speeds just 50 feet off the deck were the unhappy exception. Braving "curtains of death" to crater heavily defended Iraqi runways, the RAF lost eight crewmen and six of their 36 Tornado fighter-bombers in just four days. More than twice that many RAF jets would eventually be hit. On January 22, British high command scrapped further low-altitude attacks against airfields.

At 0957 that day, an entry in the 101st Air Assault Division's operations log read: "6th French has detected 'light' traces of chem agents tabun and sarin." A follow-up entry at 1350 noted: "French chemical alarms activated in French TAA [tactical assembly area]. The French report finding GA [tabun], GB [sarin]and H [mustard] blister in 'sub-lethal quantities.' The French assess incident to be result of bombing of chemical agent storage in as Salman [Iraq]." Sometime later, the 101st's own chemical alarms started going off.

Later on the 22nd, the writer of the "Dear Mom" letter observed many dead and dying animals while patrolling the perimeter of Camp 13. Members of Seabee Roy Morrow's unit who had been hit by a SCUD near King Abdul Aziz air base two days before, now began to suffer from rashes, diarrhea, and fatigue. Morrow's numbness would persist for a week. The aching joints, he says, began a couple of weeks later.

William Brady was by now too ill to carry out his duties. He had been taking the nerve agent pretreatment pills since about January 17 and had been getting severe headaches from them. Three days after the attack on Log Base Alpha, the sickened survivor of the SCUD attack on al Jubayl developed a high fever. His eyes began to burn, and "taking a breath of air made his lungs feel like they were burning up."

Brady also suffered from diarrhea, open sores, nausea and a persistent runny nose. Two days later he went to the 13th Evacuation Hospital. But no beds were available. The hospital was completely filled with people that seemed to have the same illness that he had. Brady's January 26 diary entry read: "I'd rather die than feel like this." The noncom was convinced his unit had "got hit with a nerve agent."

* * *

Chris Alan Kornkven wasn't sure whether to believe his own eyes or Iraqi prisoners of war. A Staff Sergeant with the 340th Combat Support Company, Kornkven had been told by a US military doctor at the 312th Evacuation Hospital that captured Iraqi officers had told the doctors that although they had chemical weapons at the front, and authorization to use them, the surface winds in their area were blowing the wrong way.

* * *

CNN's Peter Arnett didn't stop to gauge the political winds when he pointed his cameraman toward a bomb-gutted factory on the 23rd. His Iraqi guides said the factory had produced formula for hungry infants. But angry CENTCOM spokesmen insisted the factory had been producing "biological weapons."

Why such a facility would be located in downtown Baghdad when all other CBW plants were situated miles away from population centers wasn't explained. Also curious was the lack of concern by plant personnel who handled the white powder for CNN's camera, and the guests who returned to the al Rasheed hotel with powder salvaged from the wreckage to feed babies and stir into their coffee.

* * *

While Arnett waded through a controversy over spilled milk, the Iraqi lieutenant was making a short diary entry: "O God, protect! O God, save us! The planes came back to bomb again." M8 chemical alarms were also sounding at Ras al Khaki, and at a Division Supply Area about 20 kilometers away. According to Staff Sergeant Norman Camp, the Saudi-based marines were told not to go to MOPP 4. Many became sick the following night. At 2100 hours, the Czechs reportedly detected an "unknown substance".

But according to former CIA intelligence analyst, Patrick Eddington, CENTCOM was still not taking seriously the problem they had predicted. Central Command's computer model was programmed with only low-level surface winds. Fallout dispersal patterns from upper atmospheric winds were omitted. After the January 23 Czech detection, CENTOM ordered all units to "disregard any reports from the Czechs."

At 1438 on the 24th, the 101st Airborne's G-2 reported a "possible chem strike in the tri-border area." USMC Staff Sergeant Norman Camp was stationed near Ras al Khaki on the 23rd when the M8 chemical alarms went off, not only at his position, but also at the Division Supply Area about 20 kilometers to the east. Division passed the word not to go to MOPP-4.

That same day, another marine message warning of continuing gas mask shortages was sent to the Albany facility. That night, Sergeant Norman Camp's entire platoon began falling ill. Camp himself experienced headaches, nausea and diarrhea all the next day. Most of the others, he says, were sick for about a day and a half.

* * *

French logistics officer Jean Paul Ferrand remembers nerve and mustard agents being detected on January 24 or 25 to the south of King Khalid Military City. Ferrand told Agency France wire service that two chemical weapons alarms went off after a desert storm blew in from Iraq.

* * *

Joseph Boccardi was a driver/loader/gunner in a US 1st Cavalry M1A1 tank. Injured by a fall from the tank, Boccardi was recovering in a medical holding area in northern Saudi Arabia, when a lieutenant there invited Boccardi to accompany him on a short drive to a Saudi basic training camp. Located near King Khalid Military City, the facility, known locally as the "glass palace," appeared beautiful and palace-like to Boccardi. When they encountered two soldiers carrying Kalashnikovs at the top of a staircase, the lieutenant began speaking a foreign language which sounded Russian. But the lieutenant explained that he was speaking Czech.

Boccardi and the lieutenant entered a room to find eight or nine soldiers smoking, drinking vodka, and playing cards. On learning that all were members of an elite NBC team, Boccardi asked someone: "if we were kicking their butts so bad, why didn't they hit us with chemicals?"

Sudden silence greeted this remark. Speaking broken English, a Czech colonel said, "they did hit us with chemicals." According to the colonel, an incoming SCUD had recently penetrated KKMC and hit nearby. Donning their chemical gear, the Czech chemical detection and decontamination team went out onto their balcony and measured traces of sarin and another gas which sounded like "tabun."

The Czech colonel who commanded the unit said that when he called CENTCOM with their findings, he was told to keep quiet about it. A number of the soldiers broke out in skin rashes shortly after this incident: at least 18 Czechs later became sick with the same symptoms suffered by British and American troops.

* * *

When his Hercules touched down at al Jubayl on 24 January, 1991, Canadian medic David Prestwich didn't know he'd landed on what US Senate investigators would later confirm was an active bio-battlefield. "You saw what was at the end of your nose," he recalls. "That was all you knew."

By the time they got the C-130 unloaded, Saudi Arabia had turned from exotic supposition into an endless expanse of dirt. Prestwich found it "a desolate place." Even the sky seemed alien. Iraqi troops had set alight storage tanks and oil wells at al Wafra field in southern Kuwait and at the al Shuaiba refinery complex just north of Mina al-Ahmadi. As an ominous widening pall from a thousand burning oil wells spread across the sun, an ocean of fine sand clogged uniforms, M-16s and immune systems with equal impartiality. Insects attacked like insurgents. Some carried Sand Fever. Like everyone else, Prestwich bought some DEET to keep the bugs at bay.

The overpowering din and confusion of war were not so easily repelled. Prestwich remembers "massive amounts of people, aircraft, equipment" accompanied by "overpowering noise, sights, smells – and the urgency of getting your own job done." He credits his training for helping him face "stress, stress, stress."

Half-choked by the desert dust, he could have used a few beers. While people back home "were sucking back Molson Canadian, I was in my 20th hour of a grueling day sucking back my 20th cup of coffee," Prestwich says today. Even in the rush to establish Canada's only Mid-East medical presence in the middle of the Saudi desert, his superiors made sure the 34 year-old Sergeant-Major and his men took their Pyridostigmine Bromide three times a day.

"That PB was weird stuff." Prestwich remembers. Some of his people vomited when they took the small white tablets. Prestwich himself would awaken from "crazy, wild dreams" to find himself wringing-wet in his sleeping bag under an unfamiliar sky. "Being there seemed to be the dream," he recalls. "And the dream seemed to be the reality."

The basic idea was to save lives and not get killed. But as an oil spill 25-times bigger than Exxon Valdez began washing ashore at al Jubayl, the allies' key port and runway complex drew SCUDs like magnets. Three nights before Prestwich's arrival, a missile exploding over the harbor had set off chemical alarms throughout the area. The American's 13th Evacuation Hospital quickly overflowed with sick marines.

The Canadian contingent was not briefed on the attack. They were too busy moving 1 Canadian Field Hospital to Al Quamsumah, just 50 klicks from Iraq's border. "Conditions were deplorable at best," Prestwich remembers. "Pretty dismal. Filthy." He shrugs. "That's soldiering. It was the desert, what can you expect?" As the Canadians labored to set up Triage and Resuscitation centers, three 33-bed wards and four high-tech operating theaters, all under canvas, the sky began to weep oil. Black rain fell for a week, turning roads "into a soup" that "dried on boots like concrete."

Casualties were already coming in. Most of the patients Prestwich treated were stunned and starving teenage Iraqi conscripts emerging from ã round-the-clock barrage. Lindane was used to control lice. To discourage carrion-birds, all body parts, dressings and feces were burned.

* * *

American soldiers more worried about dressing for possible chemical combat than parade review were running out of reliable NBC wardrobe. On January 25, Albany's Defense Personnel Support Center warned all units serving in the Gulf that MOPP-4 "suits manufactured by Camel Mfg....should not be used, and are to be considered suspect." The next day, the 101st Division Artillery reported NBC alarms going off.

The day after those fresh alarms, US Marines in Oman rehearsed for amphibious landings on the Kuwait coast. As an oil slick spread from opened valves at the Sea Island loading terminal off al Ahmadi in Kuwait, US Air Force F-111s bombed the oil manifolds in an attempt to blast them closed. "My mind and heart are with my relatives, and only my body is with the army," the Iraqi lieutenant wrote. "I had a dream yesterday and it was not a good omen at all."

The Iraqi officer's dream was prescient. The next day, January 28, he recorded... "enemy air raids continue and I am in a (shelter). The top of it is only tent canvas. God protect us all. After sunset, a flock of sheep came up to us. Apparently the owner of the flock had been killed in the air raids. The enemy with his modern planes has launched air strikes on a shepherd. Maybe the enemy took the sheep for nuclear or chemical or petroleum sheep. For shame."

But the "enemy" had their own problems. During the early morning hours of January 28, the 101st's Brigade log recorded an M8A1 alarm at approximately 0045. The detection was confirmed by M256 kit. At approximately 0130, the log notes that D Company "reported an MA81 alarm and detected nerve agent using two separate M256 kits." About 20 minutes later, a chemical team reported hearing another M8A1. But this unit was unable to detect nerve agent using an M256 kit.

Following allied air strikes on the chemical weapons storage bunkers at Mosul Airbase, NOAA thermal imaging showed smoke plumes coming from an area close to the south of two large lakes west of Baghdad, extending to the southeast.

Arnett ignored the city's ubiquitous smoke as he followed his Iraqi handlers to a house in the suburbs of Baghdad. All he'd been told was that he was being given a rare opportunity to interview a "high-ranking" government official. After being swept by a metal detector and having disinfectant poured over his hands, CNN's star reporter was introduced to Saddam.

The tyrant had dispensed with gold braid. But he had not backed down from previous promises to make American troops "swim in their own blood." More than mere rhetoric, this phrase – and others like it – was intended to remind his Arab audience of the Abassid empire. The high water mark of Arab conquest saw the 9th century Muslim world stretch from Morocco to the Khyber Pass. As Newsweek later noted, "The blood-swimming passage was taken word-for-word from al-Tabar, the Herodotus of the Arab world who chronicled the jihads of the Abassid Empire."

Arnett was used to strongmen and their convoluted rationales. In Greece, Angola and Afghanistan, Salvador and Guatemala, he had always covered both sides. Now CNN's most controversial correspondent was acutely conscious of being seen as a propaganda mouthpiece by a dictator the world urgently needed to hear from. As he put his questions to Saddam Hussein, Arnett was careful never to respectfully address his temperamental host as "sir" or "mister president."

But the broadcast ignited another uproar. As US military personnel throughout the Gulf screamed for Arnett's head, Senator Alan Simpson touched off anti-Arnett furor back home when he denounced the newsman as an Iraqi "sympathizer." While enhancing Simpson's stature as a tough-talking Senator, the widely televised stance was somewhat contradictory. As People magazine reported, the Wyoming Republican "had junketed to Baghdad just four months before the invasion of Kuwait to praise Saddam."

* * *

While Saddam awaited the arrival of Arnett and his camera crew, a group of tired RAF personnel was filing into a stifling room at an airbase outside Dhahran. The heat weighed heavily. So did rumors concerning chemical warfare. As the *London Observer's* Tim Sebastian later described the scene: "Nerves were shaky, tempers short." As the door was secured behind them, a sergeant read out from a single piece of paper. The base was facing imminent biological attack from Iraq, he intoned, and there was little or no protection.

Around the room, Sebastian reports, "stunned faces stared ahead in silence. The sergeant held out one last chance. The RAF, he said, was pinning its hopes on a new biological warfare vaccine which would greatly increase the chance of survival." The men were strongly urged to take it. Refusal could mean a gruesome death. As they reflected on two bad options, the air crews were given an unequivocal order: Don't breathe a word about the vaccine to other British personnel on the base. "There isn't enough of it to go round."

The British sergeant was not exaggerating. About the time he was delivering his "take this or die" speech, American G-2 was reporting to CENTCOM that Saddam Hussein had given brigade commanders authorization to use chemical weapons. The intelligence officers might have been watching CNN. In his interview with Saddam Hussein on January 28, CNN's Peter Arnett had asked, "Will you use chemical weapons in a land war in Kuwait?"

Saddam's reply had been succinct, and scary. "We will use weapons that match those used by our enemy against us. I believe that you have had experience with us now. I believe that you have now found out that we have done everything we have said."

* * *

The Iraqi dictator need not have bothered making CBW threats; coalition targeters were still conducting CB warfare against their own troops. During a nine hour period on the 28th, at least three other American units reported M8A1 alarms going off. One infantry unit followed up with a positive M256 reading for nerve agent. The fallout, says Patrick Eddington, "was undoubtedly coming from chemical warfare storage sites well south of the Euphrates River."

The American high command continued to insist that the CW agents being lofted skyward by allied high-explosives were completely incinerated before posing any threat to troops positioned downwind. But according to the US Army Field Manual 3-9 Potential Military Chemical/Biological Agents and Compounds, sarin is nonflammable. Other agents like mustard have flashpoints high enough to also survive conventional attack.

As allied ground forces moved toward their jumping off points for the simultaneous invasion of Kuwait and Iraq, the SCUDs followed the main axis of their advance to Hafir al Batin, less than 20 miles from David Prestwich's bunk. Just after dark on the 28th, the chemical alarms went off at 1 Canadian Field Hospital. In a split second, some 60 startled people lining up for anthrax shots instead ran to don bulky rubber suits, gas masks, gloves and boots. Prestwich apparently escaped unscathed. At least, nobody in his detachment heard anything. Nothing landed nearby. The all-clear sounded and everybody went back to their posts.

* * *

Would the Iraqis fight? Betting by Arabs around the region was that the shell-shocked conscripts would surrender in droves. On Tuesday, January 29, Schwarzkopf's field commanders got a chance to test their enemy's mettle when nine brigades of Iraq's 5th Mechanized Division swept into al Kahfji, a small town just inside Saudi Arabia.

Two eight-man squads of US Marines infiltrated a ghost town abandoned by 20,000 fleeing residents two weeks before. Just after dark, Corporal Jeffrey Brown and his heavily outnumbered companions heard a high-pitched whine. Peering from an upper window, they watched a column of APCs roll into town. "It's the Iraqis. Great," thought Brown. "We are basically surrounded. If they spot me, they're not going to yell, freeze!"

As the armored column passed by about 40 yards away, the marines' view was blocked by a building further down the street. Shutting the doors carefully behind them, they slipped out a back gate into a side street. Dodging from cars to telephone poles to doorways, they reached the intervening building and "flew up the steps." Just as they set up behind a low parapet on the roof, an Iraqi patrol entered the side-street.

From the south wall, Brown could see the Iraqis preparing to ambush the allied counter-attack. They must have wondered what hit them as the marines began calling in air and artillery strikes on top of their own position. Brown was knocked down by a shell fragment that "felt like somebody had hit me with a baseball bat. What it did to the Iraqis," he says, "it vaporized them."

* * *

While the fight for Kahfji raged, Tallil Airfield's outdoor

chemical weapons storage areas were heavily bombed, spreading toxic black smoke along the coast. On January 30, the thick smoke plume still pouring out of Samarra extended even farther toward the southeast. US Navy intelligence reported: "Unconfirmed Iraqi defector information indicates chemical and biological weapons have been dispersed to forward areas."

Six SCUDs hit Tel Aviv and Haifa; at least one struck Riyadh. Four Israelis and one Saudi were killed; at least 130 Israelis and 30 Saudis were injured. During the first 10 days of the war, Iraq had fired about 50 SCUDs.

On Thursday. January 31, air and artillery-supported troops from Saudi Arabia and Qatar retook Kahfji from the invaders, who surrendered en masse when the marines attacked. A diving A-10 nearly hit a radio tower before firing a stream of DU-tipped cannon shells into an APC. The look-alike troop carrier with its identifying inverted-V symbol on each side was filled with US Marines. Once again, "friendly fire" was proving more menacing than Iraqi tanks and armored vehicles, which American officers at Kahfji observed were in terrible shape.

That night, marine units operating with night-vision gear near Khafji spotted a FROG rocket battery capable of launching either an explosive or chemical barrage. A US Air Force Special Operations AC-130 was called in to eliminate the threat. First used in Vietnam, the four-engine Hercules transport mounted a multibarreled Gatling gun firing out the side of the circling plane. Each "puff" of fire directed a deluge of shells scything any target within range. As it maneuvered to attack the FROG site, the multi-engine PUFF was shot down by Iraqi ground fire. All 14 crew members were killed.

A Joint Surveillance and Target Attack Radar System aircraft later detected an Iraqi convoy carrying more FROG rockets fitted with chemical munitions. This convoy was destroyed by F-6 fighter-bombers.

The next day, the chemical production plants Habbaniyah-1 and 2 were bombed again. Chemical weapons storage areas at as Shuaybah were also hit.

On February 2, recorded the Iraqi lieutenant, "I had breakfast and afterwards something indescribable happened. Two enemy planes came toward us and began firing at us, in turn, with missiles, machine guns and rockets. I was almost killed. Death was a yard away from me. The missiles, machine guns and rockets didn't let up. One of the rockets hit and pierced our shelter, which was penetrated by shrapnel."

The Iraqi soldiers cried "Allah, Allah, Allah" over and over again as one 3rd Company tank burned and three others blew up. "That was a very bad experience," the shaken officer wrote. "Time passed and we waited to die... How hard it is to be killed by someone you don't know, you've never seen and can't confront. He is in the sky and you're on the ground."

While many Iraqi soldiers waited to die that day, General

Norman Schwarzkopf was deciding against amphibious landing in Kuwait. DIA bomb damage assessors also reported to CENTCOM that 37 ammunition storage buildings had been destroyed at the huge Tal al Lahm Ammunition Depot in Khamisiyah. Approximately 10,000 tons of munitions had been lofted into the air, upwind of American and other coalition forces.

American M8 alarms had been sounding constantly for weeks. First Brigade finally had enough. At 1745, brigade headquarters notified all battalion elements to operate their M8 alarms just two hours a day "due to battery shortage."

* * *

During the weekend February 2nd to 3rd, the US lost four more aircraft, including a B-52 heavy bomber. (This reported loss by accompanying aircrews does not show up in official records listing six of the eight-engine bombers hit before returning safely to base.) Flying in another aging Superfortress out of a RAF base in Fairfield, England, Captain Brian "Disco" Liso caught the flash of surface-to-air missiles being launched 30,000 feet below. Liso couldn't believe people were shooting at him.

On Sunday, 18-gun broadsides from the battleships USS Mississippi and Wisconsin lofted 16-inch shells weighing more than a ton against targets in Kuwait. Over the next three days, coalition air strikes would also be flown against chemical munitions storage areas at Iraq's ad Diwaniyah and Karbalah, as well as airfields at al Taqaddum and Kirkuk. French Ministry of Defense spokesman General Raymond Germanos confirmed that chemical fallout – "probably neurotoxins" – had been detected in small quantities, "a little bit everywhere." Germanos blamed the sickening fallout on "allied air attacks of Iraqi chemical weapons facilities and the depots that stored them."

Later that day, the 101st's NBC element reported: "Iraqi forces have been observed placing 55-gallon drums along specific locations on the border." About 70 drums had been observed being placed along a trail and defensive berms. Though it was hard to be certain, American forward observers thought the Iraqi forces moving the drums had covered their faces and hands with masks and gloves.

Weeks later, an American marine would discover several olive-drab green and gray 55-gallon drums labeled with both Arabic and Cyrillic writing segregated inside a marked-off area within a captured Iraqi munitions area. UNSCOM inspectors would later find identical drums containing chemical precursors and bulk chemical agents at the Muthanna chemical production establishment.

Were the Iraqis preparing to use their aerosol generators to add more toxins to already poisonous nighttime winds? Kirkuk Airbase was bombed again on February fifth. As disturbing discrepancies in estimated Iraqi casualties cropped up during intelligence briefings given in Washington and Riyadh, NOAA satellite photos showed braided smoke plumes extending from Kuwait into Saudi Arabia. The following day, coalition bombs heavily damaged the CW storage depot at Kirkuk. Secretary of Defense Dick Cheney and the Chairman of the Joint Chiefs General Colin Powell arrived for an eight hour briefing by Schwarzkopf and his commanders on the imminent ground assault.

* * *

When he arrived at his Riyadh bunker every morning, General Schwarzkopf immediately made for the big situation map updating enemy positions in the tri-border area. Every day he watched the Iraqi's web of oil-filled trenches, minefields and other obstacles thicken. Multiple rocket launchers were deployed in the the Rumayah area, and symbols for two dozen decontamination sites spotted the KTO. The worst scenario, he told his staff, was for their troops to "get hung up on the wire and have chemicals dumped on them."

As the American general watched the map's day-by-day unfolding, he noticed that the Iraqi defenses were not going any further west. He remembered how the British General Montgomery and his "Desert Rats" had defeated Rommel's Panzers in another desert with a deceptive feint.

Studying the Iraqi defenses, Schwarzkopf began considering a "Hail Mary" play. This football ploy sends a player to the far sidelines as if returning to the bench. But when the ball is snapped, he sprints downfield behind the surprised defenders to receive a pass deep in the enemy end zone.

Schwarzkopf's staff was sure he'd lost his marbles. A single pass receiver was one thing. But 150,00 soldiers, they argued, equipped with 60 days of fuel, ammunition and supplies could never be moved that far that fast.

That was the beauty of his plan, Schwarzkopf shot back. When the Iraqi high command considered that coalition tanks would have to travel 325 kilometers in just two days to achieve surprise on their undefended western flank, they would never believe it. "I'm sure that at some point, somebody said, hey, what about the great big open flank over there? And the Iraqi generals or Saddam Hussein said, hey, nobody could drive over all that desert that far without their tanks breaking down and they're equipment going to hell. They'll never make it."

Still, splitting his forces and sending the bulk of his troops away from Kuwait was a gamble. By the time he met with Cheney, Colin Powell and the rest of his generals for the final briefing, Schwarzkopf had grown increasingly jumpy. Why had his Iraqi counterparts left such a vast stretch of the southern Iraq desert completely empty? Schwarzkopf worried. What does Saddam know about that flank that I don't? Why doesn't he have any forces out there?

His intelligence staff's suggestion that "maybe he plans to pop a nuke out there" was not reassuring. Even worse was when they started to refer to that bafflingly empty sector as a "chemical killing sack." As Schwarzkopf later related: "I had a nightmare vision of Fred Franks and Gary Luck hitting that area only to have the Iraqis dump massive quantities of chemicals while the Republican Guard counterattacked and fought us to a stalemate."

In the end, Schwarzkopf elected to throw the "Hail Mary" pass rather than commit his main thrust into the heavily-fortified Iraqi center in Kuwait. VII Corps would be the linchpin of the allied attack. Along with the "Desert Rats" of Britain's famed First Armored Division, General Frank's Seventh Division was to lead the daring end run around Iraq's western flank. His mission: cut off Saddam's Republican Guard at the Euphrates River.

During the last 16 days of the air war, 150,000 mounted coalition troops had successfully shifted 500 kilometers inland, away from the sea. But as the final briefing got underway, Schwarzkopf scowled at his top field general's "too deliberate" plan, and seemingly squeamish insistence on still more reserves.

It took 600,000 gallons of fuel a day to keep a single armored division of 348 tanks rolling forward. General Franks was worried about outrunning his logistical support across a vast expanse of trackless desert. The careful plan he had prepared called for his huge force to advance, stop, regroup, advance and regroup again.

Schwarzkopf, who was notorious for getting angry enough to throw things, got sore. As military analyst Roger Young writes, the CENTCOM commander "strongly felt that the best chance for success would be a maximum effort, all-out dash across southern Iraq, severing supply and communications lines, cutting off lines of retreat – and convincing an enemy force already demoralized by weeks of round-the-clock bombing that further resistance was futile."

In the end, the law was laid down according to Schwarzkopf. "I do not want a slow, ponderous pachyderm mentality," he declared. "This is not a deliberate attack. I want VII Corps to slam into the Republican Guard. The enemy is not worth shit. Go after them with audacity, shock action, and surprise."

Turning to General John Yeosock, General Schwarzkopf reiterated his orders: "Let me make it clear, John. I do not want a mechanical grind-it-out operation. We must be flexible enough to capitalize on things as they occur. The idea is not to get to intermediate objectives and then stop to rearm and refuel. If you have divisions around, you will present a huge target for chemicals, and you will lose. You cannot have VII Corps stopping for anything."

CHAPTER 5

DOG SOLDIERS

The American army preparing to slam into Iraqi forces entrenched in Kuwait was the same Seventh Cavalry that had once followed a long-haired dandy after "redskins" into a place called Little Bighorn. Certainly the cavalry troops pushing canvas-topped Humvees hard across the Saudi desert were as malodorous as their forebears, whose hard riding and rough living had taken the fierce appellation "Dog Soldiers" from the Cheyenne they pursued.

Custer's elite troopers never saw the Great Spirit come riding over the South Dakota plains astride a coal black pony. What was one more assailant among whooping warriors war-painted with fork-tailed swallows and dragonflies? Seeking vengeance for cavalry massacres of women, children and elders across the Southwest, braves from six lodges overran five companies of dismounted troopers in a fierce fight that lasted just 20 minutes.

Schwarzkopf was no Custer. This time, the Dog Soldiers were going into methodically scouted terrain whose defenders had been disheartened by 38 days and nights of bombing. But the general continued to worry about an opponent who had not hesitated to use chemical weapons against superior forces in Iran. Was he about to send his troops into a trap?

The ancient land of Sumeria and Mesopotamia was no stranger to war. But as the cradle of all civilizations reeled under the first gusts of a gathering desert storm, the scale of destruction quickly eclipsed any bombardment the world had ever seen. Ironically, the dark-skinned desert descendants of Earth's first city-builders who had given the West its first laws, its alphabet, the notion of zero which made arithmetic possible, the modern calendar, even "Western" notions of time divided into units of 60 now bowed under explosive concussions born from those 2,000 year-old concepts.

Lifting a page from General Sherman's crop-burning march to Atlanta during the American civil war, Schwarzkopf's aerial "scorched earth" campaign targeted at least 21 power generating plants and hydroelectric dams. Some targets were hit by more than 20 bombs.

Power failures crippled the world's first city. Short-circuits and power surges also burned out irrigation pumps which could not be easily replaced in a country whose ports were blockaded. As low-flying jets attacked croplands, barns and grain silos, irrigation floodgates were torn apart in cataclysmic combustions. Seawater poured in from the Gulf, once again sowing that fertile crescent under a mantle of salt.

At least four nuclear facilities had also been struck on the first night of bombing. Though they declined to release their test data, US government officials confirmed the presence of radio-activity in Baghdad following the bombing of a nuclear power plant in a northern suburb.

Further north of that stricken city, the diary-jotting Iraqi lieutenant grabbed an opportunity to wash up inside an armored troop carrier. He didn't linger over his ablutions, however, since "these vehicles are usually targets for aircraft." On the 9th, the war-weary soldier noted in despair: "The air raids began, and with them began my descent into the grave."

From February 8 to the 10th, chemical weapons storage sites were bombed at Kirkuk, H-3 Airfield, Nasiriyah, K-2 Airfield, Qayyarah West Airfield, Taji and al Qaim. CW stockpiles at Tikrit were bombed on February 13, followed by Habbaniyah-1 and -2 again on February 17. According to official military announcements made in the latter half of January (and subsequent on-site inspections), coalition air attacks blew up thousands of tons of bulk chemical nerve agents and mustard gas, as well as tens of thousands of pieces of chemical munitions. The amount of chemical warfare agents dispersed on high altitude winds vastly exceeded Saddam Hussein's wildest fantasies of a sustained chemical attack against his adversaries.

As the air war continued, satellite photos tracked dense smoke plumes over western, eastern, and southeastern Iraq, as well as Kuwait. Gun camera videotapes of exploding bunkers, as well as imagery beamed from orbiting satellites, showed debris from the bombings dispersing upwards into the upper atmosphere, where south-flowing winds disbursed trace amounts of CBW fall-out over allied ground forces operating miles away downwind.

* * *

Baghdad's citizenry also suffered from the deadly fallout. On February 10, the Soviet news agency TASS reported: "Following a coalition forces' air raid on a bacteriological weapons producing facility not far from the Iraqi capital, 50 guards of the plant died of an unknown and rapidly progressing disease."

A Cairo newspaper reported that an Egyptian physician working in a Baghdad hospital had fled across the Syrian border. The doctor told how about 100 plant guards had been brought to the hospital immediately after the air attack. Half of them died shortly after being admitted. Survivors suffered sustained injuries to their respiratory, circulatory and intestinal systems.

The physician also reported that attempts to disinfect the hospital were unsuccessful. Biological infection, he said, was spreading in Baghdad. Incidence of disease in Basra, Mosul, and Tikrit, where air strikes were being carried out against chemical and bacteriological facilities, was assuming a "massive character," perhaps even an "epidemic."

US Air Force General Richard Neal had virtually declared Basra a "free-fire zone". On February 11, Neal told reporters,

"Basra is a military town in the true sense... The infrastructure, military infrastructure, is closely interwoven within the city of Basra itself." Without explaining where they'd gone, the general claimed none of the city's 800,000 civilian residents remained in Iraq's former capital.

Even as General Neal spoke, the country's second largest city was being carpet-bombed by B-52s. Cluster and other anti-personnel fragmentation bombs were dropped on Basra, as well as other Iraqi villages and population centers. The CBU-75 canister carries 1,800 bomblets called Sadeyes. Each Sadeye unleashes 600 razor-sharp steel fragments lethal up to a radius of 40 feet; grenade-like Sadeyes from one CBU-75 can spray an area equal to 157 football fields with deadly shrapnel. But many do not explode against soft desert sands. They kill later, when children or nomads stumble over the Sadeyes, or stoop to pick them up.

The Iraqi lieutenant was worried about his family. "We went to the trenches or, rather, the graves," he wrote. "I was very upset when I heard that people born in 1973 are being drafted. That means my brother..."

* * *

While Cheney and Powell continued to insist that a ground offensive was needed to dislodge Iraqi troops and armor in Kuwait, senate leaders worked to head off an all-out ground war.

On February 12, 26 Iraqi soldiers from a single division were condemned to death for deserting the front-lines. They were caught near Samawa and executed at 2nd Division headquarters. Also on the 12th, Soviet President Mikhail Gorbachev complained that allied actions were exceeding the UN mandate. Also on the 12th, his right-hand aide met for the last time with Saddam. Yevgeny Primakov reminded the Iraqi dictator that politics is the art of the possible. "The Americans are determined to launch a large-scale ground offensive to crush Iraqi forces in Kuwait," Primakov warned.

Saddam seemed to get the message. At two the next morning, Tariq Aziz returned with a written statement from Saddam Hussein declaring that "the Iraqi leadership is seriously studying the ideas outlined by the representatives of the Soviet President and will give its reply in the immediate future."

Just two hours later, American stealth bombers scored direct hits on Baghdad's al Firdos bunker. Orbiting satellites had photographed construction work to further harden the bunker, while electronic eavesdroppers had overheard orders going out to Iraqi military units over new communications aerials installed on a roof painted with camouflage and fake bomb holes. No civilians had been spotted entering the fenced security area. But when the 2,000 pound "bunker busters" penetrated 11 feet of reinforced concrete and exploded, more than two hundred women, children and elderly civilians were killed. Arnett's televised exclusive caused a worldwide uproar, while earning him the everlasting enmity of American forces in the Gulf.

By then, at least 50 oil wells were already burning in Kuwait's Great Burgan oil field. Early allied air raids against oil installations in Basra had also begun sending an oily "black rain" over Iran, poisoning water supplies, killing crops, fish and forests. Thick oil smoke cast the entire region under a growing pall.

The petroleum smokescreen helped hide Iraqi troops dug into the Great Burgan from napalm-dispensing US marine Harriers, and other marauding jets. The blow-torch heat from blazing high-pressure wellheads was so intense, aircraft were doused with ozone-destroying Halon fire retardants before flying missions over the oil fields.

* * *

Despite the allies' best efforts, the SCUDs were still flying. On February 14, 1st Cavalry communications specialist Michelle Hanlon of Killeen, Texas, was eating lunch somewhere in the desert between Hafir al Batin and King Khalid Military City when she was startled by a loud explosion overhead. It sounded to her as if another incoming SCUD had been intercepted by a Patriot missile.

Richard Voss saw the missile Hanlon heard. The 1st Infantry Division intelligence specialist was driving in a road convoy east of al Batin when he watched the SCUD fly in from the north-northeast. The missile struck the desert about a mile from Voss's vehicle, sending up a large dark-brown cloud. Within minutes, MPs came by giving the gas alert signal. Voss drove on, dressed in full MOPP gear, for almost two hours before getting an "all clear" near Log Base Echo.

Patricia Williams, a civilian mechanic with the 1st Cavalry Division, also remembers a late afternoon, mid-February explosion in the desert near Hafir al Batin. The blast was so powerful she felt the concussion echoing in her ears. After spending 20 harrowing minutes at MOPP-4, her unit was told that it was just a practice drill; the explosion was only a sonic boom. But five civilians were so frightened, they left that night.

By then, Williams was experiencing headaches, diarrhea, and sensitivity to light. The Iraqi Revolutionary Command was also growing anxious. On February 15, as Schwarzkopf's armored VII Corps moved into final attack positions, the IRC announced that it was willing to comply with UN Security Council Resolution 660, calling for an unconditional withdrawal.

"I heard that Iraq has decided to withdraw from Kuwait, Saturday, 16 February, 1991," the Iraqi lieutenant wrote. "I feel so fatigued that I can't breathe. The only thing that you can find everywhere in the world is air, and yet I can't breathe it. I can't breathe, eat, drink or talk. I have been here for 39 days and have not yet gone on leave."

Washington did not reply to Baghdad's formal announcement that it was withdrawing its forces from Kuwait. The Times of India later called Washington's steadfast refusal to negotiate a revelation of the West's "unrestricted appetite for dominance, its morbid fascination for hi-tech military might, its insensitivity to 'alien' cultures, its appalling jingoism."

Unfortunately, the very same attributes applied to Saddam Hussein.

* * *

On the 17th, FOX mass spectrometer operator Darren Siegle was told by Iraqi POWs of "many chemical mines" in the minefields his unit would soon be assaulting. Other mines drifted close offshore.

On the 18th, Electrician's Mate Scott Smith was below-decks listening to his captain announce that *USS Tripoli* had struck a mine. Even before the *Tripoli's* trauma, two Silkworm missiles fired offshore by the Iraqis had caused a stir in the fleet. Both missiles had been aimed at *USS Missouri*. One fell into the water. The other was knocked down by a Sea Dart air-defense missile fired by the battleship's British escort, *HMS Gloucester*. But who could spot a mine tethered 20 feet underwater?

A drumming *boom!* cut short the skipper's address. Smith slammed into a bulkhead as his guided missile cruiser reeled from a hit forward. As red lights began flashing, Smith struggled to his feet cursing like a sailor. The *bong bong bong* of General Quarters reverberated through the compartment. A second detonation directly beneath *USS Princeton's* superstructure nearly capsized Smith again.

As damage control parties hurried through listing passageways, Smith ran to turn valves for fires and flooding. He and a shipmate opened a hatch to make sure the generator was not afire. Splashing through water covering the deck, Smith made his way to the switchboard. Dogging the hatch shut, he picked up a phone and reported in: "Flooding in three switchboard, two feet of water and rising." The electrician specialist could not tell that the seawater was coming from a ruptured fire main. Standing in that conductive medium, he should have been made incandescent by a switchboard carrying 6,000 amps of high-voltage power. Switchboard covers designed for just such an eventuality saved his brave but silly self.

* * *

While seaman Smith and his shipmates splashed through flooded compartments, President Gorbachev was meeting with Tariq Aziz under drier but nearly as stressful circumstances in Moscow. Primakov was also on hand as the Soviet leader tendered a formula that would see the withdrawal of Iraqi forces from

Kuwait without preconditions, and without prolonging the war. Though it "de-linked" Iraq's unconditional withdrawal from Kuwait from all other preconditions, the Soviet president pledged to pursue action on other Mideast disputes – including Israel's West bank.

Instead of his usual outburst, Aziz listened quietly to the Soviet solution. Then he flew immediately back to Baghdad

* * *

Back in Basra, Air Force Lieutenant Jeffrey Fox was discussing John Wayne movies with a MiG pilot after being shot down and captured. He was lucky. Other downed pilots were being beaten repeatedly in a dank, dark Baghdad prison by people who hoped to score propaganda points after persuading battered "war criminals" to make televised "confessions."

The results were televised worldwide. Body held rigid, staring fixedly ahead through a bruised and bloated face, US Navy A6-E bombardier-navigator Lt. Jeffrey Zaun declared in a drug-like monotone: "I think our leaders and our people have wrongly attacked the peaceful people of Iraq." As 10 more allied air crewmen made similarly stilted statements, this pitiful parade of perfidy convinced American and British TV viewers of the brutality of Saddam Hussein's regime.

Despite these video games, there was still hope Bush would accept the Soviet peace plan. As former President Jimmy Carter advised Time: "We should not reject the option of a cease-fire...or demand unconditional surrender."

But Bush wasn't buying a negotiated settlement that would leave Saddam's armies intact. On the 19th, a frustrated King Hussein told *Village Voice* reporter, Michael Emery, "I believe that every attempt that I made, that anyone made in this region to eliminate this bloodbath, this destruction, was unfortunately blocked."

The Jordanian leader concluded by saying, "I believe a ground war will take place soon. I believe it is imminent. Obviously it goes way past the liberation of Kuwait." Emery elaborated, explaining to his readers that the king was convinced that the US and its British partners had jointly decided to neutralize Iraq "and impose an American-designed regional security system, one that would ensure US control of the region well into the 21st century."

* * *

As King Hussein predicted, the next day President Bush rejected Iraq's offer to withdraw. Bush said the Soviet peace plan assured Saddam's regime that it would not be dismantled, while holding out the possibility of later linkage to pressing Mideast issues. As Bush spoke, the US 1st Cavalry Division was feinting up the Wadi al Batin to test Iraqi defenses. Riding mechanized steads against weapons far more fearsome than revolvers and sabres, the First Cav pulled back after losing three dead and nine wounded to probing fire in the dry riverbed.

That evening, a Soviet aircraft flew Tariq Aziz back to Moscow. Saddam's shuttling envoy told Gorbachev and Primakov that Iraq would withdraw, but not surrender.

"Your stand seems very inconsistent," Gorbachev replied. "On the one hand, you agree to an unconditional withdrawal. On the other hand, your position seems to include preconditions for that withdrawal."

Gorbachev also wanted to know why the Iraqi statement did not mention Kuwait. The Soviet leader insisted that the withdrawal begin immediately after the cessation of armed action, "with no strings attached." In return, Gorbachev guaranteed that Iraqi troops leaving Kuwait would not be "shot in the back." As Aziz prepared to leave once again for Baghdad, the creator of Glasnost warned the Iraqi ambassador, "Timing is crucial. If you cherish the lives of your countrymen and the fate of Iraq, then you must act without delay."

By 0330, Gorbachev's press spokesman Vitali Igantenko was informing a hastily convened press conference that "points of agreement" had been reached with the Iraqi leadership, who had already informed its forces in Kuwait that they would be coming home. As hope rose for a settlement short of war, Gorbachev got on the phone to Bush. After conversing for an hour and a half, the US president thanked the Soviet president for his initiative, saying he doubted whether the Iraqi government's latest maneuverings would lead to anything.

What was going on? Was the Iraqi army really leaving Kuwait? As Aziz flew back to Moscow with a reply from Saddam Hussein, Radio Baghdad carried the Supreme Leader's latest public statement. In an emotional address meant to reassure subjects alarmed by the country's weak resistance to fierce air attacks, Saddam explained that Iraq was holding back its air and ground forces. "When the war is fought in a comprehensive manner, using all resources and weapons, the scale of death and the number of dead will, God willing, rise among the ranks of atheism, injustice and tyranny."

The fiery rhetoric masked Aziz's secret request to Gorbachev to allow Iraq six weeks to withdraw 500,000 troops from Kuwait. The Americans were giving Iraq just four days to vacate Kuwait City, and three weeks to complete the pullout. Washington suggested their timetable could be met if the retreating army left its tanks and artillery behind.

But Aziz also wanted UN sanctions lifted once Iraq lifted its siege of Kuwait. He told Gorbachev that he had "a rigid mandate" from Saddam Hussein concerning sanctions, beyond which he could not go. Gorbachev reminded the Iraqi envoy that removing the sanctions was a Security Council decision. Aziz then proposed that Primakov accompany him immediately back to Baghdad. But the Soviets warned that the clock was ticking on the UN's deadline for withdrawal, and urged the envoy to call his boss instead. At two in the morning Moscow time, February 23, the Soviet government received a favorable reply from Saddam. At 1000, Aziz announced to the press that Iraq had agreed to an immediate and unconditional withdrawal from Kuwait. But first, he added, all resolutions adopted by the Security Council after Resolution 660 would have to be declared invalid.

Gorbachev had already dispatched telegrams to the heads of the Security Council countries. He also phoned Bush back, as well as all other coalition leaders and the government of Iran, insisting that Iraq's agreement to withdraw its forces unilaterally from Kuwait had created "a new situation." The Soviet leader suggested convening the Security Council as soon as possible to mesh Iraq's agreement with American demands.

* * *

But Bush had already given Iraq a final ultimatum. Its army must withdraw completely from Kuwait in a week, and from Kuwait City within 48 hours – beginning no later than noon that very day. The coalition ground attack was set to commence just 14 hours later.

Earlier on the 23rd, an American ambassador relayed to the CIA a warning from "someone in the Iranian air force or air force-related industry" that chemical weapons were being stored at a site in southern Iraq called Khamisiyah. This was not news to the American spy agency. In May 1986, its analysts had obtained a translated copy of an Iraqi CW production plan that discussed the transfer of 3,975 mustard-filled 155-millimeter artillery rounds, and 6,293 mustard bombs to Khamisiyah. Neither report was relayed to the soldiers preparing to assault Iraq.

Also on the 23rd, the British intercepted another disturbing Iraqi message. "We were tuned into the Iraqi command radio net," said a British signals officer. "We heard them give the release order to their front-line troops to use chemical weapons against Rhino Force if it crossed the border."

* * *

Even close up to the Iraqi border, the only shots Canadian medic David Prestwich heard were rifles being "cleared" into a sandbox in front of the triage tent. But on the 22nd, just two days before the coalition ground offensive was due to push off, Patriot missile defenses intercepted another SCUD over Hafir al Batin. Something on the night breeze made Michelle Hanlon's eyes water. Tuned to the British command net, the Canadians never heard the American radio net buzzing with speculation about the anthrax found in hundreds of dead sheep and camels outside al Jubayl.

As late afternoon gave way to early evening, medical secretary Charlene Harmon Davis was on assignment at King Khalid Military City when Patriots intercepted three SCUDs directly overhead. Chemical alarms sounded immediately. Still reeling from the rapid succession of thunderclaps, Davis felt her face, eyes and throat begin to burn. Her nose began to run, and she felt suddenly nauseous. There was also a funny taste in her mouth. The immediate symptoms lasted for about 20 minutes beore gradually abating.

Fearing allied air strikes, the Iraqis spent the next day transferring 6,000 155 mm mustard rounds from a bunker at an Nasiriyah to an open area at Khamisiyah, 59 kilometers away. The leaking rounds were buried and camouflaged with canvas.

* * *

As the allied buildup neared completion, personnel from several National Guard and Army Reserve units in Florida and Michigan worked long hours applying CACR coatings to US military vehicles. The toxic protective coatings were strong enough to resist the chemicals used to decontaminate military equipment exposed to chemical or biological warfare agents.

After cleaning with these decontamination chemicals, CARC-treated vehicles can be returned to service immediately, without stripping and repainting. Many soldiers detailed to prepare thousands of US vehicles for Desert Storm worked 12 hour days in poorly ventilated enclosures – initially with no respirators. Only later would those soldiers learn that unprotected exposure to CARC can have neurotoxological effects similar to exposures to other neurotoxins.

* * *

While coalition soldiers prayed in many languages to their individual gods, US marines staged amphibious rehearsals for an anxious Iraqi army audience. As the assault timer ticked toward zero hour, a formation of 31 naval vessels appeared off beaches that less than a year before had been crowded with bathers. No beach towels were in evidence as USS Missouri opened up with her triple-turret long-guns. After an hour's sustained salvos, USS Wisconsin took over while the Missouri's guns cooled. As the recommissioned World War Two-vintage battlewagons took turns stripping the nerves and masonry from Kuwait City's captors, Iraqi army units that might have been sent to bolster the southern border remained dug-in to repulse a sea borne assault. But the 17,000 marines on board the circling assault ships never waded ashore.

While Kuwait City awaited its fate, bomb-dazed and starving Iraqi conscripts contemplated the latest RSVP invitations from Fort Bragg. Since the beginning of Desert Shield, the US Army's only active psychological operations unit had dropped some 29 million PSYOP leaflets. Printed in Arabic, one side of the 4th Psychological Operations Group's latest offering read:

CEASE RESISTANCE – BE SAFE:

To seek refuge safely, the bearer must strictly adhere to the following procedures:

1. Remove the magazine from your weapon.

2. Sling your weapon over your left shoulder, muzzle down.

3. Have both arms raised above your head.

4. Approach the Multi-National Forces' positions slowly, with the lead soldier holding this document above his head.

5. If you do this, you will not die.

Tomorrow the Seventh Squad troops will be bombed, leave this location immediately and save yourselves.

The reverse side of the express invitations emphasized what many frightened Iraqis already knew:

You are isolated! All your supplies have been cut, and you'll never get help. Saddam doesn't care for your fate and he left you to meet your end. Drop your guns and join your Arab brothers in love and peace. Staying here means death.

CHAPTER 6

THE HIGHWAY TO HELL

History records that the 28 nation assault on Iraq began a few hours before dawn on February 24, 1991. This is incorrect. The invasion actually began three days earlier when Jeffrey Ford and company parked their Humvees and pitched their tents at assembly area 17, just north of Rafha, Saudi Arabia. While waiting for the start of the ground war, the bored GIs finally got around to trying out their Global Positioning Satellite system. It was then that the startled troopers discovered that they were already 17 miles inside Iraq.

The war caught up with them on the 24th when American units attacked in driving rain along a 500 mile line. As a mechanized storm of unprecedented size and ferocity rose out of the desert and rolled over Iraqi forward positions, Saddam Hussein's engineers ignited more than 600 high-pressure oil wells deep in Kuwait.

Because of severe gas mask-carrier shortages, some marines crossed the departure line carrying their masks in plastic bags tied to their war belts. They would soon be needing them.

At Jaleeb and al Shuyukh, just south of the Kuwait airport, 250 Ababil missiles loaded with CN, CS, AC, mustard gas and phosphorus had escaped allied detection. As coalition forces swept over the border into Kuwait, the commander in charge of the missiles was given the order to launch. The officer, a Shi'ite, refused. Instead, he and his missileers withdrew from the area, leaving the missiles for coalition capture.

But US Marines were already under chemical attack. At approximately 0635, during initial breaching operations on the Kuwait-Saudi border, a FOX sniffer vehicle from B Company Sixth Marines detected chemical agents in Lane Red 1. The FOX's chemical detection supervisor, warrant officer Joseph Cottrel, checked his computer screen. In less than six seconds, humming microchips had identified the substance picked up by the vehicle's probes. Blister agent! But just a trace. The concentration readout showed "IC+50", a level below "IMMEDIATE threat to personnel."

As a nearby M-60 tank fired on a shape-shifting shadow that might have been an Iraqi armored troop carrier, a second FOX vehicle crammed with chemical detection gear confirmed the initial chemical agent report. Following chemical detection, the usual procedure is to stop and take more readings. But this was not the time to break the tempo of the assault. The marines were ordered to keep rolling.

Master Sergeant Michael Bradford rode the fifth FOX through the breach. He quickly sounded the alarm. John Laymon's on-board computer recorded chemical readings for 16–

minutes as the armored chemical detection vehicle sped on. "There were chemicals in that breach," Bradford later stated.

Cottrel figured they were being hit by chemical mines. If so, it was likely that the mines' once-lethal contents had been degraded after baking for months under intense summer heat. He called in the alarm, but recommended that continued rapid movement through the breach lanes would pose no threat to friendly troops. Since everyone had been suited up in their protective outer garments and boots since the previous evening, it took less than a minute for soldiers advancing through the lane to pull on gas masks and gloves.

They were just in time. Twenty-one minutes later, both FOXes detected more blister agent drifting invisibly over the desert. After another half hour, as the marines continued clearing lanes into Kuwait, the chemical alert was reduced to MOPP level 2. British troops were also reporting Iraqi chemical mines as they attacked to the north of the marines.

Back in Saudi Arabia, the US Army's 513th Military Intelligence Brigade confirmed that King Khalid Military City had been hit by anthrax. At 1024, the Marine 1st Battalion's S-2 staff reported intercepting an order given nearly an hour earlier for a unit of self-propelled Iraqi artillery to fire chemicals. Friendly forces reported no incoming rounds; chemical agent monitors (CAMs) showed "all clear."

At 1135, XVIII Airborne Corps sent an urgent "Flash" message: "IZ III Corps preparing chemicals." At 1143, S-2 was back on the air reporting a nerve agent detection by the Marines' 26th Air Group on the Kuwait-Saudi Arabia border.

Eight minutes later, Marine Air Group 26 reported another nerve agent detection at 28 degrees North, 47 degrees E on the Kuwait-Saudi border. Later that evening, the US Marines 2nd Division encountered more chemical mines. At 2210, the 3rd Battalion, 6th Marine Regiment reported two chemical casualties from a lingering mustard agent strong enough to blister the exposed arms of two Amphibious Assault Vehicle crewmen. At the combat operations center, marine reservist Al Stenner heard the casualties being reported over the command net. At least three chemical mines, he recalls, were reported during the initial breaching operations.

By midday, smoke from burning vehicles and oil wells was so thick it brought a spooky darkness. "The sky has murder in her heart," said one American soldier. Advancing across the blazing oil fields, coalition troops were soon covered with oil and soot. Many of them had no clean uniforms to replace their oil soaked clothes.

* * *

Face blackened by a sticky petroleum rain, Captain Blake Crowe led a company of marine assault vehicles into Kuwait. In his shirt pocket he carried a letter from his father. Within its well-thumbed pages, Admiral William Crowe, former head of the Joint Chiefs of Staff, told his son to "stay calm."

It turned out to be helpful advice, when his battalion came under intense fire in an agricultural area about three miles from the Kuwait International airport. Captain Crowe was ordered to keep moving toward the vital runways. "We drove our battalion right through the middle of them," he later recalled. "There was heavy machine gun fire. We just continued to drive. Nobody got killed."

At the airport, a major tank engagement was already underway between Iraqi and American armor. The smoke from nearby blazing oil fields was so thick Major General Michael Myatt had to use a flashlight to read his map. All 100 tanks the marines engaged on the airport aprons and runways were destroyed.

1st Division destroyed another 50 or 60 Soviet-built tanks in the nearby Burgan oil field. Marine losses were zero as intense, sustained air and artillery attacks caught the Iraqi tanks in their revetments.

While Crowe and Myatt ducked Iraqi bullets, many more pumped-up GIs were already declaiming "the war that wasn't." As sporadic opposition melted away, some described the coalition attack as "a cakewalk." Others called it "a nature hike."

But the driver of a stuck Humvee wasn't so sure as a clanking Iraqi tank and an accompanying APC came straight at him. He figured he was dead. But instead of blowing him away, both enemy vehicles jerked to a stop. Their crews freed the stuck jeep before surrendering to the wide-eyed American boy.

Another band of Iraqis gave themselves up to a CNN camera crew. At least 40 other soldiers attempted to surrender to a remotely-operated drone. From a location miles away, astonished controllers watched on video as Saddam's young soldiers turned around and around, waving an improvised white flag at the circling, pilotless craft.

At least 30,000 of their bomb-stunned and starving comrades would surrender during the first two days of the ground war. While Saddam's elite Republican Guard was being held back in Iraq, conscripts as young as 11, 12 and 13 years old had been given just six weeks of military training before being thrust into the maw of a Desert Storm.

Forbidden to have portable radios capable of picking up American programs, these frightened kids were thoroughly demoralized by months of isolation, no pay and little food. *Life's* Roger Rosenblatt described older veterans worn down by years of pointless fighting as looking "childlike and desperate." Some tried to kiss the hands of captors whom they regarded as liberators from a gruesome death. "Where have you guys been?" they asked the startled Americans. "We've been waiting for you for two weeks."

* * *

Night-vision goggles and thermal-imaging sensors, as well as extensive "after dark" combat training, gave American helicopter and tank crews an uncanny advantage over their ill-equipped adversaries. That night, the first of the advance, British First Armored Division turned a third of the Republican Guard tanks confronting them into smoking junk. The T-72s were badly outgunned as American MI Abrams stayed out of range, using computer-aided laser gunsights to plink the hapless Iraqi tanks with "penetrator rounds" that turned their crews, as the GIs indelicately put it, into "crispy critters."

Not all the action involved bullets. At 0319 on February 25, Task Force Ripper detected gas at grid coordinate 756862. At 1735 on the afternoon of the 25th, another Ripper artillery unit also reported a chemical detection. Other chemical incidents were reported by that unit at 1908. This detection was confirmed by a FOX chemical reconnaissance vehicle. Just 14 minutes later, another FOX vehicle attached to Tiger Brigade found lewisite miles away from Ripper.

* * *

Sergeant Jeff Haley was serving with the 2nd Marine Division forward headquarters on the 25th when a nearby Remote Sensing Chemical Agent Alarm (RASCAAL) sounded.

Haley jumped. Though he'd been tense for days half expecting it, he couldn't believe the alarm had actually sounded. But the RASCAAL was a good gadget. Extremely reliable, easy to maintain and operate, the automatic chemical agent detector was known to have a low false alarm rate. It never responded to common battlefield pollutants like oil smoke or fuels.

Haley figured his buddy, Corporal Karl Gobel had hit the test button. Gobel thought Haley had set it off. After resolving their mutual misunderstanding, Haley went into Combat Ops and informed the noncom on duty that the RASCAAL had gone off in blister mode – and that it was a bona fide "no shitter."

The division went to MOPP-4 immediately. Venturing outside in their protective suits, Haley and Gobel took out separate M-256 kits. Both tests proved negative. "Maybe a cloud of agent had blown through," Haley later surmised. "Or maybe it was a false reading. You know it takes so long to do a 256 kit test."

Another marine remembers hearing an M21 RASCAAL go off. "It put the fear of God into us. For all of our training, the first thing we did was jump up and run out to check the thing – without our masks or anything." The marine ruled out malfunction because two different detectors went off in separate sectors. An M21 placed in-between never sounded.

At 1900, an Iraqi POW warned his captors of a chemical minefield buried around the Jalib Ash Shuyukh police post, west of Kuwait International Airport. Even as a translator was relaying his remarks, Task Force Ripper was reporting more lewisite wafting silently through the windy Kuwait night. This latest detection was confirmed by a FOX. Minutes later, at 1922 local, another FOX attached to Tiger Brigade picked up more lewisite at a location miles from Ripper.

In a war-turned-sportscast for a captive media, the Iraqis had yet to score. Instead, that demoralized Third World army had lost a reported 3,700 tanks in less than three days. The American psyops unit set up concert-amped loudspeakers and began broadcasting in Arabic: Iraqi soldiers would not be attacked if they stopped shooting. Stunned Iraqi conscripts did not need further encouragement; already US field commanders were complaining that they were running out of things to shoot at.

But some Iraqi units were still firing back. Not long after Task Force Ripper took up positions for the night around Kuwait's Ahmed al Jaber airbase, Sergeant Robert Maison's recon team observed an Iraqi artillery attack. The shells were landing off to the northwest, about four kilometers away. The NBC specialist remembers the bright flashes and a canvas-rattling wind, "40 or 50 knots steady", blowing toward the American position. Five or six minutes later, Maison says, a FOX-mounted mass spectrometer sounded a chemical alarm. Two other chemical reconnaissance vehicles also detected mustard gas readings similar to the first FOX report of agent "H".

* * *

Marine Staff Sergeant George Grass was driving the first FOX. Grass had been called in to monitor chemical agent vapors at the Iraqi III Corps' ammunition supply point located on the airfield next to the 5th Marines.

"It wasn't easily accessible," Grass remembers. As they bumped across the second breach lane near the airfield, the sky was black with smoke from the surrounding oil fires. The FOX's MM1 probe sounded an alert for sulfur mustard in the air. The chemical was present for at least 30 seconds and possibly a minute as the MM1 locked on the reading. Capable of detecting 60 known chemical agents, the computerized mass spectrometer can identify individual chemical elements – such as sulfur, hydrogen and chlorine – by assessing their molecular composition and molecular weight. The result is a detailed and highly precise picture of "weaponized" chemical substances encountered by the FOX and its crew.

Grass reported the chemical detection to the 3rd Tanks NBC warrant officer. Betenbenter passed the alert up through the First Marine Division. Grass was careful to report that the sulfurous oil smoke readings had been separated from the sulfur-mustard readings his operator had obtained. The vehicle's mass spectrometer, which could easily discriminate between oil smoke and chemical agents, had just been calibrated by General Dynamics Land Systems the previous day.

The FOX kept moving. To reach the suspect bunker, Grass drove his FOX off the road along a path through an open area. He guided the buttoned-up vehicle up over a hill and around a couple of other hills before reaching the entrance to an area walled by high berms. A fancy looking Winnebago was dug in beside the abandoned gate. "Grass had found a major chemical weapons storage site," the CIA's Eddington explains, "complete with a Corps-level C3 vehicle."

Grass didn't get a chance to explore the possible luxuries, or booby-traps, inside the big motor home. The FOX's computer alarm was already ringing. A distinct spectrum scrolling across the monitor indicated a lethal concentration of S-mustard vapors.

The NBC specialist immediately drove his FOX toward the bunkers. "Fully visible were the skull and crossbones either on yellow tape with red lettering or stenciled on the boxes. On top of the boxes were artillery shells," Grass later recalled. While the driver notified his regimental NBC supervisor Joseph Cottrel of the "honey" he'd found, the FOX's computer operator obtained and printed a full and complete spectrum of mustard gas readings.

Cottrel ordered Grass to return to Ripper Main. But the alarm sounded again. This time, the chemical agent H-mustard came up across the monitor, showing a lethal dose. Another complete spectrum was printed out as proof of detection. As Grass started to egress the area the alarm sounded once more. This positive reading showed the presence of benzene bromide. Grass waited while the spectrum was printed as evidence of vapor contamination. "All positive readings were within 100 yards of each other," Grass recalls.

Headquarters was not happy to get the news. They radioed back that the FOXes had been foxed by thick oil smoke obscuring the battlefield. But that was unlikely. Oil smoke almost always accompanies modern warfare; the FOX's computers automatically separate all petroleum compounds from other compounds such as the H blister agent identified by the on-board mass spectrometer. Cottrel asked division headquarters what to do with the confirming printout. "I was told to forward the tape up the chain of command," he later recounted. "Which I did." Like so many others, Cottrell's computer tape was subsequently "lost".

* * *

While the marines probed chemical minefields inside Kuwait, General Schwarzkopf decided to advance General Franks' VII Corps main armored attack by 15 hours. The angry coalition commander chivvied Franks to hurry his column around Kuwait's west flank and strike deep into Iraq. But Franks worried that his gas-guzzling M1A1 tanks and Bradley Fighting Vehicles would outrun their maintenance and fuel convoys.

Hurrying forward on the Tapline road near the Iraq border, a 101st Airborne fuel convoy was intercepted by MPs. Speeding up and down the road in Humvees, the Military Police signaled everyone to don their gas masks. Continuing down the road, the convoy passed a SCUD that had apparently detonated after hitting the desert. The area around the missile was flagged with chemical warning tape.

John Jacob was with the 1st Infantry Division as Task Force 216 drove into Iraq. The mechanic was sitting in the driver's seat of his Humvee when something wafted in through the driver's side window and drifted into his face. Jacob "got a whiff" of what smelled and tasted sweet, like almonds. Almost instantly, his throat and lungs began to burn. His eyes watered and his vision turned blurry.

Squinting against the suddenly painful desert light, Jacob donned his mask and gloves and sounded the alarm. His buddies looked at him as if he was crazy. Jacob's own M9 detector registered nothing. But the nausea and diarrhea that followed were real enough. A pounding headache started soon afterward. It never did go away.

The Iraqis were also learning how quickly chemical weapons can turn to bite their handlers. Later on the second day of the allied ground offensive, Iraqi III Corps radioed warnings of trace amounts of chemicals blown back from coalition air attacks, or perhaps their own CW shells. The Iraqis couldn't be sure just what was in the air because their own detectors weren't working.

* * *

While III Corps struggled with a potentially deadly "fog of war," coalition forces were experiencing growing difficulty in finding anyone to fight. "Only 40 hours after a half-million allied troops had gotten orders to fight a half-million Iraqis," *Life* magazine's Lisa Grunwald reported, "there was not a battle in sight."

Instead, Grunwald found thousands of Iraqi prisoners sitting in the rain on the sand. "Bedraggled and relieved, they inspired shock and pity. The allies who captured them saw exhaustion, hunger, bare feet, lice, filth, prostration and relief." Some soldiers, Grunwald found, had been eating grass and drinking rainwater.

* * *

Many others were making for the nearest exits. On the night of the 25th, as VII Corps pushed to the Euphrates and decimated Republican Guard tanks in the "Battle of 73 Easting," an English teacher named Jehan Rajab was frightened by the sky over a city where she had lived for many years. Underlit by nearly a thousand blazing oil wells, the petroleum overcast "throbbed red" over Kuwait City. "There was a tremendous bombardment," Rajab later told the BBC's recording team. "It went on continuously, and everything was shaking and shivering."

There was also, Rajab related, a "scuffling and shuffling" all around the blacked-out city. At 0200 Kuwait time, February 26, Baghdad radio announced that Iraq's Foreign Minister had accepted the Soviet cease-fire proposal and agreed to comply with UN Resolution 660. All Iraqi forces were ordered to withdraw to positions held before August 2, 1990.

President Bush responded immediately. White House spokesman Marlin Fitzwater told reporters that "there is no evidence to suggest the Iraqi army is withdrawing. In fact, Iraqi units are continuing to fight...We continue to prosecute the war."

Saddam Hussein then announced over Baghdad radio that Iraqi troops had already begun to withdraw from Kuwait. Iraq's supreme commander pledged that the withdrawal would be completed that day.

This time, Bush reacted in the Rose Garden. Addressing hastily assembled reporters, the American president called Hussein's announcement "an outrage" and "a cruel hoax." Bush's bluster was followed by a televised briefing from Saudi Arabia. Grim-faced US military spokesmen told viewers that Iraqi forces were not withdrawing, but were being pushed from the battlefield.

In fact, allied forces were still 36 hours away from Kuwait City. Jonathan Alston and Stephen Schaefer awoke from a cold and rain-filled night to an even nastier morning. Though their watches claimed it was after dawn, the acrid darkness around them remained pitch-black from oil smoke. To make a rotten morning worse, as the two Army infantrymen began checking Iraqi bunkers, a sniper opened fire on them. Alston and Schaefer traded cover fire, keeping the Iraqi soldier's head down until Alston got close to lob a grenade. Deciding that more is better, the American pitched a second grenade into the bunker, touching off a massive secondary explosion.

By then, more than 10,000 of Saddam's soldiers had decided to heed their leader's withdrawal order and beat feet for Basra. Before dawn on the 26th, Kuwait City's hostage citizenry awoke to the sound of revving tanks and trucks.

"They were in a hurry. They were shooting at each other," one resident later recalled. Fleeing soldiers stole the last cars, trucks and school buses remaining in the looted capital; even the city's fire trucks were commandeered. Every vehicle that still had its wheels and engine attached was quickly crammed with panicky young men. Most clutched hastily "liberated" dresses, dishes, or small TVs for wives and sweethearts back in Iraq.

Fearing reprisals from returning Kuwaiti government forces, thousands of Palestinian workers joined the eclectic cavalcade. Jordanian civilians eager to escape the city's coming siege also climbed aboard buses. The impromptu convoy quickly swelled into a torrent of motley military and civilian vehicles spilling onto the two main roads leading north to the border.

Sardar was one of those left behind. Like the other conscripts milling around him, the native of a village in northern Iraq had been forced into the army just before the invasion of Kuwait. He didn't know what the war was about and he really didn't care. He just wanted to go home.

But the young Iraqi villager wasn't exactly sure where he was. All the cars had been taken. There was no petrol. All he had was a carton of cigarettes. Sardar flashed the smokes at a man driving past in a small car. The driver instantly pulled over and stopped. Cigarettes were even harder to come by than cars in KC.

"Where you heading?" the traveler asked in Arabic. Sardar begged the man to take him to Basra.

* * *

More than anything, General Norman Schwarzkopf wanted to smash an enemy he would never have to fight again. At the start of the ground assault, the coalition commander had ordered "not to let anybody or anything out of Kuwait City." Now a top priority call came through to an American airbase in Saudi Arabia.

The commander of the allied bombing campaign was on the line from US Air Force command headquarters in Riyadh. He told General David "Bull" Baker that "an emergency situation" was developing in Kuwait City. The enemy was escaping from the city. The bombing commander told Baker that it was imperative to stop them at any cost: "Take whatever means you need to take and stop these people from leaving. We have to stop them!" he insisted.

"Bull" Baker grabbed the two closest pilots. Speaking urgently, he convinced Joe Seidl and Merrick Kraus that they needed to "put some hate in their hearts" and go out and "stop those sons of bitches" from getting out of Kuwait.

A startled Seidl and Kraus paused. Then they both said, "Yes, sir," and dashed in the darkness to their waiting airplanes. Minutes later, as they dove out of low clouds, the pilots were blown away – not by anti-aircraft fire, but by the sight of thousands of headlights jamming every road leading north out of Kuwait City.

"It's almost like hitting the jackpot," Seidl later told the BBC. "There are vehicles all over the place. It is a very lucrative target. We could actually go out and really do some damage... Because I mean, there are thousands and thousands of vehicles out there and they're all heading north, and you know, they're probably all bad guys. Or they are all bad guys. And we can really put hurt on 'em."

Seidl and Kraus swooped down and pickled three bombs on the "probable" bad guys. It was a perfect delivery. As the bombs burst in a string right across the main highway, the center bomb blew up between two trucks, causing both vehicles to erupt into flames.

Two of the "sons of bitches" they were aiming at watched both big military lorries explode directly in front of them. Sardar and his newfound companion could not believe their eyes. "They were just totally destroyed. It was chaotic." There was no room on the road to swerve. His driver hit the gas and they scooted between both blazing trucks. As they passed, Sardar saw two people trapped in the burning cab of one of them. Flames leaped around their faces. "I didn't know what to think," Sardar later told a BBC Radio 5 interviewer. "I just wanted to get away from that terrible scene. I felt sorry for those men, who were trapped, of course. but all I could care about was myself. I just wanted to get out of there alive."

But escape was proving difficult. As his wingman pulled out of his run, Kraus saw a traffic jam forming below him. Cars were pulled off to the side of the road. Some doused their headlights. Others kept their lights on. Gunfire winked up at him. But the small caliber shots were random, spraying in all directions. Kraus picked a spot ahead that looked like the center of the traffic jam, and dropped more bombs there. The pilot pulled back hard on the stick as shooting erupted off his nose. Then the bombs exploded. Headlights went out for miles in every direction.

Both pilots gaped in disbelief when the headlights snapped back on. "I don't believe it," Kraus chuckled over the radio. "They turned their headlights back on."

There was no choice. As wrecked vehicles were flung across the highway, others were crushed by tanks trying desperately to flee. Headlights were needed to pick their way through. Sardar's little car was by now crammed with frightened people. Some of the injured on the pavement and encroaching sand tried to crawl toward them. But there was no more room in the car. Sardar saw one man gather his remaining strength. As they drove slowly past, he slapped the side of the car, leaving a bloody smear down the side window.

* * *

Tracers were now arcing into the sky searching for the cause of all this pain and fear. Seidl radioed Kraus: "Hey, it's getting pretty hot down here. We need to get out of here."

Kraus replied, "Yeah, we've got one more pass and then we're out." This time Kraus held his jet straight and level after pickling his last bombs, hammering the throttles against the stops as he made for open water ahead.

When they landed back at the Saudi airbase, General Baker was on hand for their debriefing. "God, that's murder!" exclaimed a lieutenant listening in the back of the intelligence tent. As everybody turned around, Baker corrected that outspoken conscience. It's not murder, Baker said. It's war, with all the horrors that go with it. And that was their job tonight – to win the war.

But with the precipitous flight of Iraq's army from Kuwait, the war was already as good as over. Instead of retreating to regroup and fight again, the soldiers and refugees on those horror-filled highways were fleeing for their unhaqppy lives. Afraid of being left out of the action, other coalition pilots soon swarmed over a road that one Canadian flier likened to "a turkey shoot."

An excited naval aviator from *USS Ranger* compared the roads leading out of KC with "the road to Daytona beach at spring break." But it was unlikely university students heading for Daytona Beach had ever been cluster-bombed or hit with phosphorous and napalm that clings to the skin as it burns through to the bone. Reporting from the *Ranger*, Randall Richard of the *Providence Journal* wrote that air strikes were being launched so feverishly, pilots were taking off "with whatever bombs happened to be closest to the flight deck." Brightly garbed armorers, working to the strains of the "Lone Ranger" theme piped over the ship's PA, passed up preferred projectiles when they took too long to load.

Commander Frank Swiggert, squadron leader of the *Ranger's* bombers, arrived over the target to find an aerial traffic jam mirroring the confusion below. So many planes were diving on the trapped vehicles, combat air controllers feared midair collisions. Their victims were not offering much resistance. "They were just sitting ducks," Swiggert said. Another pilot described the attacks as "just like shooting fish in a barrel."

Sardar was lucky to escape the allies' aerial net. His plucky driver somehow wove his way through miles of wrecked vehicles into Iraq. Just over the border, the exhausted refugees were detained at a police checkpoint by Iraq's internal security agency. Guessing that the driver's pockets must be bulging with money paid by his grateful passengers, the Mukhabarat security police brusquely ordered the driver out of the car "They told us to clear off," Sardar said. "I can only guess what happened to him."

* * *

While Kuwait's main roads to Basra exploded and burned, it was also turning into an all-nighter at al Jaber airfield. Between 0430 and 0500 on the 26th, as escaping vehicles of every description streamed out of Kuwait City, the Ripper radio net came alive with shouts of "Gas, gas, gas!" Robert Maison's men went to MOPP-4 for two hours before being given the "all clear." About a half hour later, they were told that three FOX vehicles had detected mustard agent. After that, they were in and out of MOPP gear all night. They weren't the only ones. At 0213, a company of 11th Marines had detected blister agents using two separate M-256 tests. Subsequent readings of blister agent at 0327, and gas at 0410, also came up positive. The "all clear" was not given over their sector of Kuwait until more than two hours later.

But not all 11th Marines donned protective gear. 1st Marine Division headquarters still insisted the detections were "false alarms." This meant, notes analyst Eddington, that "for the better part of two hours, elements of the 11th Marines had been operating in a chemically contaminated environment, and at least some of those Marines continued operations without going to MOPP-4."

At 1045, Task Force Shepherd detected more mustard gas. An hour later, as the marines closed on the southern outskirts of a hastily vacated Kuwait City, Task Force Ripper reported detecting gas. As the afternoon started, a FOX vehicle with the 8th Marines also detected gas.

* * *

General Schwarzkopf was still berating a reluctant General Franks to speed up his armored advance as David Prestwich's detachment headed back south to prepare for 300 arriving Canadian hospital staff. But the medic never made it. Somewhere en route, his urine turned black and pain he had never dreamed possible catapulted Prestwich with dizzying speed to 33 Field Hospital in Bahrain. Two days later he was on a flight home.

Even as Prestwich was being medevaced to Bahrain, Ripper rolled over an extensive Iraqi bunker complex located at 29 degrees 14 minutes North, 47 degrees, 54 minutes East. A FOX with 8th Marines detected chemical gas. Task Force Ripper was ordered to reposition units away from "ammunition/chemical storage areas." At 1430, Ripper reported that they had "repositioned batteries away from ammunition and chemical dump hazard areas."

A half hour later, 1/11 Marines detected gas near the burning, shell-pocked Kuwait International Airport. Less then 30 minutes later, 3/23 Marines also detected gas. The division log recorded their radio call:"3/23rd under NBC attack, in MOPP 4."

In the confusion of the allies' rapid advance, it was impossible to tell if individual Iraqi field commanders were loosing chemical munitions on an ad hoc basis. But reports of chemical detection continued coming in. The next CW report, from 3/11 Marines, was logged at 1735.

At 1756 and 2035, the combat log of XVIII Airborne Corps recorded "captured chem munitions" and "captured abandoned CB munitions." At 1914, someone made an ominous notation in a handwritten log kept by 1/7 Marines: "EPWs stated that their unit was to leave Kuwait ASAP because Coalition forces were going to get hit by chemicals."

This report, like so many others, never made it into official records. As Eddington later explained, the typed notes that formed the 1/7 Marines' command chronology never mentioned the EPWs' reports of their impending evacuation. "Several of the command chronologies completely omitted any references to chemical incidents that were well known and documented by the personnel involved."

But the troops of Task Force Ripper didn't need to read between the lines. They were encountering plenty of invisible assailants between the opposing front lines. As recorded in the Marines' official After Action Review, at 2300 Ripper once again relocated "to get out of an area contaminated with chemical weapons."

By then, the Iraqis were trying to get chemical weapons out of another area. As Saddam's forces backpedaled from the coalition onslaught, they reportedly moved 1,100 chemical rockets into an open storage area at a place called Khamisiyah. Each rocket was filled with 18 kilograms of nerve agents mixed at a 2:1 mix of sarin to thickened sarin. Another thousand sarin-filled rockets already crowded bunker 73 in that same depot in southern Iraq.

* * *

On February 27, George Bush declared that "no quarter" would be given to any Iraqi soldiers remaining in Kuwait. Though it made dramatic press, the president's harsh statement violated the US Army's own Field Manual, as well as the 1907 Hague Convention, which made it an international war crime to grant no quarter to withdrawing soldiers.

The fleeing Iraqi conscripts, along with officers who had mistreated their Kuwaiti hostages and the civilians who accompanied them, had already been drawn and quartered. The morning after the air strikes, an advance unit of British soldiers crested a nearby ridge and gaped at a seven mile scrap yard of demolished vehicles and charred corpses. This was the inland highway to Iraq. Out of sight to the east, another 60-mile segment of coastal highway was littered with the remnants of tanks, trucks, ambulances, buses and bodies from the previous night's attacks.

All told, more than 2,000 wrecked vehicles and 10,000 to 15,000 charred and dismembered bodies covered what Kuwaitis soon began calling the "Highway to Hell." Attacking pilots had apparently not been briefed on the 1949 Geneva Convention, which outlaws the killing of soldiers who "are out of combat." Nor had the attackers made any attempt to distinguish between military personnel and civilians on what journalists quickly dubbed, the "Highway of Death." Cluster bomblets and napalm outlawed under the 1977 Geneva Protocols had been dropped on terrified teens and others heeding their leader's orders to withdraw.

Gazing down at an unbelievable scene of carnage, Captain Sebastian Fleming felt "an immense sense of evil there." The British officer and his men had seen corpses before. But during the three days they were told to occupy this stretch of wreckage-strewn highway, Fleming came to hate that road.

As far as the Brits could see, intermingled parts of bodies and vehicles smoldered and burned. Craters and unexploded ordnance covered the landscape. For more than 70 miles on the two roads leading north from Kuwait City, every vehicle had been strafed or bombed. "Every windshield is shattered, every tank is burned, every truck is riddled with shell fragments," wrote Joyce Chediac for former US Attorney General Ramsey Clark's postwar Commission of Inquiry. "No survivors are known or likely. The cabs of trucks were bombed so much that they were pushed into the ground, and it's impossible to see if they contain drivers or not. Windshields were melted away, and huge tanks were reduced to shrapnel."

Fleming felt like he was suffocating. The smell of burning oil and rubber was very pungent, but the scent he found most distressing, was the smell of cheap perfume. "I wasn't expecting that," he said later. "I was ready for the smell of war, but I wasn't ready for the smell of kind of everyday life and, and normality, of which, you know, this was. And it had a kind of mocking sense about it."

The party dresses, children's dolls, office files and other domestic debris only added to the sense of slaughter and desolation. Not all of it had been looted from the shops and homes of Kuwait. Many of these household effects belonged to Palestinian families fleeing with their possessions.

Fewer than 500 conscripts and civilians escaped alive. "Iraqi military units sit in gruesome repose, scorched skeletons of vehicles and men alike, black and awful under the sun," the *Los Angeles Times* reported. Time magazine did not run any photos of the blackened bodies heaped for miles along roads that resembled the world's biggest pile-up. But its' editors did not hesitate to employ a glib cliché in explaining what could only be called an atrocity. "War is hell," they told their readers.

A subsequent *Newsweek* article pointed out that prior to the ground assault, General Schwarzkopf had worried about "How long the world would stand by and watch the United States pound the living hell out of Iraq without saying, 'Wait a minute – enough is enough." He itched to send ground troops to finish the job, the American news magazine reported.

The massacre of fleeing conscripts and civilians was certainly a hellish pounding. But was it an act of war? Jehan Rajab didn't think so. When she went out into the streets on the morning after her captors had fled, she found piles of looted goods waiting for lorries that never came.

"They'd obviously been thrown down, and the people who had these things had run as fast as they could," the English teacher said, "leaving behind rolled up mattress, a piece of material, stolen material, for the wife. A toy for the child." Rajab says she felt great pain – "not sympathy, but pain" – for people "who had been put into this terrible position of doing what they did."

Major Bob Nugent echoed her assessment. "Even in Vietnam, I didn't see anything like this," this US Army intelligence officer later stated. "It's pathetic." Clark's war crimes commission would later charge that "Bush and the US military strategists decided simply to kill as many Iraqis as they possibly could while the chance lasted."

After being briefed on the carnage in Kuwait, the US president was having second thoughts. At 1430 Washington time on February 27, President Bush called his war cabinet into the Oval Office. "I want to stop the killing," he announced. After consulting by phone with General Schwarzkopf in Riyadh, the president and the coalition commander agreed on a midnight cease-fire. As Bush hung up the phone, American tanks were less than a day from Baghdad.

CHAPTER 7

"OBJECTIVE GOLD"

Later that night, Private Frank Braddish was riding in a five-person cavalry vehicle deep inside Iraq. Six other vehicles in his scout platoon were moving cross-country, completely blacked-out, a mile and a half apart. Braddish later told *People* magazine that they'd taken prisoners all day: kids in tattered uniforms, 11 and 12 years old. "Among the 30 of them, they had three or four rifles and 20 rounds of ammunition." The starving kids were happy to surrender. Luckily for them, Braddish's crew, like every other coalition unit, were thoroughly sick of their instant MREs (Meals Refused by Ethiopians), as military slang described them. The adolescent EPWs scarfed the instant dinners down.

Allah continued to smile on those Iraqi child-soldiers, who were no longer onboard Braddish's Bradley when an Iraqi tank loomed out of the darkness. "We shot at it and hit it," Braddish recounted. "Then it shot at us."

There was a resounding *boom* as the shell struck the Bradley's turret, rocking the APC back on its tracks. Private Braddish scrambled to the rear of the armored vehicle as a second tank fired a burst of heavy machine-gun into the thick steel ramp.

The rounds whisked through six inches of layered steel, turning Braddish's M-16 into puree before igniting the ready ammunition stored in the turret. In the confusion, explosions and shadows, Braddish felt someone tugging at him. When he realized he was hit, he became "extremely pissed."

Feeling around the inside of his legs, Braddish swore. "It was all numb down there and felt like Jello where the bullets went through – mushy and stuff." The Bradley's interior had been repainted in blood.

Then adrenaline kicked in. "Feeling like Superman," Braddish pulled the other dismount out of the wreck. Both of his partner's legs and an arm had been blown off. The Bradley's commander had become an integral part of the turret. The driver was gone.

Braddish swore again. Wasn't anything going to go right? Climbing down from the burning Bradley, he heard moaning about 50 feet away. The gunner was in agony from a chest wound. With bullets ricocheting off the side of the vehicle, Braddish got on the horn. But the radio net was flooded with urgent calls. Nobody heard his. So Braddish coolly sent up a star cluster before brandishing a handheld GPS. A geosynchronous satellite located a quarter of the way to the moon gave their position to within a few yards. He heard the platoon's lieutenant scream for everyone to clear the net before telling Braddish he'd be there in five minutes.

Two minutes later the driver walked out of the darkness asking, "What happened? What do I do?" Braddish instructed him to start firing bursts toward one flank while he probed the other. The other dismount, a black dude from California with a fondness for sixties rock music, was in really bad shape. "Am I gonna make it out?" he asked Braddish. "Tell me the truth." So Braddish gave it to him straight. "No, you're not gonna make it out of here." None of his stumps were big enough to take a tourniquet.

* * *

Back in Saudi Arabia, US Army mechanic Nicholas Wright was asleep in his helicopter when he and the rest of the crew were awakened and ordered into Kuwait to medevac some amputees. It was just after 0330 when they cranked. They flew four miles before someone very sharp with small arms shot them down. Wright was thrown clear on the chopper's first bounce. The pilot burned.

* * *

Earlier on the 26th, XVIII Corps had gone for the GOLD. The first US troops to reach this Khamisiyah objective were mechanized members of the 24th Infantry Division. Racing up Highway 8 without pausing for border formalities, Lieutenant Commander John Craddock directed his armored battalion toward a canal just north of the highway. Overrunning a vast ammunition storage area, Craddock's battalion herded its demoralized defenders into the weeds near the canal.

Not long afterward, XVIII Corps notified subordinate divisions of the discovery of "possible chemicals on Objective GOLD." The next afternoon, CENTCOM ruled that blowing up small quantities of chemical weapons found in the field would be permissible. As Schwarzkopf's NBC log notes: "Subject: Commanders Guidance for Disposition of captured chemical and biological munitions. Field destruction is OK, but bulk destruction may have international implications."

The next day, XVIII Corps pushed eastward to cut off retreating Republican Guard divisions. In a big tank battle near Basra that night, allied forces shattered the heart of the Iraqi army as 1,500 coalition tanks and 150,000 soldiers destroyed 700 Iraqi tanks and at least five of the Republican Guard's eight divisions.

Computer-coupled to the Abram's gimbaled, longer-range cannon, the American's laser and infrared range-finders picked off hundreds of smaller Iraqi tanks without sustaining serious casualties in return. At least not from Iraqi guns. "Friendly fire" was feared more by allied tankers than enemy artillery. In the nighttime melee, as hundreds of tanks closed to "knife-fighting" range, the ability to instantly identify targets became a high-stakes guessing game as shapes suddenly charged out of the darkness. An American officer saved the situation by ordering all American tanks to turn on their running lights.

It seemed suicidal, but the few Iraqi tanks that managed to take their best shots saw their rounds detonate harmlessly against the Abrams' depleted uranium hide. Twice as dense as lead, DU armor and cannon shells were proving spectacularly successful in their first combat trials. By war's end, almost 1,400 blackened, burnt-out Iraqi vehicles would attest to the deadly effectiveness of depleted uranium shells fired by M1A1 and M1A2 tanks, Bradley Fighting Vehicles and A-10 Warthog aircraft.

The A-10 ground-attack jets proved particularly devastating. Though smaller in diameter than a belt-fed machine-gun bullet, their 30 mm cannon shells burned right through hardened steel armor, barbecuing thousands of crew members trapped inside. Coalition soldiers quickly came to recognize rows of precisely melted holes as DU's telltale signature.

Army combat engineer Dwayne Mowrer identified DU hits on nearly half of the thousands of burned out and rapidly rusting buses, cars, trucks and tanks he encountered on the Highway to Hell. "It leaves a nice round hole, almost like someone had welded it out," Mowrer recalled. He and others discounted radioactive rumors. "We really thought we were in the new enlightened Army. We thought all that Agent Orange stuff and human radiation experiments were a thing of the past."

So Mowrer and his comrades didn't sweat it when a 40-ton transport truck crammed with DU rounds accidentally blew up near their camp. "We heard this tremendous boom and saw this black cloud blowing our way," Mowrer remembers. "The cloud went right over us, blew right over our camp." Before they left the Gulf, Mowrer and other soldiers in the 651st Combat Support Attachment began experiencing strange flu-like symptoms.

US tank crews feared DU-tipped "friendly fire" more than their Iraqi opponents. And with good reason. DU penetrator rounds fired out of the darkness by frantically maneuvering tanks or spit out by rapidly reacting Warthogs at Khafji and other desert skirmishes disabled more American tanks and armored troop carriers than less effective Iraqi weapons.

During the 100 hours of the February ground war, US tanks and aircraft fired close to one million large and small caliber DU rounds. One commander reported to General Schwarzkopf that his unit "went through a whole field of burning Iraqi tanks."

Before the brief ground war ended, at least six American Abrams tanks and 15 APCs would be hit by "friendly fire." All 21 combat vehicles were contaminated by direct DU strikes, or by their own DU munitions "cooking off" after being struck by Hellfire missiles loosed by Apache attack helicopters whose uncanny ability to pop up from masking terrain left little time for target recognition. Five other Abrams tanks were contaminated during on-board fires involving their own DU rounds. In the end, at least 35 American soldiers were killed and 72 others wounded by DU rounds and shrapnel.

The debris were radioactive. Classed as low-level nuclear waste, DU had developed as a combat-effective means to "recycle" leftover uranium used to make nuclear bombs. Depleted uranium penetrator rounds are as toxic as lead – a heavy metal whose neurological dangers are well documented. Containing about .2 percent U-235, as well as potent U-238 isotopes, DU rounds remain radioactive for hundreds of thousands of years. While these radiation levels vary, the Encyclopedia of Occupational Health and Safety states that depleted uranium can cause lung cancer, bone cancer and kidney disease. This information was never passed along to American tank crews.

Some learned this lesson when depleted uranium penetrators struck their vehicles. In a split-second, as the shell's aluminum covering was stripped away and its kinetic energy converted to heat, as much as 70 percent of the uranium and magnesium charge was transformed into an aerosol of fine uranium particles and radioactive gas capable of drifting on the wind for miles.

"This is when it becomes most dangerous," says Arjun Makhijani, president of the Institute for Energy and Environmental Research. "It becomes a powder in the air that can irradiate you." DU particles can also be picked up by later contact with contaminated vehicles and sites.

* * *

Robert Sanders' tank was maneuvering in Kuwait's desert when a single uranium bullet sliced through its DU armor. Splinters of radioactive shrapnel drove into Sanders' face and shoulders. As he bailed out of the Abrams, a horrified Sanders watched the faces of his crew members turn "charcoal black and crispy." Sander's first thought was that "this is what the people in Hiroshima looked like after being exposed to radiation from the atomic bomb." He has been sick from that memory, and Gulf War Illness, ever since.

At least 25 American GIs later helped prepare DU-contaminated tanks for public display and shipment back to the USA. A maintenance sergeant with the 24th Infantry Division Mechanized was in charge of recovering three Bradley Fighting Vehicles hit by DU rounds fired by "friendly" Abrams tanks. He and his people were never warned or trained to avoid the risks of depleted uranium contamination before they unloaded the DU ammunition and stripped the tanks of usable parts and highly-sensitive equipment. Another maintenance sergeant who helped repair one of the vehicles didn't know it had been contaminated. He wasn't even aware that the Abrams fired shells containing radioactive uranium. After the vehicle was repaired, the sergeant lived in it, along with other buddies, for several days until the ground war was over.

* * *

Sensing a decisive victory after the night engagement at Basra, Schwarzkopf pressed the president for permission to crush the encircled Republican Guard. But Bush demurred. Despite branding Saddam Hussein as a modern-day Hitler, George Bush knew that Saddam was the only "strong man" ruthless and capable enough to keep the defeated country's ethnic and religious factions from splintering into Beirut-style anarchy. Unless he was left with enough elite troops and tanks to keep Kurdish and Sunni separatists in check, the ensuing struggle between competing religious factions could spread throughout the Gulf all the way to Oman, where there were already reports of religious unrest. On February 28, less than five days after their broad blitzkrieg across the Kuwait and Iraq borders, the desert war was over.

An American journalist led the liberators into Kuwait City. Instead of encountering jubilant crowds, *Life* magazine's Edward Barnes was startled to find the city's outskirts deserted. No cars were parked on streets once clogged with traffic. As Barnes fretted over stepping on a mine – or being shot by frightened Iraqi soldiers heading out of town – a white Chevy pulled up alongside. To the reporter's relief, there were two Kuwaitis in the Detroit car. Barnes stepped closer as the driver rolled down his window. "Thank you for coming," the Arab said politely. "Is there anything I can do for you?" Then he handed Barnes a gin and tonic.

Life's Lisa Grunwald wasn't offered a drink. And she was not exactly thrilled to be a tourist in what had once been the Gulf's most opulent city. "The ground was black," Grunwald reported. "Rats fed on garbage. Windows were broken, doors hung down, rubble was strewn throughout. The city lacked drinkable water, electricity, telephones. Everything was ruined."

Her co-worker had also made it into town. As Grunwald gazed at scenes of desolation, a blind old man was running his hands across Barnes' face. Then a woman came up and thrust her baby into his arms.

As crowds began forming around the leading Kuwaiti and American troops, the flag-waving and cheering began to swell. But not all the gunfire that would continue for months throughout city and suburbs was celebratory. Weapons were plentiful. And there were scores to settle. With Saddam championing the Palestinian Liberation Organization, the city's Iraqi occupiers had treated many of the Kuwait's 300,00 Palestinian "guest workers" as de facto collaborators. Regardless of their true allegiance, Palestinians who had been denied citizenship in the country many of them had been born and raised in soon found themselves manning checkpoints and selling scarce consumer goods in small street stalls – concessions outlawed by their Kuwaiti overseers before the war. Early reports listed 628 Palestinians killed without trial by Kuwaiti death squads.

Other early estimates pegged the costs of rebuilding the shattered city at more than $200 billion. For Bechtel, Kuwait's destruction was a windfall. A Gulf veteran with 40 years experience operating in Kuwait, the California-based construction giant had been hired by Baghdad before the war to build a chemical plant known as PC-2.

According to a Bechtel official, the company received "direct encouragement" from the US Commerce Department to help construct a plant to produce ethylene oxide, a chemical precursor of mustard gas. Lummus Crest of Bloomfield, NJ, also worked on the PC2 project. Alcolac International of Baltimore sold the thiodiglycol used as a SCUD rocket propellant to NuKraft Mercantile Corporation of Brooklyn, which then shipped it to Iraq.

As the oil fires continued to rage over chemically-contaminated battlefields, the Kuwait government looked to Bechtel to rebuild its shattered infrastructure. Bechtel easily won a $150 million contract to oversee the rebuilding of Kuwait's ruined oil industry, now that the war was over.

* * *

Or was it? At Log Base Charlie later that month, near a Saudi town called Rafha just seven miles from the Iraq border, a native of Columbia, South Carolina, was fast asleep. US Army telecommunications specialist Valerie Sweatman was taking a break from her duties with the 2nd MASH Hospital when she was awakened by a sergeant and told to go to MOPP-4. She put on her MOPP suit and mask and began going outside while she was still putting on her gloves. Later that night, after the "all clear" had been given, a soldier came into the hospital with symptoms of nerve agent exposure. The next morning, Sweatman's hands itched. The little blisters that developed went away about a week later.

Sweatman had seen this scenario before. During the opening nights of the air war, Sweatman had been in King Khalid Military City when she heard a blast and felt a mist envelop the same area. Soon after this incident, she became nauseous and began suffering from diarrhea and bloody stools. Her unit's NBC noncom claimed the alarms were sounding constantly because of defective batteries, not because of chemicals.

Jeffrey Ford, whose small unit had accidentally led the invasion of Iraq, was also stationed at Rafha. A qualified Field Sanitation NCO, Ford was not impressed when the supply sergeant failed to latch the lid properly after filling his unit's "water buffalo" at the division's watering source some 15 miles away. "The trail had been pounded to fine dust after weeks of heavy travel," Ford recalls. "And on the return trip the lid bounced open for several miles and then bounced back shut."

Nobody at battalion command was too concerned about field sanitation, Ford says. But "being the conscientious troop I was...I checked the contents of the buffalo to find about two inches of sludge" in the bottom of the water tank. "Fortunately I checked before anyone got to it but I had to raise hell to the First Sergeant." Ford's entreaty was treated like any other desert pest. "Ah, it's just a little dirt," he was told. "No one will care." But Ford wasn't satisfied with such a Government Issue response. When no one was looking, he pulled the plug, spilling the tanker's contents on the ground.

This wasn't the noncom's first act of self-initiative. Ordered to bring the unit's supply of lindane along on the deployment, Ford had removed the harsh disinfectant and hid it. When the lindane was located and shipped anyway, Ford says, "I found it and hid it again. I wrapped the boxes in several trash bags, taped it up and told my command I didn't know what happened to it and it must have 'accidentally' been left back at Bragg." Ford made sure that this time the lindane was never found and issued to his troops. He also kept tight control over his unit's insect repellent. "If a troop kept asking me for it, I knew he was using it too much."

Others weren't so well served. Sandra Rigdon served as a Preventive Medicine technician at the 403rd Military Police POW Camp. Among other duties, she and her teammate were responsible for food, water, pesticides, procurement, waste disposal, mess halls and immunizations for about 1,500 US personnel and up to 15,000 prisoners. The two technicians also conducted all "de-lousing".

Because of intense sandstorms, the lindane spraying took place inside enclosed tents. "The lindane is a very, very fine powder, much finer than talc," explained Rigdon. Because only two respirators were working, the Iraqi prisoners were given gauze surgical masks to wear. "There was no directive from 'higher up' to tell us how to handle this," Rigdon related. The US Army's own Material Safety Data Sheets lists lindane as a strong carcinogen.

A number of military police units also had close and continuing contact with the EPWs they were assigned to guard. One veteran who served with the 401st MP's prisoner processing team at the same EPW camp, remembers the tent where lindane was used: "Often untrained members of our company would be asked to help with the de-lousing," Jennifer recalled. "I don't remember any warning signs in that tent. The Lindane was open and exposed to the air in the tent. I did get one warning from an intelligence/interrogator officer type, who told me to wash my uniform carefully after making any contact with the stuff, and to wash and put in plastic, any souvenirs that I might trade."

The 300th Medical Brigade was responsible for the prisoners' health care during and after the war. The malnourished, shell-shocked soldiers exhibited a variety of ailments. "Many

Iraqi enemy prisoners of war suffered skin rashes, sores, nausea, vomiting, coughing and other medical problems while they were being detained in Saudi Arabia," one unit member recalls.

Reservists with the 371st Chemical Company were also deployed on several occasions to decontaminate buses used to transport Iraqi enemy prisoners of war to detention camps inside Saudi Arabia. They were never told why the buses required decontamination.

Insects were another plague. Ford took the time to instruct his people never to apply DEET to bare skin. But laundry clerks at log base Charlie used drums of DEET to repregnate cleaned uniforms from all log bases and any unit passing through. Oklahoman Tony Newcomb remembers "the gross smell of the laundry when it came back...and getting sick after wearing it."

Though he had never heard of the hazards of DU, Ford also discouraged his troops from approaching wrecked coalition and Iraqi vehicles. Hundreds of thousands of other GI's scrambled into disabled Iraqi vehicles. Chris Kornkven recalls a lot of curious soldiers (about eight out of 10, according to a post-war survey) climbing on and inside DU-disabled Iraqi tanks. Not one of the soldiers veteran Dan Fahey spoke with "donned a respirator, gloves, or protective clothing before approaching damaged vehicles, or thoroughly washed their hands or face afterwards, as Army guidelines prudently suggest."

While some soldiers posed for snapshots atop radioactive trophies, or paused to hang fragments of DU around their necks, John Stewart was traveling on the MSR toward Kanajar. The US Marine Reserves road master remembers passing a "bomb-type crater" with dead animal bodies lying nearby. Stewart still wonders, "Could this have been chemicals or gas?"

* * *

There was no doubt what 3/7 Marines encountered on February 28. At 1641 a FOX from 3/7 Marines identified the presence of a mustard agent at coordinates QT 753393910.

Corporal Santos of the 2nd Marine Division Alpha Command, suffered chemical injuries in a separate incident. A few days later, Santos showed FOX mass spectrometer operator Darren Siegle five or six blisters on his right arm. As Siegle set the FOX's computer to high sensitivity mode, Santos put his right arm beside the MM-1 mass spectrometer probe. After cogitating briefly, the computer identified the agent as lewisite. Santos told Siegle he probably picked up the chemical agent while clearing bunkers and touching enemy prisoners of war clothing.

* * *

As 3rd Brigade moved toward Objective GOLD, the Airborne's 82nd Division was located west of the 24th Infantry

Division. Kamisiyah was reached and secured on March 1. Locally known as Tall al Lahm, Khamisiyah is situated along the southern side of the Euphrates River, about 25 kilometers southeast of the city of Nasiriyah. The site borders Highway 8, a major artery clogged with US troops transiting the area before and after the cease-fire took effect.

The 82nd had not received specific warnings from XVIII Corps of possible chemicals at Objective GOLD. But on February 24, CENTCOM issued all allied commanders with "Commander's Guidance for Disposition of Captured Chemical and Biological Munitions." Part of that directive ordered that: "Prior to destruction, all necessary measures to preclude collateral damage or down-wind hazard to friendly forces and civilians will be accomplished."

Following standard EOD procedures, the division's Chemical Officer sent FOX vehicles and unit reconnaissance teams ahead to check for evidence of contamination or chemical weapons. As the scouts moved into the 35 square-mile ammunition storage complex they gawked at stacks of munitions piled high in scores of sheds and bunkers. More munitions were stacked in a large open pit.

More than a dozen warehouses and several ammunition bunkers had been hit by allied fighter-bombers. During this cursory inspection, the recon unit reported finding riot control agent CS and white phosphorus artillery rounds. Other shells were inscribed with a yellow band. These were empty. No chemical contamination was discovered.

* * *

As the 82nd Airborne continued their cautious sniffing at Khamisiyah, Sergeant David Allen Fisher was warily proceeding through bunkers, hunting stray "ragheads" in another ammunition dump south of Basra. Iraqi artillery pieces still in place around the site had only recently been firing shells taken from the same sand bunkers whose shadows held an especially nasty surprise.

The 3rd Armored Division cavalry scout didn't find anyone from Saddam's defeated army. But he did discover a cache of chemical weapons where the Department of Defense insisted none were deployed. Fisher hardly noticed brushing up against some wooden crates stamped with skulls and crossbones. Eight hours later, his left arm reddened and began to sting. Several hours after those first symptoms, Fisher was stricken with painful blisters on his upper arm.

Bob Wages commanded the FOX vehicle called in to check out Fisher's find. "My MM-1 operator was one of the best in a FOX," Wages later declared. After cleaning the probe by burning off all residue, the operator reapplied the sensor to Fisher's flak jacket. A few taps on the FOX's computer keyboard and the screen lit up, showing an HD-mustard agent detection. After examining Fisher, Colonel Michael Dunn diagnosed his injuries as having been "caused by exposure to liquid mustard chemical warfare agent."

A career medical doctor, Dunn would later became commander of the US Army Medical Research Institute for Chemical Defense. Fisher would receive a Purple Heart for his CW-induced injuries. And the FOX operator would win a Bronze Star for "the first confirmed detection of chemical agent contamination in the theater of operations."

* * *

Dale Glover, the Military Police staff sergeant who had survived a chemical attack in Saudi Arabia on January 20th, was unaware of these developments. On the same day Fisher received his chemical wounds, Glover's unit was checking out another destroyed artillery site between as Salman and Basra, about 75 miles inside Iraq. Entering a bunker half-exposed by allied bombing, the men were assailed by a very strong odor of ammonia. Looking closer, they discovered chemical inserts for artillery shells packed inside aluminum cases. The munitions were leaking. Another 7th Corps trooper said the leaking crates "made you choke, made you want to throw up, burned your eyes. It smelled like ammonia, only a lot stronger." He could not approach the crates without experiencing immediate breathing problems. A test confirmed the presence of blister agent.

Another American GI named Darin Bokeno was also disturbed by what he was seeing. "As my unit advanced, I saw a lot of frigin' Iraqi personal decon kits opened and scattered about the ground," Darin says. "This particularly was observed by me outside of Basra. Many Iraqi positions, including bunkers, trenches, and fighting positions had decon kits opened and many appeared to have been used. They looked like they came from the 'Fifties or 'Sixties and were contained in round bottomed army green containers. Some as big as binocular cases. Probability is high that this unit, specifically the Ticonderoga Unit of the highly trained Republican Guard, did not get out their decon kits for fun and games. They used them. And they used them because they had to." Bokeno also believes the engineers he was with blew up several ammunition sites they found.

* * *

Back in KC, as American GIs referred to Kuwait City, a heavy dark "oilcast" continued to block the sun. The smoke from the oil fires was so thick, visibility was severely reduced and the smell and taste of oil permeated clothing and skin. On two occasions immediately after the ground war, GI Tom Hare remembers the sky opening up and pouring black rain for nearly an hour. "Everything, I mean everything, uniforms, food, equipment and us would be soaked in oil," Hare said.

Sergeant Jeff Haley had recovered from his earlier fright. On March 1, Haley was examining gray colored artillery rounds with double green bands stacked neatly in bunkers southwest of Kuwait City. The shells showed Jordanian stamps. King Hussein's peace-loving country had played a key role in funneling arms from the US to Iraq during the Iran-Iraq war.

* * *

During that same week, immediately following the cease-fire, Staff Sergeant Grass was also assigned to check out thousands of small ammunition bunkers dotted among the trenches which snaked for miles through the desert just west of Kuwait City. Before their violent eviction, the bunkers had belonged to the Iraqi 3rd Armored Corp.

While driving his FOX through this former Iraqi strong-hold, the vehicle's chemical alarm sounded outside a bunker. The precision mass spectrometer readout indicated the presence of HD or S-mustard agent. After checking the seals of his MOPP gear, Grass dismounted to check it out.

Inside the earthen bunker he found blue 55-gallon barrels. Some were opened. Additional white and striped 55-gallon barrels were segregated nearby. Grass's neck hairs prickled. Before becoming an NBC specialist in 1984, the career soldier had served as an ammunition specialist. The color-coded barrels could be holding chemicals. But there could be no doubt what the skull-and-crossbones marking stacks of artillery rounds signified.

Coming closer, Grass saw that these chemical rounds had flat bases and lacked the stabilizing fins found in high explosive shells. He also noticed that the blue, red and blue, green and white, and green 55-gallon drums were grouped according to solid and striped colors. Blue, red and green colored fire extinguishers accompanied each group of barrels in their own specific areas. "No other area that my FOX vehicle checked was designed or set up like that area," Grass says.

The FOX team obtained positive readings for S-mustard and HT mustard. Markings on the shell casings indicated they had been manufactured in Jordan, Holland, and the USA. The following day, EOD specialists wearing spacesuits checked Grass's find with instruments and clipboards. A marine master sergeant with the explosives demolition unit confirmed that there were chemicals in the bunker. But he explained to Grass that their real interest lay in verifying specific lot numbers on the weapons and boxes.

Someone in CENTCOM was worried about a different kind of leak. If it became known back home that American-made ammunition was being fired against America's sons and daughters, there would be political hell to pay. The only question for Grass was whether the artillery rounds he'd found were US-manufactured chemical rounds or conventional shell casings, which could be easily refilled with chemical agent by the Iraqis. The inserts of white phosphorous rounds, he knew, could be changed with little difficulty.

* * *

Back in the USA, political damage control was already underway. A March 1, 1991, memorandum from the nuclear weapons complex at Los Alamos, New Mexico, suggested that after-action reports of Operation Desert Storm be carefully written to "legitimize the continued use of depleted uranium penetrators while downplaying the environmental risks posed by depleted uranium contamination."

Even as the memo urging a DU cover-up was being drafted, the 307th Engineer Battalion's 2nd Platoon, Charlie Company was trying to deal with a large number of locals and animals inside sector GOLD. Many civilians and animals were sheltering inside bunkers filled with munitions made temperamental by neglect and the desert heat. It wasn't long before 2nd platoon concluded that any demolition at Khamisiyah would require additional engineer support. XVIII Corps quickly cut fresh orders for the 37th Engineer Battalion to assist in blowing what looked like a hundred bunkers at Khamisiyah.

* * *

Some Iraqi units never got the word concerning the two day-old cease-fire. While Charlie company chased bleating goats at Khamisiyah, a column of 140 Iraqi tanks and armored vehicles ran into US forces and started firing. The Americans counter-attacked with tanks and helicopter gunships, destroying 60 tanks and capturing the remainder.

Despite that unexpected victory, US casualties continued to mount. That night, Major Marie Rossie and her three crew members died when their Chinook chopper flew into a Saudi microwave tower obscured by bad visibility. The first US woman combat helicopter pilot had written home saying that flying up to the Euphrates to pick up EPWs was like flying back in time. "Tribes of camels, Bedouins, camels, sheep. Living in tents and mud houses. It was wild," Rossie wrote. Now four pairs of boots on a canvas-draped box were all that remained of young dreams at the memorial service held on the parking pad of the downed chopper.

On March 2, the US 24th Infantry Division engaged the Iraqi Army's fleeing Hammurabi Division just west of Basra. In four hours, the 24th destroyed more than 750 vehicles and killed thousands of Iraqi soldiers. "We really waxed them," one US.

commander exulted. Another American officer called it a "Turkey Shoot" for Apache gunships, in which one crewmember cried, "Say hello to Allah" as he launched a laser-guided Hellfire missile.

* * *

Washington was already gearing up for next month's victory parade. But some observers were having second thoughts. Writing in the *Toronto Star*, Gerald Caplin, asked, "Was Gulf War Really The Mother Of All Deceptions?" Caplin pointed out that a battle billed as "the biggest tank battle in history" cost two destroyed allied tanks. Iraqi "bunkers" were, in reality, flimsy trenches covered by corrugated roofs and some sand. Most Iraqi soldiers, including many "elite" Republic Guards, were raw conscripts with little military training. "If this monstrous plot is true," Caplin wrote, "it would make a mockery of every casualty on both sides and every fleeing refugee and every moment of horror and panic in the last six weeks."

American troops clearing enemy personnel from GOLD sector and destroying captured equipment were more concerned with staying alive than with contemplating the war's gruesome harvest. On March 3rd, the XVIII Corps logbook noted: "Divisions are discovering large numbers of bunkers/underground complexes containing weapons, ammunition and other materials. Destruction of these bunkers has already begun; however, the enormity of the task before us and amount of resources required is still unknown."

As the last elements of the 37th Engineer Battalion from the 60th Explosive Ordnance Disposal (EOD) detachment arrived at Khamisiyah, vehicles sported M8A1 chemical alarms mounted on their fenders. Suiting up in MOPP-4 protective gear, the battalion's NBC officer-used an M256 kit to check some of the bunkers for chemical agents. The results were negative. But the engineers did find one rocket with possible intelligence value. Two bunkers, 98 and 99, were wired with demolition charges and blown in place to test demolition techniques.

Elsewhere that day, G-3 operations attached to the mechanized 1st Infantry Division logged an incident in which an Iraqi had been exposed to a possible chemical agent: "Defector had blisters 1/2" to 1" on his upper arm. Tests was conducted. Results positive for blister agent."

The log entry stopped there. But Gulf War veteran Jim Brown found it "very interesting that both this defector and David [Fisher] acquired the same type of blisters, in the same place on the arm, around the same timeframe, and in the same area. Quite the co-ink-o-dink, yes? Not if you consider that the defector got the blisters first, came in for treatment, and the cav-scouts were sent out to investigate said bunker on the strength of said defector's testimony, it isn't."

Not far from Khamisiyah, at Tallil airfield, NBC Sergeant First Class Robert Bashaw drove past bunkers cordoned off by yellow chemical contamination marking tape. Staff Sergeant Grover Trew, a member of Bradshaw's company, saw what appeared to be well over a hundred 155 mortar rounds scattered in and around the Iraqi bunkers at Tallil. "The base color of the rounds was either OD [olive drab] or gray. I saw both – with two yellow stripes toward the nose." According to UNSCOM and DoD code books, the yellow bands indicate a blister agent round.

* * *

After reaching Tallil on the morning of March 4th, Jeffrey Ford was put to work blowing up three large caches of aerial bombs situated just north of the airbase. The clearly marked bombs, the Combat Engineer saw, were of American, French and Russian manufacture.

Later that afternoon, Ford's unit arrived at Khamisiyah just as the engineers from 37th Engineer Battalion and 60th EOD finished priming 38 bunkers with high explosives. Taking time-out to watch the fireworks, Ford and his buddies positioned their vehicles on the banks of the same canal where Craddock's armor had chased frightened Iraqis only a few days before.

Since no chemical alerts had been given, the American engineers did not don MOPP gear before climbing on top of their trucks to watch the show taking place about two-and-a-half miles away. A few minutes later, around 1400 hours, firing circuits closed on nearly half the bunkers at Khamisiyah. The entire complex seemed to vanish behind a shattering detonation. Shock waves shook the trucks and the men standing on them. Spectacular secondary explosions followed immediately.

This was all very satisfactory. But the onlookers became dismayed when Iraqi rockets began "cooking off" inside the burning bunkers. "The first few went overhead, but then they began falling on us," Ford later related. "I jumped from the top of a five-ton dump truck to hit the ground. All the soldiers began scrambling for cover."

Ford and the others around him had failed to anticipate the hazards "of such a large single detonation." Several rounds landed within 20 feet of American soldiers who were scrambling to get clear. Ford and another soldier took cover under the engine block of his dump truck to get out of the steel rain. As the detonations continued, the engineers who had arranged such a spectacular show saddled up their vehicles and left the smoldering area.

Ford was told that his unit would be staying. No reason was given – orders don't require explanations – so Ford just watched the cloud from the blazing bunkers continue to grow long after the other units had departed. "I remember the sun setting at our backs in the late afternoon. The plume of smoke soon mixed with an approaching storm front and soon the sun was blocked off."

Then something went haywire with his memory. Ford's next recollection is pulling guard duty around 0100 the next morning. "We blocked and restricted traffic to the bunker complex and secured the area," he says. "I recall explicitly that the bunkers continued to burn throughout the night, as well as rockets flying out although with less frequency. I have no knowledge of close proximity impacts as night conditions deterred visibility."

The secondary explosions would continue for 24 hours. But Ford could not guess that Khamisiyah's biggest detonations would continue for years to come.

CHAPTER 8

KHAMISIYAH

On March 4, the three line companies of the 37th Engineer Battalion, assisted by the two teams of the 60th EOD, were each assigned 12 to 14 bunkers to inventory, wire with high explosives, and demolish. According to Charlie company's commander, "the explosive ordnance guys came through and said, here's what you're looking at. These are safe to destroy." About 770 troops from the 505th Infantry secured the area as the engineers rigged their demolition charges for conventional munitions. Among the 38 bunkers they strung with primer cord was Bunker 73. The Wal-Mart size bunker was stuffed with Iraqi chemical munitions.

At approximately 1400 hours, the engineers blew 37 bunkers with a roar that rocked the surrounding area. A faulty time-fuse spared Bunker 92. The weather was clear, with the flag on a nearby "hummer" pointing southeast directly toward US positions in Iraq, Kuwait and Saudi Arabia.

About 45 minutes later, one of Bravo Company's M8A1 chemical alarm sounded at an observation point set up by the engineers about a mile away. Some soldiers went to MOPP-4 status. Others only donned their masks while company and EOD teams performed several M256 tests. Two NBC noncoms later said they got "weak" or "slightly" positive results on M256 tests designed to show only positive or negative results. After Bravo Company's commanding officer and another NBC specialist registered negative readings, the "all clear" was given.

The next morning Jeffrey Ford awoke to a heavy rain. Vehicles began getting stuck in a quagmire thickened by oil falling from hundreds of burning oil wells at Rumayah.

"The complex continued to burn," Ford recalls, with secondary explosions continuing from the night before. "We moved to protective cover in a building in the town of Tall a Lam, nearly 24 hours after the initial detonation." Though he does not recall any of his buddies displaying acute symptoms of nerve agent poisoning, "many were very agitated. Later that afternoon we pulled back to Tallil as the complex continued to burn and we could not continue the mission."

No one at Khamisiyah suspected that they had just detonated hundreds of unmarked, sarin-filled rockets. Army manual FM 3-6, Properties of Chemical and Biological Agents, warns that "sarin is miscible with water. Further raising the pH of Sarin [with rainwater] will increase its persistency." The Army's Material Safety Data Sheet further notes that GB [sarin] reacts with steam and water to produce toxic and corrosive vapors."

A day or so later, Ford says, "we returned to Khamisiyah to continue operations as the two EOD men had given the all clear to reenter. Ford began hauling tons of C-4 demolition charges that had been airlifted to his unit. But the extra explosives weren't enough to complete the destruction of the huge munitions storage center. "When we ran out of C-4," Ford continues, "we used Iraqi materials confiscated by the 37th engineers."

While demolition teams re-fused Bunker 92 and lit it off, Alpha company blew the warehouses in the northwest sector of the depot. Bravo Company focused on the bunkers. As Ford drove through the area delivering demolition supplies to each units, he ran over rockets, shells, shrapnel and artillery casings strewn all over the ground.

"Some were split open and leaking their contents on the ground. I ran over a few by accident, as they were heavily concentrated, perhaps one every 10 feet or so." After working to demolish Khamisiyah during the day, the engineers drove about 40 klicks to Tallil, where they spent their nights. The sky regularly erupted with debris from Iraqi munitions sites detonated by 82nd Airborne around Tallil airbase and nearby Jalibah.

Like so many others at Khamisiyah, Ford was not in the military command's "need-to-know" information loop. "At no time was I aware of any chemical alarms either being deployed or having sounded off," he later told Senate investigators. "At no time did I don any chemical protection gear whatsoever. At no time did I see anyone conduct any chemical testing, nor through-out the entire operation was I aware of any specially trained chemical personnel in the area. In fact, I knew nothing of chemicals having been at Khamisiyah until I saw it on *60 Minutes*.

The following afternoon, armored elements of the 24th Infantry Division maneuvering in the Rumayah oil field logged the discovery of "a jeep with chem ammo and documents." One of the Iraqi Army's biggest chemical weapons storage sites was located nearby, in what had been the rear area of the Republican Guard command.

At 2129 that evening, 1st Armored Division logs recorded a radio call to all stations on the unit's net: "Effective immediately, all destruction of ammunition stocks in country of Kuwait is to stop. Those stocks will be left in place. Destruction of ammunition in Iraq will continue."

On March 6, the 37th and 307th Engineer Battalions blew up bunkers to test new demolition techniques. The idea was to implode the bunkers, collapsing them inwards to reduce the number of secondary explosions and conserve the amount of explosives required. When the test shots failed to achieve either result, it was decided to connect all of the charges being set in each bunker into a single "ring main" linking all of Khamisiyah's remaining warehouses and bunkers. The new plan was to go for one super-explosion instead of a series of individual blasts timed to go off at roughly the same time.

The weather fought them harder than the Iraqis had. Rain continued so heavy that demolitions scheduled over the next three days were canceled. The engineers spent this time rehearsing the big blast and inventorying Khamisiyah's remaining bunkers and warehouses. Some videos were also made inside the bunkers. But the brief hiatus was insufficient for demolition teams to complete an accurate count of all the munitions stored in the vast aboveground and underground complex. It didn't help that almost every ammunition container was labeled with indecipherable Arabic script.

"The shells were not marked, they were not special," a senior US defense official later insisted. "The only way you could tell it's a chemical shell is to open it. Mustard rounds out in the field had words on the outside of the crates. But these sarin agents were not marked."

* * *

On March 7, as American engineers puzzled over unfamiliar lettering, Chief Warrant Officer 3 Gerald Jones was checking out a former Iraqi chemical brigade headquarters located near a cement factory in the vicinity of the Kuwait International Airport. As Jones scoured the area, his FOX sounded the alarm for lewisite. A close search soon revealed empty containers used for chemical mines. Jones also found 55-gallon drums filled with chemical warfare precursors. The MM1's operator, SSG Lawless, obtained mass spectrometer tapes for lewisite.

But four days later, Jones was blocked when he tried to obtain the results of his soil samples in order to determine his FOX's effectiveness. As Eddington relates, "The samples had been handed over to a highly centralized and secretive Joint Staff chemical warfare analysis cell, which refused to share the results of their analysis with troops whose equipment had repeatedly detected chemical agents during their reconnaissance mission."

Marine commanders were already telling reporters back in Washington that there were no indications of chemical weapons being stockpiled on the battlefields of Kuwait – or anywhere south of the Euphrates River. A US military intelligence official told the *Washington Post*: "It was a matter of not deploying chemical weapons, rather than not having them. My guess is they never managed to get it down to division level."

* * *

On March 9, the Khamisiyah Operations Officer discovered crates containing more than 1,000 Katyusha rockets transferred by Iraqi personnel on February 26th and stacked in a huge open air pit situated in the southeast corner of Khamisiyah. The officer did not know the rockets contained sarin. Nor did he know that 6,000 artillery shells moved from an Nasiriyah to the "pit" on February 17th were chemical rounds. A noncommissioned officer was ordered to destroy all 13 stacks of rockets.

The next day, at approximately 1540 hours, approximately 859 5-inch rockets rigged with demolition charges were detonated, along with Khamisiyah's 60 remaining bunkers and additional warehouses. Overcast skies and poor visibility were suitably gloomy for the tragedy about to unfold.

The wind was blowing almost due south as the 37th Engineers completed their mission at Khamisiyah and began driving south on Main Supply Route 8 toward the US and British positions. Stopping after about half an hour, the engineers closed the switch on a radio-detonator. An epic explosion rattled windows in Tallil. Khamisiyah's last stupendous detonation sent the contented contingent driving south towards Saudi Arabia for another four hours. Mission accomplished, they were looking forward to winging their way home to Fort Bragg.

* * *

Many of the officers involved in the demolishing of Khamisiyah figured that any chemical agents present would be incinerated by the ensuing explosions and fires. If they had consulted the US Army's Materials Data Safety sheet, they would have learned that instead of neutralizing this nerve agent, flames convert sarin to an easily dispersed aerosol. Under the heading "Waste Disposal Methods" for sarin, the manual specifies: "Open pit burning or burying of GB or items containing or contaminated with GB in any quantity is prohibited."

It was already too late. Like an evil jinn released from its bottle, an invisible cloud of sarin nerve gas mixed with talc-like desert sand was already pursuing the engineers south. The silent plume drifted over elements of seven US Army divisions. These included the 1st Mechanized Infantry, the 82nd Airborne, the 24th Mechanized Infantry, the 1st Cavalry, the 1st Armored, 2nd Armored and 3rd Armored Divisions, as well as support units comprised of reservists and state national guard units. More than 130,000 front-line American troops who had routed Saddam Hussein from Kuwait wound up being exposed to the most unfriendly fires of all.

CIA computer models later showed that the sarin fallout may also have passed over parts of the British 1st Infantry, as well as unsuspecting civilian populations as distant as Saudi Arabia.

* * *

Not far from Khamisiyah, a full-scale Shi'ite rebellion was underway. Street fighting was reported in six southern Iraqi cities, where Islamic fundamentalists battled Saddam Hussein's Republican Guard. On March 6, the uprisings spread from southern Iraq to the north, where Kurdish rebels claimed they had seized several towns.

As they tramped down a soggy road past burned out Iraqi tanks, a young soldier named Jabar and his buddy Hussein shared a bag of spoiled dates. "Food for cattle," Jabar called it. Jabar, Hussein and the other defectors had shed their uniforms to join another 5,000 or so Iraqi Army defectors and Shi'ite fundamentalists waving photographs of Iran's top cleric. Arrayed against the mutineers were perhaps 6,000 troops still loyal to Saddam.

The wily dictator quickly raised Republican Guard pay by one-third. After the Guard began laying down artillery barrages, many defectors reconsidered their earlier decision. "Everybody who tries to undermine security," warned Baghdad's Baathist newspaper, *al Thawra*, "shall regret it. They will pay." Hastily redonning their uniforms, many deserters rejoined Saddam's ragged army.

Fearing American intervention in the uprising, Iraqi Air Force headquarters in Baghdad ordered helicopter pilots to take their choppers dispersed along a road near Army Aviation School number 5187 at as Suwayrah and attack "US airborne commandos" operating at Nasiriyah. As nearby Khamisiyah burned, the Iraqi Army pilots took off as ordered. But instead of American troops, they found only local residents of Nasiriyah. In following President Bush's exhortations to rise up against Saddam Hussein's regime, the Nasiriyahns were considered enemies of the state. But they were still Iraqi citizens. When the fliers realized they had been tricked into attacking their own people, they held fire, returned to base and immediately departed their leader's employ.

The order went out again. This time, other elements of the 84th and 106th helicopter squadrons carried out the attack missions. Flying light Alouette helicopters and a handful of Soviet built Mi-8 Hind helicopter gunships, Iraqi air force pilots began firing what were reported to be chemical rockets at the Shi'ite civilians.

As Iraqis fired on Iraqis, distant observers began expressing doubts about a war that wasn't what it had seemed. Writing in the March 10 edition of the *Toronto Star*, Linda Diebel asked "Was Saddam Set Up For The Kill?"

Go figure, suggested Diebel. "Huge chunks of this war don't add up. Jordan's envoys scrambled from city to city. President George Bush turned an official-laden plane around in mid-air, Arab kings and presidents made promises, then refused to take phone calls, people were cursed, deals were made, then unmade." Diebel quoted a weary King Hussein saying, "I've been convinced for a while that there was no effort to dialogue, there was no effort to reach for a diplomatic solution, and there was preparation from the word go for war."

James Aikins, a Washington based energy and Middle East specialist, believed that the United States had enacted a long-term plan to assert military control over the region's region's oil wealth. Shortly after the 1973-74 "oil shock," articles appeared in *Harper's* and *Commentary* advocating a military takeover of that oil-rich region. As the US ambassador in Jeddah at the time, Aikins says he was "appalled by the cynicism and immorality of the suggestion." Aikins now believed that Saddam had fallen into a trap. The potential paybacks to US oil interests are enormous, the Mideast expert noted. "Only the Spanish conquest of the New World was so richly rewarded."

On March 15, 1991, Kuwait's emir returned home. Appearing dazed as he stepped from his aircraft, his highness ostentatiously kissed the battle-blackened tarmac. His touching gesture did not play well with many of his royal subjects, who had remained behind when the emir fled. Even though the emir was known to rise each morning at 0400 to pray and partake of a simple herder's breakfast of bread and camel's milk (with a spoonful of honey), there was nothing humble in his refusal to return home until crystal chandeliers and gold-plated bathroom fixtures could be refitted to his opulent Bayan Palace.

* * *

In late May, 1991, US Marines entering Ahmed al Jaber Airfield searched the Iraqi brigade commander's bunker and found plans for an earlier chemical attack against the Marines. Their "Command Chronology" reveals several reports of chemical detection as well, starting the first day of the ground war and occurring every day thereafter.

Many official unit logs had already been destroyed in the theater. A government official later confirmed that "many chemical incident reports were destroyed in Saudi Arabia during the Spring of 1991 under direct orders from Central Command."

As Eddington notes: "This is a violation of standing military regulations: units are required to maintain such records for at least two years." According to the former CIA intelligence expert, such a "fundamental lack of integrity among senior leadership of the US armed forces" proved that "the pernicious careerism of the officer corps in Vietnam had not been purged at all."

But confirmation of chemical munitions and attacks could prove extremely damaging to coalition government and military leaders, who were insisting that no such events occurred. The Pentagon also worried about possible health effects from the pyridostigmine bromide that hundreds of thousands of US troops had been ordered to swallow. An Army safety bulletin issued on April 25, 1991, instructed supply officers to collect all unused PB from soldiers before they departed the Gulf. The memo warned: "Nerve agent antidotes present an unnecessary health and safety hazard to soldiers, their family members (especially children), and the general public."

Even without the added hazards of a drug that amplified the effects of sarin, there was no shortage of that chemical nerve agent wafting through the KTO. On March 12, CENTCOM logged a report from a FOX vehicle whose sensors picked up chemical agents at a chemical mine filling depot. Also on that day, elements of the 307th Engineer Battalion who had remained in Iraq stumbled on "another enemy bunker complex of more than 400 revetted bunkers with large caches [of munitions] inside."

Two days later, Iraqi civilians were observed fleeing west along the highway leading from Nasiriyah past the town of al Khidr. According to US intelligence, an Iraqi defector angered by what he was witnessing told them that "many of the refugees bore wounds characteristic of chemical weapons, particularly khardel." These mustard agent-induced wounds included skin lesions and swelling last seen by this eyewitness during the Iran-Iraq War.

By this time, the road and towns from al Kut and an Najaf, south through as Samawah all the way to al Khidr were under the control of anti-Bathist, anti-Saddam forces. Iraqi helicopters attacking the local populace were being brought down by Roland anti-aircraft missiles launched from the shoulders of Iraqi soldiers, apparently on the orders of a lieutenant upset over the aerial attacks on fellow civilians. As resistance fighters maneuvered to cut government supply lines, three pro-government infantry brigades moved quickly along the road running through as Shatrah, al Gharraf and ar Rifa, north of an Nasiriyah. Soon their heavy artillery was firing chemical rounds into the town of Nasiriyah. In between barrages, Iraqi air force helicopters armed with chemical weapons swooped over that hapless town.

* * *

Unmindful of this mayhem just down the road, over the next six days hard-working 307th Engineers finished rigging explosives on yet more munitions discovered earlier in outside pits southwest of the still smoking Khamisiyah ammo depot. Around 1530 on the afternoon of March 20, these detonated munitions were dispersed on winds blowing directly toward American and British positions.

Three days later, VII Corp's 2nd Armored Cavalry Regiment assumed responsibility for Khamisiyah. The next day, the 82nd Airborne, 307th Engineer Battalion, and 60th EOD departed for Saudi Arabia and long-awaited rides home.

On March 27, the 2nd Armored Cavalry was ordered to check 100 revetments located in the southern sector of Khamisiyah for possible chemical or biological munitions. A day later, the unit reported back to VII Corps that their reconnaissance had yielded negative results.

Demolition continued at Tallil airfield. On April 2, the 82nd Engineer Battalion, located south of the 2nd Armored's area of operations, reported hearing a large explosion in the vicinity of Tallil. Four days later, members of the 84th Engineer Company and 146th EOD reexamined bunkers at Khamisiyah and determined that six bunkers required additional detonations to destroy remaining munitions. The last American units departed Khamisiyah in late April, 1991.

Almost in their wake came UN inspectors tasked with examining Iraqi NBC capabilities throughout that shattered country. By July, after checking a nuclear site, two biological and seven chemical weapons facilities damaged by allied bombing, UN scientific monitors began voicing fears for their personal safety. Their anxiety was not lessened by secret Iraqi studies that revealed how some of the technicians working in those same biological and chemical weapons plants had become ill before their deadly contents had been scattered across the heavily bombed sites.

Just being in Kuwait could compromise your health. Oil fires and suspect drinking water were bad enough. But in July, a major fire broke out at a US Army ammunition depot in Doha, about 12 miles from Kuwait City. Approximately 660 rounds burned, releasing black clouds of DU particles.

Many of the 3,000 US troops stationed at the base took part in the cleanup without wearing protective gear. No one was briefed on the potential dangers of breathing uranium oxide dust and uranium hexafluoride. Kuwaiti residents living within a radius of 25 miles of the huge DU blaze were also dusted with heavy metals that had long been linked to cancers, birth defects and serious kidney ailments – which would not show up for years.

* * *

In early August, five months after a cease-fire that did not formally end the Gulf War, Lt. Colonel Saleh al Ostath of the Kuwaiti Army requested the British Army to investigate a mysterious container the Kuwaitis had found a few kilometers northwest of the Kuwait Port of Mina al Ahmadi. Upon entering the Sabbahiyah High School for Girls on August 7, Major J. P. Watkinson and his 21st Explosive Ordnance Disposal Squadron were led to a large metal container standing alone on the school grounds.

The 2,000 litre storage tank was leaking a brown vapor through entry and exit bullet holes apparently made by an AK-47. A Sabbahiyah security guard told the British that the tank had not been there before the school was turned into an Iraqi defensive position soon after their invasion the previous year. Major Watkinson immediately ordered all personnel to move upwind. Donning his own chemical-protection "spacesuit", Watkinson walked up to the tank and tested the brown colored vapor with a Chemical Agent Monitor. The CAM gave a reading of eight bars – the maximum concentration – for H mustard agent. Watkinson was relieved to see no bars lighting on the G setting, indicating that no nerve agents were present. When the British Major tested the vapor with tricolor detector paper, the litmus test turned telltale pink, confirming the presence of mustard agent.

Returning with a length of wire, Watkinson poked it into one of the bullet holes. Withdrawing the probe, he recognized the brown, oily residue to be consistent with mustard agent. Wiping the sample on two types of detector paper, Watkinson watched as the one-color paper turned brown and the three-colored paper turned pink, once again confirming mustard agent. The major covered both holes in the container with masking tape, sealing the deadly vapors inside the tank.

On his third visit to the ominous container, Watkinson briefly uncovered the holes and tested the escaping vapor with an M18A2 chemical detector kit. This test was repeated six times. All six tests immediately turned blue – indicating an H mustard agent. Watkinson resealed the bullet holes with silicone wrapped in plaster of Paris bandages. A radio call was then made to the Commander of the 11th Armored Cavalry Regiment, requesting two FOX chemical reconnaissance vehicles as back-up to the British effort.

Captain Michael Johnson arrived on the scene the next day. Before commencing "live agent" chemical detection, detailed rehearsals were carried out by the British and American teams to ensure that no foul-ups would occur. One FOX team inserted their vehicle's detection probe into the ground to a depth of about four centimeters. The onboard spectrometer showed that microdoses of chemical mustard agent had permeated the soil.

While this test was underway, another collection team in full MOPP-4 gear approached the storage tank carrying Chemical Agent Monitors and other chemical detection equipment. When the team removed the tank's seals, amber-brown vapor shot into the air. Tests were conducted using the CAM and chemical detection paper. These tests, too, showed maximum positive readings for chemical mustard agent. Following their practiced drill, the team then inserted a medical syringe with a catheter tube into the container and extracted liquid agent for further testing by detection paper, chemical monitors, and the waiting FOX.

Within six seconds, FOX's the mass spectrometer detected and identified the liquid as highly concentrated mustard agent. Full spectrum readings were obtained and printed out on the computer's paper tape. Further analysis indicated traces of phosgene, a non-persistent choking agent, as well as the blister agent phosgene oxime. The FOX found mustard agent for the 17th time. Phosgene and phosgene oxime were also reconfirmed.

Matching the British commander's thoroughness, Captain Johnson ordered yet another mass spectrometer test, utilizing the second FOX. After repeating the tests made by the first FOX, the second team reported the same findings – except this time the reported levels of phosgene oxime were much higher. A second test confirmed their initial findings.

So far, professionalism and good luck had protected the soldiers gathered around the sinister storage tank. But when a British team member went forward to collect yet another sample, some of the liquid splashed on his left wrist. Captain Johnson reported that "the soldier had an immediate reaction to the liquid contact. The soldier was in extreme pain and was going into shock."

The stricken soldier was quickly doused with decontamination powder and cut out of his chemical protective clothing, which was burned on-site. Within a minute, a small blister the size of a pinhead formed on the Brit's left wrist. About five minutes later, the blister had grown to the size of an American fifty cent piece. Medics on the scene checked the injured trooper for residual liquid contamination and evacuated him to a hospital for further treatment.

The soldier's wound seemed minor. But without prompt attention, he could have died within minutes. According to Military Chemical and Biological Agents: Chemical and Toxicological Properties, mustard agents acting alone can take hours to form blisters. But phosgene oxime acts within 30 seconds to form a red rash-like ring. Anyone exposed to phosgene oxime can die quickly from systemic shock or trauma.

After the casualty's departure from the schoolyard, the remaining team members decontaminated themselves and their equipment using special decontamination solutions. The disposal of those contaminated liquids was not logged.

The confirmation of chemical agents at an Iraqi chemical munitions "filling station" in Kuwait threatened the American central command with grievous credibility wounds. Before Captain Johnson's team left the girl's high school, the chemical officer assigned to Task Force Victory ordered the FOX commanders to turn over their mass spectrometer tapes and all samples to personnel who arrived at the school wearing desert camouflage uniforms with no rank or distinguishing patches. Lt. Colonel Killgore explained that the mysterious personnel were members of a special UN team from the British Chemical and Biological Defense Establishment at Porton Down.

The tapes have since disappeared. Captain Johnson was subsequently awarded a Meritorious Service Medal for his conduct at the Saabahiyah high school. The Army Commendation Medal was also presented to Sergeant James Warren Tucker for "participating in the mission that located stores of chemical agents." Six other members of the 54th Chemical Troop, 11th Armored Cavalry Regiment were also given Army medals and cited for making "the positive identification of suspected chemical agent."

Despite the chemical warfare medals, and 21 separate, positive tests for mustard gas and phosgene, the Army would later claim that British and American chemical warfare experts had found fuming nitric acid at Sabbahiyah high school. Iraq stored both mustard agent and fuming nitric acid. That volatile rocket fuel oxidizer was often stored in similar metal tanks. But no rockets or launchers were found at the hastily vacated high school.

And the National Institutes for Standards and Technology notes that mustard agent and nitric acid have dissimilar "peaks" on chemical monitor tracings. An extremely flammable oxidizer, fuming nitric acid would have burst their detector paper into flames.

* * *

In November, 1991, the Kuwait government announced that 1,100 broken and burning oil wells had been extinguished and capped. Almost the same number of captured tanks, artillery pieces, missile launchers and trucks were still being washed and prepped in Dhahran for shipment back to CONUS as display pieces.

Wayne Clingman was a platoon leader in charge of a 170th Maintenance Company's "pit crew" cleaning Iraqi military vehicles in a special holding area near the Port of Dammam's northernmost pier. The Kansas National Guard unit, says Clingman, "cleaned and retrograded no enemy equipment that had been taken out by DU rounds." But Clingman remembers a single T-72 tank "that was at our location for about a week that had been taken out by DU before it was taken away."

He also recalls cleaning approximately 40 M-1 Abrams tanks and Bradley Fighting Vehicles which had been taken out by DU rounds – a figure much higher than the official count of 27. Delivered on flatbed trucks, some of the burned out American vehicles were tarped. "All were supposedly sealed so none of the contamination on the inside could get out."

During one nighttime cleaning session, Clingman spotted water leaking onto one of his men working underneath an M-1. The wastewater was coming from inside the turret. "I almost had a revolt on my hands," Clingman says, when his hole crew refused to continue washing vehicles hot enough to be loaded onto a ship for transport back to what Clingman thought "could have been a nuclear power plant in Alabama" for decon and eventual disposal.

"As soon as the brass found out about our refusal to finish prepping the vehicles," Clingman continues, "I received a visit from a very irate DoD civilian who threatened to end my career if I did not get the mission done." The angry official explained that while the vehicles were technically "hot," the radiation from incinerated DU was contained in the vehicles' interior surfaces. Unless the maintenance personnel ate a handful of dust or metal from the contaminated vehicles, they were safe. The stranger used a Geiger counter to show the skeptical cleaners that the vehicles were not "hot" to the touch.

Clingman grabbed the Geiger counter's probe and stuck it inside one of the vehicles. It registered no radiation readings. "You're more at risk from the radium that coats the dials on the azimuths of the artillery pieces and gauges in the vehicles," the DoD consultant told Clingman.

A general later told Clingman's unit that the destination of the display pieces was not their concern and to stop taking pictures of vehicles ostensibly bound for public display. A four-man team from a Pentagon museum acquisition unit told Clingman that they were eager to take possession of some of the rare Iraqi vehicles for display. They did not know the vehicles' destination or controlling authority.

* * *

UN disarmament inspectors had by now inspected 18 chemical sites, 12 biological warfare facilities and an undisclosed number of nuclear power plants and weapons development labs. The CW materials which survived intensive allied bombings included:

- •13,000 155-mm artillery shells loaded with mustard gas
- • 6,200 rockets loaded with nerve agent
- • 800 nerve agent aerial bombs
- • 28 SCUD warheads loaded with nerve agent sarin
- • 75 tons of nerve agent sarin
- • 60-70 tons of nerve agent tabun
- • 250 tons of mustard gas and 153,983 litres of thiodiglycol, a mustard gas precursor.

Besides cataloging some 5,000 tons of stockpiled chemical agents, UNSCOM inspectors also found more than 46,000 CW-filled munitions, including 30 ballistic missile warheads and many mustard-filled bombs. Sixteen of the sarin-filled al Hussein missiles were ready to launch; the other 14 warheads held precursor chemicals. At least 25 other al Husseins had been deployed before the war tipped with botulinum toxin, anthrax and aflatoxin. No one was sure how many had been fired.

While 170th Maintenance was washing down DU-contaminated vehicles, UNSCOM inspectors were also examining about 300 damaged and intact 122mm rockets in Khamisiyah. Running tests on the intact rockets, the UN team found that their warheads held sarin and thickened cyclosarin. Their Iraqi guides claimed that the chemical munitions in the bermed pit had been salvaged from Bunker 73 after its destruction by coalition forces. When UNSCOM inspectors visited the damaged bunker, their chemical agent monitors remained silent. They did not conduct a thorough search of the bunker.

The Iraqis also led the UN weapons experts to another site about a mile and a half away. The open storage area, which had apparently not been discovered by coalition forces, contained 6,300 intact artillery shells that had been moved from an Nasiriyah the previous February. Each 155mm round was filled with mustard agent. Under UN supervision, these munitions were later shipped, along with hundreds of rockets, to the destruction facility at al Muthanna.

A classified UN report coming out of Khamisiyah as late as November, 1991, had been "red-flagged" for White House, CIA and State Department attention. These government bodies were alerted that chemical weapons had been stored in a big Iraqi ammunition depot that was blown up by American troops in March, 1991. The UNSCOM report was also marked "priority" and circulated to US military commanders worldwide. The "priority" designation is reserved for intelligence considered to be of moderate importance. Commanders filed the information among a deluge of post-war assessments pouring out of the Gulf. It was never shared with the troops themselves.

Despite the UN's latest contribution to a growing stack of disturbing reports indicating the coalition forces had been repeatedly exposed to accidental and deliberate releases of deadly chemical agents, the assumed immediate lethality of sarin, mustard and other nerve agents indicated that these exposures were not serious. To a relieved Schwarzkopf, Cheney and Powell, it looked like American troops had emerged from Saddam's nightmarish CBW threat with a few minor blisters, short-lived nausea and soon forgotten headaches.

As one CIA analyst put it, if sarin had really been present in the bunkers and battlefields, thousands of coalition troops would have died quick, nasty deaths. "The primary known symptom is death. This is really lethal stuff. But it can range from that down to watery eyes and runny noses."

Another analyst looked at the UN findings of sarin at Khamisiyah and shook his head in disbelief. "Assume that the purity of that agent was 100 percent – which we have never seen in Iraqi chemical munitions, but if you assume that – and if they all exploded nearly simultaneously and you got a maximum kind of aerosol cloud out of that. Under that scenario, your lethal zone is three to five kilometers. Anybody that close should have died. We know nobody died as a result of chemical release at this time. Outside of that lethal zone is the zone of health effects, where it would be very visible if you were exposed to chemical weapons you would know it. Runny nose, blurry eyes. Visible health effects. Incapacitating health effects, presumably. We, at present, have no reports of anybody experiencing those effects at the time."

Like many officers, this intelligence specialist was sure that everyone involved was clear of potential scandal – or danger. "One of the puzzles of Khamisiyah," he later told congressional investigators, "is that supposedly some amount of sarin and cyclosarin was released into the atmosphere. That's a very toxic substance and we have no reports of any symptoms."

* * *

What if assumptions of CBW's instantaneous lethality were wrong? A US Army material safety data sheet noted that because "the inhibition of cholinesterase enzymes throughout the body by nerve agents is more or less irreversible," their effects are prolonged. During the following weeks or months, victims of nerve agent attack are especially susceptible to additional nerve agent exposure. "During this period the effects of repeated exposures are cumulative; after a single exposure, daily exposure to concentrations of nerve agent insufficient to produce symptoms may result in the onset of symptoms after several days. Continued daily exposure may be followed by increasingly severe effects."

Injuring soldiers with difficult-to-detect weapons could replace resolves with fear, even as it tied up hospitals and logistics and discouraged counter-attack. The Iraqi Air Force Academy manual, *A Course In NBC Protection*, notes that nerve agents "have a cumulative effect, if small doses are used repeatedly on a target, the damage can be very severe." As Eddington noted, and the Iraqis understood very well, low-dose attacks would often escape detection and the medical diagnosis of affected personnel. "Not causing immediate casualties would also minimize the possibility of similar retaliation, since the classic signs of a chemical attack, grossly disfigured corpses, would not be present."

Just prior to Desert Storm, a US defense analyst admitted that "Perhaps the greatest problem is created when soldiers are physically or mentally incapacitated in such a way that renders them unfit for combat, and without the commander necessarily realizing what has happened or why."

Once considered abhorrent, the utility of chemical weapons and their potential for exposing friendly troops to their own chemical weapons had been hotly debated for decades among both US and Soviet military planners. Soviet doctrine questioned the advisability of initiating chemical attacks that could slow or even block advancing friendly forces.

But Iraqi military planners clearly understood that it is much more disruptive to injure rather than kill enemy troops. While hard on morale, corpses require far less attention and resources than wounded personnel. Years of intensive research, as well as impressive results at Marjnoon and other targeted locales during their long war with Iran, had also taught them that mycotoxins are especially well suited to debilitating enemy forces. Three non-lethal variants developed by the Iraqis could produce these militarily-desirable results:

- Hemorrhagic conjunctivitis virus produces extreme eye pain and temporary blindness.
- Rotavirus causes acute diarrhea severe enough to lead to serious dehydration.

- Camelpox induces fever and skin rash in camels and may cause debilitating illness in non-natives of the Middle East.

Iraq's offensive biological-warfare manuals stress the use of chemical or biological agents to produce non-fatal casualties rather than deaths. Because their effects accumulate over time, slow-acting bioweapons ideally suited Iraqi war-fighting doctrine, which calls for non-fatal casualties to swamp an enemy's hospitals, logistics and resolve.

The large gap between an incapacitating and lethal dose of tricothecenes means that most casualties will become sick but not die. Though the long-term incubation period required by biologicals is less immediate than acute-acting nerve agents on the battlefield, their slowly accruing effects are extremely difficult to diagnose and detect. The ability of toxic organisms to reproduce inside their host targets allows these living weapons to cause widespread pandemics weeks, months or even years after an initial and seemingly inconsequential attack.

"It is possible to select anti-personnel biological agents in order to cause lethal or incapacitating casualties in the battle area or in the enemy's rear areas," explains the 1984 Iraqi Chemical Corps field manual on *Chemical, Biological and Nuclear Operations*. "Incapacitating agents are used to inflict casualties which require a large amount of medical supplies and treating facilities, and many people to treat them. Thus it is possible to hinder the opposing military operations."

The long-term effects of toxin-warfare agents fit neatly with Iraq's overall Gulf War strategy. Baghdad believed that large numbers of dead or injured Americans would generate a resurgence of anti-war sentiment that had curtailed the Vietnam war. Iraq's military command hoped that the ensuing public pressure would bring an end to a war of unacceptable attrition, even if meant reaching a settlement favorable to Saddam.

CHAPTER 9

KC

Night falls over a city awash in perpetual twilight. Framed in the apartment's high picture window is a kinetic monstrosity so incomprehensible, I find myself mesmerized by a scene that has remained unchanged for weeks.

Blazing oil wells ring a blacked-out skyline. Backlit by hundreds of unquenchable torches, distant high-rises loom unevenly, like the heads of an audience enraptured by capering giants. The huge flames writhe demonically, dancing on the graves of a half-million dead – and every wild and human survivor who inhales their poisons.

Shifting my gaze upwards, I eye a thin but steady stream of black smoke pouring through a neat round hole high in the window. Unable to reach punctures in either the glass or my own sense of dread, I simply watch this dubious haven fill like a foundering ship with a petroleum pungency whose reek I've grown as accustomed to over the past month as the scent of flowers in spring.

I'm told by the only other occupant of this building that the hole was made by bored Iraqi gunners manning an anti-aircraft battery at the intersection below. For five months they had stared at empty sky. There was a Kuwaiti family in this room when the Iraqis fired into it: husband, wife, daughter. They are not here now. Their uncaring assailants also fled a city that suddenly provided too much excitement. Or perhaps those soldiers have left the planet. The emblem of their ennui remains, pouring carcinogens into a living space that, like this entire smoke-shrouded city, has come to resemble a gas chamber.

As usual, I'm wearing my jury-rigged respirator against oil particles that would otherwise lodge in my lungs. Except for Thorpe and Bailey, who occasionally followed my example, I have never seen anyone else take similar precautions here.

But the toxicity of sweet Kuwaiti crude is not my biggest concern. It's the nearby buzz of bullets, not cancer's ticking time-bomb, that commands my attention now.

A sharp burst of gunfire broke out just a few minutes ago. Like the surrounding oil fires, sporadic gunplay has become an unremarked feature of everyday life in Kuwait City as unglimpsed trigger-fingers disperse tension, triumph or traitors. But this is the first time I've heard gunfire directly below my window. The next shots come like unwelcome questions: Friend or foe? Who goes there?

It could be rival factions fighting over neighborhood turf, or uniformed "liberators" taking advantage of the opportunities that always accrue to armed men bursting into family dwellings. I've interviewed enough frightened Hindi women, and corroborated their stories with a British television crew, to share a producer's on-air certainty that Saudi and Egyptian soldiers are filling the vacuum left by an exiled government by looting and raping Pakistani and East Indian guest workers who once performed all manual and most managerial work for their overseers.

Every type of small arm – including the ubiquitous Kalashnikov, Rocket-Propelled Grenades, even a few shoulder-braced rocket launchers still in their shrink-wrapping – could until recently be picked up as easily as asthma by anyone audacious enough to evade the check-points, and the desert's drifted dangers.

An RPG discarded in an Iraqi bunker, and a crate filled with screw-together propellant and armor-piercing projectiles, provided exceptional stress release one night for a trio of volunteer enviros who had been daily risking mines, booby-traps and unexploded cluster-bombs. The flash, crash and bang of that blunderbuss shaped RPG purged our jangled nerves, offering each of us momentary control over the explosive power waiting in hair-trigger concealment to abort our lives.

I wish I had that RPG with me now. The next crash of gunshots reaffirms my yearning for Canada's west coast and my seagoing home. The only hitch is that no commercial flights are coming near a sandbagged and burning international airport whose control tower and concourses are blackened, shell-pocked husks. The Persian Gulf is heavily mined. And forget driving out. The border remains closed in both directions to infidels without visas, which no one seemed to be handing out when I arrived.

How I got here is another story. More compelling conundrums are what I'm doing here tonight – and why everything's gone quiet eight floors below. Are people I've never met on a distant Pacific island really moving on my request for immediate evacuation?

With our health falling to bits and the other two team members sick, I've asked Earthtrust to relieve me after a stint more than twice as long as CNN is now allowing its news teams. All the other news agencies have begun following Atlanta's example, and are limiting their employees' exposure to this highly carcinogenic city to two weeks or less.

CNN never did air our findings and no test data are being released by French, American or Chinese monitoring teams. But the readings I took using an expensive, one-shot pocket gas analyzer on the roof of the Kuwait International Hotel exceeded Boston's National Toxics Campaign findings. That independent organization had measured hazardous levels of dichlorobenzene, arsenic, zinc, cadmium and lead in Saudi Arabia – 175 miles away from the oil fields burning in KC's front yard.

* * *

Allah help the oil field workers and their families unable to leave ground zero. Driving through the oil-soaked suburbs of Ahmadi the day after meeting up in KC, Bailey, Thorpe and I had passed a city hospital besieged by people troubled by strange rashes and difficulty in breathing.

It was not difficult to understand why. Just across the street from that tree shaded suburb stretched the Great Burgan. Kuwait's biggest oil field contained more than 400 wells. Many were alight, and the rest were fountaining geysers of black crude when we arrived around noon. As Bailey attempted to keep the taillights of our oil-worker guides in sight close ahead, we were horrified to find ourselves driving in almost total darkness. The only light came from hundreds of towering flames spearing out of the earth. How would just three teams whose Canadian and American companies shared a fire-fighting monopoly ever put them out? The reservoir that fed these drastic oil lamps contained nearly a tenth of the world's known oil reserves.

The sun had fled to another planet. In this alien world, there was no sky, no stars, no sun – only a roiling black "oilcast" that spread a twilight pall all the way into Iran. Dismounting from the battered GMC "Jimmy" that Bailey had somehow scrounged for a daily rental commensurate with a private vehicle's rarity in this ransacked emirate, we ventured on foot into this burning ground. Alert for signs of wildlife, we kept looking up for low-flying jets until we realized that the turbine-like shriek all around us was the roar of high-pressure oil venting from the ground.

Nothing could have prepared us for such bleak satanic surroundings. Though we looked closely, no life stirred in a place many outsiders thought of as "just dirt." But these desert sands had until recently formed a skin and a skein of creeping, crawling, flying and flowering lives. Not any more. The creosote coating our arms and hair covered every shrub, soaking every square inch of sand so that even the winds being sucked into this firestorm could not dislodge a single grain.

I don't remember who suggested we hire a fleet of buses, print posters, provide box-lunches – and charge visitors fortunes for a one day package tour of hell. Adrift in a landscape shrieking in agony, we tried to make sense of the nonsensical. Ringed by roaring fires, splattered by crude oil geysers vomiting into a petroleum sky, we eyed burned-out Iraqi tanks and a mound of blackened camel bones and told each other that this must be some extravagant film set, left over from some ultimate attempt to depict catastrophic desolation.

There was no way this could be real. No way to absorb this experience. My body cringed with an existential terror that went far beyond mere physical fright. I wanted to flee. But there was no place to run. This is how the world will end, I thought. In fire and darkness, with the air turned to poison.

What could three environmentalists hope to accomplish in the midst of such overwhelming devastation? If the entire coalition army, now waiting for transit home, traded their tanks for bull-dozers, pumps, hoses and shovels we might begin a cleanup that would tax even those resources.

Our mission had seemed straightforward when Michael Bailey called me in Dammam. "It sounds like we're doing the same thing," an unfamiliar voice suggested over the phone.

Bailey explained that he was with a group called Earth-trust. He and a New Zealand ornithologist named Rick Thorpe had flown into the Gulf to assist millions of migrating water birds. More than 200 species of grebes, plovers, herons, flamingos and other long-distance fliers were now winging their way up from Africa and the southern Gulf, bound for destinations as distant as Persia, northern Europe and Siberia's short spring. Some species, like the Socotra Cormorant, were already endangered. Others soon would be, Bailey said, if no one intervened.

I told him I would be happy lending a hand to rescue oiled birds. And delighted to use my journalistic talents documenting Earthtrust's latest campaign. I had seen the slicks coming ashore along the Saudi coast and knew the gauntlet those flocks faced.

How had Bailey gotten my room number? Simple, he said. After flying commercial into Bahrain, he and Thorpe had learned of another lone environmentalist who had been assisting the government with oil spill contingency plans as a slick bore down bigger than that entire island nation.

That explanation tracked. As a member of a hastily formed Gulf Environmental Emergency Response Team, I had been one of the first to reach a country appealing frantically for help. Located next to the sea that posed such menace, the upper floors of Bahrain's environmental agency were soon crowded with oil-spill experts, and charlatans selling everything from absorbent pads to oil-eating bacteria, modular oil-booms, big-ticket skimmers and some well-oiled pipedreams.

Maybe I stood out from that crowd by offering direct access to Canadian oil-spill know-how without charging any "finder's" or consultant's fee. The small band of concerned people in Vancouver and Amsterdam who had raised enough money to get me into Bahrain were checking oil-spill technology submitted by Canadian companies and forwarding the simplest and most thoroughly tested options to me in Manama. Bahrainian officials told me that I was the only emissary to respond to their requests for assistance not trying to profit from their predicament.

Or maybe Bailey had met someone who remembered a short, intently focused blond guy who was worried about the dugong. Many of this watery planet's last surviving dugong (or manatees) whose flippers and female breasts had given rise to sailors' first sightings of mermaids, congregated in Bahrain's western mangroves – directly downwind of the oncoming slick.

With all the emphasis on fire-power in the Gulf, it seemed only right that someone should be concerned with the critters who had settled here long before armies arrived. Every morning I watched from my upper floor hotel room as flights of bat-winged British Vulcan bombers and Saudi Mirage fighter-bombers took off from Manama's main airport. Many afternoons I watched them return from bombing Kuwait and Iraq.

The warplanes must have done something to get Saddam's attention. Around three o'clock one very quiet morning I was lifted from my bed by three nearly simultaneous blasts. The first soul-shattering *bang!* catapulted me from deepest dreams into blinking disorientation. A Patriot missile launched from a battery hidden near the hotel had accelerated to supersonic speed within seconds.

The next nearly simultaneous *bang!* came like the voice of Allah demanding retribution even for sins I had neglected to commit. The sound of two missiles clapping meant I was still alive. But before I could choose between repentance or celebration, a third ear-splitting thunderclap signified an incoming SCUD that had arrived ahead of the speed of its flight.

There had been no warning. But a few days later, air-raid sirens began wailing from the muezzin's minaret above the royal palace across the street. Flipping on the TV in my room, I stared at the letters spelling "MISSILE ALERT!" across a red screen. Espresso-drinkers in the souk downtown must have stopped with their small cups halfway to their lips as the entire city waited to learn who would die. Minutes later, the all-clear came without any sound effects.

Being shot at was definitely disconcerting. I seemed to have found the front lines in a war without fixed boundaries, rules of engagement, or strictly military targets. One afternoon, a dull distant *thump!* sounded like a warship firing a single salvo far offshore. But within hours, the entire country knew that another SCUD had struck a US barracks over the causeway in Dammam, causing heavy loss of life.

More missile alerts interrupted the Mideast Emergency Oil Spill Conference in downtown Manama. The day-long session featured frightened representatives from states as distant as Oman pleading with their Gulf neighbors to stockpile oil response equipment, or at least pledge the loan of oil booms should roving slicks wash ashore on their beaches.

But no one in possession of such scarce prophylactics wanted to give them up when their own coastlines could just as easily be hit. The Iranian delegate was particularly angry. The damage to his country was not hypothetical. More than half of the trees and crops in Iran's westernmost province were already dead or dying. Fresh water supplies and many inshore fish stocks, the Iranian added, had also been decimated by something called "black rain," and massive oil slicks sweeping down from Iraq.

As the world's biggest oil spill closed on Bahrain, no one seemed certain of its exact size or location. American military officers at the conference explained that sophisticated airborne Side-Aperture Radars could not distinguish oil slicks from the dark, waving masses of eel grass that nourished the Gulf's fish, rare turtles, dugong and shellfish.

Few people fighting in the desert were giving fish much thought. But damaged ecologies invariably impinge on economies. Before the bombing started, fish feeding in the mangroves, and in the seagrass beds whose shallow waters extended for miles offshore, had provided this region's second biggest export after oil.

The seawater temperatures to which the Gulf's coral reefs and other sealife were so extremely sensitive had already plummeted by more than four degrees Fahrenheit. Even before the war, the Arabian Gulf was the world's most polluted waterway. With 25 large oil terminals loading more than 20,000 tankers a year, annual spills totaling 150,000 tons were regarded as "routine." Fishmongers at Bahrain's sprawling indoor market joked that the 20 varieties of Gulf fish they offered were "already oiled."

American marines landing at Kara Island had cleaned the beaches before the first Green and Hawksbill turtles began coming ashore to bury their eggs. Despite the grunts' considerable efforts, hundreds of these endangered turtles were later found floating dead in oily inshore waters. So was a pod of dolphins.

Widespread die-offs of oiled mangroves, salt marshes and seagrass beds also wiped out the anchovies, sardines and other small bait fish on which the popular barracuda, king mackerel and Hamour fed. The entire Saudi and Iranian shrimp, pearl and cod fisheries would soon fail during this first spring after the war. Some Saudi fisheries experts warned that the Gulf would never recover.

No one in March of '91 could foresee the full extent of this war's environmental cost. But its bleakest outlines were already emerging from the ominous pall that covered Bahrain's north and eastern sky. When powerful currents swerved the oncoming slick away from Bahrain onto the Saudi coast instead, I determined to go there.

But the Saudi consulate turned down my request for a visa. I was informed that up to a year's wait is required before a foreigner can secure an official invitation to visit that secretive sultanate. The Saudi sheiks also understood the power of TV. Before boarding a bus in Bahrain, I learned that all video cameras were being confiscated at the border.

* * *

Five days later I found myself purchasing an unpronounceable dinner from a street-seller in Dammam. I had been lucky to meet someone sympathetic to my mission who had been willing to "arrange" my paperwork, no questions asked. It seemed that synchronicity – that uncanny magnetism that attracts tools, guides and resources exactly as required by worthy and focused endeavor – was still interceding on my behalf. Ever since an art student unknown to me had overcome a flat tire and heavy traffic to thrust a still-boxed Canon Hi-8 camcorder into my hands at the Vancouver airport, a succession of strangers had kept coming forward to assist an enterprise they must have sensed was mad, but with which they deeply identified.

Still clutching that brand new camcorder, I had boarded a KLM 747 with "Dr. Nuko." As the engines started we looked at each other, bewildered by our own audacity. When I'd discovered the lanky, doom-laden sketching his "Joules of Baghdad" in a Salt Spring Island cafe, Carl Chaplin informed me that he was going to take the completed air-brushed painting to Baghdad. It would be among an exhibition of works which had earned Disney's wrath and startled audiences around the world by depicting Disney World, *"Explo"* Vancouver and many of the world's most recognizable capitols under nuclear attack.

His intention, Chaplin explained over coffee with the matter-of-fact reasonableness of geniuses and the truly insane, was to warn Saddam and anyone else who would listen that the hundreds of nuclear weapons arrayed in that theater of war could easily trigger an intended or unintentional holocaust. Both the US and Israel, he reminded me, had promised a devastating "un-conventional" response if the Iraqi leader launched poisoned missiles at their troops or cities.

I told Chaplin that my book, *Scorched Earth* had also detailed a joint, inter-service study called JEMI. American military leaders were deeply worried that the effects of electromagnetic waves given off by high-energy US military radars, transmitters and jammers. The unpredictable interference caused by those overlapping electromagnetic waves with rapidly dividing human cells meant a real cancer risk for anyone regularly swept by those beams while exposed to other environmental toxins.

But the Joint Electromagnetic Interference investigation showed that the hazards of electromagnetic radiation included unexpected malfunctions of military hardware. US jets had exploded while refueling near AWACS radar-surveillance planes. Others had found their fuel systems shut down, or had suddenly flipped into uncontrolled dives and crashed when their electronic flight-control systems had been disrupted after flying near high-energy radio transmitter towers. Most ominous of all, bombs had been inadvertently dropped, rockets fired, and "fail-safe" circuitry on nuclear weapons partially tripped by intersecting interference from increasingly powerful military transmitters.

Given these risks, I told the artist that his latest scheme was the craziest thing I'd ever heard. "I want to go with you," I quickly added. The artist's quixotic quest would be one hell of a story, I explained. I also wished to add my own voice to Chaplin's cry for peace from the eye of a gathering storm.

Still, I was relieved when a KLM flight attendant informed us in mid-Atlantic that the airport in Amman had been closed due to the imminent threat of air strikes. As it turned out, she was nearly right. After a tremendous hassle with machine-gun toting Dutch security forces who insisted that Chaplin's paintings would cause a "riot" among excitable Arabs aboard the airplane, we boarded the last flight into Amman.

It didn't require any artistic provocation to turn that last leg into Amman aboard a badly dented Jordanian 727 into an aerial madhouse. While American and British camera crews loudly discussed the attack everyone expected would soon befall Jordan's capital, returning residents babbled in near hysteric anticipation of reuniting with families and spouses in a city bracing for blitzkrieg across its east and western borders.

As the aging jet began a series of abrupt climbs, turns and dives, the pilot's announcement that we were following Syrian radar commands to evade SCUDs streaking through the darkness toward Israel only added to the bedlam. By the time we touched down in Amman with a bounce that sent hundreds of hearts into clenched throats, no one on board doubted that Iraqi armor would soon be arriving to challenge an Israeli army and air force enraged by continuing missile attacks on their cities.

* * *

But it was Dr. Abdullah Toukan who frightened us even more. After watching Toukan's televised presentation a few nights after our arrival, Carl Chaplin quickly arranged a private audience with King Hussein's top scientific adviser. We wanted to know why he was predicting a possible worldwide catastrophe if the allied ground attack went ahead on its fast-approaching deadline.

Focusing on the quiet-spoken scientist and his small team of chain-smoking smoke and climatology experts, I videotaped the entire briefing. Toukan emphasized that many unquantifiable variables could influence his most dire predictions. But some things were known. "Escaping Kuwaiti engineers have told us that more than a thousand wells are mined," Toukan related. "If the Americans invade and the wells are blown up, our calculations show that the resulting oil cloud could circle the Earth, disrupting the Asian monsoons, destroying the crops on which millions of lives depend and altering weather patterns worldwide."

Carl Sagan, the American scientist who had coined the term "Nuclear Winter" after solving the calculations for the aftermath of atomic holocaust, agreed with the essence of Toukan's warning. So did Joe Farman, discoverer of the Antarctic ozone hole. But Toukan said that he had been told to keep quiet by the Secretary General of the UN. His appeals to allied governments had similarly been rebuffed by warmakers determined to roll the planetary dice.

The result of a ground war, Chaplin and I immediately saw, could be worse for the planet than the frightening prospects that had brought us here. Crossing and uncrossing his legs, the agitated artist told Toukan of our plan to form a Gulf Environmental Emergency Response Team. Our immediate goal would be to find a ship to carry scientists into the Persian Gulf to draw world attention to the unprecedented ecological disaster about to unfold there.

On the way back to the hotel, our taxi driver turned on the news. Listening intently, he grew more agitated with each Arabic phrase. "What's he saying?" Chaplin demanded. In halting English, the Palestinian told us that the first allied bombing raids against oil refineries and storage tanks at Basra had taken place the previous day. Now something called "black rain" was falling on Iran. Chaplin immediately decided to set up his easel in the Marriott Hotel lobby and begin a new work titled, "Black Rain." That night, in between incessant interviews with Canadian newspapers, radio and TV networks back home, the worried artist also began burning up international phone circuits to reach other far-flung eco warriors.

Greenpeace had three oceangoing vessels berthed in English Channel ports. But the world's biggest environmental organization was not keen on sailing into a war zone; floating mines and randomly exploding SCUDs were bad enough. But Greenpeace was even more afraid of being somehow seen as a Saddam sympathizer. While an international contingent of conscience was interposing their bodies between the front lines in a Gulf Peace Camp, GP's European headquarters was locked in internal discord. Even those opposed to ecological mayhem did not want to appear disloyal to fellow Westerners risking their lives to liberate Kuwait. Greenpeace feared that drawing attention to ecological damage in the Gulf would brand them as "traitors" by a jingoistic American press.

It was hard to grasp their reasoning. Everyone knew that Kuwait was being held hostage by a madman holding a match. Surely, when it came to protecting a shared space colony called Earth, every sane crewmember ought be able to rally around their common self-interest. In addressing impending calamity on an unimaginable scale, I told the director of Greenpeace's maritime division that it was imperative that his organization move quickly to highlight, and possibly head off, a disaster that would rival the radioactive poisoning of Ukraine and Belarus following some late-night tinkering at a place called Chernobyl.

Few enviro groups own seagoing vessels. After Greenpeace passed, we tried Jacques Cousteau. But the famous ocean explorer and his son held French naval commissions. There was no way they would take Calypso near such politically sensitive waters.

As Chaplin described something he'd dubbed "eco war" to his pal Paul Watson, I watched the artist listen, then smile.

Watson promised to sail Sea Shepherd from San Diego immediately. Unfortunately, the self-appointed "eco cop" who had done so much to discourage pirate whalers ran out of fuel and funds in Florida.

Our personal treasuries were also running low. Chaplin and I had taken off from Vancouver with 80 dollars between us, and a credit card that promised friendship in times of need. When the front desk called to inform us that Chaplin's card had been canceled, we headed downstairs feeling as shaky as two make-believe Aladdins whose flying carpet is about to auger in. Though nonscheduled flights out of Amman were rumored to be restarting soon, mandatory wartime insurance was now running more than the exorbitant cost of those tickets. Even more worrying was the bill for a room Chaplin had insisted we book because all of the media was staying at Jordan's most expensive luxury hotel.

When we knocked and walked in, the Marriott's manager was examining our 10-day tally. The printout of our room, meals, and nonstop phone and fax charges spilled over his desk, unscrolling across the carpet toward our feet.

By now, most of this news-hungry country was aware of the efforts of two Canadian "peace activists" who had voluntarily flown into a war-threatened capital to plead internationally for Palestinian justice and a negotiated settlement to a war rapidly escalating toward what everyone feared would be a cataclysmic crescendo. But even the best intentions carry a price. So far, the Jordanian manager informed us, we had managed to ring up a tab well over two thousand US dollars.

"Er, ah..." Nervously, I cleared my throat and tried again. Hadn't my Honsu wife taught me to mask extreme anxiety with excessive politeness? *Sumi-masen*, I thought. "Excuse me," I said. "We're a little short of funds. Could you perhaps give us a discount on our bill?"

The manager looked at us and smiled. Then he picked up the printout, folded it neatly, and tore it in half. "Thank you for helping my country," he said. "Please stay as my guests for as long as you like."

* * *

It seemed I was still on some synchronistic beam as a visa arranged outside the usual channels passed muster at the Saudi border. I held my breath anyway as a sharp-eyed guard somehow missed the camcorder hidden in the bottom of my bag. The tripod, I explained to him and a succession of suspicious soldiers manning highway checkpoints, was for the Nikon worn like a talisman around my neck.

I had to appreciate the irony of the Saudi secrecy laws when the director of that country's environmental agency in Dammam leapt at my offer to provide aerial still and video coverage of an oil slick coming ashore along that country's entire eastern coastline. Just down the hall, I poked my head into a room as the first hard numbers listing all known sources of oil washing into the Gulf scrolled across an American scientist's computer screen. Tapping his keys, he announced the total: "five and a half million barrels."

Exxon Valdez' quarter-million barrel spill had devastated a sound regularly scoured by high winds and tides. But the shallow, nearly landlocked Persian Gulf barely flushed at all. While I tried to grasp a disaster more than 22 times bigger than Alaska's nightmare, the National Oceanographic and Atmospheric Administration (NOAA) was obtaining data that would later double this figure because of the incessant carbon rain falling into the Gulf.

Both sides had contributed to this mess. The oil-loading manifolds at Kuwait's Sea Island terminal had been opened by the Iraqis to the sea, then bombed by US Air Force F-111s in a desperate bid to blast them shut. US Navy warplanes had also earned Schwarzkopf's wrath by attacking a loaded tanker. The American adviser resumed tapping his computer keys, then looked up at me. "One third of the oil spills," he told me, "are the result of allied bombing."

But statistics are not the same as seeing. Within days, I had talked myself aboard a Royal Saudi Air Force helicopter. Strapping in with a handful of American scientists and Saudi observers, I checked my batteries and tapes, preparing to point the only video camera ever allowed over the world's biggest oil slick.

Flying through an eerie midday darkness, I shivered in the chopper's open doorway as an impenetrable "oilcast" absorbed all sunlight, dropping temperatures by more than 20 degrees with the stench of crude oil clogging our nostrils, we flew for hours at an indicated airspeed of 110 knots. Not for a single moment did the American and Saudi observers fail to see heavy black crude washing ashore on oiled beaches. As far as we could glimpse to seaward, vast slicks extended beyond the horizon. Half of the Saudi coastline was heavily oiled; half of its precious mangrove and salt-marsh "nurseries" destroyed. After the helicopter landed, no one could speak.

Before handing over hundreds of slides and a copy of my videotape and departing the royal kingdom, I made a second survey flight along Saudi Arabia's northeastern seaboard. Onboard this mission was NOAA's chief scientist, the famous deep-diving Sylvia Earle. Neither of us could know it then, but Earle would soon be resigning her post in protest over NOAA's falsifying the height and extent of the smoke plume. The faked "official" figures would later appear as gospel in National Geographic and other equally reputable publications.

* * *

Bailey's call to Dammam had come during a low point in my journey. Alone in Arabia, nearly broke, without allies or friends in a city almost completely unaware of huge oil spills washing ashore at al Jubayl, I was weary from the constant stress of living by my wits during a "10 day" trip that was stretching into its fourth month. Now it appeared, I once again had an ally.

"We ought to hook up in Kuwait," Michael Bailey was saying.

"Kuwait?" I responded. "No one's going into Kuwait. The border's closed. The whole country's on fire. The only people getting in there are military."

"Don't worry," said a man whose resourcefulness never failed to produce marvels. "We'll get you in. We met some pilots in a bar. I'll set it up and meet you at the Kuwait International Hotel. It's the only place that's open in Kuwait City."

I told him to count me in, just as soon as I figured out how to pay my thousand dollar room bill. GEERT's student and citizen backers were having difficulty finding more money. And this time, I knew, the hotel management was not even aware of my mission.

The next morning, there was a knock on my door. I opened it to find an Arab gentleman standing in the hallway. His flawless manner and business attire seemed out of place for a messenger. Yet he held out an envelope.

"Mr. Thomas?"

"That's right."

He handed me the letter-size envelope. Closing the door on his receding back, I found my knife and slit it open. There was no message inside. Just 11 US hundred dollar bills.

* * *

Michael Bailey possessed a leader's ability to make quick decisions and follow through. He also had a knack for making instant friends with everyone he met – which included anyone in range of an effervescent manner that never hesitated to introduce itself, and our mission. Time and again, I watched complete strangers, including important officials, quickly become enthusiastic allies in seemingly impracticable projects.

Back in Kuwait's swanky Hi Hon International Hotel, where electricity and a trickle of cold tap water had recently been restored, Bailey segued easily from Great Burgan tour leader into an earnest environmental diplomat. Within the hour, he had cajoled the hotel management into providing us with a large conference room off the main lobby for something he was already calling the "Kuwait Environmental Information Center."

The room boasted several large tables, dozens of chairs, and a wall map of a country I had never heard of a year ago. The only thing our new information center lacked was information. While Bailey continued lobbying out in the lobby, Rick Thorpe and I were instructed to take the truck and drive out to the Kuwait Institute for Scientific Research. The slim, almost birdlike ornithologist wanted to check out the beaches there for signs of arriving seabirds. Bailey figured we might uncover reference materials describing an ecology none of us was familiar with.

* * *

Parking in front of a bullet-shattered building, we crunched across a courtyard covered in broken glass to find a seaside campus that must have been one of the most breathtaking academic settings on the Gulf. It was completely trashed. Like most of the rest of Kuwait's buildings, every window was broken, nearly every room blacked by fire. Desks were overturned, cabinets and shelving ripped from the walls. We choked on oil smoke and the fumes from a greasy tide washing listlessly up on an oil-blackened beach.

Mindful of mines, Thorpe and I skirted abandoned Iraqi defensive positions dug into the manicured lawns. Though we could not read its identifying sign, a distant building drew our attention. "For God's sake," I warned my Kiwi companion, "and your own, don't open any doors or drawers without checking for trip-wires first."

Nothing blew but my held breath as we pushed open a broken door and entered a once bustling office corridor made gloomy by rage and abandonment. Here, too, everything had been wrecked by people with a serious dislike for Kuwait. A distant creaking made me jump. But Thorpe chose a door in the middle of a long row of identical doorways and, with the air of someone who knows exactly where he is going, turned the knob and walked in without the slightest regard for what might be waiting on the other side.

I was amazed when that portal did not blow up in his face. Following my colleague inside, I entered what must have once been an orderly academic stronghold. Now it looked like someone had turned a scholar's office upside down and shaken. The room was knee-deep in ransacked books and papers.

The first book Thorpe grabbed was a large illustrated volume printed in English. "Hey, look at this," he said, holding the title toward me: *Flora and Fauna of Kuwait.*

Allah akbar, I thought. God is truly great. Setting the wildlife atlas aside on a remarkably messy desk, Thorpe reached again into the rubble. This time, the Kiwi magician unearthed a thinner, wide-format book. It was filled with detailed coastal maps. Like the first volume, its Arabic text was translated into English. Together, we examined the cover: *Kuwait Oil Spill Contingency Plans.* Like a pair of lottery winners, Thorpe and I started whooping, hollering and dancing around that paper-strewn office.

CHAPTER 10

ECOWAR

Bailey was delighted with our finds. Hardly pausing for sleep in our smoky hotel room, we immediately resumed our field surveys, crisscrossing the heart of Kuwait's flaming darkness to gauge the task before us. From the deserts north and south of KC, to the oil fields up near the Iraq border, it soon became clear that few of the expected migrating flocks had reached Kuwait. Trekking almost daily through heavily mined coastal areas, over the following weeks our three man survey party would count only a couple of thousand confused and dying birds.

None could be saved. Weighted by oil until they could fly only a few feet above the ground, the few raptors we found had been blinded by the same thick crude that covered their wings. We could only watch helplessly as the big birds flew erratically into the heat of Kuwait's great conflagration.

We had to get airborne ourselves. Augmenting our skimpy wardrobe with camouflage shirts donated by American and British officers who were increasingly frequenting our information center, we cruised highways emptied by Arab military checkpoints. With just our close-cropped hair and cammies showing through the truck's open windows, we must have looked like a band of American advisers on some important mission. I don't know whether it was my casual salute, or Thorpe's respectful *salaam alakem*, but we were waved right through the last checkpoint directly onto the runway where a US Navy turboprop had dropped me only days before.

The only intact aircraft in sight was an American air force C-130, its fans already turning. No matter. That Herc was too big for what we had in mind. Across the field, a gaggle of helicopters squatting on the grass in front of a Royal Kuwait Air Force hangar looked perfect. Without hesitating, Bailey swerved onto the main runway and fast-taxied over there.

A colonel came out of the operations center to find three maniacs dressed in blue jeans and camouflage shirts jumping down from a truck splashed with crude oil from wheel wells to roof line. Being familiar with the military mindset, I stepped forward and quickly introduced us as three members of an environmental emergency response team. Then I got right to the point. "Colonel," I said. "This is an emergency. We need to get into the air immediately to begin assessing the extent of the environmental damage to your country."

It was impossible to tell what was going on behind his Ray-Bans as the officer looked us over. "Come with me," he said. Almost at a trot, we followed the colonel inside to the squadron briefing room. Tapping an aerial wall chart with his pointer, the flight commander asked, "Where do you want to go?"

That was easy. Everywhere would do for a start. No environmental reconnaissance had yet been made of a country covered in oil. After a brief consultation, we laid out a mission that would take us upcoast before turning inland over Rumayah and the Great Burgan.

Within 20 minutes of making our request, three unlikely musketeers were strapping themselves into an ungainly contraption that we were assured would actually fly. Up front, we could see both pilots punching overhead switches. As we donned our headsets and checked in, the drooping rotors of the Super Puma were already beginning to turn.

This was more like it! There were no land mines up here. No worries at all except a few flashbacks to the flight safety posters of wrecked choppers adorning the ready-room walls. After what we'd been through on the ground, we could finally relax inside one of the most accident-prone flying machines ever devised.

Thorpe was soon pointing out of the open hatch past sunk and listing shipping to a sprawling seawater desalination plant just north of the city. Speaking into my boom mike, I asked the pilot to circle. As the camcorder whirred, we were relieved to see the wide concrete intake arms were completely boomed off.

The receiving waters inside appeared to be oil-free. But as the Puma straightened out and continued its low, clattering flight, we could make out glistening sheens of crude streaming downcoast from a bombed Norwegian tanker with decks nearly awash. More oil seeped from the bombed-out Sea Island loading terminal not far offshore.

Levitating at 90 knots at a thousand feet or so, we swung inland over the ruined city. Oil fires winking like hundreds of birthday candles spotted the desert just beyond. As we flew closer, those firelights grew fierce and drastic. Within minutes we were encircled by menace. Columns of white and black smoke poured through the Puma's open side, rocking the aircraft in thermals that made us cough. As the French machine bucked and tilted, we stared straight down into circular blast furnaces burning like Satan's own forges.

As far as we could see, the entire desert appeared to be burning. Black rivers of oil coursed through low dunes crosshatched by hundreds of miles of trenches, tank tracks and revetments. These tributaries, we saw, were coalescing into broad lakes as vast underground reservoirs sent freshets of oil through demolished, high-pressure wells.

NOAA satellites would later count 252 oil pools containing 150 million barrels of oil, covering more than half of Kuwait's land surface. The biggest measured more than six miles in length and as deep as 30 feet. Kuwait's agricultural ground water, I knew, lay half that distance beneath the surface.

NOAA's orbiting "birds" also showed that the effects of this eco war were spreading far beyond the immediate region. In early March, while I was still in Dammam, the Hawaiian observatory on Mauna Loa measured soot levels five-times above normal.

By May, California's Lawrence Livermore laboratory was tracking the smoke from Middle East oil fires three times around the Earth at altitudes exceeding 31,000 feet. Kuwaiti crude coating Kashmir's Lake Dal would soon startle Japanese skiers trudging through six centimeters of black snow high in the Himalayas. Germany's Zugspite Mountains were also being oiled, as orbiting American astronauts made headlines describing a "haze-shrouded" globe.

Precipitation occurs when moisture condenses around dust and dirt in the air. By June, as soot levels five- to 100-times higher than normal were measured over China, Japan, and the western US, record breaking rainfalls, storms and disastrous flooding would hit Iran, Bangladesh, Indonesia, China, Britain, Europe and the west coast of Canada. Before the bizarre weather patterns ended, more than 500,000 people would die. Some four million others would be left homeless by freak storms triggered weeks before Mount Pinatubo erupted.

No scientists were suggesting that the oil fires in the Gulf caused these deaths. But Dr. Krishnamurti at Florida University later crunched the numbers showing that oil fallout from this "world war" greatly amplified seasonal storms.

* * *

For now, our information on the ongoing ecological effects of the Gulf War was confined to what we could see, taste and feel. As our ground and aerial surveys continued, the Kuwait Environmental Information Center began drawing a steady procession of fire-fighters, medical doctors, military officers and journalists. Bucking ages-old discrimination, we stubbornly insisted on hiring two East Indians to "woman" the desk and answer newly restored phones during our frequent field forays. A lingering sense of terror, and miles of charred and rapidly rusting vehicles, left me badly shaken on the Highway of Death.

Other excursions frightened me down to my toes. Whenever Bailey announced daily missions into mined areas that every week were claiming dozens of camels and Bedouin lives, I told myself that I would not be returning to the hotel that night.

Despite long odds and serious craziness, some stronger force appeared to be protecting us. One dark night as we bumped off-road near al Jahrah, Thorpe got out to water the desert. "Hey look at this," he called. "You've got to see this." Joining the excited Kiwi by the right rear fender, I looked down to see our tire tread imprinted on an unexploded cluster-bomb. As Thorpe swung the flashlight beam, we saw that we were surrounded by the white casings of these USAF shrapnel-dispensers. How we drove out of there, I still don't know.

There were other close calls. One afternoon out in Ras al Mishab, I shouted a tardy warning at Fatima, Jassim and other KISR friends as they walked within inches of partially exposed mines. Some looked like tin can lids. Other saucer-shaped anti-personnel devices possessed a nipple-like plunger – just like the one Rick Thorpe later discovered hidden under the papers we had cavorted around inside that KISR office.

Though not as immediately dramatic as stepping on a mine, breathing oil smoke could be just as deadly. A special United Nations Environment Program press briefing insisted that Kuwait's persistent pall posed "no danger to human health." But our own readings showed otherwise. When Dr. David Snashall of the UK Commonwealth Health Department dropped by the center to brief a group of Kuwait's top scientists, he described the "potentially catastrophic health effects" from the toxic smoke and gases that had filled the city for months.

UNEP was bowing to political pressure not to "alarm" people with reports that would discourage residents from returning home to rebuild. Even harder to understand were repeated reassurances broadcast over Armed Forces Radio that the oil smoke posed no danger to US personnel, who did not have to wear protective masks. All of those authoritative denials were hard to accept when the lungs of autopsied sheep at Ahmadi were found to have the consistency of shoe leather.

As flocks of birds began falling dead onto Kuwait City streets, we lobbied hard to get gauze surgical masks flown in for the residents of a suburb that would make Mexico City on its worst day resemble a mountain health spa. But even when we talked our way past the tanks ringing Kuwait's state television station, no local newscasters were willing to risk government wrath by issuing common sense warnings. I hadn't met anyone yet who seemed concerned enough to fashion even rudimentary protection.

"Why are you wearing that respirator?" a Kuwaiti gentleman asked me one afternoon as I left the hotel. "Do you see that?" I asked him, pointing from the brown rivulet of oil running down his snow-white robes to the oil-streaked windshield of a parked car. He nodded. "Well, what you see, is what you breathe." For just an instant, I saw a spark of recognition in his eyes. Then it died, even faster than his lungs. The implications of actually living in this deathtrap were simply too much to handle. As he walked away shaking his head, it was the foreigner who received the revelation. There was no denying it: denial is the strongest human propensity.

* * *

At our urging, doctors al Hassan, Fatima al Abadali and al Harbi organized their KISR students into the Kuwait Environmental Action Team. KEAT carried out the first door-to-door public health survey in Ahmadi. Their statistical tally showed almost everyone suffering adverse health effects from living in close proximity to the blazing Burgan.

Inside the Ahmadi Hospital, I noted that the incubators were intact. None had been stolen from the city, I was told. But illiterate Iraqi soldiers had taken radioactive isotopes used in medical procedures from their lead-lined vaults. (Another radioactive shipment had been opened at the airport.) Of more immediate fascination were the burning oil wells framed in the windows of the hospital administrator's office. I watched them writhe and boil in torrents of thick black smoke as the chief medico assured us that oil fumes and smoke had absolutely nothing to do with his patients' chronic and acute complaints. His presentation took a while to translate, interrupted as it was by frequent bouts of violent coughing.

"Tell me doctor," I said, putting away my notebook, "do you smoke?" The smug MD looked stricken at the thought of such unhealthy practice. "Absolutely not," he exclaimed. But of course he did. Other medical doctors told us that anyone breathing oil smoke that was blackening buildings as far away as Riyadh was inhaling the equivalent of a thousand cigarettes a day. When I later tried to get my pal Jim Logan to stop lighting up, he just looked at me and laughed.

* * *

Though we lobbied strenuously with the few Kuwait government officials we could find, our pleas to evacuate Ahmadi were ignored. There were more pressing matters, they intimated, than worrying about stateless Palestinians and other guest workers.

Our three-man response team was more successful in helping convince officials to extend exclusive fire-fighting contracts beyond three original contractors to nearly a dozen other fire-fighting companies whose frustrated representatives were daily besieging our hotel command post.

Out in the Great Burgan, and in the Randhatain and Mutriba oil fields to the north, the biggest difficulty came from providing enough water to cool and cap each well. Using oil pipelines to carry water from the Gulf eventually helped, but the Canadian's self-contained water trucks seemed the most efficient solution.

It took a lot of water to cool a well below the point where its own heat would stop drawing oil out of the ground. When another team arrived with a jet engine mounted on a flatbed truck, their proposal to simply blow the fires out was met with hoots of merriment by oil-soaked professionals who thought they'd seen it all. The jet-propelled innovators were soon snuffing fires faster than anyone else.

A few Dutch oil spill recovery crews were also at work at al Jubayl, where I'd filmed them dipping a pair of hoses like soda straws into a sea of oil. But Kuwait lacked even a token response. Flying into Bahrain, I'd noticed a small ship lying stationary out in the Gulf. On inquiring at the environmental ministry, I was told that she was the region's only oil-spill recovery ship. Now Bailey and Thorpe's began beseeching UNEP to dispatch that vessel to Kuwait.

UNEP moved quickly on this request. Within a week, *al Wasit* tied up at the port of al Shuaiba. This was the place, the port captain told us, where an Iraqi soldier had been ordered to open a manifold and redirect an oil field into the sea. Listening to his heart instead of ruthless Imams, the officer had instead stenciled "OPEN" above the closed valve, leaving the oil in its storage tanks.

When we went aboard al *Wasit*, there was plenty of crude to recover without shifting her berth. Stabbing his finger at a sea-chart, Thorpe told the captain that his first priority ought to be checking coastal desalination plants for signs of crude oil contamination.

The amiable Dutchman was ready to steam immediately to Kuwait's biggest water-making plant at al Khiran. But the US Navy responded to his radioed request with a curt order to stay put. Though shipping channels had supposedly been cleared, there were too many mines loose in inshore waters for *al Wasit* to proceed along shore.

As the little ship's crew laid out booms in a well-practiced routine and commenced sucking oil, Thorpe and I drove down to al Khiran. Under a bruised and brooding sky, we checked out the area's resort community of beachfront homes and condos for a boat and trailer. There were plenty of exotic craft to choose from, but in the end, we salvaged an aluminum skiff, stepping carefully around the mines we could see. Borrowing an outboard motor from a KEAT scientist, we were soon underway.

It felt grand to be back on the water. Despite the danger, I thrilled to the lift of a hull beneath my feet as I opened the throttle and charged the cresting Gulf swell. Up in the bow, Thorpe kept a lookout for drifting mines. At the speed we were traveling, we both knew he would not even get a chance to shout before the explosion took that famous last profanity from both our mouths.

After stopping to check out a demolished Iraqi gunboat, we fetched the big striped stacks of al Khiran in the early afternoon. I drove us right into the intake arms and cut the engine. As we drifted on an uneasy swell, a stain black as a bathtub ring at the high-water mark told the story. Thorpe collected water samples, wrinkling his nose at the acrid fumes as I stood in the rocking boat and videotaped the scene. Back at the hotel, a visiting doctor was dismayed by our findings. "If you want to induce cancer in mice," Dr. Schamadan of the US National Cancer Research Institute told us, "about the worst thing you could give them is hydrocarbons mixed with chlorine."

Chlorine is routinely mixed with the drinking water produced by all desalination plants. "But don't worry," plant officials assured us. "The seawater intakes lie two meters below the surface." Right. An Aramco oil company rep had already taught me that floating crude oil soon weathers and thickens. The resulting "tar balls" become neutrally buoyant, submerging to drift randomly on Gulf currents two to three meters below the surface.

But carcinogenic tar balls in Kuwait's drinking water was not the most pressing problem. On April 26, soon after *al Wasit* begin sipping oil, I joined other KEAT observers aboard our twice weekly Royal Kuwait Air Force survey flight. As we flew north along the coast a few miles offshore, sea and sky seemed to merge in the oil-saturated air. Only slightly more distinct was a new slick moving down from Iraq.

This one was huge. Kuwait had so far escaped the brunt of oil slicks sliding south to cover the Saudi coastline. Now it appeared that despite a cease-fire, Saddam's sadistic environmental onslaught was continuing.

Attempting to trace the slick to its source, we flew up the Shatt al Arab waterway. The further we flew into Iraqi airspace, the more nervous our Kuwaiti pilots became. There were plenty of pissed off people down there, they pointed out over the intercom.

We backseaters breathed easier as we swung back over the Gulf. Neat as a conjuring trick, a US Navy gunship materialized out of thin air and took up position alongside. I could see the helmeted command pilot clearly as the menacing blue machine kept station off our open hatch. Over my own headset, I heard an unmistakably American voice demand immediate identification from a helicopter whose desert markings exactly matched its Iraqi air force counterparts.

Our pilots were having trouble keeping their voices under control as they called out in military jargon that basically meant "Don't shoot!" Frantically switched frequencies, they could not locate the US "guard" channel.

Our escort was not reading us. I could tell because their requests for ID were becoming increasingly suspicious and peremptory the closer we got to KC. The phrase "friendly fire" began taking on new and personal meaning.

The heavily armed gunship was about to do something I was sure I would regret when someone got lucky in the front office and dialed the right numbers. I heard something that sounded like: "American Navy helo this is Kuwait Air Force seven-six-three Kilo Lima X-ray inbound on authorized survey mission, over." Our driver must have added the correct password because our range-riding Navy escort abruptly banked away.

This was an excellent sign. Less encouraging was the fact that al Khiran lay directly in the path of that massive new slick. According to the oil spill plan we'd salvaged from that booby-trapped KISR office, al Khiran was Kuwait's most important seabird sanctuary. The Kuwait Environment Ministry finally had a working phoneline. But when we called we were told there was no staff, and certainly no vehicles to respond to our latest alarm.

UNEP, on the other hand, was replete with shiny new trucks. The high-paid bureaucrats had brought their own spotter aircraft and plenty of personnel. Money was not a problem, they assured us. But when we asked for a few extra hands and some help in booming off al Khiran's critical wetlands, we were informed that the UN agency would "study the problem" that we had already thoroughly documented – and get back to us in the fall.

Energized by urgency and disgust, Thorpe and I raced back to al Shuaiba, where we managed to scavenge an oil boom. But when we dragged it up onto a breakwater littered with twisted weapons and wreckage, the oil-smeared floating fencing proved too big and far too heavy to load into "Jimmy".

Leaving the oil boom on the ramp, we drove next to the compound of the US Army's 352nd Division where a guard listened to our story and took the initiative to wave us through the gate. Though beset by bedlam, a captain directing a rapid demobilization in a warehouse filled with harried people, also took time to listen to our tale of an approaching oil slick, heavy booms and threatened seabirds. The US Marines had given us MREs, as well as some real food. Now the US Army came through. Within minutes, the captain had issued a series of orders, dispatching the biggest open truck I had ever seen and two armed escorts to al Shuaiba.

The port captain had already gotten into the spirit of seabird rescue. When the army truck pulled up, a gang of Egyptian dockworkers was on hand to load the boom into the back of the big transport. There was plenty of room left over for our skiff to ride on top of the load.

Back at al Khiran, the two Army drivers helped us drag the heavy oil boom out of the truck. But it took Rick Thorpe, myself, and an Egyptian chef from the hotel, five more days to drag the heavy boom across the fast-flowing estuary. It was hard, frustrating work. The more boom we slid into the water, the less able was the tender's tiny outboard to overcome its drag. But at least I was safe. It made me very nervous watching the wiry chef stagger up sandy slopes as he gamely hauled on the rope rigged to the end of the boom.

All around us, anti-personnel mines had been sown for some bloody harvest. Some of them we could see. Barbed-wire right down to the water indicated that more of these hideous devices had been liberally sown in the face of an anticipated seaborne assault. This hunch was confirmed by the only locals living in the area, who warned us over small cups of strong coffee about a returning resident who had ignored posted "Keep Out" signs. Deciding to take a dip in front of his house not a mile from here, he had been propelled into the next kingdom by the explosion that followed.

In the end, after the chef had returned to less hazardous duties and the oncoming slick began coming ashore just north of us, our plucky little skiff was fought to a standstill by the inflowing current. Without hesitation, Rick Thorpe jumped into the water and began dragging the boom the last few yards toward shore.

I froze in horror, every nerve-ending shrieking alarm. I had not the slightest doubt that I was about to see that crazy, courageous Kiwi blown to bits before my widening eyes. As far as one of those indiscriminate slaughtering machines was concerned, the next few steps he took toward the barbed-wired beach would be indistinguishable from the tread of an American marine.

Even more terrifying was the realization that my straining companion was making no headway with the boom. I would have to get into that murky water and help him.

Well, Thomas, I addressed myself. Are you willing to give up your life – right now – for a flock of birds?

I looked quickly around. The desolate landscape offered no advice, consolation or reprieve. Carbon-caked beaches, shell-splintered homes, a dark choking sky portended only doom. It looked like a lousy place to die. Yes, I decided in a burst of sudden clarity, I am.

It wasn't, I saw in that instant, that human and wild lives can somehow be weighed one against the other. It simply seemed that my small gesture, regardless of its outcome, might begin to redress the terrible karma of a war whose full measure was being ignored, but must someday be repaid in full.

Lowering myself into that water to place my hands next to my friend's was the hardest thing I had ever done. Things became much easier after that, after we secured the boom to the opposite shore and returned to the ruined city.

* * *

Like Michael Bailey and Rick Thorpe, I had come into the Gulf because I could not imagine being any other place. Because I could not believe that anyone who called him or herself an environmentalist would not respond immediately to the biggest ecological disaster in modern times.

But where was everyone else? Where were the big environmental groups, with all their expertise and resources? Joe Walsh, of the World Federation for the Protection of Animals, was here saving the few zoo animals that had not been eaten or released by the Iraqis. I was here for GEERT. But the first organization to interpose themselves between harpoon guns and whales was the only major respondent to a war that would wound the world.

Michael Bailey got my vote as one of the Gulf War's true heroes. As an Earthtrust project director charged with saving dolphins and tigers, it was Bailey who moved when everyone else hesitated, grabbing the ET checkbook and taking off for the Gulf.

But I had to give Earthtrust credit, too. Despite an unorthodox campaign whose political implications were giving its directors nightmares even as they worried over our lives, that organization fully backed Bailey and the two campaigners he had hired.

I soon learned that for an organization so rarely in the press, Earthtrust could count on some first-class directors and contacts scattered throughout Europe and the USA. This was good. For we were still almost entirely cut off in a country that until a week ago could count just one working international phone line.

Other amenities were just as scarce in a city whose jealous jailers had not bothered to douse the lights when they departed, but simply stolen the bulbs and light fixtures, along with everything else that could be pried loose or unbolted. There were few unbroken windows, unblemished facades or vehicles with their motors and wheels intact in the entire city. Even a fleet of teak dhows, the last rakish descendants of the lateen-rigged sailing craft that had once traded as far as Africa, had been burned to their waterlines in what witnesses described as a night of frenzied Iraqi laughter, cheering and torchlight.

As a seaman, I found it hard to forgive the scuttling of the dhows. But ET, at least, never let us down. Somehow, after Bailey thrust the wrong prong of a multi-plug into a wall-socket and fried the one I'd brought, they even got a new printer to us. Jim Logan brought another Hi-8 camcorder and fresh tape when he arrived to relieve Thorpe, who was needed by his own government back in the antipodean land its original inhabitants called Aotearoa.

In contrast to the seriousness of Thorpe's dedication, Jimmy was a wise-cracking, can-do, all-American boy whose ability to fix anything mechanical became instantly indispensable. Logan arrived in time to dislodge and outrun an exploding booby-trap, fix the other "Jimmy" that did the outrunning, and help check out a report of four thoroughbreds trapped in the Emir's summer palace.

The horses must have been of the apocalyptic breed. After a harrowing drive through a little-traveled corner of the Great Burgan, all Logan and I found inside that ruined estate were exotic plants either aflame or dripping creosote. Out in the oiled orchard, the blackened aviary hung open and empty. A pair of distraught pigeons strutting on a nearby wall were coated in crude so thick it was dissolving their flesh.

Logan and I didn't find out until later that Joe Walsh had rescued the horses. We also couldn't guess that we were about to become bonded as brothers in a way even wives cannot know.

It happened just after we regained the main road through the blazing Burgan. Angling close to a roadside wellhead, we felt a blast of heat through the windshield. Traveling fast, both road and visibility disappeared in a sudden petroleum squall.

In less than a heartbeat the big GMC was spinning. As we turned to look at each other across the wide bench seat, a small sun rotated from Logan's side window. It stopped in the center of the windshield and grew rapidly larger. As we skidded toward a petroleum-fed volcano, Logan held up his hands in a "what the hell" gesture. We were both passengers now.

While we waited for that wellhead to embrace us, I had just enough time to appreciate the irony of our predicament. Logan must have had the same thought. It showed in his face, where I caught a hint of sardonic amusement. We were about to duplicate exactly an accident that had barbecued a carload of Arab engineers near this very spot just a few days before.

We had argued loudly about how anyone could possibly be dumb enough to drive into a burning oil well. Now, unless our four-wheeled "Jimmy" could regain its original course, we were about to find out. As Jimmy and I looked at each other, waiting for whatever came next, it seemed important not to speak. So we used our eyes.

* * *

Is someone shooting back? I can't tell. Darkness has a way of amplifying and distorting scary sounds. If there are more bad guys out there, I could be hosting unwelcome visitors soon. Diligent Earth protector that I am, mine is the only light burning in this nearly vacant apartment block.

I can't go to black-out because I've got to finish the report that is my ticket out of here. Though I've been growing steadily sicker with intense flu-like symptoms and that beyond-exhausted state that comes from constant stress, wakefulness and despair, my Earthtrust employers in Hawaii had begged me to stay on for one more week.

They want me to finish an environmental assessment they hope will earn their organization enough royal reimbursement to save other wildlife campaigns whose budgets have been fed like fiscal fodder into the extravagant and insatiable maw of this distant, desperate, rear-guard action. Earthtrust's entire operating budget would be pocket-change to a royal family worth billions. Not to mention a government whose country we'd come so far to assist after so many had run.

But all this shooting is starting to make me nervous. Bailey and Logan aren't due back for hours. And even the most imagin- aive paranoids are sometimes proven correct.

Fortunately, a soothing exercise is close to hand. Spread across the table before me like a jig-saw puzzle in reverse, is a growing collection of closely-machined metal parts. Receiver group. Trigger assembly. And a long metal tube that efficiently recycles the explosive gases from each loud discharge to slide the next tapered round into place.

I'm not entirely comfortable admitting this. But with its metal folding stock and curved banana clip, the AK-47's wicked, rugged simplicity borders on the beautiful. My hands snap the weapon apart as if born to the task, never fumbling as they twist and pull and tear down unfamiliar components without benefit of written or oral instructions.

I've fired more than a thousand rounds through this piece, plinking away at the detritus of a still-smoldering war or loosing entire clips in loud lunatic exhalations. At 100 yards over open sights, the single-shot accuracy of this heavy, unbalanced rifle is far too frightening to be placed in the hands of an angry teenager. Unlike its problem-plagued American counterpart, this stolid Soviet gift to a blood-drenched developing world has ignored a steady buildup of carbon and sand. Clip after hot smoking clip, it has never jammed.

But the Kalashnikov's best feature is the incredible racket it makes. Unlike the toy-like M-16, recently modified so nervous soldiers can fire only four rounds with each trigger pull, the AK can unleash 30 much bigger bullets in less than three seconds. Of course, its panicky operator isn't going to hit anything either; after the first few rounds, hand-held automatic weapons pull sharply skywards despite every effort to counter that lunge. But who cares? There is nothing quite like the sustained crash of an AK to keep unfriendly heads tucked down.

If those gunmen below come calling, I'll unload an entire clip into the building's deep stairwell. The resulting reverberations and ricochets should prove powerfully distracting while I run like hell.

That's Plan A. I don't want to think about Plan B, the one where I run of out exits. Working quickly now, I clean each component with a squirt of gun oil liberated from an Iraqi trench like the one where I'd found the letter. A KISR companion had translated the note addressed by a young soldier's sister in Basra:

Dear ----,
     We are sorry to learn that you have no food, and that you have not been paid in months. Here is some dinar to buy food...

Was the recipient of this letter the same starving teen my translator had watched rip the lid off a jar whose label he could not read and gulp the face cream inside? Or had he been one of the young Iraqi boys for whom Kuwaiti residents had put aside their anger and resentment, and brought water to drink? Was he still alive? Had he seen his sister again?

Assembling the Kalashnikov's two-piece ramrod, I take an oily swath of torn T-shirt and swab the barrel, just like a marine "Gunny" taught me the year before I became an anti-war protester. As I snap each lightly oiled part back into a completed sculpture of instant carnage, I reflect that this is a hell of a thing for a peace activist to be doing. Just as I've always suspected, and even suggested to a packed student assembly during an anti-Vietnam war rally at Marquette University, philosophizing ends when the shooting begins.

Just before that speech, I had resigned my US Navy commission, putting away a uniform I had worn proudly – and a lifelong goal of flying carrier jets. It was an inglorious end to an illustrious line of relatives who had served and died in American uniforms from Valley Forge to the Colorado "Indian Wars," a Yankee prison camp, and the Battle of the Bulge.

But patriotism was no longer so simple. Like the Shi'ite officer who walked away from germ-filled missiles and the French Legionnaires who threw their Gulf war medals into the dirt in disgust, didn't a true patriot have a duty to try to stop immoral and inept leaders? I had to face the realization that I could soon be ordered to napalm families not unlike my own. I had to acknowledge the fact that I could no longer march in lockstep obedience to a Commander-in-Chief as craven and disingenuous as a Nixon or an LBJ.

I sent my letter of resignation to the Chief of Naval Ops with a lighter heart than I'd known for years. If being exiled from the land of my birth turned out to be the price for not killing people I had no quarrel with, so be it. It remained my most fervent desire to depart this planet without taking a human life.

Certainly not tonight.

But you never know. In a place where corpses have become such common currency, my own life could jingle like small change in the pockets of someone for whom sentiment has become an unaffordable indulgence.

Besides, my body carries a three million year-old imperative. And more recent memories. If cornered, I had not the slightest doubt it will know what to do. For I have been there before, in a paradisiacal yet perverse place called Pago Pago, where a pocketed rigging knife appeared open in my hand before the first synapse of conscious volition could begin to overcome the shock of an attack intended to kill.

That move left me wandering dazed for hours under bowing palms, high on adrenaline and its unexpected atavistic grace. It also saved my life, continuing as it did in a single fluid upwards curve that slashed savagely at the leader of a loping pack of feral dogs just as he lunged snarling for my throat.

Dogs are not men (though the reverse is not always true.) But when I turned with a curse to bloody my assailant, I learned in that primal moment that it makes absolutely no difference if mortal threat is borne on two legs or four.

The only true pacifists are martyred saints, or those who have never been threatened with immediate extinction by aggressors unmoved by protestations of peace or reason. When the karma collectors are pounding on your door, who but the most coddled armchair pundit can argue against self-preservation?

And yet, despite my experience in Samoa and a seemingly unassailable rationale, how to explain the way my fingers linger over the Kalashnikov, enjoying its curves and its heft, the rigorous frame of its sight-picture?

The next gunshot hardly bothers me at all. For I've found the perfect anodyne to the fear of armed attack. With almost sensual pleasure, I rip open a cardboard box labeled in Arabic and begin pushing 7.62 mm cartridges into empty, spring-loaded clips. Each click of a round seating home carries a reassurance as seductive as it is false. No tracers tonight; I load only solid shells capable of shattering an arm in passing, or spreading some stranger's entrails hot and steaming over pants he'd donned, like me, this morning.

It's important to remind myself of these things, for it seems incredible – even impossible – that such a calming, almost domestic chore could have such brutal consequences. Or attract similar violence to itself.

Isn't this the seduction of all wars? Turn on testosterone-addled teenage boys with made-for-the-movies uniforms, place the god-like power of life-taking weapons in their unwise hands, and point them toward an "enemy" they'd probably be happy sharing a beer with if met in other circumstances...

The catch is – and each generation seems to have to relearn this lesson for itself – by the time the impetuous and the indoctrinated discover they've fallen for a lie, it's way too late to change their minds.

The point of no return was crossed back at the recruiter's desk, when a life of conscious volition was traded for the robotic responses absolutely essential for taking lives – and staying alive, if possible – in the chaos of combat. From Sparta to Collodan, Gettysburg to Basra, full realization comes with an explosion that ends thought – or the splash of your buddy's brains across your forehead. War is not fun when it's in or all over your face. The adventure ends in your first minefield, where life becomes random and promises of glory are revealed as sham.

In that searing moment of attack and counter-attack, debate and regret are irrelevant. The only choice is to kill or be killed. And if you're heavily outgunned – as were more than a hundred thousand terrified Iraqis in their teens and early twenties – there is likely to be a great deal more dying than shooting back.

Which is where I find myself tonight. Or near enough at least, to glimpse that shadow-side within and discover a few more things about my peace-proclaiming self. I load two more 30-round clips and shove a third into the AK. It engages with a loud click. I check the safety "On" and push the selector-lever to Rock 'n' Roll, placing the assault rifle within easy reach before taking up an even more formidable weapon.

As I reboot the donated Macintosh, my thoughts return to the environmental impact statement I've pledged to finish before leaving this crucified city. While attention has been focused on the oil slicks, lakes and fires, I'm very concerned about microscopic fungi.

It's hard to imagine countries mobilizing around mold. All of our entreaties to CENTCOM, requesting General Schwarzkopf to order thousands of idle soldiers, bulldozers and earthmovers into fresh combat with a crumbling ecology have been met with what I can only guess is embarrassed silence.

The fungi anchors the desert sands. From the drafty Super Puma I had gazed down on a desert desecrated by tank treads, tire tracks, trenches, ditches, bomb craters, shell holes, berms and revetments. A poster in our environmental info center shows a tire track made in the Sahara by a jeep during World War II, still as plainly delineated and un-grown over as the day it was made.

Farouk al Baz, an expert in Arabian deserts and director of Boston University's Remote Sensing center, will later employ sophisticated environmental satellite imaging to zero in on this devastation.

After careful analysis, al Baz will call Kuwait's war-accelerated desertification, "a more severe long-term problem" than either the oil spills or oil fires. The desert-imaging expert will warn that the disruption of as much as a quarter of Kuwait's land area by a war many TV viewers had thought took place in a sand box, would cause a doubling of the region's already severe sand storms. The searing overpressures from "fuel-air" bombs, al Baz added, had further pulverized precious topsoil, extinguishing all vegetation over wide areas. Even as I tap on the Mac, disrupted dunes are marching on roads, towns and cultivated areas, threatening human routines with an aptly named "desert war" that seems to have no end.

Typing quickly now, I warn the royal family and the cabinet members Logan and I will soon be briefing, that "ordnance pollution" will remain another considerable "environmental impact" for generations to come.

French mine-clearing teams, along with their Canadian counterparts and carefully probing Arab teams, have just declared KC's beaches to be free of sudden surprises. But at least a third of the 100,000 tons of explosives dropped on Kuwait by coalition air forces have failed to explode in the soft desert sands. In the first year after the formal cessation of hostilities, some 1,600 Bedouins and other civilians would be wounded or killed by unexploded mines, rockets, and cluster bombs that will only become even more unstable in the returning desert heat.

I omit mention of depleted uranium in my report. If I had heard of DU, I would not have been so eager to explore burned out Iraqi tanks whose small, windowless compartments resembled the coffin it became.

My final concern is for Kuwait's fresh water aquifer. The benzene, toluene and naphthalene found in the oil saturating those sands are some of science's most potent carcinogens. Even tiny amounts are enough to poison groundwater.

That's the theory anyway. Reality had intruded in our information center one afternoon when a thirsty Thorpe uncapped a bottle of "pure, distilled" Saudi Arabian water, tilted it toward his mouth – and recoiled in confusion. Instead of taking a sip, I watched as he held the open container to his nose. "Smell this," he offered, thrusting the bottle toward me. I took one whiff and gagged on the stink of kerosene.

Hurriedly uncapping more bottles, we found the entire case of "pure, distilled" water to be contaminated. An American Army officer immediately crossed the crowded room. His face registered shock as he read the bottle's label. "Can I have some of this to run some tests? he asked. "Sure," I told him. "Take the case." As he bent to heft the box, the shaken soldier must have read the question in our eyes. "This is the same water I'm giving my men," he explained.

* * *

Though ugly enough to make grown pilots flinch, the US Navy transport that plucked me from Kuwait flew as lovely as a swan. I would have enjoyed staying onboard to make my first "trap" aboard a carrier that cost a million dollars a day to sail around the Gulf. But the twin-engine Carrier Onboard Delivery plane dropped me COD in Bahrain.

The hotel manager in Manama did not waive my room bill. But he had cleaned out my room, and held onto the rest of my gear. It did not take me long to grab a meal, get some clothes pressed, pack a pair of sturdy Iraqi duffel bags and hail a cab to the airport.

As I approached the immigration desk to board my flight, I realized too late that I had no visa stamp showing that I'd been legally cleared into Bahrain. How would I explain my unofficial presence to Arab authorities so inordinately strict about such niggling formalities? Visions of long interrogations and dank prison walls swam before my feverish eyes.

Screw that! I was not in the mood. Suddenly, I was not even myself. It must have been someone else who straightened his laminated Arabic ID, pulled out dark glasses, and stepped forward to slap his passport on the immigration counter.

The inspector's quick glance at the tight-lipped expression beneath the blank pits of my Ray-Bans was followed by a snap appraisal of the rest of my ensemble: Shined shoes. Creased khaki slacks. Desert camouflage tunic without rank or insignia, topped by a haircut short enough to pass a parade-ground inspection. "Do you have military ID?" the official asked, not bothering to open my passport.

"No," I replied curtly. "I'm a special consultant."

Just what kind of "special consultant" and exactly who I was consulting for, I did not volunteer. And the immigration officer didn't ask. Deciding that he'd rather expedite my exit than know any more about this grim foreigner, he flipped open my passport to a blank page, stamped it with the flourish I'd seen government mandarins imitate from Tonga to Swatow, and waved me through.

I wasn't faking either impatience or anger. Being back in "the world" was turning out to be even more confusing than the oil fires and miles of rusting, blasted school buses lining the Highway to Hell. I knew how to shut off an oil pipe valve in a trench open to the sea. But I could no longer negotiate an airline terminal.

I kept wanting to go up to people and shake them until their eyeballs rattled. Didn't they know what I'd been through? Didn't they care that the mass bombings and sanctions they had sanctioned had killed hundreds of thousands of small children? Didn't they grieve over some of the planet's last big wildlife migrations winging into terror and oblivion?

Of course they didn't. They hadn't been told. A news media almost entirely controlled by the same corporations which had manufactured the jets and engines and bombs had neglected to mention "collateral damage" – along with a few other details.

Though drastically disoriented by normalcy, I was also discovering a wonderful new way to travel. My hybrid uniform, augmented by distinctly "been there" vibes, garnered me preferential treatment all the way back to Amsterdam. In that fair city, surrounded once again by my adopted GEERT family, I gave interviews and watched my footage air nationwide on Dutch TV.

But I was not pleasant company. Sneaking off for an hour, I tried to get a grip on myself by going for a walk around a quiet lake. The instant my feet hit the beach, my entire body went rigid. It would be months before I could walk in sand without that accompanying reaction.

I don't know where she came from. A friend of Bo's, I guess, who must have heard that the guy who had gone into the Gulf just five weeks before had come back a very different dude. However it transpired, this local manifestation of the goddess showed up right on some cosmic cue. Angela took me into a darkened bedroom, lit candles and incense while I numbly undressed, and then began massage.

It was that angel of Amsterdam whose wise eyes and wiser hands brought me back from the edge. Her full identity must remain as private as the ways her fingers dug deep into muscles locked so long against the spit-second occasion of their violent rending. Something more than my tears was released when she resurrected another part of me deadened by despair and a folly so long unrelieved by any hint of the feminine. It seemed evident to me then, as it does now, that all men carry an impulse for destruction made virulent by their own close company – and women's banishment or abdication.

When Angela said goodbye that week, I was not whole. But I could function. I hardly noticed badly scaring a long-time friend who greeted me when I landed in Vancouver. Of more concern were the ferries, which seemed to be running much slower than I remembered. After days of numb drifting, I was suddenly in a hurry to get out to the islands of another gulf, back to the patient lady who waited there.

I had promised to return in two weeks. Lucky for my foolish self, as my eyes ranged over the masts of sailing craft, seiners and trawlers secured to the wharf at Ganges Harbour, I spotted my broad-winged seacraft out to seaward, still swinging to twin anchors where I'd left her five months before.

Sighing in a way that seemed to close a circle, I strode down the dock and threw the heavy Iraqi duffels into the dinghy someone had kept bailed. As I bent to the oars, rejoicing in the water's clean welcome, it seemed as if I had been away for years.

Or much longer. The rage I felt for an uncaring world daring to go about its mundane daily tasks would not abate for months. And my thoroughly trashed immune system would keep me constantly sick and exhausted for a year.

I was lucky.

PART II

COVER-UP

CHAPTER 11

WHEN JANEY CAME
MARCHING HOME

When Julia Dyckman went to war, she never expected to become a casualty herself. Even though Fleet Hospital 15 was the most forward-deployed US Navy hospital, its location just west of the Saudi city of al Jubayl seemed safely removed from the front-lines.

Dyckman is proud that her unit set up a 500 bed hospital ready for surgery within 12 days of arriving on Saudi soil. As one of four department heads, Dyckman was responsible for the Casualty Receiving area and out-patient clinics. She was also in charge of about 15 nurses and 40 corps personnel stationed at the al Jubayl airport. Each 12 hour shift presented a panoply of problems, from supervising nurses to direct patient care, data collection and forwarding, even general housekeeping.

Before Dyckman's tour ended in April, 1991, her hospital would administer 8,211 out-patients, as well as 697 in-patients and 90 combat admissions. Before Fleet Hospital 15's tents were folded, more than 8,000 Medical Encounter Data Sheets would be filled out and submitted to the Naval Health Research Center in San Diego.

During this time, battle-damaged Iraqi and US tanks were cleaned near the hospital. Oily "black rain" occasionally fell as she made her way to her tent. Sometimes, mysterious clouds passed directly overhead.

Dyckman's duties took her to the Casualty Clearing company at Camp 53, south of al Jubayl. She also traveled to other areas and hospitals in Saudi Arabia and Bahrain to assist with discharge physicals, which she still considers "inadequate." Her unit handled its own "sick call," treating a troubling series of respiratory problems, inexplicable fevers, vomiting and diarrhea, persistent rashes, heart problems, and undiagnosable stomach and abdominal pains. There were also numerous adverse reactions among her staff to various unspecified vaccinations, as well as the pyridostigmine bromide tablets everyone was ordered to take.

This array of constant medical complaints would have been worrying back home. But the patients they were seeing were young soldiers who had been in top physical condition when they arrived in the Gulf.

Then Dyckman sickened, too. Soon after the first SCUD attacks shook the hospital tents, the navy nurse began experiencing strange rashes, stomach problems and flu-like symptoms. Blisters opened on her right foot. She contracted bronchitis, and developed high blood pressure and a rapid heart rate. Despite these disabilities, Dyckman and other sick members of her staff continued to work long shifts.

Today, like so many other veterans of that forgotten war, Dyckman's health continues to slide downhill. She still suffers from hearing loss, hypertension, aching feet, a recurring rash, a stomach ulcer, foot and abdominal pain. In addition to these ailments, chronic headaches, joint pain and diarrhea still dog Dyckman.

"Each day starts with uncertainty," she later explained to a House Committee on Government Reform and Oversight. "When you eat you are constantly sick and have intermittent diarrhea. Mobility is difficult due to swollen joints and muscle aches. Severe headaches are intermittent. Sometimes you forget what you are doing and what you were going to do. Pain and fatigue are constant companions. To complete your day you are forced to deal with constant denial from the Pentagon that 'nothing happened' during the Persian Gulf war. These statements confuse medical providers who then doubt your credibility."

Joint pain, rashes, fatigue, severe depression and kidney problems are common among sick veterans, many of whom returned home aching, out of breath and too tired to carry out household or military duties. Despite painkillers and ointments, the headaches and rashes did not go away.

* * *

Joyce Riley was a retired Air Force flight nurse when she heard about a war that could claim many Americans if they did not receive adequate care. Deciding to once again serve her country, Riley returned to Kelly Air Force Base in San Antonio, Texas. Though she volunteered for duty in Saudi Arabia, the cease-fire saw her flying missions on a C-130 for about six months instead. Following that active duty stint, Riley went back to her job in Houston as a heart, lung, kidney and liver transplant nurse. When she became ill, Riley later told a national radio audience, "I could get no answers. I didn't know why I was sick. No one would talk with me about it. No one would help me with it."

Riley had heard about medevac aircraft returning from the Gulf filled with sick GIs. But the only thing she saw that she had in common with those who made it overseas was that she had received the same immunizations and had a great deal of contact with Gulf War veterans returning to the states. "Little did we know at the time that the biologicals that were used were impregnated in the equipment they had, such as tents and duffel bags," she says. "It was being spread to all of us and we didn't even know it."

For Joyce Riley, words like "aching joints," "chronic fatigue," "night sweats" or "declining memory" do not begin to convey the real suffering experienced by many returning veterans, and later, their families. "When I am talking about memory loss," Riley said, "I am talking about one young man who told me, 'I can only remember today. I can't remember what happened yesterday.'

"He was 27 years old. We are talking about a problem known as night sweats. Any Gulf War veteran who has the mycoplasma knows about night sweats. You have to change your linens twice a night. The muscle spasms get so bad that you can't stand it and people scream in pain. There is also loss of eyesight, breathing problems, and chest pains because the mycoplasma settles in the atrium of the heart. All of these are problems that become worse."

* * *

Like Riley, Heather Moore was also never deployed. But she did come in contact with many co-workers, receive some of the same vaccines and operate some of the equipment just returned from the most toxic battleground ever fought over. Afraid to come forward "for fear of being called a moocher or liar" by fellow soldiers and Gulf War vets, Moore suffered from chronic ailments for two years before speaking up. "I knew something was up," Moore says now. But it took the revelations reported by another vet to click on "a light I had been looking for."

When Moore attempted to get treatment while still on active duty, she was not taken seriously by Army doctors who could not explain her illnesses. A civilian doctor told her she might have Lupus – but no lab tests were ever done to confirm or disprove his off-the-cuff diagnosis. None of the many medications she took during her last year of service life or during her subsequent ordeal as a civilian have done any good. None of the doctors she's seen has any answers.

"I have become so frustrated," Moore says today. "Even my active duty coworkers commented to me about the first noticeable chronic illness, and that these chronic problems I have never had before in my life. I am only 31." While her illnesses don't seem immediately life-threatening, she says being constantly sick from an undiagnosable illness is effecting her mentally as well as physically. Like many sick veterans, Moore fears that without competent care, her symptoms may get worse over time.

* * *

Prestwich says that when he was evacuated to Bahrain, those first kidney stones were almost worth his first beer in 40 days. But the Canadian medic's problems had just begun. "I was in top physical condition when I went to the Gulf," he relates today. "Once I got back from the Gulf, my health has gone steadily downhill."

Though he's retired now, David Prestwich's slippers seem to connote infirmity more than leisure. As the close-cropped former soldier heads downstairs, his syntax dips and bobs like the kids playing street hockey in the quiet Colwood cul de sac outside. Painkillers, he explains, and antidepressants dog his thoughts.

His small study is wallpapered with Scouting awards, military commendations and plaques from Huron and Gatineau. In the place of honor, next to a "Scud Ducker" certificate from a club whose membership we share, hangs a framed acknowledgment for completing an Ironman just before the war. With its full-pack mountain marathon and 10 kilometer solo canoe portage, this Special Forces Ironman was twice as grueling as its civilian namesake. But it was strictly no sweat for Master Sergeant David Prestwich, who now spends weeks recovering from a short jog.

Since returning home, this Canadian war veteran has undergone six operations on a pinched nerve, a bleeding rectum and a relentless succession of kidney stones. Chronic headaches, coughs and bronchitis still plague Prestwich, who, like many other Gulf War vets, constantly embarks on errands whose purpose he cannot remember.

Kidney, rectal and memory problems are common among sick veterans of North America's most recent war. So is a constellation of seemingly unrelated symptoms, including night sweats, weight gain, insomnia, incontinence, rashes, diarrhea, bleeding gums, sensitivity to light, chronic coughs, shortness of breath, hair loss, nausea, dizziness, blurry vision and blackouts. The bodies of some returning husbands are so toxic, wives say their sperm burns like ammonia.

Prestwich's wife and two young daughters are fine. But when he came home he was not the same person who had left for the Gulf only a month before. Moody and withdrawn, the ailing Sergeant Major avoided friends who "did not know what to say" about an experience they could never share. By the end of April, Prestwich was passing more stones. He was operated on twice more in Ottawa, then hospitalized again in August for yet another kidney stone.

Daughter Sara was born in 1992, as fair and frisky as her two-year old sister, Emma. In November of that year, Prestwich was operated on again for kidney stones. For Christmas of '93 he received surgery on a pinched nerve in his shoulder. Then came a series of operations to stem rectal bleeding. Army doctors were baffled. "No real correlation," Prestwich says, could be found among his many symptoms.

In 1995, Prestwich packed it in. He was sick and tired of being sick and tired. Depression weighed heavily. He was "pooped all the time" and "couldn't seem to get going." On January 25, just as the Department of National Defense was opening a short-lived 1-800 hotline for sick veterans, Prestwich retired as a sub-lieutenant after serving 25 years in the Canadian Forces.

* * *

For more than 120,000 American GIs, as well as their spouses and families, the war is just beginning. Many victims of multiple toxic exposures share a constellation of seemingly unrelated symptoms including sudden weight gain, insomnia, incontinence, bleeding gums and rectums, sensitivity to light, chronic coughs, shortness of breath, hair loss, nausea, dizziness, blurry vision, blackouts and night sweats so heavy, sheets have to be changed twice a night.

Many women veterans also suffer from chronic or recurring vaginal yeast infections and menstrual irregularities, including excessive bleeding and severe cramping.

Members of the 300th Medical Brigade responsible for EPW health care, as well as a number of military police units who had close and continuing contact with the EPWs they were assigned to guard, have since become sick with symptoms shared by other returning veterans. Jennifer, who was a guard with the 401st MPs, says that many members of since disbanded prisoner processing teams from Missouri and Indiana are ill. "I know of one suicide, and one collapsed lung, and several heart attacks," she told a veterans' support group. "I have had a total hysterectomy and one lumpectomy – they don't seem to ask about the health of female soldiers."

Charlene Davis is still plagued by the recurring rashes which began after the first explosions over King Khalid Military City. As her health continues to decline, Davis battles constant migraines, hip pain, hair loss, insomnia, night sweats, nightmares, numbness in her toes, joint and muscle pain, fatigue, gastrointestinal problems and dizziness, as well as other symptoms of an ailment that does not officially exist.

Valerie Sweatman, who felt a fine mist after hearing an explosion over the desert, currently suffers from headaches, exhaustion, fatigue, memory loss, nausea, muscle and joint pains, rectal and vaginal bleeding, and rashes. She has been diagnosed as having arthritis, headaches, and post traumatic stress disorder.

Patricia Williams, who was told by her superiors that a powerful explosion that shook her position was a sonic boom, currently suffers from headaches, fatigue, joint and muscle pain, memory loss, lumps on her arms and neck, night sweats, insomnia, urinary urgency, diarrhea, photosensitivity, gastrointestinal problems, deteriorating vision, shortness of breath, coughing, thyroid problems, abnormal hair loss, swollen lymph nodes, sinusitis, and chest pains.

Patricia Browning, who watched a Patriot hit a SCUD from her vantage at the Khobar Towers, continued vomiting until she stopped taking the PB pill. Now 38, Browning currently suffers from memory loss, severe recurring headaches, fatigue, joint and muscle pain, recurring rashes, night sweats, sleepiness, diarrhea, gastro-intestinal problems, dizziness, blurry vision and photosensitivity, coughing and shortness of breath, two duodenal ulcers, chest pains, heart arrhythmia, and erratic blood pressure. Many of these symptoms originated while she was still in Saudi Arabia.

Michelle Hanlon, who was startled by a SCUD while eating lunch in the desert, still suffers from intestinal problems, hemorrhoids, occasional fatigue, memory loss, and a rash on her finger "like little water blisters under the skin." Her cervical infections coincide with intestinal problems. The 24 year old veteran feels that she is becoming progressively more ill. Her child has been getting fevers since he was 16 months old, as well as yeast infections and rectal and penile discoloration.

Richard Voss, who watched a SCUD hit near Hanlon's location, suffers from headaches, occasional fatigue, joint and muscle pain, memory loss/inability to concentrate, urinary urgency, dizziness, photosensitivity, shortness of breath, rashes, recurring walking pneumonia, chest pains, numbness, and severe joint pains in both wrists and hands.

* * *

Regardless of gender or age, memory loss plagues many vets who find themselves constantly embarking on errands whose purpose they cannot remember. One day a recently returned vet got in his car and drove toward a town about 35 miles away. "Halfway there, I pulled over to the side of the road and began to cry," he says. "I had no idea where I was going, or why."

"It happens a lot these days," echoes Jim Dearing, who vividly recalls his encounter with dusty tarps on a rooftop Saudi villa. "I buy some tea at work, then do it again, only to hear the cafeteria guy say 'man, you were just up here!'"

Assigned to maintain computers that track US Air Force personnel, Dearing was the sole occupant of a four-bedroom villa in Eskan village on the overcrowded Riyadh air base. While looking for souvenirs on the roof of the abandoned villa, Dearing discovered several cases of bottled water that crumbled like eggshells when he touched them. He also found cots and tarps coated with yellowish dust, "like pollen from butterflies' wings." Unlike desert dust, this yellowish powder felt lumpy on his hands. As soon as he touched it, a feeling of dread came over him. "I know that at that time I had a really bad feeling about the tarps and the dusty stuff on them," Dearing later told his fellow vets. After washing his hands, he phoned his wife and mentioned an incident that spelled chemical warfare to him. "It was like a sudden light to me."

But Dearing was different from most of the other sick vets. Though his uniforms were saturated in permethrin, he did not take PB. Even more startling, he served in Saudi Arabia from October, 1992 to March, 1993 – long after the war supposedly ended.

Though his short-term memory fades in and out, Dearing distinctly remembers eating lunch one afternoon in January or February, 1993, with his buddies in their room in Khobar Towers. He will never forget their shock when the SCUD alert sounded. Similar sirens went off simultaneously in Riyadh, Dhahran and Kuwait City. After recovering their wits, the "blue-suiters" sprinted almost half a mile back to their office for their chem gear. Dearing later learned that an Air Force jet had shot down an Iraqi fighter inside Saudi air space.

The Air Force officer suffered no dramatic effects from the air attack or the yellow dust. But like many Gulf War veterans, his feces turned into "clay red bricks." Photographs from his last months in Saudi also show Dearing "puffy looking" and "bloated up."

Since coming home, he says, "I've never been half the guy I used to be." Three months after returning to St. Lake City, Dearing found himself incapable of answering a question or making a decision. Walking up to his house one day, he reached for the doorknob – and couldn't bring himself to open the door. He started to cry. Upstairs, his wife watched incredulously as her husband crumpled into a ball on the floor, crying, "I don't know. I don't know."

Dearing and his wife are now separated and about to divorce. The man who used to lift weights, practice martial arts, and backpack for days alone in Utah's canyonlands can hardly walk. He has upper respiratory problems, no energy, and his joints are "trashed." Dearing is in constant pain. Headaches, he says, regularly bring him to his knees. His joints ache so fiercely he "walks like a man on stumps." Nightmares and nightsweats leave him exhausted after only three or four hours sleep each night. "It takes me forever to get going," he says. An educated and articulate man, Dearing often finds himself becoming frustrated and angry. "I just can't put it together any more. I find myself losing my way in conversations."

Often losing patience with himself, Jim Dearing calls his short-term memory loss, "disgusting." He goes downstairs four or five times, forgetting to get the laundry. He watches the same movie three or four times before realizing he's seen it before. A crowded commissary triggers panic attacks. He can't remember his own phone number, or the short-cut home.

A big, muscular man, Dearing has also started shedding weight. In late 1997 he lost 45 pounds in just three months. The VA is treating him very well, he says. But their extensive tests have found no signs of cancer, HIV or other known pathologies. Dearing takes no drugs, doesn't drink or smoke. Mystified military doctors have thrown up their hands and classified him as an "unknown etiology."

Dearing suspects the yellow powder and the permethrin, and perhaps the two vaccine "cocktails" he took during his

Middle East tour. But it's hard to be sure, he adds. "Who knows what was latent? Who knows what?"

Isolation is as bad as his ailment. None of his military friends talk about what is happening to so many veterans. Some co-workers nervously joke about a "contagious disease" which is "communicable" among family members – but not contagious among the general public. He's lost track of almost everyone he served with – except during a vacation in Alaska in 1994, when he tracked down his closest friend from those days in Riyadh and Dhahran. Still serving in the US Air Force, this individual insisted he was fine. But when Dearing started going down the list of symptoms, every one clicked. Both men were also surprised by how short-tempered they'd become. "Slamming doors, sirens, surprises, trains, loud noises set me off," Dearing explained. "It's horrible to try to live."

* * *

After a 32-hour flight back to the States, Julia Dyckman and other reservists worrying about unresolved medical problems were told they had 90 days to report to an active duty medical facility for treatment. Many hoped that everything would be fine once they got to sleep in their own beds and began getting good food and regular hot baths. "We soon found out that we were ineligible for active duty care," Dyckman recalls, "and registering of complaints could result in release from the reserves as Not Physically Qualified."

Hoping for health care under active duty status, Dyckman volunteered to assist in the RESTAR program to welcome back reservists. Returning Navy vets told Dyckman they were concerned about their current and long term health, as well as being able to support their families. Reporting their symptoms to military doctors and superior officers, they said, could result in a quick discharge from the military that was their employer and their home. Many who were released were too ill to hold down a job, and could get no medical insurance to cover health care as civilians.

The Seabees who had been subjected to repeated SCUD attacks at al Jubayl were especially hard hit. When the *New York Times* checked in with the 750 24th Naval Mobile Construction Battalion reservists, America's "newspaper of record" found that of the 152 Seabees interviewed, 114 said they were sick with illnesses stemming from the war.

Mike Tidd, who had been on guard duty in Tower 6 when a double explosion lit the overcast above his head, now suffers from joint aches and pains, sinus infections, diarrhea, frequent urinary urgency, rashes, heartburn, dizziness, occasional low temperatures, occasional night sweats, chronic fatigue and small sores resembling mosquito bites.

Terry Avery also heard the double explosion. Late in the summer of 1991, the demobilized navy veteran began feeling tired and having headaches. A private doctor told him he was probably working too hard in the sun. Avery, who says he has "good days and bad days," does not think he's as ill as the rest of the men in his unit. He currently suffers from fatigue, headaches, weight gain, itching, muscle and joint pains, memory loss and an inability to concentrate.

Rocky Gallegos, who remembers tasting "burnt toast" after a SCUD blossomed over the Saudi port, suffers from joint pains in his knees, elbows, and hands. He is also dogged by sinus infections and nose bleeds, narcolepsy, blackouts, dizziness, rashes, hair loss, dental problems, muscle pains and spasms, fatigue, night sweats, insomnia, nightmares and blurred vision.

Nick Roberts, who noticed a yellow talc-like powder coating vehicles and tents at al Jubayl, has since been diagnosed with a cancer of the lymphatic system. Roberts claims that several other Seabees who served at al Jubayl have developed lymphatic cancers.

Roy Morrow, who felt his skin burn and go numb after seeing a flash in the sky over al Jubayl, returned home with symptoms that have since grown progressively worse. Morrow currently suffers from swollen lymph nodes, fatigue, diarrhea, night sweats, low grade temperature, weight loss, aching joints, muscle cramps, rashes, blisters, welts and short-term memory loss.

Sterling Symms, who tasted ammonia after seeing a "real bad explosion" overhead has since experienced debilitating fatigue, sore joints, running nose, a chronic severe rash, and open sores which have been diagnosed as an "itching problem." He has also been treated for streptococcus infections.

Mike Moore, who heard the same explosion as Symms, has suffered from a severe thyroid problem, a heart attack, memory loss, tired and aching joints, rashes on his feet, nervousness and muscle cramps since returning home. In February, 1992, Moore's daughter developed a thyroid problem after suffering from nervousness, headaches, and fatigue.

After surviving SCUD attacks and prowling through Iraqi bunkers, Dale Glover is also afflicted with headaches, fatigue, joint and muscle pain, recurring rashes, irritability, night sweats, insomnia, diarrhea, gastrointestinal problems, dizziness, blackouts, excessive photosensitivity, sore gums, swollen lymph nodes and an inability to concentrate that may or may not be related to a spot doctors found on his brain.

* * *

Even as she traveled extensively to hear the stories of sick Seabees and other returning reservists, Julia Dyckman was having difficulty walking. She was also having problems with Navy bureaucracy. The written interviews she conducted were discarded in favor of a "new survey" that never appeared. Dyckman says her Readiness Commander also interfered with her medical care, and succeeded in canceling her pay for more than 16 months. Her medical problems still unresolved, Julia Dyckman was finally released from active duty. Like so many out-mustered Persian Gulf reservists, she was told to apply to the Veterans Administration for help.

* * *

Jim Brown was already hospitalized. Removing the batteries from his unit's incessantly sounding chemical alarms had finally allowed Brown and his buddies to sleep. But soon after the air war commenced, Brown became a frequent face at sick call. His complaints were many: nausea, vomiting, cramps, soaking night sweats, and headaches. The doctors told Brown to "stick it out" and sent him back to duty.

After his return Stateside, the Gulf war veteran became increasingly ill. By the end of March, 1991, he was in a South Carolina military hospital, flat on his back with fatigue, insomnia, headaches, strange rashes, dizziness, abdominal pain, and blood in his stool and urine. Brown was also finding it difficult to concentrate and remember things he'd noted just a short time before. After exhaustively examining Brown, his doctors agreed that he was sick. But they were baffled by symptoms that fit no standard medical diagnosis. Telling Brown they could do nothing for him, the sawbones sent him home, suggesting that he "de-stress."

A few months later, Brown received compassionate reassignment to Fort Gordon, Georgia. But his strange illness became progressively worse. A series of tests at the Eisenhower medical center proved inconclusive, and once again the Army doctors advised Brown to go back to duty despite the fainting and nausea he was constantly experiencing.

In November, 1993, Jim Brown was carried into the post's emergency room after passing out in the line-up outside. This time the sick soldier was sequestered far from other patients, and left sitting on a bed cordoned off by curtains. Word spread quickly. A few minutes later, doctors began crowding into the cramped space. To Brown's increasing alarm, they began talking excitedly among themselves about poisoning and its visible effects on victims.

"They talked about me as if I would not understand the jargon," Brown says. "Yet I understood all too well that these people were connecting an exposure to a toxin to my condition." Brown sat up and began asking questions that left no doubt that he understood them. The conversation stopped abruptly as 10 physicians simultaneously remembered urgent appointments elsewhere.

Brown remained hooked up to an IV for two days. He'd never heard of some of the antibiotics flowing into his veins. What was really surprising was being ordered not to tell anyone that he had been given any antibiotics.

When Brown asked what was wrong with him, he was told it was pharyngitis. The inquisitive patient then wanted to know how they knew so fast, since cell cultures take time to reveal the microorganisms responsible for illness. This time Brown was not surprised when he was told to "leave it alone."

In their agitation, the doctors overlooked an attending nurse. After the flustered physicians left the room, she told her equally upset patient that many of the returning Saudi vets were coming in sick with the same symptoms as Brown's. Giving flu shots at the base seemed to spark an upsurge in admissions. She reminded Brown that he had gotten his flu shot just two days before he turned up sick.

The news made Brown reconsider what he'd learned so far. Looking at the test results his doctors were dismissing, the sick soldier suddenly saw a pattern of values "that were high or low, rather than normal" cropping up in every lab report he had.

The sicker he got, the more outspoken Brown became. Since many returning veterans from the two battalions deployed from Fort Gordon to Saudi Arabia were sick, Brown got the great idea of inviting a TV crew to interview him about the treatment program, "to let the vets know they had somewhere to go for testing and maybe treatment."

The army MDs did not enjoy the show. In order to soften the resistance he was encountering on this medical beachhead for less-informed vets behind him, Brown began filling out every medical form with combat-level care. When he inquired about the diagnostic tests he was going to receive that day, an army doctor "said it would be really extensive, a lot of stuff. Then he rattled off the basic tests listed on the phase 1 protocol. Simple stuff that wouldn't really even tell if you were alive when the test was given."

Brown then showed the physician his unauthorized copy of the mandatory three-part protocol that was supposed to be administered to returning vets. The doctor "turned a very interesting shade of white," Brown relates, "and asked me "where the ---- did I get those from?"

Brown visited all the hospital labs, had eight tubes of blood drawn, handed over a urine specimen, had an x-ray, and was asked whether he wanted any coffee or tea. If the staff thought this budding army activist had been placated, Brown set them straight with a short parting speech in which he informed the doctors gathered outside the exam room that "from now on, I would be coming back to the hospital with every vet I knew who needed testing, and would personally see to it that they received proper testing and treatment." Then he went to see the hospital administrator to tell him the same thing.

Back home in South Carolina, Brown tried to make weekend drills. But he was too sick to march. His commander ordered him to get a doctor's excuse to miss drill. When Brown went to a civilian doctor he was told that two blood tests would nail down his symptoms. Brown was skeptical, but he forked over $113 for the tests.

The results showed that he had been dangerously anemic for years, which he knew, and that he had an active infection from the Epstein-Barr virus, which was news. The doctor also told Brown that he had been able to back-track to the earliest stages of his illness, which had started during the time he had spent ducking SCUDs in the Saudi desert.

A few days after getting a civilian diagnosis, a letter from the VA arrived informing Jim Brown that all tests had been negative. "Don't worry, be happy," the army told him. Brown was not amused. The VA's diagnostic protocol had included a simple test for Epstein-Barr.

* * *

At least Brown was angry enough to still function. For countless other returning veterans, being constantly told that an overwhelming array of frightening and debilitating symptoms was all in their heads, finally got to their heads.

"Do you feel the frustration and extreme feeling of anger well up inside you when it happens?" Dearing asked his fellow vets. "Try to laugh it off and make cute little jokes about it so your peers don't think you're crazy? Struggle with the anxiety of desperately trying to recall even some of the simple things you are asked to reiterate or pass on? Then with all that 'brewing,' feel other things 'kick in'...a migraine, the fatigue increases, sleep won't come to me, body feels like its humming or something, the symptoms seem to increase and then...

"Like two nights ago for me, I sat, and cried, and wanted to scream, got a momentary grip on my senses, made a phone call, tried to act like I was just saying 'hello' and was so shook up with the uncertainty of myself I couldn't talk, just cried and repeated the words 'I don't know' and 'what's wrong with me' over and over and over."

Scorned by military doctors and superior officers, some soldiers committed suicide. "My son came back after 9.5 months in the gulf and rapidly developed all the classic symptoms, hair loss, rashes, aches and pains in all muscles, fatigue and severe chronic headaches which would render him non-functional," one parent wrote to a veterans support group. "As time went on, his personality changed, he would really verbally abuse his wife. Everybody noticed his change. When VA told him he had less than a year to live...with the conditions worsening, he couldn't take it and killed himself."

Other Gulf War veterans, Congressional investigator James Tuite noticed, "began to die of cancers, heart failure, and central nervous system diseases not normally seen in people of their age and previous physical health."

Even though cancers usually take 10 to 15 years to manifest following initial exposure, Tuite wasn't exaggerating. Just 11 months after returning from the Gulf with what had been dismissed as "hemorrhoids," Michael Adcock died of multiple cancers. His grief-stricken mother, who still believes that prompt medical attention could have saved his life, says her son was never referred to a surgeon."He had repeated rectal bleeding, rash, severe headaches, raspy voice, and pain in his joints. Upon return to the States, he, along with many in his unit, was given a very limited physical examination with no chest x-rays, no blood work, and sent on his way."

As Jim Brown discovered, when it came to taking care of sick soldiers, the government they served seemed to suffer from even more acute memory loss. An internal report by the National Guard revealed that hundreds of Gulf vets had been summarily discharged, despite the fact that their medical problems entitled them to remain in the military for the treatment their war service had earned.

Even the military's statistical surveys were flawed. Though the VA's Gulf War medical exam differed from the active duty CCEP exam, both studies were lumped together to make medical conclusions."Shouldn't they have the same criteria?" asks veteran Christopher Parrish.

* * *

Jim Dearing continued to watch his mailbox with the same intensity he had once looked for mines, alert for any letter, card or other notification from the VA regarding his disability claim. Despite his depression and growing disabilities, each request for information received his quick response. In May, 1991, Dearing returned from visiting his family in the Midwest to find a "ah-ha" letter from the VA hospital informing him that he had failed to keep an April appointment. "Having never, ever received any notification for this appointment," Dearing checked every letter he'd ever received from the Veterans Administration. He found no notification of any appointments.

Stressed out by the news that his medical lifeline had been severed, Dearing nervously contacted the VA. According to their records, he had missed three appointments in April, "all of which; I have no notification of whatsoever, at all, nada, zip..." Dearing informed his fellow vets. "Well, you see my point."

Fortunately, Dearing was rescheduled for four appointments. But he wondered if the same VA "oversight" was happening to other sick vets. Had his case not been "still pending," missing those appointments, he says, "would have closed my case or stopped it in its tracks."

Many sick veterans were being summarily dismissed after a cursory exam. After returning to Fort Bragg, Jeffrey Ford began experiencing concentration problems, especially while driving. In 1996, Ford traveled to the VA Medical Facility in Kansas City, Missouri, where he added his name to the 85,000 already listed on the Persian Gulf Registry exam. After describing his symptoms, Ford told the examining doctor that he had been just two miles from the chemical detonations at Khamisiyah. His announcement, he says, "didn't raise an eyebrow."

After a routine blood test, urinalysis, a chest X-ray, and some pointed references to "mental hygiene," Ford was sent home. When he complained to the hospital administration about the inadequate medical exam, he was told that they'd done their job and followed the existing protocol.

* * *

According to the largest US veterans organization, by 1997 as many as 180,000 American veterans were suffering from a degenerative illness connected with the Gulf War. Among the Czechs who detected sarin and mustard agents, as many as 85 percent of the members of that special unit have since been struck by many of the symptoms associated with Gulf War Syndrome.

Willie Hicks, whose face burned as he ran to his bunker at Cement City, now says that 85 of the 110 men in his unit came home sick. "We also had one guy that died by the name of Staff Sergeant Bell," Hicks adds. "And in his case he was in good physical shape. He did not smoke or drink. He came home one day feeling good, walked up the street, and came back, and dropped dead."

According to Hicks, Staff Sergeant Neal "is now nothing more than a vegetable." Hicks himself carries a notebook all the time "because my memory is gone." The former schoolteacher had to quit his job because he kept passing out and getting lost on his way to work. His other symptoms include headaches, blood in his urine, insomnia, joint and muscle pain, deteriorating vision, loss of mobility in his left arm, night sweats and sometimes bloody diarrhea. The VA says he's suffering from post traumatic stress disorder.

But Hicks' weight continues to yo-yo, dropping from 170 pounds to 126 in a single month, then shooting back up to 150 pounds. "I have no income," says another veteran who put his life on the line in the Gulf. "I lost my car. I was getting desperate for funds to support my family with. The VA tried to charge me $169 a day for being in the hospital. I went up and questioned it. I said this is service-connected. The lady said you have not proven it to be service-connected, therefore, we are charging you $169 a day. I said, I have no income. She said, it makes no difference."

For this former Vietnam veteran, it's Vietnam all over again. Once again, he's been abandoned by a government more concerned with its own lie-ability – and liability – than soldiers wounded in its service. As Hicks puts it, "I am sick and unable to work because I served my country."

William Brady, who made two separate tests confirming a chemical attack, became his own chemical warfare sensor. The NCO from log base Alpha currently suffers from severe recurring headaches, chronic fatigue, joint and muscle pain, rashes, depression, night sweats, insomnia, urinary urgency, diarrhea, gastrointestinal problems, lightheadedness, photo-sensitivity, shortness of breath, coughing, abnormal hair loss, sensitivity in his teeth, burning and itching everywhere, arthritis, worsening leg cramps, a tingling in his arms and a "bulging disc" in his neck. He is also constantly battling flu-like symptoms. Unmarked by any visible wounds, in May, 1993, Brady suffered a heart attack.

Michael Kingsbury, whose R&R in Riyadh was so rudely interrupted, began having stomach problems after returning home from the Gulf. He currently suffers from memory loss, rashes, aching joints, headaches, rectal bleeding, nausea, sensitivity to light, abnormal hair loss, high fevers, clammy skin, lumps, bloody mucous, night sweats, sore muscles and fatigue.

After running in confusion around "Expo" during a SCUD attack, Randall Vallee currently suffers from very severe recurring headaches, fatigue, respiratory problems, joint pain, memory loss, recurring rashes, depression and irritability, night sweats, insomnia, blood in his urine, constipation, nausea, dizziness, shortness of breath and coughing, thyroid problems, flu symptoms, sinus problems and sensitivity to smells. He always feels cold, and takes medication for pain.

John Stewart tried treating his physical decline with "self-denial" after getting out of the marines in late November, 1991. But ignoring his symptoms didn't work. Abrupt changes in appetite, weight gain, multiple aches in his joints, assorted skin rashes and blotches, some dyspnea and lung problems still trouble this vet, who is also easily fatigued.

Six years since Kevin Treiber served in the Persian Gulf as a medical specialist with a mobile ambulance unit in Dhahran, this nursing student at the University of North Carolina says the blurry vision, shaky hands and mouth sores he experienced after the war have subsided. But Treiber is still bothered by occasional swelling in his right shoulder, as well as aching joints. Like so many others, Treiber also had to deal with Veterans Affairs doctors who denied that his symptoms were serious.

"They told me these were just signs of aging," he told an investigating panel of VA officials. "But these are not normal conditions for a 25 year-old to endure. The last time I checked with my friends my age, they didn't need needles stuck in their elbows regularly to remove fluid."

Norman Camp, who watched his fellow marines sicken at Ras al Khaki, also currently suffers from headaches, joint pain in knees and elbows, memory loss, night sweats, occasional insomnia, urinary urgency, dizziness, photosensitivity, shortness of breath, coughing and heart problems.

Brian Martin, whose unit was plagued by "false" alarms, returned from Saudi Arabia and began experiencing memory loss, swollen and burning feet, joint disorders, muscle weakness, heart palpitations, shortness of breath, rashes, fatigue, headaches, insomnia, bleeding from the rectum, chronic coughing, running nose, burning eyes, and uncontrollable shaking of his right-side extremities.

Dwayne Mowrer, who didn't worry when a truck loaded with DU rounds exploded upwind from his tent, figured his symptoms would fade once he was back in the United States. They didn't. Even though his personal doctor and physicians at the local Veterans Administration could find nothing wrong with him, Mowrer's health worsened. Fatigue, memory loss, bloody noses and diarrhea dogged him. Then the single parent of two began experiencing problems with motor skills, bloody stools, bleeding gums, rashes and strange bumps on his eyelids, nose and tongue. Mowrer thinks his problems can be traced to his exposure to depleted uranium.

Wayne Clingman, along with other members of his maintenance crew, also suffers from what has come to be known as Gulf War Syndrome, or more recently, Gulf War Illness.

John Jacob pulled on his gas mask after smelling sweet almonds in the open cab of the truck he was driving into Iraq. But his quick reaction was not fast enough. Jacob has been sick ever since. Among his many afflictions, he currently suffers from fatigue, joint and muscle pain, memory loss, recurring rashes, lumps at joint areas, night sweats, depression and irritability, insomnia, urinary urgency, gastrointestinal problems, shortness of breath, coughing, abnormal hair loss, dental problems, swollen lymph nodes and a foot fungus that will not go away.

* * *

While American vets sicken and die, at least 1,228 ailing British veterans have also registered for compensation. Richard Turnbull, the RAF chemical alarm specialist who reported 31 positive readings following a single SCUD attack, has had two dozen separate chest infections since returning home to Liverpool. An avid scuba diver, who worked out every day before going to the Gulf, Turnbull has been forced to give up diving because he "can't take the pressure below a few feet." Turnbull, who can no longer run or swim or even take long walks, uses two inhalers to help ease serious respiratory complications.

Turnbull was also exposed to deadly organochlorine insecticides while using a high volume smoke machine, called a "swing fog" to kill scorpions and other insects inside the British tents. He has been diagnosed as suffering from angina, emphysema, asthma and arthritis. He has also been told that his life expectancy has been reduced by toxic exposures in the Gulf. Severe fatigue, mood swings and general weakness have become daily companions. Turnbull's left leg is now so frail, putting pressure on it is like "walking on a piece of string." After leaving the RAF in 1994, Richard Turnbull set up his own business. But ill health forced him to abandon it.

Corporal Terry Walker, the British driver who witnessed a SCUD attack on al Jubayl, reports that he's been ill "ever since I've come back from the Gulf." Walker's medical problems include recurring chest infections, rashes, and headaches.

Walker is furious that the military he has since left is "covering up what happened and the real risks" faced in the Gulf by allied forces. "When they sent us out to fight the war, we expected them to look after us. Instead, when we came back they just tried to cover it up. They said there was nothing wrong at all because the general public would go against them if they found out about the exposures to chemical and biological warfare and how it gets into your whole family."

* * *

Fred Willoughby, the soldier who had been "hanging out" when the alarms went off, has also been sick since returning from the desert. It wasn't long after his homecoming that he began noticing the same fatigue, diarrhea, and aching joints in his spouse.

In the hardest hit American units, three out of four spouses are now sick with a syndrome blamed on the Gulf War. All of these stricken soldiers and their partners were in their mid-twenties or just a few years older when they became ill.

Since a sick Gallegos got home from the Persian Gulf, his wife Laurie has undergone bladder surgery, experienced a heart valve prolapse, and suffered from disrupted menstruation, headaches, yeast infections, and a swollen thyroid.

It's his family's illnesses that most angers Terry Walker. "We knew there was a risk of being killed," he says. "But we didn't know that we would come back from the war so ill, and that our families would be getting sick, too."

Soon after his return to England, Walker's wife began suffering from chronic abdominal pain. She has been hospitalized at least seven times in the last three years. "She's been cut open twice but they couldn't find what was wrong," a bitter Walker explains. The Walkers are also troubled by the health of their infant, who has been plagued with a cold and respiratory problems "from day one."

Terry Avery feels that his wife is more ill than he is. Besides sharing her husband's joint pains, night sweats, fatigue, stomach problems, itching and rashes, she now has an enlarged spleen and liver and abnormal liver functions. Two of Avery's children also complain of headaches, as well as joint and abdominal pains. His 13 year old daughter was diagnosed with mononucleosis, sinus infections and throat pains from the sinus drainage. His 11 year old son has also exhibited unusual rashes, headaches, joint pain, itching, sinus and throat infections, and fevers.

In February, 1992, Moore's daughter began developing a thyroid problem. The youngster also suffers from nervousness, headaches and fatigue. Within a year, his wife began to develop these same symptoms despite there being no history of thyroid problems in their families.

Brady's wife suffers from fatigue, yeast infections, a rash, two ruptured discs in her neck, sinus headaches, aching in her right arm and a loss of feeling in her thumb.

Soon after he was first hospitalized, Jim Brown's wife began having the same illnesses. Vallee's wife also suffers from fatigue, yeast infections and menstrual irregularities. Glover's spouse has the same symptoms, as well as joint pain, memory loss and hair loss. Norman Camp's wife suffers from fatigue, yeast infections, menstrual irregularities, joint and muscle pain and chest pain. Voss's wife suffers from recurring yeast infections, menstrual irregularities, rashes, fatigue, muscle pain and severe joint pain in her wrists.

Other family members have caught the mysterious malady from returning soldiers. Erika Lundholm is the sick sister of an American vet. "I believe that chemical and biological weapons were used in the Gulf, that my brother was exposed, and that through him I was exposed, either directly or through contamination of his equipment that he brought home," she told a radio interviewer on the Christian Broadcasting Network.

Though she can only work part-time because of her illness, Erika Lundholm is more concerned with the welfare of her brother, Dean, who she says was abandoned by the VA and the country he served. "All he gets is denials and no help from anyone, and he hasn't been able to work. And he's homeless. And it's just not right."

* * *

Even more troubling are the illnesses and birth defects in children and infants exposed or born to returning Desert Storm vets. A soldier who wishes to remain anonymous alleges that among approximately 70 people in D company, 1/327 Infantry of the 101st Airborne, 15 or 20 unborn children were lost to miscarriages within a year after returning from the Gulf.

Another disputed study found that of the 55 infants born to four Mississippi National Guard units soon after the war, 37 were born with birth defects.

In a photo exposé as shocking as its earlier exposé of Minamata disease, *Life* magazine pointed to a Senate investigation which found that among 400 sick vets, "a startling 65 percent reported birth defects or immune-system problems in children conceived after the war."

A half-dozen tragically deformed children were featured on the cover and inside that special November, 1994, issue. Jayce, who resembles a thalidomide baby of the 1950s, also appeared in *People* magazine. Born with hands and feet "attached to twisted stumps," the five year-old still has an extremely difficult time trying to walk on artificial legs without arms for balance. According to the accompanying text, the "cherubic, rambunctious blond" also came into the world with a hole in his heart, a blood problem similar to hemophilia and ear canals that were not fully developed.

Kennedi was born with tangled blood vessels, and no thyroid. Without daily hormone treatments, the little girl whose face is swollen with red knotted lumps would die. Despite repeated laser surgery, the tumors keep appearing, disfiguring Kennedi's eyelids, lips, throat and spinal canal, twisting her speech and threatening her life.

Like many stricken Gulf War babies, Lea Arnold has spina bifida. The characteristic split in the backbone results in paralysis and water on the brain. Lea cannot move her legs or roll over. Casey was born with the lopsided head and spine that signifies Goldenhar's syndrome. His left ear is missing, and his digestive tract is not connected. Casey speaks in sign language. He is fed and his wastes are removed through tubes in his belly.

Cedrick's shrunken face, missing ear and one blind eye are also the result of Goldenhar's. He was born with his trachea and esophagus fused, and his heart in the wrong location. Steve Miller's son was born with one eye and a single ear. Doctors told the former Army nurse that these severe birth defects were not only extremely unusual, but suggestive of a toxic exposure.

After that article's publication in November, 1995, the Association of Birth Defect Children identified the first cluster of defects among the offspring of US Gulf veterans. Clustering occurs when an ailment strikes one group of people more than others.

* * *

Six years after the celebrated end of a war unprecedented in its toxicity, the *Journal of the American Medical Association* reports that 80,000 US veterans are afflicted by wounds whose cause is unknown. Veterans organizations insist that the real toll is twice as big and increasing.

The death toll continues to climb. In July, 1995, the Department of Veterans' Affairs raised the official number of US combat casualties from 148 to 6,526 deceased Gulf War veterans. Tony Picou, who heads the MISSION Project (Military Issues Surfacing In Our Nation), says his organization now believes that toll to be twice as high and growing.

As Joyce Riley discovered, not everyone who got sick served in the Gulf. From the connex cleaners who scrubbed the big shipping containers coming back from the KTO, to civilian vehicle and helicopter mechanics, the mysterious contagion showed no discrimination in who it hit.

A retired Seabee named Woody now works in a computer store two blocks away from the VA hospital in Biloxi, Missouri. One Wednesday, Woody watched a man and his spouse get out of their car in front of his store. "He got out of the passenger side and had crutches, a truss around his torso, and looked like death on a soda cracker," the al Jubayl veteran relates. "Something told me he was a 'Bee' – and a victim of the Gulf."

The couple came in "and sure enough the conversation got around to the fact that he was a storekeeper with NMCB 133 during the Gulf War." When the fellow Seabee explained that he had "Gulf War Syndrome," Woody looked at him strangely. NMCB 133 never made it in-country – a fact the sick Seabee confirmed. If he hadn't been rotated himself, Woody would have met the man when he was transferred to Rota, Spain.

"It was then that I was floored," Woody continues. "He explained that he had never entered 'the War.' He was a member of a team that just received the connex boxes from in-country and was to clean them." He was also "very, very, very ill."

Turning the tables as well as his body, the former 'Bee faced Woody and said, "What's really scary, senior, is how are you doing? You were actually in there."

Woody had to go to the back of the store and cry for a moment. Fortunately, he explains, his employer is "retired military and understands." The storebound Seabee says his heart broke for this young man, who was about 26 years old. "Compared to how he is doing I don't have any problems. He has hemorrhaged from within, is starting to lose mobility in his lower extremities, and is generally ill, night sweats, can't sleep, depression etc. etc. etc."

Thomas House, the US Air Force sergeant who served as an aircraft mechanic with the 48th Tactical Fighter Wing in Taif, is currently beset by recurring headaches and rashes, fatigue, joint and muscle pain, memory loss, lumps under the skin, depression, irritability, night sweats, insomnia, urinary urgency, diarrhea, gastrointestinal problems, dizziness, blurry vision, photosensitivity, shortness of breath, coughing, bleeding gums, swollen lymph nodes, seizures, shaking, vomiting, fevers, chest pains, sinus infections and sinus growths.

His wife suffers from nearly all of the same symptoms. Seven other members of this unit have also reported experiencing similar symptoms from exposures to returning combat aircraft.

* * *

Not everyone who was sickened by the Gulf War wore a uniform. Little Lea was born to a civilian helicopter mechanic who worked with the Army's 1st Cavalry Division. Herman Piceynski had been hired by the US Army to repair its helicopters in northeastern Saudi Arabia. While working there, Piceynski was jolted by nearby SCUD missile detonations, as well as the pyridostigmine bromide he was told to take. In good health before the war and working full time, Piceynski has become a living catalog of Gulf War Illness symptoms.

Besides the joint pain, dizziness, loss of balance and memory and poor concentration suffered by so many returning vets, this civilian aircraft mechanic also suffers from chronic diarrhea, stomach problems, fatigue, impotence, cough, muscle spasms, soreness and headaches. His ears ring and he has been diagnosed with progressive diabetes. His persistent skin rashes have left permanent scaring. Bleeding gums have cost him all of his teeth. Despite this disastrous and demonstrable litany, Piceynski's employer, as well as his employer's insurance company, continue to insist that his medical problems are unrelated to his work on contaminated aircraft during the war.

A number of Department of Defense civilian personnel assigned to Army depots at Anniston, Alabama and Sharpsite, California, during Desert Storm have also been found by a special presidential investigating committee to be showing symptoms consistent with those of other ailing Gulf War veterans. These individuals were assigned to clean, repair, and upgrade military vehicles and other equipment returning from the Southwest Asia theater of operations.

Even a little bit of contamination goes a long way. Though still in his twenties, US Marine veteran Chris Newman feels like he's 50. "I brought home some Iraqi equipment and it made my dad and two uncles, all healthy prior military guys, sick a few days after looking at it." Newman burned it all. This was back in the summer of '91, he explains, "before the GWS heated up."

Another American veteran brought back berets, canteens, books, uniforms, maps, an Iraqi General's map case, money, a couple of British land-line phones, a warbelt from a Republic Guard captain and other unique travel souvenirs. After packing it all away, "Mustang" says he's only had it out two or three times over the years. "Peculiarly, each time I took it out and my wife handled something...red blotches broke out on the backside of her hand. It was almost spontaneous, within minutes, and after an hour or so, the blotches would disappear."

Telling other vets that he's "learned to be careful with this stuff," Mustang suggests wearing plastic gloves when handling Gulf War memorabilia. He adds that he "can't help but think her reaction is caused by something like a 'mustard' chemical powder."

Whatever it was, this invisible contaminant is persistent. In June 24, 1997, Britain's Ministry of Defense warned that Girl Guides and Scouts could be exposed to dangerous chemicals impregnating Gulf War-surplus tents and sleeping bags. The Countess of Mar claimed that she knew of two Scout group organizers who had become ill after handling tents brought from Desert Storm. "They had the same symptoms," she told the British press, "nausea, tiredness, muscle pain".

Lady Mar observed that the organophosphates sprayed on the surplus desert gear are "far more potent in young people than in adults" because human immune systems do not fully develop until adulthood. Lord Gilbert, a junior Defense minister, admitted that it would be "extremely difficult, if not impossible, to identify any tents which are now in the hands of the general public."

* * *

Then there were the sailors. When Shane Jumper shipped out to the Gulf aboard the carrier *USS Nimitz*, he was the proud new father of "a wonderfully healthy year old boy." Jumper doesn't think he has any symptoms of GWS. But then he's still not clear on what those symptoms are. What worries him and his wife now is that since his return from the Persian Gulf, she has miscarried three times, twice in 1994, and again in 1997.

Another ailing vet from Victoria, Canada, knows twice as many sick shipmates as the 74 patients treated so far at the National Defense Medical Center in Ottawa. They are not coming forward, she says, because they fear ridicule, have left active service for civilian careers, or don't wish to jeopardize military pensions and careers with chronic medical complaints.

Still others, she adds, are away at sea for six months at a time and probably never read the single notification sent by National Defense Headquarters to all Canadian Gulf War vets. It doesn't take much to derail the human endocrine or nervous systems. But what could be making sailors sick who never saw a battlefield?

CHAPTER 12

PARTING SHOTS

Though there appeared to be many complex synergies contributing to a baffling epidemic among returning Gulf War veterans, it soon became apparent that the single most glaring commonality among all Gulf War Illness sufferers was pyridostigmine bromide.

Appalled by the casualties inflicted by Iraq's chemical warriors on Iranian troops and civilians, the Pentagon began testing a drug called HI-6 as a possible antidote to soman nerve gas three years before its own soldiers were sent into a similar CBW maelstrom.

When that experimental drug proved genetically damaging, attention turned to pyridostigmine bromide. Used for decades in occasional short-term treatment of patients recovering from surgery for a rare muscle fatigue disease called myasthenia gravis, it was thought that prophylactic doses of PB might also prove effective in shielding the human nervous system against exposure to soman nerve agent powders or gasses. But by the start of the Gulf War, PB use was in sharp decline among doctors who questioned its safety. Pyridostigmine bromide, they feared, could cause damage to neuromuscular junctions that could not be corrected by surgery.

Was a potential cure for soman poisoning worse than the soman damage? Iraq's dramatic demonstrations of air-dried nerve agents against Iranians and Kurds had convinced the American military that nerve agents are nasty neurological weapons. Chemically related to commonly used organophosphate pesticides derived from Nazi gas chambers and WWI mustard gas attacks, nerve agents such as sarin, tabun, and VX kill by causing a build-up of the chemical messenger acetylcholine in the critical gap between nerve and muscle cells. As increasing acetylcholine causes runaway nerve and organ activity, the drooling, excessive sweating, cramping, vomiting, confusion, irregular heart beat, twitching and convulsions that follow can quickly lead to loss of consciousness, coma and death.

When Saddam's army invaded Kuwait, US researchers still knew very little about the consequences of non-lethal exposure to chemical nerve agents. Their emphasis remained on the immediate lethality of chemical weapons such as soman.

Though it is a carbamate, rather than an organophosphate like sarin and tabun, PB is considered to be a potent nerve agent by itself. Like sarin, PB also binds to and inhibits the enzyme that normally shuts off the acetylcholine neurotransmitter. The idea is that PB-blocked nerve sites cannot be invaded by other nerve agents; when the PB wears off after four or five hours, normal nerve function should return to a third of the body's nerve junctions "protected" by PB. The danger with carbamates like PB is that if they are used after exposure to nerve agents like sarin, their ability to increase cholinesterase-blocking activity amplifies the effects of that nerve agent poisoning.

In one of several studies submitted to the FDA before the war to request "fast-track" approval for the use of PB as a chemical warfare protective agent, the defense department's Study Report 8740-86-8 described how four rats were given PB at a dosage of 1.25 milligrams per kilogram of body weight, before being sent swimming as a test of their "stress" response to the experimental drug. All four rats flunked the test by dying. Veterans were later forced to swallow repeated doses of pyridostigmine bromide at one-third the bodyweight dosage that killed the "stressed" rats. In reviewing this study, a PhD researcher named Dr. James Moss commented, "War is stressful, even if you are the supply clerk."

The Pentagon-paid researchers said the rats "drowned." But they were careful not to open three of the rodents' lungs to check their hypothesis. The fourth "drowned" rat died *after* being removed from the pool. "At 1.25 mg/kg, zero rats should have died, Moss wrote to Gulf War vets, "400,000 or so people were dosed with PB, based on real shitty science. If you make a stink about this, make sure a friendly lawyer has this first."

Undaunted by 100 percent mortality in their key PB experiment, in August, 1990, DoD scientists requested approval to study four men to evaluate PB's side-effects on vision. Unlike the 463,000 US troops the Pentagon estimates took PB for weeks or months during the desert campaign – without medical briefings or followup – all four preliminary test subjects were admitted to Lyster Army Hospital for close monitoring.

All four experimental patients were males. Even though their lower weights, birth control pills and reproductive cycles makes female's fluctuating levels of acetylcholine especially vulnerable to PB, that potent pill was never tested on women.

In later studies, other test subjects were questioned extensively about their sensitivity to bromide and similar medications. Patients found to be taking any other medication, such as birth control pills or anti-malarial vaccines, were excluded from PB testing. In some instances, smokers were also excluded. Most participants were told not to drink any alcoholic beverages while taking PB.

The army was concerned because during earlier safety trials air force pilots had crashed-landed in hospitals with serious side effects – including impaired breathing, vision, stamina and short-term memory. One pilot experienced respiratory arrest just 91 minutes after swallowing his third 30-milligram PB tablet. Another subject lost consciousness after experiencing blurred vision and a severe headache. Abnormal liver tests, unusual electrocardiograms, gastrointestinal disturbances and anemia were also reported. By the second or third day of treatment, test subjects were unable to perform tasks requiring short-term memory or exercise in hot environments.

Craig Crane was one air crewman ordered to take pyridostigmine in the 1980s. Though he is only 32 years old and did not serve in the Gulf war, Crane left the Air Force permanently disabled by memory loss, joint pain, chemical sensitivities and other symptoms that have come to be associated with Gulf War illness.

Though intended only for use against soman nerve agent, pyridostigmine is unable to enter and protect the brain. PB may also be ineffective in protecting the spinal cord. Nor does it protect against nerve agents when taken alone. It only works in combination with other drugs, such as atropine and pyridine-2-aldoxime methochloride included in the Mark 1 nerve agent antidote kits issued to American GIs.

But when DoD began its second phase of pyridostigmine research, something went wrong. The atropine and 2-Pam taken with PB were not saving the lives of animals that were exposed to soman. Ramping up the dose of atropine to 0.40 milligram per kilogram of body weight seemed to increase the survival of Rhesus monkeys exposed to soman.

Based on the monkey numbers, a 27 milligram dose of follow-up atropine would have been required to protect a 150-pound soldier from the lethal effects of soman. But even without the shock of nerve-agent exposure, the side effects from only one-twelfth of this effective dosage of atropine boosted heart rate, blurred vision and decreased sweating – which could prove fatal in a desert environment. Shying away from the prospect of incapacitating its own troops before they met the enemy, the Department of Defense elected to stay with the lower, ineffective dose of atropine when finalizing its treatment regime for Desert Storm warriors.

Once again, DoD researchers warned that PB should only be used against nerve agent soman, code-named GD. But defense intelligence officers knew long before the war that Iraq did not manufacture, stockpile, or use GD. Instead, Iraq was busy brewing very large quantities of sarin.

* * *

As Desert Shield began deploying nearly one million allied troops into position for an assault against Iraq, coalition commanders were desperate for any remedy against the chemical and biological horrors their own governments had sold to Saddam Hussein.

The FDA did more than expedite approval of PB as a nerve gas antidote. A Food and Drug Administration deputy commissioner later revealed that the FDA also gave "considerable deference" to the Pentagon's insistence that soldiers bound for the Persian Gulf not be told of the risks associated with the experimental drug they were being ordered to take. Mary Pendergast told House of Representative investigators that while the agency customarily sought "informed consent" before using an unapproved "investigational" drug on humans, the FDA had agreed to waive this stipulation as "impractical" under battle-field conditions. As Pendergast explained, "We thought it was our best shot against nerve gas. It was better than nothing."

Was it? Contrary to all known medical procedures since the time of Hippocrates, Pendergast added that the Pentagon did not keep adequate records concerning those to whom the drug was administered.

"It blows my mind," commented Representative Christopher Shays. Representative Dennis Kucinich observed that the Pentagon had known for years that nerve gas might be used against its troops in the Persian Gulf. "People should have been informed from the moment they set foot in the desert that this drug was not licensed and that it had side effects. They had time to tell the soldiers. They didn't do it. It's very clear that the Defense Department ran roughshod over the FDA and that the health of our soldiers was not protected."

* * *

Carol Picou was one of some 28,000 American women GIs ordered to take PB "to protect us against chemical attack." Within one hour of taking the experimental nerve agent, she began experiencing uncontrollable twitching in her eyes, a runny nose, drooling, and neck and shoulder pain.

By the third day of taking PB, the frightened nurse was also suffering from incontinence, shoulder pain and blurry vision. When she stopped taking the pill, the side effects ceased. But after ordering her to continue taking the pills, her commanding officer watched to make sure she swallowed them. Picou was told to take the pills three times daily for 15 days.

There is more to Picou's story than PB. Today she is worse off than the casualties treated and released for gunshot wounds in the combat support hospital when she served. Her inconvenient incontinence continues, along with muscle weakness and memory loss.

* * *

While serving with the 1454th Transportation Company, Steve Hudspeth also became very ill from taking the nerve agent pretreatment pills. If I'm going to feel like this I might as well be dead, Hudspeth thought. His severe nausea and diarrhea did not abate until he stopped taking the pills after the second day. But other symptoms persisted. Today, Hudspeth suffers from memory loss, fatigue, sore muscles and joints, insomnia, cough, occasional night sweats, diverticulitis, diarrhea, kidney stones, bloody stools, urinary urgency, growths on his eye, rashes, tingling and itching sensations – as well as depression and irritability.

About half of the 41,650 members of the XVIII Airborne Corps who were issued PB every eight hours during Operation Desert Storm noted non-incapacitating physical upsets, such as increased flatulence, abdominal cramps, diarrhea and urinary urgency. Other symptoms included headaches, runny nose, perspiration, nausea, and tingling of the extremities.

Another American vet believes that the PB he took while under extreme stress in the Gulf may have permanently damaged his central nervous system. "I don't know. I am not a doctor," he emailed a Gulf War Veterans net. "But my muscles sure do twitch an awful lot. It will occur for two or three days at a time. One area, like my leg, this one muscle just twitching along. Then, a week later, my left tricep, serious twitching. Then my eyelid. What the hell is going on with me? Oh well, who knows. God knows I don't, and neither do my doctors. If I am wrong someone please correct me."

Instead of a correction, this vet received corroboration from Vietnam and Gulf War veteran, Jim Chamberlain. While attending Physician's Assistant School, Chamberlain wrote back, "I learned that twitches such as you describe are often due to a depletion of phosphorus, in the phosphate compounds of ADP (Adenosine Diphosphate) and ATP (Adenosine Triphosphate) – both essential energy molecules for muscles and other cells."

* * *

The British "Defense" department calls PB a "Nerve Agent Pretreatment Set"– or NAPS. When it issued product license number 4537/0003 to produce NAPS for troops heading into the Gulf, a senior British defense officer later explained that lack of military medical staff and desert warfare training led to confusion in deciding what counter-measures to employ against the threat of Iraqi chemical and biological weapons.

"Our teams were not geared for war in the desert," he told the *London Telegraph*. Since British forces left Libya nearly 20 years before, training in desert warfare has been largely lacking. Or, as the British officer put it: "We had gone off the boil."

Nobody in the British command wanted a repeat of the fly-borne diseases that had ravaged British soldiers as they pursued Rommel across North Africa in 1941. Soon after landing in the Saudi desert, the 1st British Armoured Division and other UK units purchased local pesticides and began spraying their insect-plagued camps with pesticides derived from the same organophosphates used in chemical weapons.

But coordination collapsed between the Royal Army Medical Corps, front-line forces, environmental health teams and chemical warfare decontamination units. "We had to call up doctors serving with the Territorial Army, and some of the environmental health and decontamination teams were from countries as diverse as Canada, Rumania, and Czechoslovakia," said a retired British officer. "There was little evaluation of local pesticide packaging that gave little indication as to how those products were to be used."

The result was disaster. By late February, 1997, as many as 1,500 former UK servicemen and women (roughly two percent of the British forces who took part in Desert Storm) said they were sick as a result of their time in the Gulf.

At that time, Permanent Ministry of Defense Under Secretary Sir Richard Mottram, was still handling "new, and very distressing cases." One officer told Sir Mottram that he had been diagnosed with multiple sclerosis after serving in the Gulf. "He said he didn't think anything more about the connection with the Gulf," said Sir Mottram, "until he discovered that the man he shared his tent with had died of Alzheimer's disease at the age of 40."

Like many other ailing veterans, and a growing number of medical researchers, RAF chemical defense specialist Richard Turnbull believes that the allied command "used us as guinea pigs for new drugs" and chemical-weapons testing. Turnbull feels that both chemical warfare agents and experimental drugs like NAPS are responsible for his illness.

"I feel we were subject to a chemical attack that affected us," he says today. "As a service-man, I can accept that, it's my job. But I believe more damage was done due to experimentation by our government. Many people got sick after taking some of the drugs. I came down with a high fever, I was sweating excessively. I actually stopped breathing a couple of times."

After battling his illness and the defense ministry for three years, Turnbull was amazed by the elaborate denials concocted by the British bureaucracies. "We were always told that there was a 99.999 percent possibility of a chemical attack. We were expecting it. That was in our intelligence briefings. 'Inevitable' was the word used. And now they deny it."

* * *

A "French Connection" pointed the most damning fingers at pyridostigmine bromide's pivotal role in causing – or catalyzing – Gulf War Illness. Joe Viallis, a reporter for the independent Gulf War information bulletin, *Blazing Tattles*, broke the story after unearthing an Australian television broadcast stating that French military personnel in the Gulf region had been ordered by the French Commander-in-Chief not to take the pyridostigmine bromide tablets distributed to other NATO troops.

The October, 1995, Australian Channel 10 news item further noted that since the end of the Gulf War, not a single soldier among thousands of returning French legionnaires had reported any known symptoms of the Gulf War Illness which, at the time of the broadcast, was afflicting more than 90,000 other allied troops.

When Viallis checked with French authorities, the French Military Attaché in Australia confirmed that not a single French soldier or airman had contracted the Gulf War Illness. Viallis also learned that the French contingent numbered about the same as their British counterparts. But the British troops – who were ordered to take PB – had since taken ill at the same rate as US soldiers exposed to the same experimental drug.

"For any scientist or veteran, the fact that the French should be completely clear of Gulf War Syndrome... has huge and potentially horrifying implications," Viallis wrote. "After all, the French ate the same food, drank the same water, breathed the same air and trudged through hundreds of miles of the same desert. They also fired much the same weapons at much the same targets. So what were the additional environmental variables which made the French unique in their ability to completely withstand the deadly Gulf War Syndrome? The truth is there were none at all, save for the experimental American 'cocktail' inoculations and tablets."

On the day the French PB story was broadcast in Australia, a British military doctor interviewed on ITN TV World News stated that in her view, 99 percent of UK veterans' problems could be traced back to "cocktails" of anti-germ warfare inoculations, and anti-nerve gas tablets forcibly administered to military personnel in the Gulf region.

The British and Australian broadcasts were not aired in the United States, but Dr. Garth Nicholson, an American researcher in the forefront of GWI treatment, contacted the French Army Representative at INSERM, the French equivalent of the US National Institute of Health.

Nicholson learned that "one of the reasons given for the French not using experimental vaccines, anti-nerve agents or other experimental drugs in Desert Storm was that the French Medical Corps had been burned in Vietnam for using experimental drugs, as well as for their questionable use of some commonly used drugs. Since that war, Nicholson notes, the French military has been very careful about administering drugs. "Since Indochina, the apparent policy of the French Medical Corps has been to be on the safe side when it comes to prophylactic use of experimental drugs or excessive use of commonly used drugs."

Their initial deployment put the Foreign Legion's 9th Light Armor Division on the far western flank of Desert Shield, almost 400 kilometers from the nearest oil well fire and 200 kilometers from the nearest SCUD missile attacks. Randy Riggins, an American veteran whose unit supported the French before and during the ground war, points out that the Iraqi elements opposite the 9th "were widely dispersed in small units, and were far from being front line, well trained troops. The idea that these units had CW weapons is minute."

But the French did not stay "way out west." When the ground assault kicked off, 7,000 men of the 6th Light Armored raced 150 kilometers to cut off the retreating Iraqi troops and capture an airfield at as Salman. The only French casualties were two killed and 25 wounded from allied air strikes which sent cluster bombs exploding in their ranks. Despite such unneighborly "friendly fire," the thin French line soon spread across a third of Iraq.

Unfortunately for Riggins, his unit "left the French and the far west two days after the ground war started, heading for Objective GOLD. Their mission: demolish ammunition storage bunkers at a place called Khamisiyah.

By then, Riggins continues, "the 6th French Light Armor Division had obtained their objectives near as-Salman, about 175 kilometers NE of Rafha where we started. The French went little further north from here. My unit, continued another 200 kilometers (not as the crow flies) where my unit and elements of the 82nd ended up near the Euphrates River and the city of Nasiriyah."

According to Riggins, after destroying the Iraqi bomb dump at Talil Airfield, about 40 percent of the 307th was within 50 kilometers of Khamisiyah when 100 ammunition bunkers and 43 storage warehouses were destroyed. "There were no French units within 150 kilometers of these massive explosions which, as far as I know, was the largest combat engineer demolitions in U.S. history."

* * *

PB was not the only drug to sicken soldiers. The Pentagon directed that military personnel heading for the Gulf receive as many as 17 different live viral and dead bacterial vaccines simultaneously, including polio, cholera, hepatitis B, adenovirus, influenza, measles, mumps, rubella, meningococcus, plague, rabies, tetanus, diphtheria, typhoid, yellow fever, anthrax and the experimental botulinum toxoid.

Though their combat effectiveness against bio-attack remains in scientific doubt, vaccinations cannot protect against chemical weapons. They are only meant to protect against specific biological weapons. But the bacillus anthracis favored as a weapon by Iraqi forces is incredibly hardy. Just before the ground war in the Gulf, a live anthrax botulism was found in a capsule confiscated from a German Army Officer in 1918.

A US Navy memorandum assured commanders that its anthrax vaccine is "Routinely administered to Veterinarians, Cattle workers, and research personnel." To be effective, six doses of vaccine must administered over a year and a half. Among the veterans who took the Pentagon's anthrax vaccine and responded to a senate survey, 85 percent were told they could not refuse it; 43 percent experienced immediate side effects. Only one in every four women to whom anthrax was administered was warned of potential pregnancy risks.

Like the anthrax shots given to US troops, their botulism vaccine was produced by the Michigan Department of Health. Intended to protect against five of seven neurotoxins, the botulism vaccine was not licensed and could only be used as an Investigational New Drug.

Under US law, unapproved vaccines can only be administered by the DoD under an Investigational New Drug process. This procedure legally requires that individuals about to be administered an investigational drug must give her or his consent after being informed of the potential risks and benefits of the product, orally and in writing. Patients must then "choose freely" whether or not to participate. The Investigational New Drug law further stipulates that all investigational drugs must be distributed under carefully controlled conditions ensuring that safety and effectiveness can be fully evaluated.

Despite these legal strictures, during the preparatory stages of Desert Shield, the Pentagon rushed to review experimental drugs and vaccines. At a meeting of the Informed Consent Waiver Review Group on December 31, 1990, a representative from the FDA's Center for Biologics Evaluation and Research expressed concern about the existing supply of anthrax vaccine, which was nearly two decades old. The FDA advised DoD that there would not be time to adequately test the botulism vaccine for efficacy. The watchdog drug agency added that the vaccine's effectiveness against inhaled anthrax remains unknown.

But FDA safety tests were not completed until after the air war had commenced in late January, 1991. To be effective, the recommended schedule for immunization calls for a series of two additional injections given two and 12 weeks after the first, followed by a booster shot 12 months after the initial shot. This lengthy protocol was not followed for the approximately 150,000 US military personnel who were eventually inoculated with the anthrax vaccine. Nor were pregnant personnel warned that the vaccine's Michigan Department of Public Health manufacturer did not know if the anthrax shots were safe for them or their offspring.

British military authorities also defied standard medical procedures by ordering multiple vaccinations given on the "hurry up." Defense Minister Earl Howe and the Countess of Mar found that some British servicemen were given up to five doses of anthrax treatment, designed to be spread over nine months, in barely three weeks. Their claims were supported by documents disclosed by UK veterans Ray Bristow and Shaun Rusling, as well as senior officers at the MoD. The British injections included a serum that the US military considered too dangerous to be administered to American personnel.

According to an MoD memorandum on the "UK Vaccination Program," the anthrax vaccine produced by the

Public Health Laboratory and the Center for Applied Micro-biology and Research was intended to be given in four shots at three, seven and 32 week intervals. Instead, some soldiers were given three vaccinations in three weeks, plus two extra anthrax shots included in other biological warfare vaccines. In addition to an anthrax overdose given to 150,000 British troops, British medical person-nel also administered a Pertussis adjuvant – hopefully to enhance the effect of the hastily given anthrax vaccine.

British troops were inoculated against four known biological warfare agents: anthrax, Pertussis, bubonic plague and botulinum toxin. But many UK veterans say they were also injected with an additional "five or six" secret vaccinations.

American GIs were also inoculated with the botulism vaccine known to cause unwanted side-effects in many recipients. An FDA reviewer examining DoD's application for use of the botulinum toxoid in the Persian Gulf observed that in 1973, the Centers for Disease Control had considered halting distribution of the botulism vaccine because of the large number of individuals who reacted negatively to the injections. The FDA reviewer added that "there are no efficacy data in humans" inoculated with guesstimated dosages derived from guinea pigs. But potency testing suggested that the experimental vaccine would not be effective against two of the five known botulism toxins.

Even worse, the effects of this "prescription only" botulism vaccine on pregnant women had not been studied prior to its injection into the bloodstreams of British, American, Canadian and Anzac troops during the Persian Gulf War. The FDA's Informed Consent Waiver Review Group recommended that pregnant women be excluded from receiving the vaccine and that information about the vaccine be "posted at places where vaccine is administered."

But DoD demurred, arguing that pregnant women would be at greater risk from exposure to botulism toxins than to the same bugs injected in a vaccine. Instead of excluding pregnant women, the FDA agreed to tacking a sentence onto the vaccine's information sheet stating: "If you are pregnant, it is not known if this vaccine will hurt the unborn baby, however, most vaccines do not."

During a pivotal meeting on December 31, 1990, DoD officials agreed that the controversial botulism vaccine would be administered by trained health care personnel. The Pentagon's people also agreed that information on the vaccine's risks and possible side-effects would be given orally "at minimum, and in written form if feasible, to all personnel receiving the vaccine." When faced by skeptical FDA questioning, the desperate DoD officials retreated, saying that at least verbal information would be provided to each person receiving the vaccine.

Among American personnel who took anti-botulism plague vaccines and responded to a post-war questionnaire, 88-

percent were told not to turn it down; 35 percent suffered side effects. None of the women given botulinum toxoid were told of pregnancy risks. One government report admits that the prescription-only plague vaccine's "safety remains unknown."

Injecting the immune system with dead anthrax, polio or plague germs is intended to raise the recipient's level of antibody recognition and resistance. As their dosage protocols indicate, all vaccination programs require repeated injections given over months to build up the body's defenses. But American GIs received only one or two inoculations of botulism vaccine, starting seven days after the onset of the of the air war – dosages too low and too late to protect them against a plague attack.

This timing was sufficient, however, to make many people sick. After getting his hands on the data sheet for the American-made plague vaccine, which the British call "Cutter," Terry Walker noted that the directions warned of "accentuated side-effects" if plague shots were given with cholera or typhoid injections.

"When I got my Cutter shot," Walker relates, "it was at exactly the same time as I got the second anthrax and whooping cough shots and I was also taking pyridostigmine bromide. The effect of all these shots at the same time was to put me on cloud nine for about 24 hours. In fact I was walking around and I could not feel my feet touching the floor; other people got really sick and bad stomach cramps."

Though approved by the FDA in 1971, the botulinum toxoid is still listed as an investigational drug. The British military eventually injected 8,000 soldiers with the American-made plague vaccine.

* * *

When it comes to germ warfare "antidotes," many Iraqi soldiers apparently felt that the "cure" was worse than any possible bite. While combing battlefields west of Kuwait City, my Earthtrust companions and I found thousands of discarded vials from Iraqi nerve gas antidote kits strewn across the desert. Maybe they'd picked up on Alexis Shelikoff's remarks. It was the considered opinion of this virologist and director of research at Salk Institute's biowar lab that "No physician would recommend that you subject yourself to a live virus vaccine."

Nevertheless, US personnel were reportedly given simultaneous vaccines for cholera, polio, typhoid fever, meningitis, Pertussis, tetanus, diphtheria, yellow fever, hepatitis B and influenza. Two experimental vaccines referred to in medical records as VAC-A1 and VAC-A2 were also administered, along with "investigational" anthrax and plague vaccines. The effects of this potent but little-known "cocktail" were further heightened by repeated, eight-hour doses of the experimental drug, pyridostigmine bromide.

The National Vaccine Information Center, which helped write the National Childhood Vaccine Injury Act of 1986 to insure federal compensation for individuals injured by mandated vaccines, has long criticized the simultaneous administration of multiple viral and bacterial vaccines.

"The question that must be answered immediately," said NVIC co-founder and president Barbara Loe Fisher, "is whether a significant minority of Gulf War veterans responded with immune suppression to the potpourri of live viral and killed bacterial vaccines given to them and were subsequently vulnerable to further immune and neurological damage when they were given drugs and came into contact with environmental toxins in the Gulf."

Soon after the allied "victory" in the Gulf, evidence mounted that the forced administration of pyridostigmine bromide and experimental vaccines had permanently sickened tens of thousands of soldiers by working alone or in combination with exposure to chemical or biological weapons unleashed by Iraqi forces and allied bombing attacks.

As Whitehall and Washington scrambled to suppress these findings and deny the claims being made by tens of thousands of suffering soldiers who had served in their employ, an equally explosive story threatened to expose the lie of a bloodless allied victory.

CHAPTER 13

SUFFER THE CHILDREN

Gaunt with hunger, wracked by coughing and diarrhea, they stare vacantly past their teachers with the fixed, "thousand-yard stares" of veteran combat survivors. Girl or boy, the pictures they draw invariably showed the same scene: a line of child-scale airplanes filling the top of the page, dropping bombs on the houses below...

"The children strive to understand what they saw," reporter Evelyn Leopold told readers of the *Manchester Guardian*. "Planes bombing, houses collapsing, soldiers fighting, blood, mutilated and crushed bodies. The children fight to forget what they heard: people screaming, desperate voices, planes, explosions, crying people. They are haunted by the smell of gunfire, fires and burned flesh. Many children are still struggling with the memories of what they touched: remains of planes, blood, carrying dead bodies and wounded relatives."

At night, Leopold continued, millions of Iraq's children would go to bed remembering "the terrible, shaking ground and the prospect of the whole family being buried in the ruins of the house." Along with the trauma, grief, loss and lack of prospects came a deeper, more persistent fear that it would all start again...

Three days after the cease-fire reopened Baghdad to outsiders, Canadian physician Dr. Eric Hoskins led a Harvard Medical Study Team into Iraq. Stunned health workers found survivors "like the living dead." After examining hundreds of dazed children, Professor Magne Raundalen of the University of Bergen found "they have eradicated all their feelings and have no joy."

Almost six million children experienced bombing at close range; one in every four children lost their homes in what Hoskins, after an extensive tour of Iraq, described as the "most intensive suburban bombing" in history. Nearly two thirds of the children interviewed by the study team believed they would not live to become adults.

A team of psychologists were among 87 professional health and social workers who accompanied Hoskins on his second of three visits. Though all were veterans with decades of war experience in Uganda, Sudan and Mozambique, the war-trauma specialists were appalled to find the children of Iraq to be "the most traumatized children of war ever described." Likening the physically and emotionally damaged residents to the survivors of Hiroshima, the psychologists found that three quarters of the children interviewed felt sad and unhappy. Four out of five expressed the fear of losing their family.

Along with other members of the Harvard Study Team, the psychologists visited 30 of Iraq's largest cities and rural areas.

Besides inspecting 92 hospitals, clinics, electrical, water and sewage plants, team members also conducted 9,000 random household surveys. Instead of the "smart bombs" and "surgical" war described by Schwarzkopf and his targeting staff, the stunned Harvard team found entire neighborhoods flattened by the bombing. Out in the countryside, crops, barns and grain silos had been strafed, and farm equipment was twisted into scrap by the same munitions used against tanks.

United States aircraft alone had flown 110,000 sorties against Iraq, dropping 88,000 tons of bombs on a country the size of California. Most of the bombs fell on Iraq's two biggest cities: Baghdad and the former capital, Basra. Despite allied assurances of surgically-aimed "smart bombs" targeting Saddam Hussein's Republican Guard and command centers, almost all aerial munitions were free-falling bombs dropped from high altitudes. Among the seven percent of guided "smart" bombs, one in four missed their intended targets. Mass-deployed, dumb "iron bombs" fared far worse, causing widespread damage beyond the suburban communication, electrical, water and sewage facilities they were aimed at.

But even the smartest robots kill without compassion. The first made-for-television images of the 42 day air war showed the cross-hairs of a stealth aircraft's laser centered on the rooftop of the Iraqi Ministry of Defense. Seconds later, a 2,000 pound bomb plunged out of the darkness over Baghdad and blew the building apart. Hundreds of military news reporters watching the videotape in Schwarzkopf's Saudi Arabian briefing room laughed nervously, trying to connect this Nintendo game with the deaths of hundreds of office workers. While Pentagon briefing officials stressed that coalition targeters were taking great pains to minimize injury to civilians in heavily populated areas, tens of thousands of women, children and elderly civilians were soon dying in a push-button war ending in real slaughter.

As the Institute for Peace and International Security's Paul Walker would later write in his "Myth of Surgical Bombing," the sheer weight of explosives expended over Iraq and Kuwait, "tends to undermine any assumption of surgical strikes." More than 3,000 bombs, including 200 Tomahawk cruise missiles fired from ships offshore, struck downtown Baghdad.

The numbers are numbing. Among the quarter million additional bombs dropped by allied aircraft, between 60,000 and 80,000 were cluster-bomb canisters. Each of these maiming weapons scattered hundreds of "bomblets" over a wide area. Another 170,000 weapons were 500, 750, 1,000 and 2,000 pound free-falling "iron bombs." Artillery shells from battleships and rocket launchers contributed an additional 20,000 to 30,000 tons of high explosives.

Massive amounts of phosphorous fire bombs and napalm were also used to ignite oil-filled trenches, as well as Iraqi troop concentrations in Iraq and Kuwait. While at least one American officer refused to call artillery strikes on the Great Burgan, explaining that "good guys don't wear black hats," tactical support "jump jets" used napalm with great effect against the central Iraqi command dug into Kuwait's biggest oil field.

Besides consuming large stocks of aging ammunition, the Gulf War was also used as an open-air laboratory to test new NATO weapons against human targets. Fuel Air Explosives were an immediate "success". Packing the punch of a tactical nuclear warhead without any residual radioactive fallout, FAEs spray nearly a ton of gasoline-like ethyl oxide in a fine mist over the target. When the aerosol cloud is touched off, the resulting shock wave is powerful enough to suck all of the oxygen out of the air, while flash-frying all living creatures within an area of 50,000 square feet. The explosion's extreme overpressure can detonate pressure-sensitive mines, even as it ruptures the eardrums and internal organs of every creature within range. Desert minefields were also detonated by dropping 15,000 pound "daisy cutters" left over from the Vietnam war.

As Walker writes: "What all of this means to anyone who thinks about the numbers is simply that the bombing was not a series of surgical strikes but rather an old fashioned mass destruction. This is not surgical warfare in any accurate sense of the term and more importantly in the sense that was commonly understood by the American public."

B-52s cruising almost unchallenged through the stratosphere carried out 30 percent of the bombing campaign. Flying out of bases in the Indian Ocean's Diego Garcia, Spain, the United Kingdom, the United States and Saudi Arabia, each of the eight-engine bombers released between 40 and 60, 750 and 500 pound bombs. In raids reminiscent of attacks against Cambodia during the Vietnam war, a single formation of these heavy bombers could obliterate a "box" more than half-a-mile wide by about two miles long.

"The targets we are going after are widespread. They are brigades, and divisions and battalions on the battlefield. It's a rather low density target," US Air Force General McPeak explained. "...carpet bombing is not my favorite expression. Now is it a terrible thing? Yes. Does it kill people? Yes."

B-52s were used against chemical and industrial storage areas, airfields, troop encampments, and Iraq's former capital. The *Los Angeles Times* reported that the air war had brought to Basra "a hellish nighttime of fires and smoke so dense that witnesses say the sun hasn't been clearly visible for several days at a time." The paper reported that entire city blocks had been leveled, leaving "bomb craters the size of football fields and an untold number of casualties." Raw sewage submerged the streets of Basra and poured into Baghdad's rivers.

The Geneva Protocol's prohibition against area bombing was no consolation to more than 200,000 Iraqi conscripts who were systematically cut-off, killed and later bulldozed into 49 mass graves. Nor were the dazed and dying citizens of Basra and Baghdad reassured by misleading reports of "surgical strikes."

When the border that had kept Chaplin and I from reaching Baghdad reopened, UN observers fanned out through the Tigris River valley. The "cradle of Western civilization" is also the principle source of the entire region's drinking and irrigation water. After finding once life-giving waters contaminated by radioactive and chemical fallout from the bombing of nuclear reactors and Saddam's principal nerve gas factory at Samarra, just 25 miles upwind, the UN inspectors declared the Tigris "dead."

General Dougan's stated intention to leave Iraq in a preindustrial state was achieved by systematically destroying the infrastructure on which the country's civilian population depends. United Nations inspectors entering the country just after the war declared that the allies' aerial scorched earth campaign had left Iraq in "a near apocalyptic" condition.

At least 21 power generating plants and hydroelectric dams were attacked, some by more than 20 bombs. Water treatment, pumping and distribution systems, and reservoirs were destroyed – along with sewage treatment plants, telephone relay stations and transmission facilities, buses and bus depots, bridges, railroads, highways and highway overpasses, trains, trucks and private vehicles.

Inspection teams found that oil wells, oil pumps, pipelines, refineries, storage tanks and gasoline filling stations had also been bombed. So had factories producing cars, textiles and infant formula. Other food processing, storage and distribution facilities were also demolished in a campaign that targeted a civilian population held virtually prisoner by the "Butcher of Baghdad's" military and secret police.

The first winter after the Gulf war was harsh. Short-circuits had sent surges of electricity through the nation's power grid, frying transformers and irrigation pumps throughout the Tigris-Euphrates river valley.

When the pumps failed and irrigation floodgates were ruptured by bombs, the Persian Gulf came surging into the low-lying farming delta, turning fertile soil to salt. The war's "end" was followed by the catastrophic failure of Iraq's harvests. While Saddam Hussein's inner circle continued to eat well, for Iraq's 14 million people – nearly half of whom were under the age of 15 – one meal per day without protein became the norm.

"Biowar?" asked Edward Pearce in the Manchester Guardian. "If you bust the water supply and sewage plants of a country...cholera is what you get. We know about cholera but we destroy electricity plants and power supplies and we deny by embargo the means for immediate repair. That is different from deliberately seeding and spreading the cholera virus only in the most etiolated fashion."

By the first November following history's most intensive urban bombing campaign, typhoid, brucellosis, hepatitis, gastroenteritis, meningitis, hepatitis and cholera were endemic throughout Iraq. The rates of rare cancers and birth defects were also rising sharply. Preventable diseases like polio and measles surged, and children with treatable diabetes and leukemia continued dying from lack of medicine.

Since the cease-fire, Hoskins and his team found that deaths among children under five had jumped nearly fourfold. By March, 1991, 55,000 Iraqi children under the age of five had died. Close to a million children were malnourished and more than 100,000 were starving to death. Hoskins predicted that if sanctions prohibiting food and medicine from entering warshattered Iraq were not immediately lifted, at least another 170,000 children under five would die in the coming year from the deliberate targeting of the country's civilian infrastructure.

Commented Pearce: "Putting aside everything done by his recent enemies to build the man up, arm him, and turn this same obvious villain to useful account, the struggle against him falls upon innocent heads."

* * *

Ramsey Clark also toured Iraq. The former Attorney General under President Lyndon Johnson was gathering evidence for an International War Crimes Tribunal that would later charge CENTCOM and the Bush administration with war crimes against the people of Iraq. Like Hoskins and his Harvard medical team, UN inspectors and the unnerved psychologists, Clark was stunned to find supposedly spared neighborhoods flattened by coalition bombing. *Why did they shoot up the farms?* he wondered.

Clark's Citizen's Commission counted on moral integrity more than legal weight. Its distinguished members included the Panamanian president of the National Human Rights Commission in Panama, Pakistan's former deputy prime minister, a former Japanese judge imprisoned for opposing Japan's invasion of China, a former director of the Center for Constitutional Rights, a Jordanian Parliamentarian, an Egypt medical doctor held as a political prisoner for 14 years, a former director of the National Conference of Black Lawyers and a representative for the International Indian Treaty Council at the UN Commission of Human Rights.

Also included on the panel were Puerto Rico's Secretary for Foreign Relations, an Arusha High Court magistrate, the Canadian president of the United Steel Workers of America, a Quebec attorney, a member of the New York Newspaper Guild's Executive Committee, a former Malaysian Auditor General, several lawyers, a former Chief Justice in India's High Court, a Vietnam vet who had led the protest against US attacks on Iraq, and a former Lieutenant Colonel in the German Army,

Over the following year, this citizen's commission heard testimony from other commissions of inquiry held throughout the US and Southwest Asia. Eyewitness statements, photographs, videotapes, expert reports and analyses were compiled in thick volumes of evidence showing the havoc wreaked against a hostage and nearly defenseless nation.

* * *

Many visiting doctors were by then preoccupied with the effects of malnutrition and spreading epidemics of waterborne diseases throughout Iraq. Among them was an epidemiologist who specialized in infectious disease with Austria's Yellow Cross. While making the first of what would become many forays through the ruins of what had been the world's first nation, Dr. Siegwart Horst Gunther stopped on the bomb-pocked highway from Amman to stretch his legs in the desert. Attracted by some shell fragments, Gunther pocketed several pieces of twisted metal and continued on his journey.

On returning to Berlin in July, 1993, with the depleted uranium souvenir shell in his luggage, Gunther took the spent DU round to a lab to see if German technology had been involved in its manufacture. But when monitored with radiation detectors, the DU "bullet" gave a radioactivity reading of 11 to 12 microsieverts per hour.

German police garbed in full protective gear arrived in short order. After seizing the projectile for safe containment, the cops grabbed Gunther for illegally "releasing ionizing radiation." Gunther was arrested for "exposing the populace to radioactive material." Upset German authorities claimed that one DU projectile emitted more radiation in five hours than the 50 millisieverts allowed annually under German regulations.

Later that year, during another visit to Iraq, Gunther noticed that many of the hundreds of children dying each week in the southern part of the country had collected shells similar to the one he had found. The symptoms he was seeing resembled the strange illnesses coming to light among US Gulf war veterans and their children. It looked to Gunther as if many youngsters with huge, swollen bellies were suffering not just from malnutrition, but from kidney and liver failure.

By 1993, typhoid, gastroenteritis and cholera were still endemic across Iraq. Meningitis, hepatitis, malaria and polio rates were also up sharply.

In September of that year, Saddam's army also stepped up their brutal suppression of some 10,000 suspected Shi'ite rebels, and hundreds of thousands of marsh-dwellers living on floating islands in southern Iraq. Washington complained that Baghdad was "systematically destroying" the region's ecology in order to exterminate "marsh Arabs" who had inhabited that part of Iraq since Sumerian times.

Middle East Watch's Andrew Whitely revealed that in their pursuit of simple fishers and reed-dwellers, the Iraqi Army had built earthworks to block the Tigris from replenishing the marshes. A canal had also been dug to drain water from the marshes into the Persian Gulf. Satellite photos confirmed that vast stretches of the confluence of the Tigris and Euphrates Rivers were being transformed into desert.

In malicious mimicry of the "poisoned earth" tactics practiced by the Soviet Army against the inhabitants of Afghanistan, Saddam also ordered the marshes poisoned by dumping toxic chemicals into tributaries and lakes.

On September 26, Shi'ite survivors told a *New York Times* reporter that an early morning attack by Iraqi artillery had landed shells with a thud, "not the usual explosion," sending up white clouds. Iraqi troops wearing gas masks attacked behind the barrage. Shi'ite rebels claimed that when they entered a disabled Iraqi armored troop carrier, they found battle orders calling for a chemical attack.

Rebel leaders provided a copy of the captured orders to the *Times*. Written in Arabic on the twenty-sixth of September, orders numbered 1-15 directed Iraqi soldiers to use chemical weapons to "retake the village." Unit commanders were reminded that "each soldier must be instructed on how to respond during the chemical attack." After the attack, when a few villagers returned for their belongings, they found nothing but withered and yellowed trees and plants. Their cats, dogs – even the birds and water snakes – had died. Human victims had been removed by Iraqi troops.

* * *

Dr. Gunther never saw the silent, dying marshes, but he did return to Iraq in time to witness a lambing season like none he had ever seen. As many as one in 10 newborn "kids" could not walk, or were born with distorted faces.

Between 350 and 800 tons of depleted uranium fragments still littered Gulf war battlefields around Basra and the deserts of Kuwait. Back at the US Army's Aberdeen Proving Ground, soils were found to be contaminated with radioactive DU toxins at a depth of nearly eight inches below a single corroding penetrator round. An Army study suggested that the poisons found saturating the Maryland soil could migrate further from their source.

Gunther had already guessed that rainwater was carrying depleted uranium particles into the groundwater in Iraq, and possibly into Kuwait. If so, chances were high that DU debris had infiltrated the food chain. "We must investigate all of this," the MD decided, "because this is affecting the children. They don't know if they are Iraqi or American, Muslim or Christian. They're just children."

* * *

In February, 1995, Iraqi news reports cited health statistics showing that Iraqis were experiencing high rates of birth defects, including eye disorders, mongolism, bone deformities, and brain and central nervous system disorders. The reports said that since the war, many children were dying of cancers and neurological disorders – and even more were suffering a bewildering variety of diseases.

Six months later, Iraq presented a study to the United Nations showing sharp increases in leukemia and other cancers, as well as other unexplained diseases around the Basra region. Iraqi scientists attributed some of the cancers to depleted uranium. Another study by Dr. Siegwart Gunther reported that DU projectiles "were gathered by children and used as toys." One little girl who collected 12 of the projectiles died of leukemia.

By late 1995, the Iraqi health ministry was reporting frightening increases in child leukemia and aplastic anemia. The number of congenital birth defects had also rocketed from eight percent before the war to 28 percent of newborns. Late-term miscarriages were also up sharply. Gunther's earlier observations were also proving correct: liver and kidney disease were now ranked as the fourth and fifth causes of death among children over the age of five.

But health ministry officials warned that the frightening figures were low because most Iraqi women no longer gave birth in hospitals, or were unable to take their children there for the most basic treatment. With the ongoing economic blockade making it nearly impossible to keep diagnostic equipment running, there was no way to confirm either the statistics or the diagnosis. The UN embargo also effectively denied sick children lifesaving or even pain-relieving treatment. Four years after the war's supposed cessation, children were dying in large numbers from failed immune systems and lack of food and safe drinking water.

Gunther was sure that the symptoms surfacing in Iraqi children could be linked to hundreds of tons of depleted uranium fired by allied tanks and warplanes. As Francisco Lopez Rueda, co-author of a 1993 GAO report on "uranium battlefields" noted, "Children are especially vulnerable to uranium poisoning because their cells are rapidly dividing. DNA-altering alpha rays from decaying uranium are also known to pass through the placenta into the developing fetus."

According to Rueda, if a child picked up a spent DU shell weighing two-thirds of a pound and held the shell close to her body for just one hour, she would receive the equivalent of 50 chest x-rays. "Now if a child has several of these and brings them home and puts them on a shelf, everybody in the room is getting irradiated at a low level."

By the spring of 1996, Gunther had taken German and Japanese film crews into Iraq to document his findings. "I am

~ 203 ~

very concerned about this," he told reporters. Five years after the war, Iraqi health officials were reporting alarming increases in rare and unknown diseases, mostly in children. Anecephaly, leukemia, carcinoma and cancers of the lung and digestive system were continuing their dramatic rise. So were late-term miscarriages and incidence of congenital disease and deformities in fetuses.

What about exposure to chemical and biological fallout? Shortly after the first bombing raids against Baghdad, members of the Gulf Peace Team who had bravely camped between the opposing armies fled to Jordan after a "chemical cloud" enveloped streets near the al Rasheed hotel. It was later found that cyanide, toxic organochlorines, nitrogen dioxide, dioxins and heavy metals had been released in massive quantities during tens of thousands of bombing raids.

* * *

Iraqi families were not the only civilians suffering the after-effects of the world's most toxic war. Within months of his country's liberation, Dr. Saleh al Harbi, an immunologist with Kuwait's Ministry of Public Health and director of the immunogenetics unit of Kuwait University Medical Center, reported that many people in Kuwait and Iran were suffering from what appeared to be illnesses relating to exposure to chemical and biological warfare agents.

"After the war we were getting diseases, respiratory diseases and unknown blood diseases such as leukemia, but not the typical kind, and for unknown reasons," Dr. Saleh said. "Birth-related problems increased dramatically after liberation."

Saleh al Harbi is currently working with US researchers looking into the causes of the many medical conditions that have plagued Kuwaitis since the war. A 1994 Defense Intelligence Agency report reveals that burning wells released approximately 2.5 million barrels of crude oil into the air, generating some 1,500 tons of particulates. Particles less than 10 microns in diameter are capable of deeply penetrating respiratory systems, the report warned, increasing risk of disease. Readings taken at three locations in Kuwait 16 months after the last oil fire was supposedly snuffed out, showed "particles in the hazardous diameter category were still present at levels significantly higher than prewar values."

Just after the war, the most commonly diagnosed conditions at Kuwaiti primary health care clinics were acute respiratory illness, headaches and skin and eye irritations. Children one to 12 years of age suffered the most from respiratory problems. From 1989 to a year after the war, deaths from respiratory and lung diseases were up more than 54 percent. Victims of heart failure increased by 43 percent.

During a 1994 conference on post-war environmental health problems in Kuwait, doctors Sabah al Mumin, Saleh al

Harbi, Jassim al Hassan and Fatima al Abdali pointed to what appeared to be increased instances of chemical sensitivity among the people of Kuwait, including multiple chemical sensitivity-(MCS) patients sick enough to require hospitalization. The researchers wondered if US troops exposed to unspecified toxins during the war, "which normally would have no effect on long term health," experienced a "synergistic effect...in the presence of some other environmental toxin – perhaps produced by the burning wells."

If this proved to be the case, the researchers went on, "information from Kuwait becomes extremely important for the US study since the secondary toxin exposure almost certainly was from a war related source. Moreover, such a mechanism implies the potential for long term health risks to the population of Kuwait, for there is no way of predicting at the present time what latent effects exposure of a large number of people to the secondary toxin or toxins may have."

These were not the findings Kuwait's rulers wanted to hear. Like other former members of the Kuwait Environmental Action Team, the Kuwaiti immunologist is under intense political pressure to suppress his embarrassing findings and concerns. "The authorities here are also standing with the Europeans and Americans' point of view, but we believe that this is something political," said Dr. Saleh. "I'm independent in mentioning this, and hopefully I will not get any threats from the superiors regarding this matter. They don't want the bad news and rumors to go around." Dr. Saleh al Harbi characterizes the syndrome as a form of multiple chemical sensitivity.

The people of Kuwait were not alone in their post-war misery. A follow-up survey found that fully 15 to 20 percent of the populations of Kuwait and Jordan currently suffer from GWI. This US study was independently confirmed by Dr. Charles Hinshaw, past president of the American Academy of Environmental Physicians.

* * *

In March, 1995, Harriet Leverett visited a neighborhood that had been a middle-class suburb of Baghdad before the war. The Amariyah shelter, an underground bunker built to shield more than 2,000 community residents, had been turned into a shrine for thousands of mourners. Some distraught mothers wore pictures of their dead daughters and sons around their necks.

Leverett learned that "When the missiles entered through the roof, exactly on target, the impact blew the doors shut, incinerating and drowning those inside in boiling water" from burst water mains. Flames and heat drove back would-be rescuers from the cement doors. Leverett, a grandmother participating in the Interfaith Pilgrimage for Peace and Life, stood outside the gutter shelter-turned-shrine, experiencing "the same sense of raw pain I had felt outside the crematories at Birkenau."

In December, 1996, Illinois resident Chuck Quilty and a group of Catholic volunteers calling themselves Voices In The Wilderness made their second trip into post-war Iraq bringing desperately needed medicines. Driving through Saddam City, a densely populated suburb of Baghdad, streets awash in raw sewage blurred through a haze of tears. Goats grazed on garbage heaped everywhere in the neighborhood after the city's fleet of garbage trucks became immobilized for lack of parts.

The pediatric ward at al Manaur children's hospital held too many mothers with "piercing, pain-filled eyes." Too often their emaciated, pain-wracked children were dying. Suffering on this scale exhausted Quilty. After meeting young Noora Talibi, he later told the readers of a Catholic newspaper: "Noora is in her third relapse with acute lymphoblastic leukemia, and there is no treatment available for her. Many children die from severe infections because there are no antibiotics. Many parents sell their homes to buy treatment for their sick children, only to discover no treatment is available."

In the cancer ward, youngsters who should have been in their most carefree years were dying at five and six-times their prewar numbers. Dr. Salma al-Haddad and her colleagues stood by helplessly, unable to medically intervene in the fear and pain of children like Dhuha (Sunrise), Khalid (Eternal) and Muhammad. When Khalid's mother heard that there was no more medicine, she beseeched the Americans saying, "But my son, he is going to die."

What possible good could come from making so many children suffer? "It's a pleasing fiction that the economic sanctions on Iraq mean that its sadistic dictator is living on bread and water and running out of aspirin," wrote columnist Colman McCarthy. "He isn't. No evidence exists that Saddam is personally hurting."

The following spring, Quilty again risked imprisonment and heavy fines to make his third trip to war-ravaged Baghdad. The Catholic relief team found al Mansur in even more desperate straits. The hospital was out of nearly all therapeutic agents required to treat children, many of whom could be saved with a course of antibiotics. The $60,000 worth of donated medicines brought by the Voices In The Wilderness volunteers "was a drop in the ocean for the treatment of children's cancers," Quilty saw. Cancer had become as endemic among young Iraqi children as it was among Belarussian children of Chernobyl. Chuck Quilty and his Catholic companions wept when they learned that Mohammad had died two days before. Little Noora had succumbed to leukemia two weeks previously. Dhuha was at home, in a remission her doctor was sadly certain was only temporary. Khalid was even sicker, but still alive.

Their pediatrician, Dr. Salma al Hadid was in an untenable predicament. How should she apportion the few remaining medicines? Give them to the sickest, or to those more likely to live? "There is only one solution," Salma said. "End the sanctions."

Conditions were even worse in Basra. In one malnutrition ward, Dr. Tariq Habah Hassim told the Christian visitors that the only difference between him and his patients was a white coat. There are no supplies of any kind to treat helpless children or even clean mattresses which grew dirtier with the secretions of each frail victim. Even if some survived, Quilty realized that he was seeing an entire generation of children condemned to growing up "mentally and emotionally traumatized."

Quilty thought it strange that it was okay for Iraq to invade Khomeini's Iran, but not to invade Kuwait, a country with whom it had legitimate, long-standing and increasing grievances. Chicago priest, Father Bob Bossie, criticized the press blackout on the genocide of Iraq's children. Bossie had been a member of the 100-strong Gulf Peace Team that had interposed themselves between opposing armies in the desert.

In May, 1997, while the Voice In The Wilderness volunteers were being overwhelmed by human misery, Iraq's Minister of Health, Umeed Mubarak, protested to the UN that the mortality rate for children under the age of five had gone from 540 deaths per month before the embargo to the current rate of 5,600 per month. UN officials estimated that seven years of murderous sanctions against Iraq had resulted in the deaths of 600,000 children.

Air Force Brigadier General William Looney, commander in charge of the air patrols which prohibit Iraqi aircraft from flying below the 32nd parallel, responded to the plight of Iraqis by saying: "They know we own their country. We own their airspace. We dictate the way they live and talk. And that's what's great about America, right now. It's a good thing, especially when there is a lot of oil out there we need."

"Isn't Christianity largely a calling to human compassion on behalf of one's neighbors?" asked VIW's Steve Woolford. In September, 1997, a group of American humanitarians risked a dozen years in prison and one million dollar fines to deliver another $15,000 worth of medicines to Baghdad. One Baghdad surgeon told Detroit bishop Tom Gumbleton: "Can you imagine trying to do an operation without anesthesia or without muscle relaxants so the body will remain still?" At Baghdad's St. Raphael hospital, the director wept quietly after telling the Catholic delegation that for most people in Iraq, "hope was a thing of the past."

President George Bush with King Fahd of Saudi Arabia, November 21, 1990. Photograph courtesy of George Bush Presidential Library.

President George Bush with returning troops, June 8, 1991. Photograph courtesy of George Bush Presidential Library.

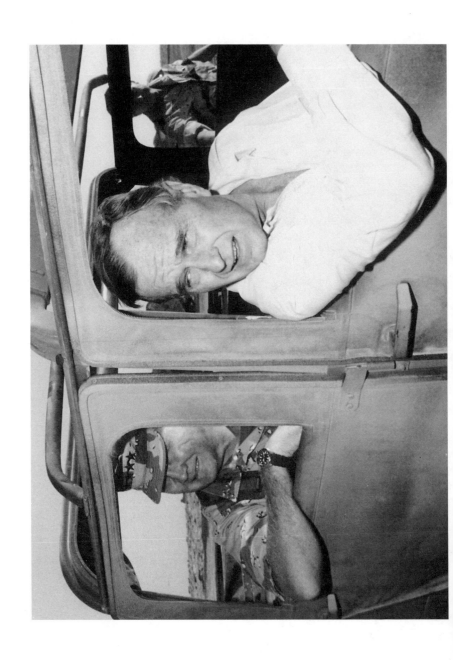

President George Bush with General Norman Schwarzkopf Jr.
Photograph courtesy of George Bush Presidential Library.

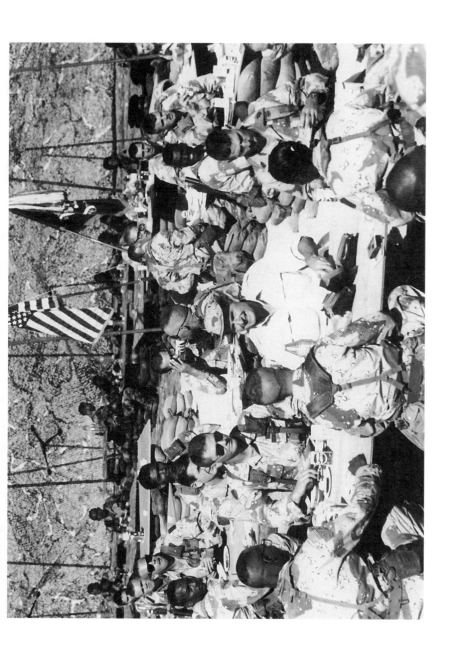

President George Bush with Troops, November 22, 1990. Photograph courtesy of George Bush Presidential Library.

Oil fires, Greater Burgan oil field, Kuwait. Photograph by William Thomas.

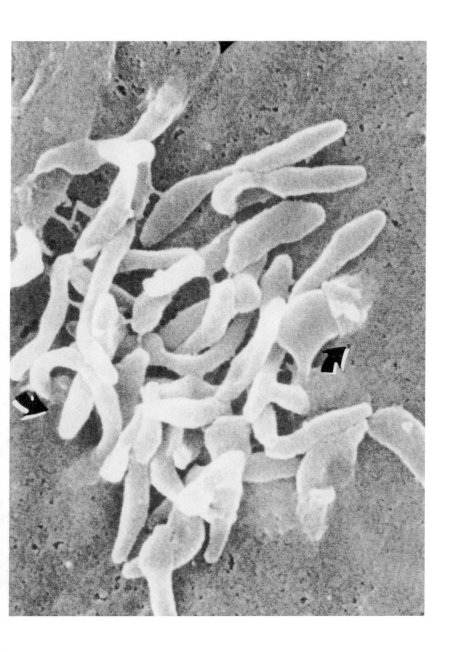

Mycoplasma Incognitus. Photograph courtesy of Dr. Joel Baseman of the University of Texas, Health Science Center at San Antonio.

Dhuha (Sunrise) and her mother, Al Mansur Hospital, Baghdad, December, 1996. March, 1997, the cancer had spread to her bone marrow and no treatment was available. Photograph courtesy of Chuck Quilty, Voices in the Wilderness.

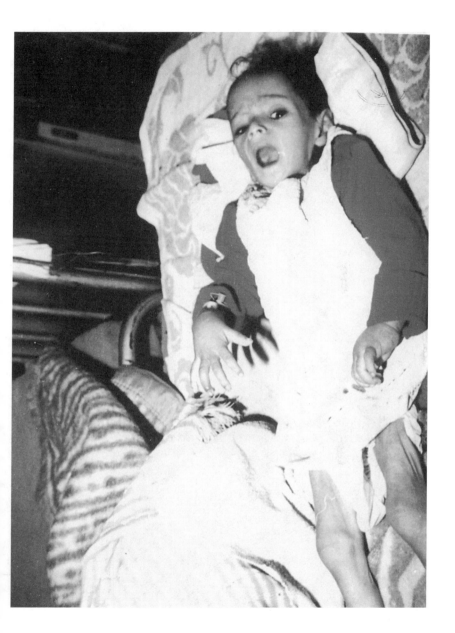

Nassar Feyath, about 1 year of age, at Basrah Pediatrics and Gynecology Hospital, December, 1996. He has severe malnutrition. His weight was 9.47 pounds and ideally would have been 22 pounds. Photograph courtesy of Chuck Quilty, Voices in the Wilderness.

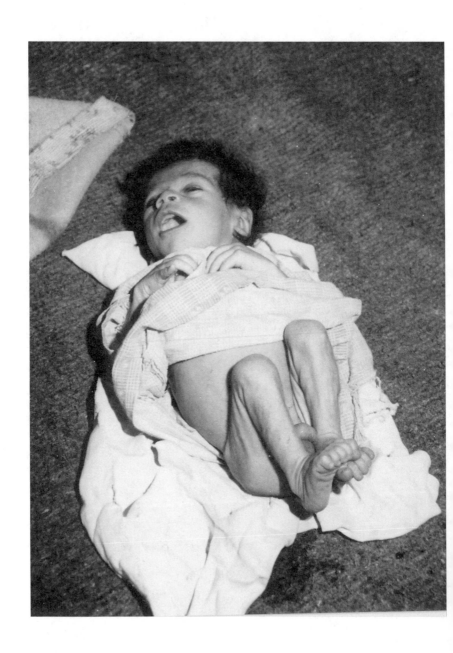

Hassam Dehie, 2 months, at Basrah P & G Hospital, March, 1997. He was malnourished and weighed 4.4 pounds. His ideal weight was 11 pounds. Photograph courtesy of Chuck Quilty, Voices in the Wilderness.

Bishop Thomas Gumbleton, Detroit, MI, and two friends at the orphanage of the Missionary Sisters of Charity in Baghdad, September, 1997. Photograph courtesy of Chuck Quilty, Voices in the Wilderness.

Desalination plant intake arms, al Khiran. Photograph by William Thomas.

Michael Bailey, Field Director, Earthtrust. Photograph by William Thomas.

Risky business: US soldier inspects Iraqi tank hit during battle in Great Burgan oil field. Photograph by William Thomas.

Michael Bailey, Field Director, Earthtrust. Photograph by William Thomas.

The world's biggest oil spill coming ashore on the Saudi Arabian coast. Photograph by William Thomas.

Great Blue Heron trapped in a pool of oil in the Kuwait desert.
Photograph by William Thomas.

Demolished airliner after tank battle at the Kuwait International Airport. Photograph by William Thomas.

CHAPTER 14

SEE NO EVIL

If a half-million dead or dying Iraqi children were not an acceptable news item for North American viewers, documented incidents of chemical-biological attack against US and UK soldiers in the Gulf threatened to expose the complicity of governments who had sold those weapons and production capabilities to Saddam Hussein.

Treason was a charge that came to many wounded soldiers' minds. Not to mention financial liabilities that would make the $280 million paid out to the American GI victims of Agent Orange look like parking meter change.

As reports of troubling post-war symptoms continued to mount, Dr. Gunnar Heuser proposed a universal protocol for diagnosing a disease loosely categorized as Persian Gulf Illness. A civilian physician specializing in chemical injury, Heuser called for an extensive series of tests aimed at analyzing symptoms of low-level chemical weapons, as well as other toxic impacts. Heuser's high tech brain scans, and more than a dozen tests of the central nervous, respiratory, autoimmune, hormonal and gastro-intestinal systems would cost about $13,000 per patient. Thorough radiation "body-burden" testing to determine the level of uranium byproducts in the lungs and other organs would add another $15,000 to the tab for each veteran tested.

But expenses would not end there. Albert Donnay, Executive Director for Multiple Chemical Sensitivity Referral & Resources estimated the costs for diagnosing chemical, biological and radiological exposures at a very conservative $30,000 per year in disability and medical benefits paid to each of just 100,000 sick veterans, and came up with $3 billion per year. If veterans in their mid-to-late twenties lived another 40 years, Donnay figured, the Pentagon's total liability could exceed $120 billion dollars.

Even measured against the US military's $265.3 billion arms budget request for 1998, (up $3 billion from the previous year despite the collapse of the former Soviet military machine and admission of some WARSAW pact nations into NATO), paying out such a large indemnity to ailing veterans would put a big crimp in future weapons procurement.

Such an admission of medical culpability and catastrophe would also certainly cool the enthusiasm of young women and men lining up outside recruiting centers for an education not fully described in armed forces brochures.

US and British Gulf policy might also suffer serious setbacks if the truth regarding Desert Storm ever came out. Would the governments of Kuwait, Saudi Arabia and other Arab emirates agree to back future "de-fanging" operations against dictators armed and encouraged by the West?

On the international scene, a message meant to intimidate future tyrants might have already backfired. Just how credible was a $300 billion nuclear "deterrent" if Baghdad ignored repeated warnings of nuclear retaliation for carrying out chemical attacks – and got away with it?

The whole simmering fiasco was a nightmare eclipsing Watergate, Irangate, Iraqgate and other recent abuses of presidential power. If Washington and CENTCOM admitted lying to their own soldiers about the pills they took and the attacks they endured, what would happen to morale among those still in uniform? How willing would volunteers be to carry out medical and military orders that could result not only in their own incapacitation, but serious injury to their children and spouses as well?

George Bush's successor was not about to ask those questions. In a military where loyalty counts far more than discomfiting truths, senior staff officers would not welcome a probe into their conduct by a draft-dodging president who knew not to inhale, but did not know how to salute. No wonder, Eddington says, that John Deutch, "one of Clinton's most trusted advisors, became intimately involved with the management of the cover-up."

That cover-up was underway before the shooting stopped. By the end of 1991, 2nd Marine Division was still awaiting the results of chemical and soil samples taken by Captain Johnson's team at the Sabbahiyah high school. As Eddington points out, the fact that these and other samples were never reported most likely indicates that they were "positive" for chemical agents. A further tip-off came when an officer involved in the Sabbahiyah mustard gas tests was repeatedly intimidated by DoD investigators for responding to Senate inquiries. The soldier was led to believe that his career was in jeopardy.

According to Eddington, sampling operations conducted during and after the war were conducted by special units controlled by Schwarzkopf's own staff, with "guidance" from Powell and the Joint Chiefs of Staff. In his ground breaking book, *Gassed In The Gulf*, the former CIA staffer identifies the personnel in unmarked battle dress taking soil samples in and around ammunition bunkers in Kuwait as members of a US Army Technical Escort Unit. Based at the Edgewood chemical warfare facility in Aberdeen, Maryland, these special units were responsible for the transport of chemical agents or munitions. In a mission reportedly dubbed, "Steel Box," other secret teams were responsible for identifying and recovering "Made In USA" munitions from Iraqi bunkers..

* * *

Even before war broke out in the Gulf, Washington's dealings with Saddam Hussein's germ warfare program came perilously close to being revealed by ABC TV's 20/20. Smelling a sensational scoop, in March, 1990, an ABC camera crew had descended on the officers of the International Security Group in Pompano Beach, Florida.

But the story proved hotter than ABC could handle. Though Ted Koppel and co-host Alan Friedman eventually aired three different segments detailing the role of the Product Ingredient Technology plant in Boca Raton, Florida, in arming Iraq, 20/20 never aired their full interview with security consultant Peter Kawaja.

Kawaja claims ABC executives told him his revelations, "might have toppled the US government." Operating under a government-issued code name, the security specialist had uncovered an eight-year string of shipments of biological agents from US manufacturers to Iraq. All had been approved by Washington. Kawaja believed that the sale of germ warfare pathogens, chemical agents and CBW production technology to a would-be enemy amounted to a betrayal of American lives.

The troubled agent informed the CIA, FBI and the US Customs service that chemical warfare agents were being made in Boca Raton. When Washington officials told him to stay on top of the situation and keep them informed, Kawaja was perfectly placed to carry out those directives.

As the head of security at the Product Ingredient Technology plant, he was already well acquainted with PIT's major investor, a former Iraqi architect named Dr. Ishan Barbouti. Shortly after signing a security contract with Barbouti, Kawaja received a letter from PIT instructing him to provide a cyanide detection system. One of the by-products from making cherry flavoring is ferric ferrocyanide, a chemical used to manufacture hydrogen cyanide.

Kawaja learned that in 1969, soon after the Ba'ath takeover in Iraq installed a peasant's son named Saddam Hussein as second-in-command, Barbouti had boogied out of Baghdad. The shadowy architect resurfaced several years later in Lebanon, before making his way to Rabta, Libya, where he claims to have designed Mu'ammar Qaddafi's German-built Pharma 150 chemical-weapons plant.

Between 1987 and 1989, three US companies also received the attention of Ishan Barbouti. TK-7 of Oklahoma City, Pipeline Recovery Systems of Dallas, and Product Ingredient Technology of Boca Raton all became Barbouti investments. They seemed innocuous enough. TK-7 made a fuel additive, the pipeline people made an anti-corrosive chemical that preserves pipes, and PIT produced food flavorings.

But Barbouti had sought these companies for some special applications. TK-7's fuel formulas could extend the range of liquid-fueled SCUDs. And Pipeline Recovery knew how to coat pipes so they could carry the highly hazardous liquids found in nuclear reactors and chemical weapons plants.

Besides PIT, Barbouti also owned other specialty chemical companies. Cross Link was headquartered in Belgium. An engineering company in Frankfurt held a $552 million contract to build airfields in Iraq. The mysterious architect also owned about $100 million worth of real estate and oil-drilling equipment in Texas and Oklahoma.

Assisting Barbouti in these ventures were business partners James Tully and Jack Brennan. Both Brennan and Tully had been involved in a $181 million deal to supply uniforms for the Iraqi army. The uniforms were made cheaply by using forced or indentured labor in Ceausescu's Rumania. Other Barbouti partners included Watergate felon John Mitchell and Sarkis Soghnalian. Soghnalian had introduced Saddam Hussein to Gerald Bull, inventor of the so-called "Supergun." Currently serving a prison term for selling 103 military helicopters to Iraq, the Lebanese arms trader was considered by the super-security firm, Wackenhut, to be a "valuable client."

It was New Orleans exporter Don Seaton who introduced Barbouti to Wackenhut. Also assisting Barbouti with his US investments was a business associate of Seaton's named Richard Secord. The former US Army general turned war-profiteer had been deeply entangled in the Iran-Contra scandal.

Barbouti used the Middle Eastern Bank of Commerce and Credit International as his banking "middleman". The corrupt BCCI would later be featured on the covers of America's biggest news magazines for laundering drug money, bribing high-ranking officials, arms trafficking, fraud, financing CIA and Mossad covert operations, selling nuclear technologies, managing prostitution, facilitating income tax evasion and illegal immigration and smuggling. Only George Bush's alleged dealings with BCCI would be omitted from that coverage.

Shell corporations, bankers' confidentiality, buy-back arrangements, kick-backs, bribes, witness intimidation and the use of offshore banking havens enabled BCCI to commit its many crimes. Payments to prominent political figures in most of the 73 countries in which BCCI operated also helped its officers evade prosecution and call in favors as needed.

At the time of Barbouti's dealings in Houston and Boca Raton, BCCI had just opened branches in both cities. In late April, 1990, Hill and Knowlton, the giant public relations firm that had ensured American intervention in Kuwait with the fake incubator story, was hired to defend BCCI against charges that this distinctly malodorous bank also owned First American, a bank used by another unsavory character named Manuel Noriega.

The world of deceit can be as small as a cesspool. Barbouti met with Richard Secord in Florida on several occasions. The retired general-turned-arms-dealer became partners with a Washington businessman named James Tully, and Jack Brennan, a former Marine Corps colonel and longtime aide to Richard

Nixon. Brennan later became director of administrative operations in President Bush's office.

* * *

In the "old boy's network" that runs this planet for profit, every contact eventually makes a circle. In late 1989, Barbouti met with Ibrahim Sabawai in London. Saddam Hussein's half-brother became excited about Pipeline Recovery's products. The European head of Iraqi intelligence urged Barbouti to rush the company's special pipe-coating technology to Iraq so that it could be in place by early 1990.

Barbouti began pressing all three firms to ship not only their products but also their manufacturing technology to corporations he owned in Europe. From there, he told the American businessmen, their products and machinery would be forwarded to Libya and Iraq. Sending anything to Libya violates US law. So does shipping any sensitive material to an intermediate instead of a final destination.

None of the three companies whose technology Iraq was so eager to acquire would play ball with Barbouti. In 1990, 2,000 gallons of a crucial chemical-warfare ingredient called ferrocyanide vanished from the Boca Raton cherry flavoring factory.

The US defense department subsequently learned that five 55-gallon drums of ferrocyanide had been sent to Iraq from PIT prior to the Gulf War. In a briefing memo #IIR 2 201 0243, the Department of Intelligence noted that:

"BOTH LIBYA AND IRAQ HAD DIRECT TIES WITH A US PROCESS COMPANY WHICH PRODUCED FERROCYANIDE AS A BYPRODUCT... ONE OF THE SOURCES OF THE INVESTIGATION WHO SPECULATED THAT THE COMPOUND WAS TO BE USED IN MAKING "BLUE-ACID." BLUE ACID IS REPORTEDLY THE MIXTURE OF MUSTARD GAS AND HYDROGEN CYANIDE OR MUSTARD GAS, HYDROGEN CYANIDE AND A G-NERVE AGENT.
"TWO 55-GALLON DRUMS OF THE FERRO-CYANIDE COMPOUND WERE SENT TO CARLOS CARDOEN INDUSTRIES IN CHILE. CARDOEN IN-DUSTRIES MAY HAVE BEEN TESTING THE CHEM-ICAL MIXTURE IN MUNITIONS. ONE FOREIGN SOURCE IN THE INVESTIGATION CLAIMS THE FERROCYANIDE COMPOUND WOULD BE CON-VERTED TO SOMETHING ELSE PRIOR TO WEAPONIZATION – THE MIXTURE OF TWO OR THREE ORGANIC CHEMICAL WARFARE AGENTS IS NOT NEW AND MAY HAVE SYNERGISTIC

EFFECTS ON THE BATTLEFIELD. BUBBLING AT
LEAST MUSTARD GAS INTO HYDROCYANIC
ACID MAY CHANGE THE VAPOR PRESSURES
YIELDING A MIXTURE WHICH HAS GOOD DIS-
SEMINATION CHARACTERISTICS AND PER-
SISTENCY. THIS BLUE ACID MIXTURE MAY BE
RESPONSIBLE FOR THE UNIQUE SIGNATURE OF
CASUALTIES IN THE IRAQI ATTACKS ON
KURDISH VILLAGES IN THE 1988 TIME FRAME –
BLOODY VOMIT WITH BLACKENED SKIN.

Was Wackenhut helping Barbouti ship chemicals and
chemical weapon production equipment to Iraq? Kawaja traced
the trail from Texas to Chicago and Baltimore, then on to
Baghdad.

British investigative journalist David Guyatt delved deeply
enough into the Wackenhut connection to confirm Kawaja's links.
"Oddly enough," Guyatt wrote, "this is one of the enduring
aspects" of a story "involving engineered bio-organisms supplied
to Iraq by Wackenhut Corp, the giant US private-sector security
company whose board of directors reads like a roll call of military
and intelligence alumni."

But the Bush White House remained a suspect in the
shadows. What is known is that Washington approved the licensed
transfers of germ cultures to Baghdad from the American Type
Culture Company in Maryland.

Also clearly on record is how President Bush bucked
strong Congressional objections to renew funding for "agricultural credits" for Iraq just months before that country invaded
Kuwait. Records from a House Banking Committee investigation
initiated in 1990 show that some $5 billion in Agriculture Depart-
ment loans was sent to Iraq. The catch, of course, is that "dual
use" chemicals ostensibly intended to produce pesticides and
herbicides can just as easily be used to produce organophosphate
chemical weapons.

If the agricultural loan transfer was legitimate, why was it
"laundered" through another scandal-ridden Italian bank, the
Banca Nazionale del Lavoro? In October, 1990, as the congres-
sionally unauthorized buildup in the Gulf continued behind
Desert Shield, the Chicago Federal District Court heard case
number 90 C 6863. House Banking Committee investigators
headed by Representative Henry Gonzalez wanted to have a look
at BNL bank records. The Congressional investigators were trying
to trace "agricultural subsidies" sent to Saddam. BNL's books
would show whether or not US taxpayers had helped fund Iraq's
chemical and biological weapons programs.

The case was too controversial for the federal court.
Chicago Federal District Judge Brian Duff ordered the immediate
return of all bank records held by the Banking Committee to the

BNI. But in May, 1991, just after the Gulf War officially ended, the case involving BNI's alleged laundering of Iraq's agricultural subsidy was bumped up to Chicago's Federal Appeals Court.

Once again, the financial dealings between the White House and Baghdad proved too potentially explosive to pursue. In a move that triggered suspicions and speculation that persist to this day, the federal court refused to turn ultrasensitive banking records over to the Congressional banking investigators.

* * *

With the Gulf awash in oil money and ambition, Barbouti hoped to cash in on Baghdad's desire for weapons of mass destruction. What Kawaja discovered at the PIT plant "was very heinous." The undercover investigator found that a type of hydrogen cyanide called Prussian Blue was being tested on gas-mask filters by Barbouti more than one year prior to the Persian Gulf War. Used by Iraq in its wars against the Kurds and Iran, hydrogen cyanide has the insidious ability to dissolve the seals on gas masks and protective clothing.

Kawaja says he made this information known to the White House after bugging phone lines throughout the United States. "I intercepted the Commodity Credit Corporation, the Banca Nazionale del Lavorro, the letters of credit of the BNL, which came from Switzerland, as well as a lot of other communications regarding the Gulf War that was to come," Kawaja claims.

The head of PIT security also recorded calls "going to and coming from Baghdad, to and from the United States and London." As he listened to the wiretap tapes, Kawaja was stunned to hear his former CIA employer, as well as the FBI, US Customs, American congressmen and officials in the Bush administration, all placing calls to the corporate headquarters of Ishan Barbouti International.

Not trusting his own phone lines, the former agent sent a FedEx letter to the National Security Agency, informing them that terrorists were in the United States making biological weapons. "Tell the president," he urged.

"I was green about a lot of these things," Kawaja admits. He never realized that if key administration officials were making calls to Barbouti, they would not enjoy having their conversations recorded.

He made that connection when armed agents knocked on his door and served him with a special subpoena issued by Executive Order from the President of the United States. It was the first "War Powers Act Subpoena" issued since the Second World War.

Kawaja's grim visitors did not bother with a search warrant. Citing "national security," they emptied his office of all recordings, documents and computer files. When they left, the security man still had his pants and shirt, but not much else.

The British press erupted in with a flurry of stories: "Boca Plant Begins Trail to Washington," "Congress Probes Linking Gates to Arms Deal," "Barbouti Acted in Accord with US Plan Toward Iraq," and "Gates and Secord Linked to Iraqi Pipeline." The July 3, 1991, edition of the *Financial Times of London*, reported "U.S. Cyanide Shipped to Iraq Despite Warnings to CIA," and "Iraqi's Florida Plant Tied to Poison Gas: Export of Chemical Feared."

* * *

By then, Barbouti had once again disappeared. Kawaja later heard that the chemical arms dealer died of heart failure in a London hospital and was buried one week before Iraqi troops invaded Kuwait. He also heard that the elusive Barbouti was still alive.

Not long after Barbouti's July 1, 1990, disappearance from US soil, a grand jury in Harris County, Texas, issued a subpoena for a deposition by former president George Bush regarding dealings with Barbouti's company. The International Gulf War Illness Coalition later traced a "paper trail" showing Peter Kawaja's efforts to expose the criminal activities of federal and foreign government agents going back to May, 1989. That document trail led to the CIA, the FBI, US Customs, and FBI Counter-Intelligence.

The IGI Coalition also uncovered an "Affidavit for Search" and other government documents that prove the "US government knew what was going to take place in the war with Iraq."

As part of their evidence of "gas mask penetration chemicals" being manufactured at the PIT Plant in Florida, federal agents provided a curious letter written in 1990 to a US Senator from Barbouti's partner in PIT, Louis Champon. "I can assure you," Champon told the G-men, "if drums of Cyanide left our plant, Dr. Barbouti had his reasons, either to be used against American troops or for US terrorist acts against us here at home."

None of this evidence was ever used to indict anyone. When Kawaja was subpoenaed to appear as a star witness for a federal investigation into PIT, he was prevented from answering the most pertinent questions put by jurors. When Kawaja attempted to volunteer some politically incorrect truths, Assistant US Attorney Thomas O'Malley dismissed the Grand Jury and Kawaja.

Peter Kawaja then filed his own lawsuit in the Southern District Court of Florida. The legal action charged the Bush administration and 100 federal agents with "committing war crimes, concealment, conspiracy, corruption, aiding and abetting, fraud, obstruction of justice, tampering with a witness" – and more. Over the next two years, Kawaja would continue to insist that the accused had attempted to conceal US government dealings with "the same terrorists the Bush administration had publicly declared war against."

Instead of denying the charges, Washington simply claimed immunity from prosecution.

* * *

Washington officials weren't the only world leaders sweating out the possibility of pre-Desert Storm revelations. On March 13, 1991 a scandal erupted in Germany after it was learned that the firm which had made gas for Hitler's death camps had also shipped chemical weapons to Iraq.

Along with German companies, American firms also played a major role in helping develop Saad 16. Located just outside of Baghdad, the secret high-tech complex was responsible for designing aircraft and missiles, as well as nuclear and chemical payloads. As much as 40 percent of the equipment at Saad 16 was "Made in the USA" – including computers from Hewlett Packard, and high-speed oscilloscopes and machine tools capable of weapons-making from Tektronix. A powder press suitable for compacting nuclear fuels was supplied by XYZ Options Inc. of Tuscaloosa, Alabama.

Other politically embarrassing revelations revolved around a UN Special Commission investigation carried out in southern Iraq from October 22 to November 2, 1991. During that period, the 20-man chemical and biological inspection team found hundreds of chemical warfare rockets and artillery shells at al Tuz, Muhammadiyat and Khamisiyah.

On February 29, 1992, Ramsey Clark's war crimes tribunal laid formal charges in New York against President George Bush, Vice President Quayle, Secretary of Defense Richard Cheney, General Norman Schwarzkopf, and others. The charges included 19 separate "crimes against humanity" that violated the UN Charter and 1949 Geneva Conventions, as well as other international agreements and international laws.

* * *

Inquiries were also flooding into US government agencies from sick veterans. Dr. Joshua Lederberg, Chairman of the hastily assembled Defense Science Board Task Force on Gulf War Health, moved quickly to assure them that their crippling ailments were the result of "very fine sand," "lack of recreation" or "alcohol deprivation."

But their nagging ailments and questions would not go away. By October, 1992, some Washington officials were also starting to feel ill as the senate committee responsible for overseeing exports held an inquiry into the US export policy with Iraq prior to the war. During those senate hearings, it was learned that UNSCOM inspectors had identified many US-manufactured arms and weapons technology sent to Saddam's regime under export licenses issued by the US Department of Commerce. Much of this weaponry – which was shipped directly to Iraqi military installations – was directly related to germ and chemical warfare.

Kawaja had been right. Despite the alteration of a key document dealing with shipments to a particular Iraqi military unit, the Senate Committee on Banking, Housing, and Urban Affairs was able to contact principal suppliers and obtain records of pathogenic "disease producing" shipments to Baghdad dating back to 1985.

Among the biological agents provided under federal government license to Saddam Hussein was histoplasma capsulatum. Shipments of this Class III pathogen were made on February 22 and July 11, 1985. This microorganism, the senators found, causes "a disease resembling tuberculosis that may cause pneumonia, enlargement of the liver and spleen, anemia, an influenza-like illness and an acute inflammatory skin disease marked by tender red nodules." These signs almost exactly matched the symptoms being reported by sick US and UK veterans. "Reactivated infection," senate watchdogs found, "usually involves the lungs, the brain, spinal membranes, heart, peritoneum, and the adrenals."

Other Class III pathogens included 10 "starter" vials of Brucella melentensis sent to Baghdad on May 2 and August 31, 1986. This bacteria "can cause chronic fatigue, loss of appetite, profuse sweating when at rest, pain in joints and muscles, insomnia, nausea, and damage to major organs." These symptoms were also common among a rapidly growing number of sick Gulf War veterans.

The 19 containers of anthrax bacteria supplied by the American Type Culture Collection company on May 2 and September 29, 1988, were identified by the Department of Defense as a major component in the Iraqi biological warfare program. ATCC is located just down the road from the US Army's high-security germ warfare labs at Fort Detrick, Maryland. Also noteworthy is how, in DoD's manual, "anthrax begins abruptly with high fever, difficulty in breathing, and chest pain." Similar symptoms were experienced by sick Seabees and other GIs after coming under fire from exploding SCUDs at al Jubayl.

The 15 doses of clostridium botulinum supplied to Saddam with Washington's approval were sent from ATTC's Rockville, Maryland labs on February 22, 1985 and September 29, 1988. Clostridium botulinum "causes vomiting, constipation, thirst, general weakness, headache, fever, dizziness, double vision, dilation of the pupils and paralysis of the muscles involving swallowing" – symptoms again familiar to many Gulf War veterans.

The 16 doses of clostridium perfringens shipped on May 2, 1986, and September 29, 1988, is a highly toxic bacteria which causes gas gangrene as it rots muscle bundles, killing cells and feeding on their detritus to reproduce. "Eventually, these toxins and bacteria enter the bloodstream and cause a systemic illness."

In addition to these plagues, salmonella, streptococcus, candida, ricketts and West Nile fever virus were also sent with Washington's approval to Baghdad's houses of horrors. Several shipments of extremely infectious E. Coli gut bacteria, as well as human and bacterial DNA, were sent directly to the Iraq Atomic Energy Commission. When bombarded by nuclear radiation, these bacteria could be mutated into novel biowarfare agents that would be virtually undetectable.

"In such a program, common intestinal flora such as E. Coli could be altered to produce viral, bacterial, or other toxins and would be difficult to treat," the committee noted in their report. "If Iraq was successful in developing such agents, diagnosis will continue to elude physicians testing for traditional illnesses."

In all, at least 61 shipments of germ cultures were made to Iraq between February 8, 1985, and November 28, 1989. Even though urgently needed food and medicines were later blocked by a strict trade embargo, lists provided by the Centers for Disease Control show "biologicals" being shipped to Iraq from October 1, 1984 (when the CDC began keeping records) through October 13, 1993.

Corporate profit could not have been the motive of these germ warfare shipments. In one of many letters sent to Washington officials, Senator Donald Riegle noted that the average cost of each of the deadly biological cultures shipped to Iraq, was "less than $60.00."

Riegle's investigators also found that "these exported biological materials were not attenuated or weakened and were capable of reproduction. UNSCOM inspections later produced evidence showing that the prewar government of Iraq was conducting research on enhancing the disease-making properties of bacillus anthracis, clostridium botulinum, clostridium perfringens, brucella abortis, brucella melentensis, francisella tularensis, clostridium tetani, bacillus subtillus, bacillus ceres and bacillus megatillus – all supplied by ATTC with US government export permits.

* * *

In addition to these biological weapons, the senate committee learned of two chemical agents whose distinctive odors made indelible impressions on the memories of sick veterans. Lewisite, which causes a burning and stinging to skin, eyes and upper respiratory tract, exudes a characteristically strong odor of ammonia. Unfortunately for victims of lewisite attacks, this ammonia-like reaction is sensed by pain fibers, not smell. If you "smell" Lewisite, you are already injured.

Cyanogen chloride shipped from the US to Baghdad could be mixed in chemical cocktails to take advantage of its ability to penetrate gas mask filters. US-supplied hydrogen cyanide smells of bitter almond. Immediately effective in blocking the cell's ability to absorb oxygen, the senators learned that the "toxic and physiologic properties of hydrogen cyanide permit it to be used effectively in munitions – predominantly in rocket launched artillery."

The material safety data sheet for mustard gas – shown as "HD" on FOX mass spectrometer readings – warns of "skin sensitization, chronic lung impairment, cough, shortness of breath, chest pain, and cancer of the mouth, throat, respiratory tract, skin, and leukemia. It may also cause birth defects."

HD could not be detected by M8A automatic chemical alarms. According to the US Army Chemical and Biological Defense Command, the sensitivity threshold for M256 detector kits was useless. The Army manual warns that prolonged exposure to HD at levels as low as .003 milligrams per cubic meter requires MOPP-4 protection. But the same army's best personal detection kit could not detect mustard agent until its concentration exceeded this threshold by a factor of more than 660. Well-suited to a variety of munitions and delivery modes, the first signs of mustard gas injury appear after two to 12 minutes of exposure.

* * *

According to UN information, Iraq's biological warfare program began in mid-1986 at Salman Pak. At this facility, UNSCOM inspectors later found evidence of research into botulism, anthrax, gas gangrene, tetanus and brucellosis. During the four years prior to the war, the UN representatives noted, "These research programs focused on Iraqi efforts to isolate the most pathogenic spores." Studies were also carried out on spreading these deadly spores with aerosol sprayers, and on the longevity of certain "biologicals" once released into the environment.

Noting that the committee received several reports "of Iraqi helicopters penetrating Saudi airspace during the war by flying at low levels through the wadis and of Iraqi aircraft penetrating the area over the northern Persian Gulf," the UN inspectors said that the probability that Iraq had not successfully "weaponized" biological warfare agents was very low.

Unfortunately, their inspection of Salmon Pak on August 8, 1991, was delayed because of the need to immunize UNSCOM personnel as extensively as most allied soldiers had been vaccinated – a telling commentary in itself. While they were still getting their shots, the Iraqis razed the bombed-out remains of the Salman Pak chemical-nuclear facility.

* * *

Who else was getting sick? The congressional committee learned that many Iraqi EPWs had suffered from skin rashes, sores, nausea, vomiting, coughing and other medical problems while being detained in Saudi Arabia. Many members of units who had close contact with EPWs, as well as civilian defense workers who helped decontaminate returning Desert Storm vehicles at the Anniston and Sharpsite Army depots were also reporting "symptoms consistent with those being suffered by other Gulf war veterans." In addition, the committee pointed out, "Iraq has claimed a dramatic rise in reported cases of communicable diseases since the end of the Gulf war including typhoid, brucellosis, hepatitis and cholera."

As senate investigations continued probing the biological and chemical consequences of Desert Storm, potential senate witnesses were being contacted by high-ranking military officers looking into the same issues. But as senate investigator and Vietnam veteran James Tuite put it, "Rather than trying to seek other witnesses or corroborate their reports, these officers have called to convince them that they were mistaken, that their findings were not credible, that their statements made to congress would be refuted."

Another member of the Persian Gulf Illness Investigative Team, which was looking more and more to sick GIs like a "Gulf Illness Cover-up Team," phoned a US Army officer who had previously testified before Congress detailing the 20 separate confirmed Sabbahiyah chemical detections. The caller insisted that the officer had not found what he thought he found.

As Pentagon denials and attempts at intimidating Gulf war witnesses continued, it became obvious that whatever was going on was serious enough to merit a concerted cover-up.

But at least one US government watchdog agency insisted on doing its job. During the first month of 1993, the US General Accounting Office charged with overseeing government spending activities issued a report on DU use by the US military. "Army Not Adequately Prepared to Deal With Depleted Uranium Contamination" noted that soldiers involved in the recovery and storage of 29 combat-damaged vehicles had never been informed about the presence of depleted uranium contamination, or ways to avoid exposure to depleted uranium.

While the GAO was looking into the Army's handling of toxic materials, Baghdad was not keen on allowing UN inspectors inside Iraq to look for chemical weapons and a some 39 tons of biological agents hidden in mosques or other suspected locations throughout the country. On January 17, Washington ordered the US Navy to provide persuasion by launching 45 Tomahawk cruise missiles against an already bombed nuclear fabrication facility near Baghdad. Eight missiles missed the targeted complex. Another struck the al Rasheed hotel, killing two civilians.

~ 237 ~

Impressed by the cruise missile's ability to project hurt without endangering American lives, President Clinton ordered another cruise missile attack in June, this time in retaliation for an alleged Iraqi plot to assassinate former President George Bush. Of the 23 Tomahawks launched by a pair of US warships, 16 hit an intelligence headquarters in Baghdad. Three struck a residential neighborhood, killing at least nine people and wounding 12 others.

Saddam did not have to shoot back. Later that month, Gulf war veterans presented evidence to an Armed Services Senate hearing of what they described as confirmed CBW attacks. Senate investigators noted that many veterans were exhibiting symptoms "consistent with exposure to a mixed agent attack."

On July 29, the Czech Minister of Defense made public the detection of the chemical warfare agent sarin by a Czechoslovak chemical decontamination unit operating in Saudi Arabia during the opening phases of the Gulf war. The Czech government attributed the detections to fallout from coalition bombing of Iraqi chemical warfare agent production facilities.

The following month, Senate Banking Committee Chairman Donald Riegle Jr. began probing possible connections between Iraqi CBW development and the mystery illness being reported by thousands of returning GIs. By September, Riegle had become concerned enough by his staff's findings to introduce a budget amendment providing initial funding for research into the illness some were calling Gulf War Syndrome. Riegle noted that "hundreds and possibly thousands of servicemen and women still on active duty are reluctant to come forward for fear of losing their jobs and medical care. These Gulf war veterans are reporting muscle and joint pain, memory loss, intestinal and heart problems, fatigue, nasal congestion, urinary urgency, diarrhea, twitching, rashes, sores, and a number of other symptoms."

As more family members of sick veterans began exhibiting the same symptoms, and soldiers continued to contract grave illness after returning "safely" from the Gulf, Riegle redoubled his efforts. His investigators interviewed thousands of government officials, scientists and veterans. On September 7, 1993, during a telephone interview with Walter Reed Army Medical Center commander Major General Ronald Blanck, committee members were informed that the issue of chemical and biological warfare agent exposure had not been explored because it was the position of "military intelligence" that such exposure never occurred.

But the case was not closed. Riegle's researchers were already pointing to "a large body of evidence linking the symptoms of the syndrome to the exposure of Gulf war participants to chemical and biological warfare agents, chemical and biological warfare pretreatment drugs, and other hazardous materials and substances." During detailed interviews with 400 sick Gulf War veterans, banking committee members had learned that more than three-quarters of their spouses were complaining of the same debilitating symptoms.

The brass was looking at the same material. And what they were seeing did not jibe with their public pronouncements. Having assessed the Czech detections as "valid," the office of the Secretary of Defense, the Joint Chiefs of Staff and the office of the Army Legislative Affairs met behind firmly closed doors on October 20, to discuss a report that detonated their denials.

* * *

As American military officers continued to issue threats and arguments against potential uniformed witnesses, relentless congressional investigations led by James Tuite and Donald Riegle continued to expose a wide-ranging Pentagon cover-up. Among their most serious findings was the deliberate defacing, alteration and destruction of unit logs and FOX chemical traces. Two US Marines from Camp Pendleton, California "went public," stating on the record that they had observed "hundreds of records from the Gulf war being destroyed."

In desperation, defense department officials began ordering armed forces personnel not to testify at senate hearings. Veterans were told the Iraqis couldn't initiate chemical attacks; they were also ordered not to appear publicly in uniform while advertising their plight. A member of the Persian Gulf Illness Investigative Team told a former US Navy Lieutenant Commander that she should send her wartime diary directly to him because he "did not want the CIA to get it." When the commander asked what would be wrong with the American intelligence agency getting her war diary, she was told "it would get lost."

Former Secretary of Defense Lee Aspin was the next high-level dissembler brought forward to face the investigators. On November 10, 1993, Aspin told a Pentagon press briefing that the Czechs could not have measured fallout from air attacks against Iraqi chemical weapons facilities because the winds were blowing to the northwest – away from US positions.

No doubt hoping for the same gullibility shown by the media during Schwarzkopf's sports-like casualty wrap-ups during the war, Aspin added that after analyzing the results of the Czech report, the Department of Defense concluded that the detections were unrelated to the "mysterious health problems that have victimized some of our veterans." Aspin maintained that winds were wrong and the distances too great to suggest a link with sick Seabees serving far to the southeast of the Czech detection. But no one was suggesting such a link.

DoD did admit that the Czech unit had detected sarin. But defense officials neglected to mention that the Czechoslovak chemical detection team also detected HD that same morning. The presence of both sarin and mustard agent in the same vicinity could only have come from a direct Iraqi mixed-agent attack – or fallout from bombed Iraqi weapons and storage sites.

The Czechs insisted that they had detected a nerve agent following a SCUD missile attack close to their base at the King Khalid Military City. The assertions of the most competent and best-equipped CBW-detection team in the Gulf were confirmed by a member of the US 1st Cavalry, and an entire platoon of US Army chemical detection specialists who trained with the Czechs. Unfortunately for Aspin's own attempts at laying down a smoke-screen over their findings, declassified visual and thermal satellite imagery showed the fallout plume from coalition air attacks moving southeast, following a front and its associated upper atmospheric wind currents directly towards coalition forces.

Under direct questioning from unhappy senators, Under Secretary of Defense Dr. John Deutch also admitted that the Department of Defense was withholding classified information on the exposure of US forces to biological materials.

By this time, the Department of Defense had named Dr. Joshua Lederberg to head its research team into the causes of Gulf War illnesses. Among his other credentials, Lederberg was a Nobel Laureate and an expert in the fields of bacteriology, genetics, and biological warfare defenses.

* * *

While Lederberg looked into germ warfare in the Gulf, the Pentagon's public persona put on a "happy face." Guy Smith was hired by the defense department to defuse a loudly ticking credibility bomb. A top tobacco industry PR man, Smith had spent 15 years as senior flack-catcher for Phillip Morris. That company was about to be indicted in Florida and other states for marketing its addictive tobacco products to children.

Guy Smith knew what to do when the public smelled a rat; he had defended Miller Beer against reports of a rodent floating in one of its beer bottles. Smith and his associates began cranking out speeches and Opinion Page newspaper editorials in an effort "to mitigate fear among affected service personnel who may have received incorrect or incomplete information." But Smith's $61,500 a month Pentagon project lost a wing and crashed when word of his activities leaked to the press.

Other leaks had DoD public relations personnel working overtime to patch holes inflicted by their own crossed signals. Less than a month before the Office for the Assistant Secretary of Defense informed the Senate Banking Committee in writing that a crucial NBC log did not exist, its own public affairs office sent three pages from the same log to CENTCOM. Central command, in turn, had passed the three originals to Paul Sullivan, president of Gulf War Veterans of Georgia.

The Senate committee wanted the log for the crucial battlefield dates it covered. CENTCOM insisted it didn't have the log. That "mix-up" ended when Paul Sullivan heard the uproar and immediately turned the "nonexistent" document over to Senator Riegle's aide.

Problem was, the three pages presented to the irate investigators sported a different log header than the originals. Each of the fresh fabrications was also stamped with multiple and conflicting declassification dates.

The brass had good reason to suppress the damning document. When it was finally released, the incident log revealed:

> Jan. 18, 1805: "Israeli police confirmed nerve gas probably."

> Jan. 20, 2017: "Czech recon . . . report 'detected GA/GB [sarin and tabun, two warfare nerve gases]' and that hazard is flowing down from factory/ storage bombed in Iraq. Predictably, this has become/is going to become a problem."

> Jan. 21, 215: "Czechs were called who reported trace quantity of 'Tabun, Soman and Yperite... which was caused by fallout from bombing of Iraqi CW storage/weapon sites."

> According to congressman James Tuite, "The withholding of [the logs] not only interfered with the conduct of a congressional committee's invest- igation, but also misled medical research efforts into this issue for a period of nearly one year."

That was just for starters. As Senate sleuths continued to sniff out unpleasant truths, the Pentagon spin specialists resorted to serious denial. On May 4, 1994, John Shalikashvili, Chairman of the Joint Chiefs of Staff and Secretary of Defense William Perry sent a joint letter to the chairman of the banking committee claiming that, "There is no information, classified or unclassified, that indicates that chemical or biological weapons were used in the Persian Gulf."

Riegle realized that this assertion directly contradicted a statement given by Deputy Secretary Deutch. In his November 10, 1993, briefing, Deutch had admitted that DoD was withholding classified material relating to biological exposures in the Gulf.

What was in these classified documents? What had really happened in the Gulf that the media had never been allowed near? Although seriously compromised in Senate chambers, Pentagon damage-controllers pressed ahead, laying down a minefield ahead of their own ship of state. Riegle's investigations were about to blow the lid off the Gulf Bio-War cover-up.

CHAPTER 15

RIEGLE'S REVELATIONS

On May 25, 1993, a mixed chorus line of senators and defense department officials took their seats in room SD 106 of the Dirksen Senate office building on Capitol Hill. The room was already packed with Gulf War veterans. Some were in wheelchairs. Some had given interviews or sworn affidavits to the senate committee members who were taking their own seats at the head of the room. Shortly after 1000 that morning, chairman Donald Riegle fired the first rounds in what was soon to become a day-long barrage of accusations, denials, lies, equivocations, outbursts, diatribes and startling revelations.

Edwin Dorn was the first to face Riegle. Testifying under oath, the Undersecretary of Defense for Personnel and Readiness insisted that all chemical agents discovered in the field were located "a great distance from the Kuwait theater of operations." Dorn added: "We've concluded that Iraq did not use chemical or biological weapons during the war...There were no confirmed detections of any chemical or biological agents at any time during the conflict. And by Kuwait theater of operations, I mean those portions of southern Iraq and Kuwait that constituted the battlefield. We did not find any chemical or biological munitions, live or spent, among the thousands of tons of munitions recovered on the battlefield."

Dorn's declaration sounded unequivocal. But later in the same hearing another senior Defense Department official would be forced to reconsider his testimony after being confronted with the discovery of chemical agents by UN inspectors near an Nasiriyah. Yes, he admitted, the town of Nasiriyah is very close to areas in which US forces were deployed. In fact, it was US forces who secured this key chemical weapons storage area.

Having embarked on the road of falsehood, Dorn doggedly plowed ahead. "As you know," he told the senators – and soldiers who had seen chemical litmus paper turn pink – "there were any number of reports or alarms of chemical agent detection during the conflict. There was a procedure for verifying those initial detections. Those secondary tests did not verify the initial detection."

Senator Kerry had another thought. "Well, it's very curious," he told the hearing, "I must say. I mentioned a moment ago to the staff that I was in Kuwait about two days after the liberation as part of the observer group from the senate, and apart from biological or chemical, I found that the acridity of the air and the thickness of the air just from the oil fires. I remember turning to one of the soldiers there in Kuwait and asking him whether the air he was breathing bothered him, and how he felt about being outdoors. In fact, several people there who were from

Reserve units out of Massachusetts mentioned to me that they were very concerned about breathing the air."

Added Kerry: "I've got to tell you, for the 24 hours or whatever that I was there, I found a significant impact and discomfort from the air I was breathing, not unlike Bangkok where you can go out and you can't run. In 15 minutes, you feel your lungs searing. I certainly felt the effect of those fires and within miles around, when it rained buildings were covered, cars were covered. I mean, you had, as far away as in Riyadh, you had buildings that turned black by virtue of the rain. You had black rain. So that means you have particles in the air, and if you have particles in the air, you are clearly breathing those particles. I don't know what the air quality was. I don't even know if we measured that air quality, but I remember distinctly feeling it and having concern expressed to me by people."

Kerry said he'd been told that there were no indications of ill health among American soldiers exposed to extremely dense and potentially deadly oil smoke. "But I would personally be surprised if, for those who were there for some period of time, there isn't some kind of impact or potential for it."

Riegle hoped for more reliable testimony from Dr. Theodore Prociv. As Deputy Assistant to the Secretary of Defense for Chemical and Biological Weapons, Prociv oversaw the DoD's chemical and biological defense program. He was also in charge of the Army program to destroy its own chemical weapons stockpile while implementing chemical weapons treaties, including the chemical weapons convention which was then being considered for ratification by the senate. Prociv's office also assisted the Defense Science Board Task Force on Gulf War health effects. He was obviously a heavy hitter in the nation's CBW lineup.

Prociv was proud of his work, and of the American forces' chemical detection capabilities. "The M256 kit is very specific and very, very sensitive," he told the intently listening senators. "It goes three orders of magnitude better than the M8 alarm does. So even if materials have dissipated after the initial alarm, you should be able to pick it up with the M256 kit. I've worked with that kit and I have a lot of confidence in that kit." Prociv added that he had never seen any reports of M256 kits testing positive in the Gulf.

Senator Bennett had a question. Handing a thick transcript of post-combat interviews to the head of the defense department's chemical and biological program, Bennet pointed a passage out to Prociv. "OK. It's on page 79. Event 13. Dale Glover was a Staff Sergeant with the 1165th Military Police Company. He recalled being awakened at 3:30 a.m. The Battalion NBC NCO was announcing that they were under chemical attack. An M256 kit registered a positive reading for a chemical agent. They went to MOPP level 4 for 4 hours. Afterward, all of them had runny noses.

While Prociv digested this bombshell, Bennett bored in: "So here is the case where the kit you have described registered positive, unless you have information that Mr. Glover is somehow mistaken about what happened. But this appears to me to be an eyewitness account contemporary with the event, reporting that the kit that you have described as being very, very accurate, produced a result contrary to that which you just told the Committee occurred."

Prociv paused to recover while reviewing Glover's statement. It now appeared that he *had* seen a report on Glover's detection. "Mr. Glover and the Battalion NBC NCO conducted a 256 A1 kit," Prociv proclaimed. "Both received a positive pale red color on the nerve agent test spot, but the accuracy of this reading is suspect. Both men were using a red lens in their flashlights. This is a defensive measure. Mr. Glover stated one test kit nerve agent spot was a deeper red than the other test kit. Correct colors for nerve agent tests are blue for safe and clear or peach for nerve."

Bennett was paging through the sheaf of interviews as Prociv spoke. Now the senator looked up. "Go back to page 66 on this document. Witness number 04. I have not gone through this that carefully. I was just thumbing through it while we were going on. This kind of sprung out at me."

As Prociv flipped to page 66, Bennett helped out with a running commentary: "Witness No. 04, Mr. Harold Jerome Edwards. The chemical NCO in charge of the Nuclear/Biological/ Chemical Team for the Naval Mobile Construction Battalion 24 Air Detachment at the King Abdul Aziz Naval Air Station was interviewed by the US Senate staff on January 13, 1994. During that interview, Mr. Edwards said he conducted three M256 tests for chemical agents on the evening of this event."

Dorn broke in, blowing smoke. "Can we get a date, Senator? We have not looked at this, and so we're not quite certain what time period we're talking about here."

Bennett replied. "I don't have that here."

The chairman said, "Apparently, January 19 or January 20."

Bennett came back with the bottom line: "Two of the three tests he conducted were positive for chemical blister agents. He said that the negative test was conducted in an area in between a number of rows of tents. He also said that he reported this information to his unit commander. Mr. Edwards said that a member of the unit, Tom Muse, blistered in the area under his watch during the event. The all-clear was given from a higher command. Mr. Edwards was called out to serve on a chemical decontamination team that day, and so on and so forth.

"But here is another report of an M256 test that was positive," Bennet noted. "In this case, two positive tests." The senator paused. "We'll keep looking for some more."

After several improvised detours taken by a preoccupied Prociv, Riegle returned to the issue at hand: "I appreciate very much Senator Bennett raising the issue with respect to these testing kits. Now let me come back to my question to your two colleagues. Can you give us here today your professional certification that there were no exposures of Gulf War veterans to either chemical agents or biological agents out there in that war zone?"

Prociv: "Since I've taken this position, Mr. Chairman, I have reviewed a lot of data and a lot of cases. My statement that I do not believe that any chemical agents were used by the Iraqis..."

The chairman broke in: "No, that's not what I said. I understand double-talk when I hear it. That's not what I asked you."

The assembly broke into loud laughter.

"That's not what I asked you," the chairman reiterated after the snickering died down. "And with all due respect, let me repeat it again because I'd like an answer to my question, and then if you want to elaborate, you can. I realize everybody's designed here to veer off into the question as to whether there was an attack, a verifiable attack by the Iraqis to use these weapons. I did not pose that question. I asked you under oath for your professional opinion to give me a certification of your belief and confidence that no Gulf war veterans had any exposure to chemical agents or biological agents while they were in the war zone. Now can you give us that certification, regardless of the source?"

Prociv performed a quick shuffle: "Again, Mr. Chairman, I'm not a medical doctor. I don't understand a lot of the medical symptomology. What I do understand is that when chemical agents are used, and I understand how they are dispersed, I understand how they're detected, in all of the evidence that I have seen that I can say in my own professional certification, I can say that I do not believe that any chemical agents entered the theater of operations and exposed any of our soldiers. That I can say."

But the chairman was not happy with this non-answer from his star witness: "Well, I've got to make sure that I understand every single word in your sentence here," Riegle came back. "I want to make sure because you're putting your professional reputation on the line, and you're doing it under oath. Meanwhile, I've got a lot of sick veterans all across the country, some in the room today, who heard the chemical alarms going off all the time, even though the chemical alarms were set at a much higher level than we know can cause a problem if there's extended exposure. You know that as well."

Riegle looked directly at Prociv. "But you're telling us, in your testimony today, that it is your best professional belief that we don't have a single veteran coming back from the Gulf war who had an exposure to chemical agents or biological agents in that war zone. And you're here today under oath with your professional reputation on the line."

Prociv: "Sir, again, I'm here to say that, knowing what I know and what I've reviewed, I do not understand how any of our veterans could have been exposed..."

The chairman: "I didn't ask..."

Prociv: "I have to say it this way because I'm not a medical doctor, sir."

The chairman. "Maybe we need a medical doctor to answer the question." Turning to the Chief Officer for Ground Forces at the Defense Intelligence Agency, he said, "Let me ask the same question of you, Dr. Kriese."

Kriese was ready. "Sir, in the intelligence community, one of our, if you will, reminders is that absence of evidence is not evidence of absence. So I cannot say absolutely, categorically, that there was no chemical or biological use and nobody was affected. I can tell you that, based on all the evidence I've seen, my judgment is that it was not used. But as a professional, I cannot tell you..."

Riegle: "Now when you say, 'not used', you mean...by 'not used' you mean, what? That there was an offensive use of these weapons?"

Kriese: "Yes, sir."

Riegle: "You've not been able to validate in your own mind an incident or instances where they would have been used in an offensive way.

Kriese. "That's correct, sir."

Riegle: "But you also make the point that you're not prepared to rule out the possibility that these agents got loose in some way and may in fact have had an effect on some people. You can't comment one way or the other on that."

Kriese inadvertently admitted chemical agent exposure. "I think it's impossible to prove a negative. I don't mean that lightly, sir. This is a very difficult issue, with low levels, many people involved."

Riegle agreed. "You see, it's difficult, when you have hundreds, and now thousands, of eyewitness accounts of people who are in the theater of operations and the chemical alarms go off. The chemical alarms sound. Now the chemical alarms were not just sitting out there waiting. We designed them. We sent them out there. We put them there because we were worried that this might happen. That's why the chemical alarms were there in the first place. That's why all the gear was there in the first place."

The chairman continued his broadside: "That's why we have job titles that some of you carry that talk about biological and chemical warfare, because this is a real issue and it's not somebody's invention. Saddam Hussein has done this in the past, killed his own people with these kinds of weapons. This isn't science fiction or fantasy. So we understood that there might very well be a problem. We put all the monitors out there and then the monitors kept sounding and people keep taking their MOPP gear on and off. There's no question in your mind about that having happened, is there? "

Kriese. "No."

The chairman. "OK. How many times, to your knowledge, would you say the chemical alarms went off throughout the whole theater of operation where they were placed to try to detect the chemicals?"

Kriese dissembled. "I think Dr. Prociv probably has a better estimate than I do."

Prociv: "I can't quote an exact number, but there are times when those alarms are deliberately set off. For instance, in the regiment, the NBC platoons are required to, in fact, test those alarms. What may have fallen apart is that they may not have notified the soldiers they were testing the alarms. So, as a minimum, twice a day, they would have tested."

The room rang with applause from soldiers who'd been there.

"No, please," Prociv said..

The chairman. "Let's have order."

Prociv: "I also will admit that they are prone to false alarms. They are prone..."

Riegle: "But you can see all the possibilities. It's amazing to me how clear your mind is on all the reasons why the alarms could go off, how it could be an accident or mistake or faulty equipment." The chairman shook his head. "So now we have a new question – why are we buying faulty equipment? Why are we putting faulty alarms out there? In fact, I don't understand why we're putting alarms out there that detect a level 1,000 times higher than what we know can cause a problem over a period of time."

Prociv said he could quote some numbers on that.

But Riegle wasn't interested in numbers. "Let me ask you this question. I'm going to ask you for the record. Again, I would urge you to measure your answer. Was the M8AI automatic chemical agent detection alarm which was deployed during the war sufficiently sensitive to detect harmful exposure levels of chemical nerve agents?"

Prociv: "The M8. Yes, sir."

The chairman: "Are you saying, then, that there could be an exposure level harmful to somebody that could come in beneath the level that device was scheduled to measure? If there were chronic exposures that went on for a period of time below those levels, couldn't those cause medical problems in people?"

Prociv: "I believe that there is data that shows that chronic levels at very low levels do cause problems. But I believe it's only with..."

Riegle: "But the machines weren't designed to pick that up, were they?"

Prociv retreated. "It was only with mustard, is my understanding."

Riegle was relentless. "Well, we'll get to that. But the machines were not designed to pick up low levels on a chronic level, were they?"

Prociv: "No. The M8 detection, the range of 0.1 to 0.5. You can get myosis, which are the initial symptoms, at 0.005. But the first time that you get a runny nose is at 0.5. That's the second symptom. And 0.5 is well within the detection range of the M8."

The chairman was becoming exasperated. "We can go back and forth on this. The fact is..."

Dorn tried a distraction. "Senator."

Riegle turned on him. "Let me just finish. He and I are having a discussion. I'd be happy to call on you in a minute." Turning back to Prociv, the chairman spoke for the record. "I'm distressed about the fact that we've got a million reasons why we can't find the problem. We can't get to the root of this thing. We have all these sick veterans out there, wives and kids getting sick, and we just can't find out what's causing it. Now, we're going to stay on this trail..."

"When you talk to the sick veterans who were in the theater of operation where the alarms were going off, the ones who are now sick are overwhelmingly convinced that there is a relationship. Now maybe you're smarter than they are and maybe they're smarter than you are. The consequences for them are a lot higher than they are for you because you're not sitting here sick, with all due respect."

This time the room rang with applause.

Prociv grew desperate. "Sir, if I can just go on the record. I don't disagree that there are sick veterans. I was a veteran myself. I'm very sympathetic toward the veterans. I wouldn't be working for the Department of Defense – I just left a 20-year career in industry to work for the Department of Defense because I believe in this cause."

But Riegle was not impressed. "Let me give you another example of how powerfully real it is in the lives of real people." The chairman gestured across the room. "Colonel Smith over here who's sitting in the wheelchair spent 30 years in the military himself. He was in excellent health when he went over to the Persian Gulf, actually had prior training as a veterinarian, so he knows something about what causes people to get sick and die, and animals to get sick and die. He's no longer in the service. I'm doing this from memory, but after a long struggle, he finally received a 20 percent, I think it is, service disability related to his problems, although he can hardly get up out of the wheelchair and walk."

Riegle was choked. "When he was invited to go on the Phil Donahue Show to talk about this problem, as a guy with a background in this area who is very, very sick, he was told by somebody in the military, it would be a good idea for him not to wear his uniform and all those ribbons on his chest. I've got to tell you, I'm much more concerned right now with sick veterans than I am with veterans like yourself who I respect very much who are not sick. I think if you were sick, if you were sitting in his wheelchair, your feeling about this would be dramatically different."

The chairman continued: "I think part of the problem here is that the people who ran the operation during the Gulf war are not sick because they were not the ones out into the area of exposure and who have not come back with these problems. And so, I think it's very hard sometimes for us to put ourselves in the other person's shoes. That's why it would be very healthy for some of these interviews to be conducted directly. I'm going to ask, and we're going to bring the witnesses in here, if I have to bring in 500 witnesses and we have to do this hour by hour by hour, we're going to get the Defense Department to pay sufficient attention to this problem.

"I don't think that's happened yet, with all due respect. As Senator Bennett points out, with the atomic exposure problem years ago, and as I mentioned with the Agent Orange exposure, I think there's an enormous institutional difficulty for a bureaucracy, whether it's the Defense Department or some other agency of the Government, to ever come to terms with perhaps some grievance decision errors about equipment, about exposure, about things that maybe weren't properly planned for that happened after the fact. We have some of that here, and we're going to have to deal with it because you have a problem here that's a lot bigger than you understand right now.

"You have wives and children that are sick. I don't know how many of them you've talked to. I'm going to give you some names of spouses that are sick, whose reproductive situation has been knocked completely haywire since their husbands have come back from the Persian Gulf, and some women veterans who have come back and whose reproductive situation is completely haywire. They think, and I believe that they're right in thinking it, that they were exposed to agents out there that have caused this to happen. They had a perfect health profile before they went. In fact, they couldn't have gone without a good health profile."

Riegle returned to this point later in the day. "These veterans, I've talked to hundreds of them now directly. These are not malingerers, these are not malcontents, these are not people who are having fantasies. These are sick people who, in every case, were well when they went to the war or they could not have even gone to the war. In many cases, they are people who were among the most fit. People that have gone through survival school, paratroop training, run marathons, and various other things. The fact that their health has been turned upside down is a genuine national tragedy. We can't hold back anything that they need to get to the bottom of this and fix their problems as best we can. I do want you to talk to some of these spouses and children because you're not going to appreciate this problem until you do.

"Many of the veterans who were already out of the service tell us that if you don't get any real help out of the VA or in terms of a disability rating, and you're too sick to work, you're absolutely uninsurable, the insurance companies don't want to see you because you need the help and you need the coverage. So there's a diabolical end-game situation facing more and more Desert Storm veterans. And when you think back to the parades, the deserved parades at the time as the war was ending and people were coming back, they don't mean much now if a veteran is sick or his family members are sick, and they need a response, they need a proper diagnosis, and they need proper care.

"You need to talk to them," Riegle told Prociv and the officials he represented, "not through intermediaries and the chain of command where everybody understands that if there's a line that we're going to follow here that there were no exposures and we're all going to hue to that point of view, it gets very easy to start to tailor what's being heard into that sort of channel.

"I've seen it too many times and I think it's happening here. I want you to talk to some of these people. I want you to sit down and get right up close to them because if there is a problem where this thing is moving through families, as we now have enough anecdotal evidence for me to believe that it is, you ought to get up close to it. You ought to look at it. You ought to look at the sick kids, not just Col. Smith and the others that are here right now who have given as much or more time in uniform as you have and who are now sick and are being tossed out the side door, quite frankly."

"That's what's happening because, in effect, there's a problem but we don't know what caused the problem. It couldn't be chemical. It couldn't be biological because we can't find any evidence of that. Therefore, we're not going to aim our treatment regime down that track because if it never happened, then that can't be the cause of the problem. "So let's look for other things. Let's look for mental problems. Let's look for this. Let's look for that. This is not a mental problem. It is a mental problem, I think, in the Defense Department. I think it's fair to say that because the defense establishment has decided that this problem has to be outside certain boundaries. Yet, all of the evidence is accumulating, and we're going to go through it here today. We've gotten sidetracked here, which is a little bit regrettable because I want to nail down specific things here and we're going to do that."

At this point, the senate committee chairman demanded a DoD assurance "that no active-duty person will be sent out of the military if they come forward and indicate that they have these problems and that they won't be off-loaded for some other reason that's a fake reason. And that, in fact, if they have to leave the service because they are so sick coming off the service in the Gulf War, that they will get service-connected disability and so they're not just going to go out and land on the scrap heap and find they can't get a job and they're uninsurable."

Turning from his emotional appeal for compassion, Riegle next tried logic. "We're in a Catch-22," he told Prociv and the assembly. "If we say, on the one hand, the alarms going off in every instance was due to malfunction or misreading or diesel oil, or whatever, and then we turn around and say, on the other hand, we have absolutely no confirmation from anywhere that these agents were present. It's the second conclusion that's driving the first. If you say, just one alarm functioned properly, and what are the statistical chances that that's true, just one of these M256 readings was accurate, then we do have confirmation."

A few minutes later, the chairman complained that the "system didn't work right and we're having a very hard time, I still think, getting an honest understanding of what happened. I think Senator Bennett is exactly right... that you've come in here with a truly unbelievable assertion that every single one of these alarms going off was faulty and didn't mean anything. I think that that's clearly not the case and I would hope at the end of the day, not just today, but at the end of this, you wouldn't force yourself into believing something that is patently unbelievable."

But, Riegle warned, there was "a more serious and sinister part" to the Pentagon's prevarication. "If you're working off the premise that it can't be chemical exposure or biological weapons exposure, then you don't aim the bulk of your medical research effort with real urgency into that area of exposure. You look at other things. You can spend a long time looking at everything else that it might be. Meanwhile, you've got very sick people that in many instances, are getting sicker. In other words, their sickness isn't standing still. Their sickness in many cases is progressive."

The thing that really alarmed him, Riegle remonstrated, was that "by, in a sense, ruling out the notion that it could be chemical and biological exposure causing a lot of this difficulty, maybe in a mixture with the pretreatment pills and so forth, we are losing very valuable time and causing perhaps an immense amount of grief. If you've got a biological issue working in all of this, you may have even a bigger threat on your hands than we're accustomed to even thinking about. And so, that kind of logic or illogic, in this case, I think is what people can't accept who look at this."

Perhaps the people present in the hearing room sensed a major turning point. Or perhaps Riegle realized from the look in the witness' eyes that he was on a roll. The chairman broke through Prociv's defenses like an Abrams tank taking a barbed-wire fence.

"And to your question, how many times did the alarms go off, I can assert to you right now, based on just the first person accounts that we have had, with discussions with people who have come forward, for whom we have names, places, times, and so forth, that there would be thousands of events of alarms going off. Would any of you dispute that?"

In the silence that followed, the chairman insisted. "You would not dispute that."

Prociv protested. "We have no data."

Senator Bennett broke in. "That goes back to my question – what would you be surprised if it were fewer than? Does 1,000 strike you as much too high? You say you have no data, but you obviously..."

Prociv, hastily: "I think that I would agree to per-alarm, perhaps two to three a day. I could see that happening.

Riegle, quickly: "How many alarms were out there?"

Prociv: "We had 14,000 alarms out there."

Riegle rejoiced in the admission. "So 14,000 alarms going off three times a day."

Prociv: "Big number."

Riegle: "That's a pretty big number."

It was in fact a huge number of chemical alarms. And a king-size hole in the Pentagon's credibility. Smoke was still pouring out of this direct hit, when Riegle tried another tack.

"Now listen to this. This is just what we got after all the bombing. We went in and, as a priority target, tried to knock out a lot of these weapons storage places and weapons production places. So, presumably, we got rid of most of it in the bombing runs. But this was what was left after all the bombing. Now just think about this and think about it logically: 13,000 155-millimeter shells loaded with mustard gas; 6,200 rockets loaded with nerve agent; 800 nerve agent aerial bombs; 28 SCUD warheads loaded with sarin; 75 tons of nerve agent Sarin; 60 to 70 tons of the nerve agent tabun; and 250 tons of mustard gas and stocks of thiodiglycol, a precursor chemical for mustard gas.

"Again," Riegle implored, "just think about this, we went in with these saturation bombing raids. We tried to hit their weapons production facilities and knock them out. Presumably, we did knock a lot of them out. A lot of what they had to start with presumably went up in smoke and, unfortunately, I think a lot of it drifted down over our people and that's part of why these alarms were going off. According to the testimony here, if there were 14,000 going off three times a day, there's an awful lot of something going on. But this is what was left after the war that we managed to find.

"Knowing Saddam Hussein," the chairman concluded, "he may have more than this squirreled away some other place we haven't even found. But leaving that aside, this is a tremendous stockpile of these kinds of weapons to have at the end of the war."

Within minutes of this lesson in logic, Riegle tried this:

"Now you have to say to yourself, and especially when we're dealing with sick veterans and so forth, who feel that they were exposed to these items, is it conceivable that Saddam Hussein, with all of this stockpile – I mean, he didn't have these things by accident, he built these with a very deliberate design to have all of these things – is it conceivable that in the course of the war, he or his field commanders, and I understand some of his front-line field commanders had authority to do certain things in the war, depending upon how the war went. Is it conceivable that not a single one of these shells or weapons was ever fired? Is that conceivable? Maybe it's conceivable. I think it's very, very unlikely."

In fact, said Riegle, "We find a very high correlation between the kinds of sickness and medical symptoms and exposure to chemical and/or biological weapons. In fact, we can't find anything else that correlates highly. This is the one thing that fits."

Prociv tried to return to statistics – as if the anguish of American families who had trusted their leaders could be reduced to the cold calculus of numbers.

"I think until somebody, and maybe you've done this, I hope so and if you haven't, we're going to help you do it," Riegle promised Prociv. "When you talk to a veteran's wife whose hair is falling out and whose reproductive cycle has been knocked completely haywire who was healthy before her husband came back from the Gulf war, you're going to understand this problem in a way you can't understand it before that. You've got to put a real face, lots of real faces on this thing to understand the severity of it."

"The question," the chairman said moments later, "is what can we offer them? Let me give you some specifics. Number one: To ones that are sick and can't work, they ought to have 100 percent disability. That you can offer them. That you can fight for and that you should get and we shouldn't wait another day to do it.

"Number two, if you've got family members that are sick, showing the same syndrome, they ought to get care from the government. The Defense Department ought to be fighting to get the money for it. If you have to not build another battleship or something else in order to get the money to take care of the sick family members, you ought to stand up and say it. And so should the Secretary of Defense, because the veterans are a lot more important than the equipment."

At this point, Riegle was again interrupted by sustained applause.

"I think there should be an epidemiological study of every single Gulf war veteran to find out what's going on out there and if some are being affected now, there might be some that are going to be affected three or four years from now. We could learn something and do something about helping them at the present time."

The chairman had another suggestion. "I think it's good national policy and I think the Defense Department today, the best thing it could do for itself as it's trying to figure out what happened is to go on an all points effort to deal with the aftermath of this problem and see to it that these veterans and their families are getting the full scope of care immediately that they need and not wait to find out exactly what happened in each and every instance but to get that job done.

"I'll tell you very bluntly, that is not happening. And you can say this is way up on the priority list of the Secretary of Defense. But I've listened to the Secretary of Defense. I've listened to him on the radio. I've watched him on television. I've been waiting for him to talk about this problem. He can get a mike any time he wants it. He can step outside his office door and say, get the networks in here. I've got something to say on the Gulf War Syndrome issue. And you know what? They'll be there. They'll be happy to come. He can talk about this and he can deliver a message that's so powerful and so clear that shows where the priority is in treating these sick veterans and their families, that it's unmistakable. The silence is deafening. That hasn't happened. And there's no excuse for it. I wouldn't have a Secretary of Defense that didn't do that, quite frankly.

Dorn was squirming.

"I'll get to you," Riegle said. "Let me finish. I've seen the sick kids. You ought to go see some of them. You ought to go talk with them. It will change your thinking about this problem, I guarantee it. It will make you a lot more passionate about it and a lot more determined to get to the bottom of it in terms of at least treatment for people, because we're not treating people today. Where does the spouse and the child go today? Can they go to the VA hospital? No, the VA hospital isn't geared to take them. It doesn't want them."

By now, the Undersecretary of Defense was waving a letter, which he said promised treatment, encouraged people to come forward, and instructed all vets that there were no restrictions against what they may wish to say about their experiences. "Let me say it again loudly," Dorn declared. "If a soldier comes to a military treatment facility, he or she will be treated. If that soldier brings a member of his family in, he or she will be treated. If there is anyone in this audience who feels that has not happened, I will take the names, I will make the calls, and it will happen."

Dorn's pledge was greeted by pandemonium as sick veterans who had been subjected to years of run-around by military doctors and Veterans Administration administrators jumped to their feet .

Riegle held up his hands: "Let's have order in the room." Turning to Dorn, the chairman noted, "You have some people here that feel that way who are standing. They feel that they have been given the brush-off in that area. So we'll see to it that you have their names."

Dorn nodded.

"Let me ask you this," Riegle wondered. "When was this letter put out?"

"It's dated today," Dorn admitted.

The chairman could not believe it. "So, in other words, the letter was put out today."

Dorn quickly amended. "That is the last, as I said, of about a dozen messages coming out of DoD on this matter."

A few questions later, the Pentagon spokesman admitted that those previous messages had gone out to the upper echelons of the military chain-of-command – not to isolated, individual veterans.

Those missing missives were not the only letters to surface that day. At one point, Riegle asked Dr. Mitchell Wallerstein if that expert in counter-proliferation and export control for International Security under the Undersecretary of Defense had seen something else. "Did you happen by chance to see the letter," the chairman inquired, "which had a little bit of a frantic tone to it, from Secretary Baker in the Bush Administration, as the war was getting ready to start, that we suddenly stopped the shipments to Iraq of these kinds of items, things that could be either used in chemical weapons or biological weapons or nuclear weapons. Are you aware of that letter that was sent around?"

Wallerstein said he wasn't.

Riegle responded: "We ought to give you a copy of it, because it was a case of suddenly it dawned on people that we were going to have a real problem facing off against weapons that we had inadvertently, one presumes, helped create. And that's part of our problem here, but your testimony is that you only looked at the things that were going to be transshipped to the so-called rogue regimes that were on the bad guy list at the time. Is that right?"

Wallerstein insisted that Saddam's murderous regime was not on the government's list of taboo trading partners. Riegle found this to be almost as curious as the commanders' shyness about visiting the front lines once the fighting had been joined. "When I went back, in an earlier staff review I asked the question of how many of the senior military officers that were directing the war were up in the area where the chemical alarms were going off. I found that very few, if any, were. They were much further back, and it didn't give me a very good feeling."

Riegle had another image in mind. "I kind of like the picture of the Civil War generals that got on the horses and got out in front," he told the assembly. The fact that those generals – usually Confederate – often got shot was part of a long tradition of military leadership.

"I'd feel a little more comfortable and a little more confident in the judgments if I saw some of the major signal callers in the strategy right up in the front areas breathing the same air, working with the same chemical detectors, relying on their own advice in terms of putting their own health at risk," the senator went on. "I have a bit of bitter feeling about it because I've seen so many sick veterans. So I would hope that the people who have this level of confidence would, you know, we'd see them right up there, right up in the front when the going is unpleasant, and not back in some protected base area working out of a bunker."

Riegle also noted that "when we started out on this way back when, it was to try to understand what the control regimes were that we had within our own government that would have prevented Saddam Hussein from getting the things that he needed to make biological weapons or the things he needed to make chemical weapons."

The chairman hoped that the Director of the CIA's Nonproliferation Center in Washington, DC, could explain what had gone wrong with US export controls. Dr. Gordon Oehler was quick to admit that "With regard to biological weapons, we estimated, prior to the start of the war, that Iraq had a stockpile of at least one metric ton of biological warfare agents, including anthrax and botulinum toxin."

Had Oehler attended the same disinformation briefings as Prociv and Dorn? "If in fact a munition blows up a chemical warhead storage site and chemical agents are released into the atmosphere, the modeling that has been done on this suggests that nothing is going to go further than maybe 10 miles. So if your American troops, if the coalition troops are much farther than that, they are not going to be exposed to chemical warfare," the export expert stated.

"Biological is a very different situation," Oehler quickly added. "because particularly if it is dispersed at a high altitude the biological agents can go very long distances. But there is no evidence that any of that was ever released."

What about the presence of chemical weapons in Kuwait, Riegle wanted to know.

Oehler: "There is some evidence that some chemical weapons were moved into the Kuwait theater of operations, but then withdrawn prior to the beginning of the air attacks, with the exception of the ones that were found still in an Nasiriyah."

The chairman had trouble with this one. "They were moved in and taken out?"

Oehler: "That is what some intelligence suggests."

Riegle: "Just one instance? Several instances?"

Oehler. "No. There were a couple of instances in intelligence that suggest that. We do not know moved where or what."

Riegle wanted to know, "What would be the caliber of the intelligence source that would give you that information?"

But all Oehler would say was, "That was a generally reliable source."

Riegle: "More reliable than these sensors?"

Laughter greeted Riegle's riposte.

Oehler admitted that "At the same time Iraq was developing CW and BW agents, it was also developing the missile delivery capabilities. By the time of the invasion of Kuwait, Saddam could field up to 450 SCUD type surface-to-surface missiles. The Soviet-origin SCUDs originally had a range of 300 kilometers, but Iraq reconfigured them into a series of other missiles with ranges of up to 750 kilometers." These ranges, Riegle brought out, were sufficient to deliver chemical warheads on Tel Aviv, or US positions in Saudi Arabia.

How did Saddam's secret procurement program work, Riegle wondered.

"European middlemen brokered chemical precursor deals for Iraq under the pretext that the materials were intended for pesticide plants," Oehler explained. "A Dutch firm purchased supplies from major chemical firms around the world, supplying the Chemical Importation and Distribution State Enterprise in Baghdad in the 1970s, and in the 1980s supplying the Iraqi State Establishment for Pesticide Production, both cover names for the CW program.

"The middlemen supplied dual-use chemical precursors including monochlorobenzine, ethyl alcohol, and thiodiglycol. When the Iraqis requested phosphorous oxychloride, a nerve agent precursor banned for export under Dutch law without explicit permission, the supplier balked, and drew this request to the attention of Dutch authorities. Subsequent Dutch investigations found that two other Dutch firms were involved in brokering purchases of chemical precursors."

According to Washington's senior arms export analyst, "Iraq exploited businessmen and consortia willing to violate the export laws of their own countries. As has been indicated in the press and television reports, the Consen Group, a consortium of European missile designers, engineers, and businessmen, established a network of front companies to cover its role as project director of an Argentine, Egyptian, Iraqi-sponsored Condor II ballistic missile program."

It wasn't difficult for Saddam's CBW scientists to get what they needed. "Iraqi procurement officers, knowing full well the licensing thresholds, requested items that fell just under the denial thresholds, but nevertheless would suffice," Oehler outlined. "Prior to Desert Storm, US regulations on the export of these technologies were drafted to meet US technical specifications and standards. Technologies of a lower standard worked just as well, and permitted Iraq to obtain the goods and technology consistent with Commerce Department regulations."

Riegle broke in. "Let me just stop you again. This is again very valuable, and I appreciate your presenting it for us so we can have it on the record. Before we get too far past it, you made a reference to phosphorous oxychloride. What agent is this a precursor for?

Oehler: "Sarin."

Riegle: "Also, well, I have interrupted you here. This backs up even further, but when you acknowledged that Saddam Hussein had SCUD chemical warheads, where did he get those?

Oehler: "They made them themselves."

Riegle: "They made their own."

Oehler elaborated: "They had quite a missile refurbishment extension plant where they took the SCUDs and added in extra lengths and the fuel tanks, changed the warheads, and had a capability to make their own warheads.

Riegle wondered: "Were the Russians helping them with this?"

Oehler: "No. There is no evidence of any Russian involvement at all in this."

Riegle thought for a moment. "You see, part of the picture that emerges here – this is really an extraordinary story that you are sharing with us, because, according to your testimony, the CIA was tracking this in real time as it was happening, and had a great concern about it, and had figured out that this robust program on chemical weapons and these other areas was going forward. Yet, as we get down further in time, we are going to find out that, as Saddam Hussein needed other items to go into his war machine, that he actually came and got some from us, particularly in the biological warfare area, that required licensing."

Oehler had revealed that between 1984 and 1990, the CIA's office of Scientific and Weapons Research provided five separate memos covering Iraqis' dealings with United States firms on purchases, discussions, or visits that looked like they were related to weapons of mass destruction programs.

"So you wonder," Riegle continued, "how anybody in the licensing regime who was reading the CIA reports at the time and who could see this buildup of this kind of weapons potential, you would think that people would have been very, very reluctant to approve anything that could go into a weapons production system of this kind. You would think that this would have had everybody on full alert to be extremely careful about what is or is not licensed for shipment into this kind of a regime. Is not that the logic of learning this?"

The chairman found it "really astonishing to find that our own government had licensed a shipment of those very things to Saddam Hussein and many of them going directly to military units. There was no subterfuge, they were going to go right into his war production system. Then, of course, when we decided the necessity of going to war with Iraq, we had our own troops suddenly facing weapons that we had helped develop by providing critical items to them."

Riegle looked at Dorn. "You're nodding in the affirmative. I don't want to put words in your mouth, but that's correct, is it not?"

Dorn responded: "As my opening statement says, it appears that our export control regime was not effective."

Riegle: "Right. We helped him create these diabolical weapons by supplying a lot of the critical things he needed for them. We also knew that he had a history of using these weapons. He used them on his own people. He used them on the Kurds years earlier, gassed and killed a lot of people. So when we went into the War, we must have anticipated a real problem here. I mean we just didn't send these chemical alarms out just to have something to do in all these MOPP 4 outfits. We sent them out there because we anticipated that there was a real threat, did we not?

Dorn: "That is true, sir."

Riegle: "We understood that he had this capability and that it posed a threat to our people and we took various steps. We had the pretreatment pills, we had training, we had chemical monitors out in the field, we had teams designed to do this. All of that certainly creates a very strong supposition that we were worried about what he might do. I don't think the Defense Department did this for an exercise. There was a real worry that he might use these chemical weapons or biological weapons, wasn't there?

Dorn: "There was."

Riegle: "There was that worry. So these precautions were taken. Now, as it turns out, and this is where the firsthand statements of veterans I think are so important because they're the ones that were out there, we weren't, and they're the ones, in many cases, who are sick. When these alarms go off, I must say to you, it's incredible and unbelievable and unsustainable and shouldn't, I don't think, be offered to come here today, any of you and say, look we had all these chemical alarms and they kept going off in various areas through the War zone, but they were all misfires. It was all accidental alarms. It doesn't mean there were any chemicals in the area. There are no chemical incidents, and so forth and so on. Even as Senator Bennett pointed out, going back to some of our firsthand accounts, that in many cases the gear was picked up afterward and who knows what happened to it."

The chairman went on: "These alarms went off for a reason, and I think it's clear, it's clear in my mind they went off because the things they were designed to detect came into that zone and set them off. I mean, they didn't go off ahead of time, they didn't go off afterward; they went off during the time that things were going on in the War zone that they were designed to detect.

"I think it's very important that the Defense Department bring itself to face the reality that a lot of veterans were exposed to chemical agents during this war period. And whether they were fired in an offensive capacity in some instances, or delivered that way, as I also think they were, is really incidental here. The question is, did people come into contact with these agents, and in all likelihood some biological agents as well, and in some mixture that we don't yet fully understand, is this the foundation for the sickness that a lot of them have? I think the facts now are essentially inescapable that that is a significant part of this problem... In the end, the main losers are going to be the veterans and their families."

But they weren't the only ones. "The second loser," Riegle pointed out, "is going to be the Defense Department because you're going to end up with your reputation in ruins. I'm not exaggerating and so I don't want to be misunderstood when I say I'll bring veterans in here and have them, one after the other, and their family members, for days on end, I will do that if I have to, because I want this problem paid attention to. They don't want to come. I don't want to ask them, but we will ask them and they will come. That's not the way to solve this problem, but if there is no other way, then that's the way we will do it."

Riegle wanted Dorn, Prociv and other Pentagon proponents to make no mistake. "This is not a shot across the bow," the senator warned. "This is about as direct as the communications get between the Legislative Branch and the Executive Branch."

CHAPTER 16

MELTDOWN

Like a suddenly fast-forwarded film, Riegle's senate revelations unleashed a runaway chain reaction of official admissions, contradictions and denials. During a Department of Defense sponsored conference on counter-proliferation held at Los Alamos National Laboratory on May 6 and 7, 1994, Undersecretary of Defense Dr. Deutch admitted that biological agent detection had become a priority development area for the Department of Defense.

On June 23, 1994, as tens of thousands of sick American soldiers registered for treatment at military and Veterans Administration hospitals, the Pentagon announced that its Defense Science Board had found that "there is no evidence that either chemical or biological warfare was deployed at any level, or that there was any exposure of US service members to chemical or biological warfare agents."

But earlier that month, in response to an earlier request from Senator Riegle for a laboratory analysis on samples submitted by his Senate commission, the Lawrence Livermore Forensic Science Center reported some disturbing findings. Using advanced DNA analysis and biological screening techniques, the nation's top war-research lab found unique DNA sequences for Q-fever and Brucella plagues on the inside of a gas mask carrying case, the top of a gas mask filter, and under the rubber seal of a gas mask brought back from the Middle East battleground. When the tests were repeated, the same unique DNA "prime pairs" were isolated.

Riegle's top investigative aide, James Tuite, told Riegle and his commission that the presence of only a single DNA strand could indicate the presence of a genetically altered biological warfare microorganism. "We do know that the US licensed the export of genetic materials capable of being used to create these types of genetically altered biological warfare agents to the Iraqi Atomic Energy Commission, an Iraqi governmental agency that conducted biological warfare related research prior to the war," Tuite reminded the senators. "One method of creating these genetically altered microorganisms is by exposing them to radiation. The US also licensed the export of several species of brucella to Iraqi governmental agencies."

In preliminary testing, the forensic scientists also found other chemical compounds present in the gas mask samples, which they believed to be hazardous. Tuite told the senate fact-finding body that "the scientists at Lawrence Livermore National Laboratory Forensic Science Center believe that additional analysis of more samples may isolate and identify unusual hazardous chemical compounds, chemicals that in combination may be hazardous, chemical warfare agent compounds, or biological pathogens on the surface of collected items – and that much more study is warranted."

James Tuite also noted another anomaly in DoD's denials. "What seems to be emerging is a troubling pattern of events involving individuals who have received medals, Bronze Stars, Meritorious Service Medals, Army Commendation Medals, and Purple Hearts, in the course of coming into contact with unconventional weapons that the Department of Defense continues to insist were not even present in theater."

The General Accounting Office presented a very different government position. In August, 1994, the GAO found that American soldiers in the Gulf had been exposed to "possible chemical warfare agents," in addition to "prophylactic agents" including experimental vaccinations and pyridostigmine bromide "to protect against chemical and biological weapons, and infectious diseases." The GAO called DoD medical studies related to chemical warfare agent exposure, "insufficient."

* * *

In late September, Randall Vallee was preparing to testify at Tuite's Senate Banking hearings. The former sergeant, who had been at "Expo" near Dhahran when a SCUD attack had left him smelling ammonia before sickening him severely enough to be sent home, was still struggling with that mysterious malady when the phone rang. An officer who identified herself as Lieutenant Colonel Vicki Merriman was on the line.

"She asked me about my health and my family," Vallee told Tuite in a letter of complaint filed soon after the call. After some small talk with this high-level aide to the Pentagon's top CBW expert, Dr. Prociv, "the colonel's attitude turned from one of being concerned about my well being to an interrogator trying to talk me out of my own experiences. She started using tactics of doubt regarding my statements. She said in regard to chemical and biological agents that there was absolutely no way that any soldiers in the Gulf were exposed to anything. Her exact words were, 'The only ones whining about problems are American troops. Why aren't any of our allies?'"

The 1993-1994 Gulf War veterans intimidation program was being run out of Prociv's office. One month after Merriman's call, Senator Donald Riegle released his banking committee's findings. "These are horrendous statistics that show the true scale of this problem," Riegle told the press. Condemning "the heartlessness and irresponsibility of a military bureaucracy that gives every sign of wanting to protect itself more than the health and well-being of our servicemen and women who actually go and fight our wars," Riegle added, "To my mind, there is no more serious crime than an official military cover-up of facts that could prevent more effective diagnosis and treatment of sick US veterans."

Noting that "some licenses had been granted by our own Commerce Department to ship certain dual-use items...directly to Iraqi military installations," the senator said that when that written document was sought by the Senate and the House, "that particular document was altered. The exact text of the words on the document, which indicated that it was to be shipped to an Iraqi military unit, those words were deleted, and something else was put in its place to create a false picture. That document was sent up to the Congress as a deliberately misleading document."

Riegle also blasted the Department of the Army for withholding Captain Johnson's Sabbahiyah high school report, saying they first had to obtain clearance from the Department of Defense and conduct an intelligence review. "That would seem to contradict their claim that there is no classified information on this subject," the banking committee chairman observed. When congress received the British report of the Sabbahiyah incident, "it was dated July 14, 1994, indicating that it had been prepared in response to my request, in coordination with the Department of Defense."

"The British Chemical and Biological Defense Establishment claimed that "in their view" the substance analyzed more than 20 different ways as mustard agent was "fuming nitric acid." But Riegle sniffed out a copy of the original British report prepared by the UK unit actually present at the high school. "It confirms that mustard agent was detected, and that the substance was oily, like mustard agent. Nitric acid is not oily."

Riegle was not impressed. "In my view," he fumed, "this is an important example of a pattern of deliberate misrepresentation of the truth. It is an appalling record."

* * *

In November, 1994, the Santa Cruz city council passed a resolution calling for a ban on blood and tissue donations by Gulf war veterans until doctors confirm or confound theories that the illness experienced by so many vets was caused by viral or bacterial infections. "It will put a little pressure on the medical community to say it's not all post-traumatic stress," said Dean Lundholm, president of the California Association of Persian Gulf Veterans. "Something's going on. It needs to be looked at."

The Red Cross had lifted its blood ban on Desert Storm donors in January, 1993. When asked about the Santa Cruz call, American Red Cross representative Kristen Wilde responded that "extensive research conducted by DoD concluded that there is no evidence these symptoms are transmitted by blood."

On December 8, a report on Gulf War Illness was issued by the Committee On Veterans' Affairs. Investigating chairman John D. Rockefeller had also run into roadblocks. "Veterans' service medical records are difficult to find," Rockefeller complained. "According to the US General Accounting Office, veterans' service medical records can potentially be in thousands of locations." How could this be? Military medical files which once clung to soldiers as tenaciously as the "jacket" containing their service records, were missing in action. But who was responsible? There were now few records, or proof, that any Desert Storm soldiers had received vaccinations.

This was typical of DoD dealings with its own troops, Rockefeller's committee discovered. "For at least 50 years, DoD has intentionally exposed military personnel to potentially dangerous substances, often in secret," the report read. "DoD has repeatedly failed to comply with required ethical standards when using human subjects in military research. DoD used investigational drugs in the Persian Gulf War in ways that were not effective. DoD did not know whether pyridostigmine bromide or botulism vaccine would be safe for use by US troops in the Persian Gulf War."

That was not all. "The Defense Department and Department of Veterans Affairs repeatedly failed to provide information and medical follow-up to those ordered to take investigational drugs...The Federal Government failed to provide timely information needed to compensate military personnel harmed by various exposures." Nothing had changed, the committee commented. "DoD has demonstrated a pattern of misrepresenting the danger of various military exposures that continues today."

Also in the month of Christian good will, the government of Iraq held a conference on "Post-War Environmental Problems in Iraq" in Baghdad. Those attending heard Iraqi scientists present analyses of samples of vegetation, water and soil. All revealed high levels of five tricothecene mycotoxins. Both T-2 toxin and HT-2 toxin were reportedly found in the blood and urine of Iraqi civilians complaining of vomiting, fever, headache, backache, swollen eyes, and chest pain. Based on these findings, Baghdad accused the United States of conducting mycotoxin warfare against Iraq. But it was more likely that bio-weapons produced and stockpiled by Iraq for use against its enemies had been dispersed by allied bombing. Open-air storage pits had offered no protection from heavy air raids, and follow-up reconnaissance revealed that primary CBW manufacturing facilities had been hit hard enough to "bounce the rubble."

* * *

The new year started well for those involved with the Gulf Bio-War cover-up. In January, a burned-out Donald Riegle retired from the senate. But in early February, his protégé, congressional investigator James Tuite, rose like a phoenix from Riegle's ashes to charge that a special Gulf War Illness oversight committee had ignored evidence that the sicknesses they were studying could be traced to Iraqi chemical or biological weapons. Tuite, who had collected that evidence for Donald Riegle's senate investigations, said the 18 member medical team from the Institute of Medicine had never called on witnesses with expertise regarding Iraqi bio-warfare.

Tuite noted that Riegle's reports had been made available to the institute. But the institute, Tuite declared, "has chosen to disregard them in exchange for assurances of the policy makers at the Department of Defense that these officers and enlisted veterans of the Persian Gulf War, many of whom are the very chemical specialists who determine whether or not chemical agents are present in combat, were mistaken." Under the same political pressure that had dogged Riegle, Tuite finally left his senate research post to found the Gulf War Research Foundation.

The more he heard and read, the more troubled Patrick Eddington was becoming. The CIA analyst began asking some discrete but pointed questions. The agent's request to see a sensitive CENTCOM log was his only active intelligence gathering.

It was enough. On March 2, 1995, Eddington's division chief called him in for a chat."I'm going to ask you to cease any further information collection as they relate to this issue, at least for the immediate future. We need to try to get control of this situation."

Saddam Hussein was also having problems with nosy inspectors. As the CIA initiated its damage control, its former ally installed toxicologist Rihab Rashid Taha al-Azawi as the head of Iraq's ongoing and now clandestine CBW effort. "Dr. Germs" was hand-picked to protect Iraq's bio-warfare capability.

Eddington, meanwhile, was still on the case. As he explained to his CIA colleagues, "the VA is not even testing these people for exposure to chemical warfare-induced injuries because the Pentagon says 'it didn't happen.'"

Other journalists were also on the scent. "Many veterans' disability claims are being turned down," reported the *Hartford Courant*. "Between February and May, 1995, government doctors have allowed only 12 percent of 4,157 environmental hazard sickness claims and only 5 percent of 2,059 undiagnosed illness complaints."

* * *

Across the Atlantic, a renewed desert storm was also starting to rattle Whitehall's windows. On March 6, a senior Defense minister apologized for misleading parliament over pesticides repeatedly sprayed over British troops and tents. Junior Armed Forces Minister Earl Howe insisted that there was now "considerable doubt" over his previous assurances that flocks of camels, sheep and goats grazed by Bedouin tribesmen in the war zone had died from "natural causes." Howe's mea culpa came just one week after his boss, Minister of Armed Forces Nicholas Soames, faced loud calls to resign after being accused of presiding over a Whitehall cover-up.

The first big cracks in the Pentagon's wall of denial came on March 12, when *60 Minutes* aired a Sunday segment seen across the country. Following Captain Johnson's account of finding a mustard gas "filling station" in Kuwait, ABC Host Ed Bradley pressed Deputy Secretary of Defense John Deutch to explain the Czech detections. Deutch was not convincing. But less than two months later, he became director of the CIA. Captain Johnson was immediately reassigned to Korea. Presumably he took his Meritorious Service Medal for exceptional service at Sabbahiyah with him.

Patrick Eddington was not so easily dismissed. On March 21, the CIA sleuth presented nearly 100 specific reports to a Senate Select Committee Intelligence meeting. Almost all of the documents were from DoD sources. Eddington would later write that the book-size stack of official memoranda "gave the location of known or suspected chemical warfare storage sites, cited chemical warfare attacks or preparations for them, or gave results of the chemical warfare sampling activities."

The depleted uranium issue was reignited the following month when French General Gallois told a reporter: "If we equip these tanks with these sorts of [DU] munitions, that means that chemical-nuclear war is morally allowable." One week later, CIA office director Chris Holmes replied to Eddington's senate committee presentation with signed a memo stating: "the CIA does not plan a comprehensive review of DoD information such as troop testimony, medical records operational logs."

Eddington was more than surprised. "The CIA's refusal to contact the veterans themselves was a complete departure from normal Agency practice," he wrote in *Gassed in the Gulf*. The career CIA analyst found it strange that an intelligence agency that routinely receives "information from American business people, academics, students, vacationers and others who travel abroad" was not interested in interviewing veterans of the nation's most recent war.

In May, 1995, a special Presidential Advisory Committee was formed to keep Clinton posted on developments on the Gulf War Illness front. Eddington noted that General Frederick Franks, the VII Corps commander who had incurred Schwarzkopf's verbal shrapnel for failing to aggressively pursue and engage the fleeing Iraqi Republican Guard, "sat on the panel for the remainder of the year, but never showed up for a single meeting."

Later that month, James Tuite told reporters that many of the symptoms suffered by Iraqi adults, children and babies after the war were identical with the symptoms reported by US and allied soldiers, their spouses and children. Tuite noted that their ailments also matched the profiles of those exposed to chemical and biological weapons.

The troublesome Tuite also revealed that partially released CENTCOM daily *Nuclear, Biological and Chemical Incident* logs showed at least 15 occasions in which US or allied forces reported detecting chemical weapons agents. Six more log entries documented the exposure of soldiers or civilians to chemical or biological weapons. In one episode, CENTCOM believed that British and US troops could have become sick from anthrax bacteria loaded into SCUD missile warheads.

According to the *Hartford Courant*, "The logs have been sought by veterans' advocates, federal investigators and the news media since 1993, but pages covering entire weeks of the deployment still have not been released." The news item also noted that the wartime staff writers "consistently downplayed most of the reported discoveries of chemicals or bacteria, sometimes before an inquiry was started."

During the spring and summer of 1995, DoD spinmeisters began what Eddington termed a "public relations and damage control campaign designed to deflect criticism while maintaining control over the information flow, and thus the public debate." In July, a web site called GulfLINK appeared on the Pentagon's public DefenseLINK. Internet browsers could click on Persian Gulf news, hotline numbers, DoD updates on a Comprehensive Clinical Evaluation Program, and a listing of military medical facilities offering CCEP examinations.

But the most hit-on website also contained documents recently declassified by a special Pentagon team. To the amazement of dedicated worldwide web watches, these official reports were filled with intelligence warnings on Iraq's CW capabilities, CBW warfighting doctrine and intentions to employ chemical warfare against allied troops. Incidents of actual or suspected use of CW agents by the Iraqi Chemical Corps were also available for "downloading" onto private computers. The whirr of hard-drives could almost be heard in Washington.

* * *

Just three days before nationwide celebrations of American independence from British rule, a Department of Veterans Affairs press release giving the casualties for "America's Wars" listed 6,526 Persian Gulf War veterans deaths as of July 1, 1995.

Two months later, on September 13, the CIA informed the Department of Defense of potential chemical warfare exposures at a place called Khamisiyah. The CIA memo asked for information on any US military forces in the area.

After years of deceit and denials, things were heating up. In November, the Pentagon cover-up of an illness now affecting over 80,000 veterans and their families was suddenly splashed nationwide when the cover of *Life* magazine featured a touching and tragic shot of US Army Sergeant Paul Hanson holding his three year-old son Jayce. A victim of White House duplicity as much as the Gulf war, Jayce had hands and feet, but no arms or legs.

"Jayce shimmied up to me on his bottom, pushing along a Donald Duck toy, and broke into a beautiful smile," reporter Briggs recounted later. "I was horrified by his condition – and amazed by his courage and strength."

Briggs interviewed some 50 scientists, veterans and Washington officials and digested a mountain of documentation. Along with British photographer Derek Hudson, the *Life* reporters visited nearly a dozen families whose lives had been forever altered by a distant war.

"Like hundreds of other families, the Hansons face official stonewalling and a frightening future," *Life* reported. "Certainly, soldiers expect to forfeit their health, if necessary, in the line of duty. But no one expects that of a soldier's kids."

The magazine quoted an internal National Guard study which "revealed that hundreds of Gulf vets had been wrongly discharged as a money saving measure – let go with a supposedly clean bill of health, although ongoing medical problems entitled them to remain in the service for treatment." The Veterans Administration's repeated delays in paying even minimal compensation to sick vets angered Senator Rockefeller, who *Life* quoted as saying: "The phrase I've used is 'reckless disregard.' There's a stark pattern of Defense Department recklessness."

Instead of responding with immediate offers of assistance for unfortunate families and their children, a Clinton administration National Security Council staffer named Elisa Harris prepared a "media guide" to help DoD and Veterans Administration officials fend off the *Life* feature. "Harris's involvement meant it had become a national security issue," Eddington observed. "How many people would want to join the Army if they knew that their combat injuries might be passed on to their kids?"

Such graphic revelations by one of North America's oldest and most respected magazines were bad enough, but the Deputy Secretary of Defense and Assistant Secretary of Defense for Health Affairs was also starting to express concern about "sensitive reports" posted to GulfLINK. In a November 20 electronic memo to Internet users explaining why the defense department had decided to delete the site, DoD's Paul Wallner explained that "'sensitive' meant documents that could generate 'unusual' public/media attention," as well as "all documents that seemed to confirm the use or detection of nuclear chemical or biological agents; or could embarrass the government or DoD."

Unimpressed veterans who had flocked to the Internet to trace wartime buddies and share experiences and information on a debilitating illness for which they still could not get straight answers, immediately reposted the deleted material.

One week later, Dr. Jonathan Tucker submitted his preliminary findings on the Seabees who had come under attack at al Jubayl. "The symptoms they reported were strikingly consistent: chronic diarrhea, joint pain, muscle spasms, mysterious tumors and skin rashes, chronic fatigue, recurrent headaches, and memory loss," Tucker reported. "Dozens of veterans said they had been hospitalized repeatedly and had been forced to give up their jobs and careers. Nick Roberts has been diagnosed with non-Hodgkin's lymphoma, a cancer of the lymphatic system, and he claims that several other Seabees who served at al Jubayl have developed lymphatic cancers as well."

DoD had told the inquiring MD that the loud bang heard by the Seabees on the early morning of January 19, 1991, was probably a SCUD intercepted by a Patriot air-defense missile at high-altitude as it nosed over toward Dhahran. The new explanation contradicted the military's initial claim that the big bang had been a sonic boom. In fact, battle records logged at the time of the incident showed that a SCUD had been hit over al Jubayl at the time of the incident.

But the Pentagon told Tucker that there was no way the SCUD could have carried chemicals, since the burning skin, facial numbness, and metallic taste reported by the Seabees did not correlate with the effects of chemical-warfare agents. Mustard gas induces painful skin blisters three to eight hours after exposure. Their immediate burns were caused by a rain of rocket fuel.

Tucker didn't think so. Nitrogen oxide missile propellant is a highly corrosive acid, he noted in his report. "None of the exposed troops observed any damage to their rubber gas masks, protective garments, weapons, ponchos, canteen containers, or tents." The MD also noted that NOx produces a reddish-brown smoke. "Eyewitnesses of the al Jubayl attack have consistently reported a 'yellow-green fog or mist floating through the air.'"

This mist matched the bio-agent referred to in Iraqi chemical warfare manuals as "yellow rain." The symptoms found among all the sick sailors were also an exact fit with the medical effects from the tricothecene mycotoxins released in yellow rain attacks. Evidence that the Iraqi Army had stockpiled significant quantities of this bio-weapon had come from Iraqi scientists when they had shown samples of widespread mycotoxin contamination at the Baghdad conference the previous December.

It was no secret where they had gotten the deadly fungus. In 1986, Baghdad had paid nearly 30,000 West German marks for four tricothecene mycotoxin "sample" shipments from Sigma-Chemie in Munich, Germany. Sigma-Chemie is actually a subsidiary of a St. Louis-based company that produces "specialty biochemicals" for research institutions. Less than three years later, Iraq purchased more of the toxic fungus from the Netherlands. A classified US government intelligence report noted that "the mycotoxins are being developed in a high security laboratory at the Saddam University (332100N/04425000E), Baghdad, IZ [Iraq] for possible biological warfare use."

The only glitch in Tucker's findings were several positive M256 identifications for blister agent. "Had Iraqis used a mixed agent attack?" Eddington wondered. "The Iraqis had an entire manual dedicated to fungal mycotoxins. The manual was available as far down as the battalion level. Its wide distribution indicated that the employment and defense against mycotoxins were part of their operating doctrine."

For his significant contribution to the Presidential committee's understanding of Gulf War Illness, Tucker was fired from the PAC. Journalist Philip Shenon reported how Tucker was called into Dr. Nashimi's office in December, 1995, and told he had one hour to clean out his desk.

"What are the grounds?" Tucker asked.

Nashimi replied, "I'm not going to tell you that."

When Tucker returned to his office, the hard drive from his computer had already been removed. A supervisor kept the dangerous doctor under close scrutiny as Tucker cleaned out his desk. They wanted "to make sure that I didn't take any of the files," Tucker later explained.

Eddington viewed Tucker's termination as a warning to other truth-tellers, including himself. "Tucker's integrity had cost him his job," Eddington realized. "Dr. Jonathan Tucker was conducting a real investigation. Tucker's integrity stands in marked contrast to that of the PAC senior staff. The PAC was nothing more than an exercise in damage control."

Riegle was gone after uncovering Washington-approved shipments of biological warfare cell cultures and production technology to Saddam Hussein. Tuite would soon follow. Rockefeller had been fired as chairman of the Veterans' Affairs Committee after producing the 1994 report on PB and vaccine use in the Persian Gulf. His replacement, Alan Simpson, said he would undertake no new investigations until the hard science was in – at which point no further investigations would be needed.

* * *

Simpson's pledge to ignore GWI turned out to be premature. On January 26, 1996, the Central Intelligence Agency told the National Security Council that US engineers had probably blown up chemical munitions at Khamisiyah.

A CIA analyst listening to a March 10, radio interview with Brian Martin heard the former Army engineer describe his demolition work at a site the analyst immediately recognized as Khamisiyah. DoD had contacted Martin after he had testified before the House Veterans Affairs Committee. But it took that radio interview for an intelligence analyst to make the connection between demolitions at an Nasiriyah and the nearby bunkers and open pits at Khamisiyah. The agent notified DoD and PAC of his interpretation the following day.

Five weeks later, on April 16, 1996, James Tuite nuked Schwarzkopf's deception. Citing "the collision of science and politics, the senate investigator provided reports of "direct chemical warfare agent deployment, exposure, or limited use during and after operation Desert Storm" to the Presidential Advisory Committee on Gulf War Veterans' Illnesses.

The following month, UNSCOM inspectors returned to Khamisiyah. This time, after making a more thorough examination of the demolished Bunker 73, the team positively identified debris characteristic of chemical munitions.

On May 1, 1996, the CIA announced at a PAC hearing in Washington that UNSCOM had found chemical weapons at Khamisiyah and that "elements of the 37th Engineer Battalion" had blown up those munitions in 1991.

The CIA's Sylvia Copeland also admitted that the Office of Scientific Weapons Research had set up a 24 hour CBW "watch office" at the start of the air war, which continued to the end of Desert Storm. "On the basis of all available information, we concluded that the coalition bombing resulted in damage to filled chemical warfare munitions at only two facilities, the Muhammadiyat storage area and the storage area at the al Muthanna chemical site," she told the Presidential Advisory Panel.

The UN inspection team returned to Khamisiyah on May 16th. During this tour, their Iraqi guides told the increasingly nervous inspectors that 6,323 mustard rounds had been moved to Khamisiyah from al Muthanna in January, 1991, after the coalition air raids commenced. About 2,160 sarin/cyclosarin rockets had also been transferred from al Muthanna to Bunker 73. But the discovery of a chemical leak in the hurriedly transported munitions had resulted in about half of those nerve agent-tipped rockets being moved to the open "pit" area in February, 1991. This was the arsenal American ground forces had blown up.

A few weeks later, former Air Force nurse Joyce Riley told a nationwide radio audience that she had talked to several flight nurses who accompanied soldiers being medevaced out of the Gulf. "They told me that many of the men had no skin on them, that their skin was falling off. Evidence of a chemical burn. So, this is known information. Some of the autopsies done at Dover, Delaware, found that some of the deaths were due to chemical poisoning." Riley also mentioned that she was receiving more and more phone calls from sick surplus dealers who had been selling Gulf war clothing, duffel bags and camping gear.

She was not kidding. A year later, on June 24, 1997, the Countess of Mar told the British House of Lords that young Scouts and Guides could be exposed to hazardous chemicals linked to Gulf war syndrome after the Ministry of Defense sold tents and sleeping bags used during Desert Storm. Her ladyship said she had evidence that Scouts using the war surplus camping gear were being exposed to the same gas warfare-derived organophosphate insecticides that some British scientists had linked to illnesses among Gulf veterans.

The countess knew of two Scout group organizers who had taken ill after handling tents bought from the MoD. "They had the same symptoms," she said. "Nausea, tiredness, muscle pain." Lady Mar noted that organophosphates are "far more potent in young people than in adults because the immune system does not fully develop until adulthood."

Junior Defense minister Lord Gilbert responded that "it would be extremely difficult, if not impossible, to identify any tents which are now in the hands of the general public."

* * *

Back in Washington, the growing media furor over possible exposures at Khamisiyah forced the Department of Defense to call a press briefing on June 21. Ignoring UNSOM reports of chemical munitions found at the huge ammo dump in late 1991, Pentagon officials said they had just been informed by UNSCOM of their May findings. "Based on a new review of the available information, it now appears that one of these destroyed bunkers contained chemical weapons," a DoD spokesman admitted. The room erupted with shouted questions. How many troops had been exposed? The Pentagon briefers said they were still trying to determine which units were in the area at the time of the blasts.

The reporters did not have long to wait. During a PAC meeting in Chicago on July 8 and 9, Copeland presented the CIA's final report on the chemical exposure question. "We conclude that Iraq did not use chemical agents, nor were chemical agents located in Kuwait," Copeland declared. "We assess that US troops were not exposed to chemical agents released by aerial bombing of Iraqi facilities."

Eddington was more amazed than irate. "Despite hearing detailed testimony to the contrary, not one member of the PAC staff or panel challenged Copeland's assertions," he observed.

But Khamisiyah was detonating all over again. On April 16, Jeffrey Ford, now the Executive Director of the National Gulf War Resource Center, testified before the US House of Representatives Committee on Veterans Affairs Subcommittee on Health. "On March 4th, 1991, while serving with the 307th Engineer Battalion of the 82nd Airborne Division," Ford told the packed hearing room, "I watched along with members of the 37th Engineer Battalion the destruction of 43 bunkers, one of which we now know contained tons of deadly binary-tipped nerve agent rockets."

During pointed cross-examination by Representative Christopher Shays during subsequent congressional hearings, a senior DoD official admitted on September 19 that more than 5,000 troops may have been exposed to chemical weapons at Khamisiyah.

The next day, the *New York Times* published the results of its interviews with 152 former Seabees who had served with the 24th Naval Mobile Construction Battalion during the missile attacks at al Jubayl in January, 1991. The "official newspaper of record" reported that 114 Seabees said they were still sick with illnesses stemming from a war that had "ended" five years before.

"Good afternoon," a senior defense official welcomed the nation's press on October 2, 1996. "Khamisiyah, in our judgment, is a watershed in this search for the information and understanding of Persian Gulf veterans' illnesses. Khamisiyah is the first event where we now can place American troops in the known presence of chemical agents."

But not to worry. Eight days later, a new report released by the National Academy of Sciences' Institute of Medicine concluded that no scientific evidence had been found to link service in the Persian Gulf War with adverse health effects other than those from combat injuries, insect bite infections and psychiatric disorders.

The institute claimed that sarin exposure would have resulted in death or severe, immediate illness, not the subtle, delayed symptoms commonly reported by sick vets. Dr. Stephen Joseph, head of the Pentagon's Gulf War illness investigation, said the military had been unable to confirm some 26 "positive" field readings indicating the presence of chemical agents. No corroborating evidence was found, he stated, ignoring numerous reports to the contrary.

Two days later, during a DoD background news briefing, the number of US troops exposed to chemical fallout from Khamisiyah was increased to 20,867.

* * *

Denial was still the order of the day. A hospitalization study released by the defense department on November 14, 1996, ignored more than 150,000 National Guard and Reserve members who served in Desert Storm. In a report released in December, the Presidential Advisory Committee on Gulf War Veterans' Illnesses also concluded that exposure to depleted uranium probably did not cause the illnesses. Few soldiers were adequately trained in Army procedures for handling vehicles contaminated with depleted uranium, however, and thus "unnecessary exposure of many individuals could have occurred."

The Shays hearings into the Gulf War opened in the House of Representatives on December 10, 1996. A month later, the city of Nashville alone had 36 claim handlers for sick desert war veterans.

As Veterans Administration representatives across the country attempted to deal with an avalanche of ill soldiers, the Countess of Mar was asking the House of Lords if the British Ministry of Defense had any "documentary evidence of chemical warfare" in the Gulf conflict. At that time, the British government had admitted to some 1,500 sick UK veterans following their desert deployment. The Countess' "tough" question omitted the possibilities of chemical agent fallout or biological weaponry. The

Earl Howe replied that MoD research "does not indicate any confirmed use of chemical warfare agents during the conflict."

The key cover-up word was "confirmed." Despite Riegle's earlier revelations, tens of thousands of detections triggered by chemical alarms during the Gulf conflict, many of them backed up by litmus paper tests and FOX spectrograph printouts, were discounted by the MoD as uncorroborated "alleged detections."

A lawsuit filed on January 16, 1997, by former CIA analysts Patrick and Robin Eddington against key US defense department officials and General Norman Schwarzkopf sought the release of tens of thousands of missing combat logbooks, FOX computer tapes and other official documents relating to the exposure of US troops to Iraqi chemical and biological weapons.

Schwarzkopf took to the airwaves instead of the witness stand. On January 29, the retired general set aside his memoirs to publicly proclaim that US troops had not been exposed to chemical agents "before, during or after hostilities." This incredible statement failed to mention log entries recorded at Schwarzkopf's CENTCOM headquarters showing at least 55 NBC incident reports of chemical detections during the air and ground wars.

"I never received, before, during or after the hostilities, any report of Iraqi use of chemical weapons, nor the discovery of or destruction of Iraqi chemical weapons," Schwarzkopf subsequently testified under oath before a US Senate hearing. "When there were suspected incidents, survey teams checked them out. In every case, survey teams entered the area with the most sophisticated detection devices available and in every case I am aware of, the alarms were declared false alarms." CNN carried these statements without comment, as well as Schwarzkopf's concluding whopper: "No one showed any symptom of chemical exposure."

The general must have forgotten the Purple Hearts handed out by the US Army for chemical wounds during the Gulf War.

Even the president of the United States contradicted Schwarzkopf's story. In his State of the Union Address delivered on February 4, 1997, Bill Clinton either slipped up or deliberately laid the groundwork for future admissions when he said: "...we must move strongly against new threats to our security.... Now we must rise to a new test of leadership: ratifying the Chemical Weapons Convention. It will make our troops safer from chemical attack. It will help us to fight terrorism. We have no more important obligations – especially in the wake of what we now know about the Gulf war."

PART III

MICRO-HUNTERS

CHAPTER 17

THE COCKROACH CONNECTION

Healthy French forces pointed the finger at a little white pill taken by more than a half-million US, UK and Anzac volunteers. But the first tangible clue to the cause of the mysterious maladies affecting so many returning veterans came from the wily, unloved cockroach. In 1993, this common insect pest, whose ability to withstand repeated chemical attacks had confounded the makers of pesticides for decades, was still under intense scrutiny by the US Department of Agriculture. James Moss, a scientist hired by the AG department's Medical and Veterinary Entomology Research Laboratory, was trying to increase the effectiveness of diethyl-m-tolamide, commonly known as DEET.

DEET had been developed by the Department of Agriculture in 1950. Currently sold in SC Johnson's popular insect repellent, "OFF," DEET was used by almost all American GI's to combat insects in the Saudi desert. Another insecticide, permethrin, was also used by some US forces.

Moss was looking at boric acid. The safe, low-cost powder messed up cockroach nervous systems, but too slowly for the "spray it – kill it" demands of customers being overrun by brigades of scurrying bugs. Additional chemicals, Moss hoped, would act synergistically to amplify boric acid's toxicity. In November, 1993, Moss began dripping droplets of a defoliant onto cockroaches. They didn't like it much. But when Moss added DEET to the defoliant, the result was spectacular. Each insect instantly departed its current embodiment in an impressive "rapid kill" strong enough to discourage reproduction, if not reincarnation.

Moss was onto something. As David Olinger reported in the *St. Petersburg Times*, Moss called Donald Hildebrandt to inform the Johnson Wax executive that the defoliant-augmented DEET might be a profitable cockroach killer. The excited scientist also mentioned a "hunch" he had that DEET's affinity for adrenalin might somehow be connected with something called Gulf War Syndrome.

Hildebrandt was not happy to hear that Moss was also calling other industry researchers to discuss his findings. The Johnson Wax officer immediately called Carl Schreck, another Gainesville lab researcher and DEET expert. "Who is Jim Moss?" Hildebrandt wanted to know. And what was his involvement with DEET?

Schreck went to his boss, Richard Brenner, who bucked Hildebrandt's complaint up to Ralph Bram, the program's national director. As Olinger discovered, Bram fired a verbal rocket at lab director Gary Mount. The resulting detonation would have impressed SCUD developers. Mount called Moss in for a chat.

Didn't the scientist know that DEET was sold worldwide by SC Johnson?

This was news to Moss. He thought that DEET was a Department of Agriculture concoction, free of commercial restraints. He quickly learned otherwise. Mount told Moss to stop discussing his work with anyone outside the lab. The researcher was told to desist from further DEET research.

But that was not quite all. The lab director also asked his employee if he recognized the damage his "hunch" about DEET contributing to Gulf War illnesses could have on the reputations of SC Johnson and the Department of Defense. It would not look good for either the corporation or the government agency if DEET was found to be dangerously toxic to humans. Mount told Moss his own reputation was on the line, as well as his chances for future employment after his current contract with the Gainesville lab expired. He ordered the research scientist to adhere to his work profile.

But he was. Moss' job description included developing pesticide "synergists". He asked his boss to put his comments and directives in writing.

When Mount declined to commit his "cease and desist" to paper, Moss continued to investigate the cockroach connection. Could DEET have somehow amplified the effects of permethrin sprayed on Gulf warriors uniforms? The PhD thought so. But even if he could prove that correlation, the numbers of people exposed to the DEET-permethrin combo could not begin to account for so many sick veterans.

The following month, Moss' line of inquiry shifted abruptly when he learned that sick soldiers had also swallowed a powerful nerve agent called pyridostigmine bromide. PB's "organo" origins, Moss realized, are the same as many insecticides. Besides jamming neural gateways open, his hunch was that DEET, adrenaline and pyridostigmine bromide might "synergize" each other, triggering secondary health outcomes much different than each of those three co-factors acting alone. "If you synergize PB with adrenaline, that doesn't mean you're going to expect the outcome that you would expect just from PB poisoning," he later explained. "It accentuates the effects of PB."

"PB is a 'pesticide,'" Moss later told veterans. "PB is a nerve agent." Both PB and Saddam's favorite nerve agent, sarin, are organophosphates. Both bind to the cholinesterase enzyme that neutralizes acetylcholine. "Too much acetylcholine builds up and the bug, or soldier, dies," Moss continued. "The only difference in the PB is that it does not stick as long. So, to get a low level PB dose to have the same effects as a single low sarin or other OP dose, you would have to repeat the dose: 30 mg, every eight hours for a few days would do it."

Why would someone want to pop what was essentially a 30 mg dose of sarin into her mouth? Because PB wears off quicker and binds to about 30 percent of the nervous system's cholinesterase, while longer-lasting sarin can only attach itself to the remaining 70 percent of available cholinesterase.

The idea, Moss explained, is that as the PB starts to wear off, its blocked cholinesterase is released and 30 percent of your nerve functioning starts to come back. "You are walking around with 30 percent of your cholinesterase tied up with PB. You get hit with nerve gas and you wind up with 100 percent of your cholinesterase tied up. That is, 30 percent by PB and 70 percent by sarin. The sarin can't hit the 30 percent because it is already blocked ('protected') by the PB. In theory, the temporary 30 percent block by PB is released (PB slowly comes off the cholinesterase) in four or so hours leaving you with 30 percent of your cholinesterase, which is enough to get by on."

It takes weeks for the human body to make enough cholinesterase to replace the 70 percent lost to sarin. But at least you're still around while this internal manufacturing takes place.

At least that's the theory. The flaw, of course, is that if you block 30 percent of your cholinesterase with a PB pill, then get a whiff or touch of sarin dust that ties up the other 70 percent, you now have 100 percent of your acetylcholine-inhibitor blocked for at least four hours. This is not a good thing. As many British and American soldiers found, it is hard to function with your nervous system firing continuously on Full-Automatic for four hours until the PB wears off.

But what happens if you are never told that you have just been subjected to a low-level dose of sarin drifting downwind from an exploding SCUD, or a bombed chemical weapons dump? What if you then pop another pill as ordered? What if you keep taking the pills as soon as each one wears off? What happens if you get further low-level doses of sarin? The answer is simple: you risk permanent nerve damage.

This is why pyridostigmine bromide was never supposed to be used after exposure to sarin.

But Moss knew that sarin wasn't necessary to amplify the affects of pyridostigmine bromide. Any exposure to any other OP would be just as hazardous – even more so, if the dosage and frequency were higher. DEET is an OP. So is permethrin.

The more Moss looked at pyridostigmine bromide, the less he liked it. Carbamates like PB don't just assault cholinesterase. They also target other enzymes, including one, Moss knew, responsible for delayed neurological effects. This could explain the "delayed reactions" reported by so many veterans, who instead of getting better after getting home, became even sicker. Not every expert agreed that PB produced such long-term effects. But chances are, Moss decided, if you repeated your exposure to PB as so many soldiers did, you would "mimic the main OP effects."

Because cholinesterase-inhibition caused by exposure to PB or a related nerve agent like sarin is not long-lasting, delayed reactions surfacing months later had nothing to do with cholinesterase-inhibition, Moss decided. The delayed effects must be due to an enzyme called neurotoxicesterase."

Found inside nerve cells, not at the nerve-muscle interface, this enzyme is also inhibited by some organophosphate nerve agents. So are other digestive enzymes, which could explain the many gastrointenstinal problems experienced by sick veterans. Hit these enzymes with sarin, Moss knew, and they would be as inhibited as cholinesterase.

"Now you've got hundreds of these enzymes in different parts of the cells in different parts of the body. So you can get hit with an organophosphate and it could cause delayed neuropathy. Or it could lead to cholinesterase-induced [effects] that leave you twitching and jumping around."

Or both.

Moss recalled people walking around in the 'Thirties after drinking "Ginger Jake," a soda adulterated with an OP. "What happens with people who drank this stuff? A couple of weeks or a month later, they started to get peripheral neuropathy and brain damage." Then they started twitching like headless chickens.

None of these initial findings made a strong case for swallowing PB at any time, much less during an actual chemical attack. "Any distinction between the effects of PB, sarin, or OP pesticides is artificial. There is none," Moss told veterans. "The only reason PB did not kill directly is the dose was about one-third that needed to kill you. You were exposed to a carbamate insecticide and you washed it down your throat, if you took these pills." And if someone did swallow the little white pills as ordered? "All these delayed effects that people think an OP like sarin could do, is just as likely from a chronic dose of PB. By chronic I mean every eight hours for two weeks."

For the next six months, James Moss and lab tech Gregory Knue continued hitting cockroaches with various combinations of DEET, PB and other insecticides. Both men were under growing pressure to stop their investigations. Moss's lab notes rarely left his hands.

By the spring of 1994, Moss and his assistant had shown conclusively that when used in combination with PB, DEET became almost seven times more toxic than when used alone. Some tests showed a 10-fold increase in toxicity.

* * *

By then, another researcher had suggested a link with OP exposure and the memory problems exhibited by many sick veterans. Noting that our ability to remember items and events is regulated by the nerve impulses in our personal neural processing unit (sometimes referred to as the brain). Dr. Howard Hu proposed in August, 1993, that the effects of non-lethal exposures to nerve agents could mimic non-lethal exposures to pesticides. Hu wasn't just blowing smoke. As a researcher with Physicians for Human Rights, Hu had helped investigate Iraqi nerve gas attacks against its own Kurdish people. Whether from pesticides or chemical weapons, Hu pointed out, the resulting dysfunctions are usually neuropsychological and include nervous system disorders and memory loss.

Also that year, researchers in India reported that low levels of sarin caused chronic brain and nerve damage in animals exposed over several days. The nerve damage was not apparent until two weeks after exposure to small amounts of sarin.

Heart problems, muscle aches, fatigue, inability to concentrate and almost every other symptom lumped under the heading of "Gulf War Illness" stem from neurophysical, as well as neuropsychological malfunctions. Whatever synergy was at work involving DEET, PB, sarin and/or other factors, some of the damage done to neuromuscular junctions is treatable. The bad news, Moss knew, is that some of that neuro-damage is irreversible.

When Moss called an aide to Senator Jay Rockefeller to discuss his findings, Rockefeller's ears perked up. As chairman of the US Senate's Veterans' Affairs committee, Rockefeller was about to convene senate hearings into decades of US military research that had subjected soldiers to atomic bomb blasts, LSD, poison gas and a host of other secret and deadly experiments. After listening to Moss, Rockefeller decided that PB should be included on the short-list of deleterious experiments inflicted on GIs without either proper warnings or their consent.

Rockefeller called Moss as a US Senate witness. On May 6, 1994, Moss was asked to provide his preliminary research findings. The researcher carefully replied under oath that PB, permethrin and eight other pesticide compounds "increased the toxicity of the repellent DEET to some degree."

While thanking Moss, the senator noted; "for the record, that the Department of Agriculture was not very happy about your coming here today to testify." Seven weeks after his Senate testimony, Moss' contract with the Agriculture department expired. It was not renewed. The USDA suspended all further research into DEET and PB, saying the Gainesville entomology lab "is not geared toward doing human toxicology research." If that was true, they should never have been looking to increase the potency of pesticides like DEET in the first place.

With his initiative, insight and credentials, James Moss should have easily found another research position. Instead, he found every application for employment or research grants turned down. Agriculture Secretary Dan Glickman says he suggested that Moss go to work for the Environmental Protection Agency or the Department of Defense. Moss says the suggestion was never made. Even if he had made it, Glickman must have been joking. When Moss went to the Department of Veterans Affairs, the USDA and the US Defense Department for funding, his applications fell into a bottomless In basket.

Months went by. A year passed. Moss's work as a substitute teacher and his wife's salary as a librarian were not keeping up with house payments and the needs of three children. Two years became three years of worry and unemployment. "We're broke," Moss told the veterans who had praised his courage as well as his work, but were broke themselves.

* * *

In 1991, Garth and Nancy Nicholson were relieved when their step-daughter Sharron returned safely from a violent visit to Iraq with the 101st Airborne. But she was also sick with something she couldn't seem to shake off. Soon, her entire family had caught her ailment. When both cats got sick as well, the Nicholsons tested everyone's blood, including the felines, Yin and Yang.

Both Nicholsons were well placed to perform their own tests. As Chief Scientific Officer for the non-profit Institute for Molecular Medicine in Irvine, California, and former Cancer Research chair at the University of Texas' M D Anderson Cancer Center in Houston, Dr. Garth Nicholson had published more than 450 medical papers, served on the editorial boards of 12 medical journals and peer-reviewed research grants for the US Army, National Cancer Institute, National Institutes of Health, American Cancer Society and the National Foundation for Cancer Research.

PhD molecular biophysicist Nancy Nicholson was the Institute for Molecular Medicine's CEO, and President of the Rhodon Foundation for Biomedical Research. Author of more than 30 medical and scientific papers, Nancy Nicholson had delivered over 60 international and national scientific presentations, and would come to be cited in the Who's Who in the World International Woman of the Year for 1996-97.

While so many other researchers were looking at chemical agents as primary culprits in Gulf War Illness, the Nicholsons knew that a contagious disease capable of spreading to other family members, including their cats, had to have a viral or bacterial component. Together, they made a list of possible biological agents that could cause the complex, chronic symptoms found in Gulf War Illness.

"We started testing, one-by-one," Garth Nicholson later explained, "but mycoplasmal infections were near the top of the list." The problem for the husband-wife team of microbiologists was how to develop a generic test to detect unusual microscopic organisms that appeared in many different tissues. Initially using sophisticated "nucleoprotein gene tracking," the Nicholsons later adapted methods to track complex chain-reactions in blood samples.

Deep inside their own white blood cells leukocytes, the Nicholsons discovered a slow-growing mycoplasma. Garth Nicholson describes the mycoplasma fermentans incognitas they found as "a kind of primitive bacteria that does not contain a rigid cell wall." It is not a virus. "Though mycoplasmas are often found at superficial sites in humans, such as in the oral cavity, they are rarely found in the blood," Garth Nicholson explained. "When they are in the blood, similar to other bacteria, they can cause a dangerous system-wide or systemic infection."

The transmission of mycoplasma incognitas through repeated casual contact would also explain how Gulf War Illness was being transmitted to family members and in a few instances, to attending physicians seeing GWI patients regularly over prolonged periods. Unlike the chemical contaminants being pursued by most doctors treating Gulf War patients, mycoplasmas can reproduce themselves in victims' bloodstreams, causing "delayed reactions" of secondary effects.

Though the antibiotics doxycycline and Cipro are effective against mycoplasmas, infections as deeply rooted as the mycoplasma fermentans incognitas the Nicholsons had found in their own bodies can be very hard to treat. The cat named Yin died. Brother Yang survived because, as Nicholson explains, "We got him on the doxycycline just in time." But before he responded to repeated courses of doxycycline, Garth Nicholson lost four teeth and underwent a jawbone infection that required removal of one bone and part of another.

* * *

Peering through powerful microscopes, the Nicholsons saw spirochetes taken from the blood and spinal fluid of other ailing Gulf War veterans poking through cell walls. Like a Trojan horse, the spirochetes penetrate cells and release microorganisms. When these microscopic organisms punch back through the cell wall, they carry fragments of that membrane along with part of the Trojan host cell into the bloodstream. The immune system spots these rogue organisms and launches an all-out counterattack. Often, that over-reaction does more damage than the microorganisms that triggered it.

The result is auto-immune dysfunction. As Garth Nicholson put it: "Cell-penetrating mycoplasmas, such as mycoplasma fermentans, may produce unusual autoimmune-like signs and symptoms when they escape from nerve and other cell types and stimulate host immune responses to host cell antigens carried on the mycoplasma surface."

The Nicholsons detected mycoplasmal infections in the blood leukocytes of nearly half of the first 170 GWI patients they studied, including "two out of two" British veterans. In non-deployed, healthy adults the incidence of mycoplasma-positive tests was less than five percent.

From its extreme prevalence among Gulf War vets, the researchers concluded that "systemic infections may be a major contributor to GWI." Most often, these infections show up as auto-immune disorders having symptoms similar or identical to diseases such as Lupus, Multiple Sclerosis, CFS or Alzheimer's.

When the Nicholsons went on to study 650 more veterans of Operation Desert Storm, and their immediate family members who also suffer from GWI, they found multiple chronic signs and symptoms very similar to patients with Chronic Fatigue Syndrome and fibromyalgia. This explained why many sick vets were "relieved" to finally be diagnosed with recognizable diseases like Lupus, CFS or MS – even though they most likely did not have those ailments.

Nancy and Garth Nicholson wondered if the mycoplasma incognitas they were seeing had somehow been genetically altered to make it so virulent. The mycoplasmas prevalent in most populations are usually not a direct threat to health. "As long as your immune system is all right it will not affect you," Garth Nicholson pointed out. But if mycoplasma incognitas is "weaponized," it becomes a different, deadlier story.

When the Nicholsons probed deeper, they discovered something so heinous they were initially ridiculed for even suggesting what their lab work clearly showed: the Trojan horse mycoplasma incognitas turning up in the cells of sick vets had been cleverly hidden inside an HIV-1 cellular wrapper to evade immune defenders. The sick soldiers did not have HIV. But part of an HIV-1 "envelope" had been used to send mycoplasma incognitas Special Delivery into the bloodstreams of US and, most likely, other coalition soldiers.

Could the mycoplasma have picked up the HIV fragments while passing through cells? While not a conclusive indication of genetic tampering, the mycoplasma incognitas-HIV combo "strongly suggested" deliberate genetic tampering, Nicholson explained, "because we did not find any other HIV gene" such as Tet, Pol or Rev genes. While the mycoplasma incognitas showing up in the blood of sick vets could be either a biological weapon or a natural occurrence, to Garth Nicholson the unusual HIV gene suggested either a weapon, an experimental vaccine or both.

The Iraqi Army, he pointed out, was known to have extensive stockpiles of biological weapons "and the potential to deliver these weapons offensively, at short range in modified biological sprayers that deliver biological weapons onto the sand to create exclusionary zones or 'biological minefields' – and at long range in modified SCUD-B missiles with 'skyburst' warheads."

In addition to Iraqi BW attacks, the Nicholsons continued in their written statement, "many of the storage and factory facilities where Chemical and Biological Weapons were stored were destroyed immediately up to, during and after the Desert Storm ground offensive, releasing plumes containing these agents high in the atmosphere where they could be carried downwind ('blow-back' exposures) to our lines."

The Pentagon was quick to respond to the suggestion that a biological agent had infected its soldiers. Assistant Secretary of Defense for Health Affairs Dr. Steven Joseph and Dr. Kenneth Kizer from the Department of Veterans Affairs launched a counter campaign in the press and before Congress. Lecturing to DoD in 1994 and 1996, and to the DVA in 1995, Joseph and Kizer declared that the type of infection detected by the Nicholson's in the blood of sick soldiers is commonly found, not dangerous and not even a human pathogen. Furthermore, the DoD complained, the Nicholsons' lab results had not been duplicated by another laboratory.

"These statements could not be further from the truth," Garth Nicholson responded. Their tests had been confirmed by a certified diagnostic clinical laboratory, Immunosciences Laboratories of California. The commercial lab found the same prevalence of mycoplasmal infections in blood of GWI and CFS patients.

As for the threat posed by such a difficult-to-detect organism, the US military's own medical school, the Uniformed Services University of the Health Sciences, taught that the type of rare infection the Nicholsons had found "is very dangerous, and can progress to system-wide organ failure and death. The Armed Forces Institute of Pathology has been publishing for years that this type of infection can result in death in nonhuman primates and in man."

The AFIP also recommended treating patients hit by mycoplasma incognitas' slow growing, chronic infections with doxycycline, the same antibiotic issued to the French Legionnaires who never contracted Gulf War Illness.

The Nicholsons were soon finding success by treating veterans who tested positive for mycoplasma incognitas with multiple courses of mycoplasma-specific antibiotics, including doxycycline (200 mg/day for 6 weeks per cycle), or Cipro (1500 mg/day for 6 weeks per cycle).

Repeated courses of Azithromycin or Zithromax (500 mg/day for 6 weeks per cycle), clarithromycin or Biaxin (500-1000 mg/day per 6 week cycle) or minocycline (200 mg/day for 6 weeks per cycle) also proved effective against this stubborn infection.

"Only the types of antibiotics that are known to be effective against mycoplasmas are effective," Garth Nicholson warned, "Most have no effect at all on the signs and symptoms of GWI/CFS/FM, and some antibiotics make the condition worse."

Because this slow growing microorganism is localized deep inside tissues which are hard to reach with enough antibiotic firepower, multiple treatment cycles are required. Though all 73 patients on antibiotic therapy relapsed within weeks after the first six-week cycle of therapy, subsequent relapses were milder. After up to six cycles of antibiotics, 58 of 73 GWI patients recovered; the rest were still undergoing therapy in the summer of 1997.

Garth Nicholson also cautioned that "if a vet has as his primary problem chemical exposures, then DOX should not help and could worsen the condition. Fortunately," he added, "most patients do better on antibiotics after an initial herxheimer reaction or die-off of the microorganism and release of toxic materials."

Besides finding hope for effective treatment, sick veterans could also take some satisfaction in a life-giving spin-off from their suffering. The Institute for Molecular Medicine and other laboratories began finding similar chronic infections in a significant percentage of civilian cases of CFS and fibromyalgia. Many of those successfully diagnosed and treated patients are now recovering after years of unexplained illness. "Since there are over one million CFS/FM patients in the US alone," Garth Nicholson pointed out, "this means that hundreds of thousands of Americans may be able to regain their health using the diagnostic tests and treatment suggestions developed for GWI."

Given this remarkable success rate among sick Gulf War veterans and civilians, the Nicholsons asked congress, why did the Department of Veterans Affairs issue guidelines stating that GWI patients should not be treated with antibiotics like doxycycline? Was Washington afraid that successful treatment for mycoplasma fermentans incognitas would confirm a biological infection and point a finger at their vaccines, or previous germ weapons sales to Iraq?

The news of the Nicholson's breakthrough swept through the veterans community at the speed of Internet impulses. When the Nicholsons went to the media, the phone started ringing. More than one thousand calls came in the first week, mostly from families experiencing the same debilitating symptoms as the sick veterans in their households. In 1997, after the Nicholsons were featured on TV specials, they received over 5,000 calls in a two week period.

* * *

One of those callers was Julianne Hamden. On the first of May, 1997, Mrs. Hamden had appeared before the Presidential Advisory Committee on Gulf War Illness. She told the presidential investigating panel that soon after her husband returned home from the Persian Gulf with a mysterious ailment, she and her daughter had also become sick. Bedridden with extreme uterine pain, Hamden was told by Army doctors at Walter Reed hospital that she had "willed" her uterus to expand.

Tested by the Nicholsons, the Hamden family had been found positive for mycoplasma fermentans. Only after they began taking doxycycline did they begin feeling much better. "Without their help I believe I would not be here today," Hamden testified.

Pointing to a 1996 issue of the Journal of Occupational Environmental Medicine, Hamden declared that "What we have uncovered includes evidence that Gulf War Syndrome biological exposures may be linked to chronic fatigue immune dysfunction syndrome (CFIDS), acquired immune dysfunction syndrome (AIDS), and may have relevance for other autoimmune diseases such as Lupus and Multiple Sclerosis. In these diseases an agent, often referred to as agent X or compound X, is believed to act as a viral catalyst reactivating Epstein Barr, human herpes virus #6, and other viruses. We believe that agent X is anthrax and/or mycoplasma fermentans."

Hamden then asked the committee to check the validity of confidential sources who reported that mycoplasma fermentans is a byproduct of anthrax production. If so, the mycoplasma could have easily contaminated anthrax vaccines given to American GIs.

"Mycoplasma fermentans has been shown to cause signs and symptoms similar to rheumatoid arthritis. It can also cause cardiovascular problems, tissue necrosis, organ failure and other damage to the body," Hamden noted.

Despite the obvious risks, during basic training in the spring of 1976, more than 3,900 US Marine volunteers had been injected with experimental mycoplasma pneumonia vaccines at Parris Island, South Carolina. Identical vaccines were also administered to US Air Force personnel at Kessler Air Force Base. While these experiments were underway, the University of Maryland was also testing germ warfare mycoplasmas on civilians. Some of those volunteers subsequently developed autoimmune diseases – including Chronic Fatigue Syndrome and Multiple Sclerosis. At least one military volunteer was tested positive for both mycoplasma fermentans and anthrax. Heavily vaccinated Vietnam veterans who reported auto-immune dysfunction also tested positive for mycoplasma fermentans, Hamden noted.

The well-informed Julianne Hamden also referred to Garth Nicholson's research showing that the powerfully fatiguing effects of mycoplasma fermantans incognitas are exacerbated by high-altitude flight. With US military pilots reporting difficulty in concentrating in *Aviation Weekly* and similar journals, she expressed concern over a recent spate of military airplane crashes in the United States.

In March, 1997, the US military lost three Harrier "jump-jets," two helicopters and an F-18 in unexplained accidents. Hamden asked the panel a show-stopping question: Could mycoplasma incognitas infections be spreading through the close-knit US military flying fraternity?

Her warning became prediction five months later, when another rash of crashes and collisions, including the crash of an Air Force Starlifter transport, and the loss of three fighter jets in just three days would lead to a temporary halt to all US military training flights.

Even more troubling than Hamden's supposition was her testimony that Dr. Raymond Chung of Walter Reed Army medical center had told her in August, 1994, that doxycycline would soon be given "to all the Gulf war vets."

But it never happened. Instead, Chung "recanted," Hamden said. "So it appears that this treatment was considered and then rejected by the military," because it "might point to the use of CBW during Desert Storm."

Because of Dr. Chung's about face, and many similar incidents, Hamden went on, "We do not trust the government scientists to do the right thing by Gulf veterans. They have demonstrated their incompetence in designing these vaccines and biologicals in the first place and in withholding treatment for mycoplasma fermentans (incognitus) even from soldiers with positive test results for the organism. We fear that if they do find a cure," she added, "they may withhold it, in order to keep their weapon secret."

To make matters worse, Hamden concluded, "the FDA is making permanent the temporary ruling used during the Gulf war that allowed DoD to use these experimental treatments in the first place. Do you want your children shot up with experimental vaccines and used as guinea pigs? As veterans who have been charged with protecting our countrymen it disgusts us that our military has intentionally harmed our civilians with chemical and biological agents."

* * *

Working in a lab in Huelva, Spain, an MD named Francisco Lopez Rueda was also pondering the origins of Gulf War Illness. The Spanish doctor had became involved with Gulf War veterans after noticing similarities between their symptoms and Huelva Toxic Syndrome. This syndrome had been triggered by pollutants during a severe drought in the Huelva region of Spain that lasted from 1990 to 1995.

At that time, Rueda had been intrigued by a study done at Tulane University which had looked at the pesticides Dieldrin and Endosulfan. Neither chemical appeared to be especially harmful to humans alone. But when they were paired, Rueda noted, "the potency rose by 160 to 1,600 times, a huge leap that stunned the researchers." Though the Tulane scientists were not looking at the Gulf War Syndrome, the synergistic effects they measured had troubling implications for veterans exposed to combinations of nerve agents and pesticides derived from those weapons.

When many wives began complaining that their husband's semen "burned like ammonia," researchers on both sides of the Atlantic had reached for their microscopes. And when they peered at the seminal fluid obtained from Gulf war vets, the microbe hunters found decreased protein content and an unidentified microbial organism. Dr. W. Boone, in Greenville, South Carolina, also discovered an increase in pH in the semen samples "possibly resulting in enhanced polyamine synthesis," which could actually result in the formation of ammonia. For anyone still trying to deny the reality of GWI, Rueda thought, there could be no doubt. Bodies sweating and ejaculating ammonia are definitely toxic.

Now Rueda was looking at a semen sample taken from a sick Gulf War veteran. Zooming up the magnification in his scanned semen photograph, Rueda was intrigued by the inability of molecular specialists to identify the fungal or protozoa-like structure he was looking at. They also could not account for the loss of protein in their samples. "Fungal-like" or "Protozoa-like" was not close enough for Rueda. Which was it? Or was it something new, "maybe a strange microorganism?"

Was it a "biological weapon?"

Working with Corel Draw software, the resourceful Rueda continued magnifying the one-centimeter computer image. He also dipped it in a 7,200 pixels per square-inch can of computer-generated colors.

As he tapped the computer keys, the image on the screen in front of him resolved into a thread bent in half on itself. The capsule containing the organism showed up in red on the monitor. The body was colored green for identification purposes. The central white part of the capsule was strangely hollow.

Rueda was convinced that he was looking at "a strange biological agent." Could it, he asked again, be a biological weapon?

A second small structure seemed to have separated from the upper thread-like organism. Rueda concluded that the smaller, unstructured part had died, while the upper part of the magnified organism was still alive at the time the photo was taken.

As a practicing MD, Rueda possessed a good under-standing of basic human metabolic processes, and more than a modicum of common sense. When he turned his attention to the average 50 percent decrease in protein found in sampled Gulf war veterans' semen, the answer jumped out at him.

"Probably this rare microorganism needs to eat some-thing," he guessed. "Perhaps human proteins." If it ate proteins, this microorganism had to produce urea. And since it was digesting protein in an oxygen-rich, or aerobic environment, the resulting oxidation would alter the semen's pH levels, producing the ammonia common in urine. Semen is not a waste-product excretion. Yet the sick veterans' semen was producing the am-monia indicative of metabolic processes, along with the "burning sensation" experienced by some spouses during intercourse.

"Conclusion," wrote Rueda to US vets: "Strange micro-organism in veterans semen not identifiable for our modern technical could be a biological weapon. Are you OK?"

There was another inference to make, as well. Burning semen would not only be conjugally discouraging. The compro-mised sperm would have a perfect avenue to transfer its hitch-hiking toxic messenger directly into a loving wife's body.

Genetically-altered mycoplasma was not the only biological suspect in the medical mystery surrounding Gulf War Illness. Another common spirochete showed that biting desert insects could have also laid some soldiers low.

Lyme disease, with its characteristic "bulls-eye" rashes on the buttocks, was also showing up among some sick veterans. Frank Sauer, a retired 24-year career soldier, began having symptoms suggestive of Chronic Fatigue Syndrome and Multiple Chemical Sensitivity soon after returning from the Vietnam war.

Most of the symptoms had faded by the mid-1980s when he was posted to the Sinai Desert as a UN observer. During an operational patrol in the Sinai he became "deathly sick." All the symptoms from Vietnam came back: headaches, chronic fatigue, difficulty sleeping, back pain and other medical problems as well. But new symptoms also emerged: stiff fingers and arthritic pain that migrated into various joints. Mild memory loss was accompanied by "fluctuating vision and most of the GWS symptoms that can be identified."

When he mustered out, Sauer submitted a service claim for disability. The VA medicos diagnosed him as having chronic lubosacral strain, allergic rhinitis and mild Post-Traumatic Stress Disorder. Sauer disagreed. Almost by accident, he learned from his veterinarian that his symptoms sounded similar to Lyme disease. His family physician arranged for more blood tests – and finally referred a very sick Sauer to an infectious disease specialist. Sauer asked to be tested for Lyme Disease. "And guess what...it came back positive!" Sauer was subsequently diagnosed with advanced stage Lyme disease.

Other Gulf War veterans were also testing positive for this multi-symptomatic infectious disease whose characteristic signs are flu-like and arthritic symptoms, as well as recurring "bulls-eye" rashes on each buttock.

Named after the Borrelia burgdorferi spirochete first found in deer ticks in Lyme, Connecticut, in 1975, Sauer noted that the disease is now thought to be carried by other vectors such as the fleas and biting flies found in the deserts of the Middle East. If multiple vaccinations, caffeine overloads, unremitting stress, radiation, pesticide exposure, chemical agent fallout and attacks, toxic oil smoke, lack of sleep and other immune-stressors had shattered once healthy immune defenses, military personnel serving in the Saudi, Kuwaiti and Iraqi deserts would have been wide open to Lyme-carrying fleas and flies.

* * *

"Desert ticks" enjoyed brief popularity among DoD denials of more serious synergies responsible for Gulf War Illness. While some returning veterans had undoubtedly succumbed to

Lyme-carrying fleas and flies, they might have shrugged off these infections had their immune systems not already been seriously compromised by PB, vaccines, stress and a host of other immune-suppressing agents. Even so, the few confirmed incidents of Lyme disease were a very minor contributor to a much bigger syndrome. No winged insect could ever hope to match the toxicity exhibited by much more formidable biological aggressors: the mycotoxin weapons perfected by the Iraqi Chemical Corps in their war with Iran.

It made a macabre kind of sense that such a proven-effective bio-weapon would next be turned against US troops. Pointing to the rare cancers, recurring rashes, bloody stools and other extreme, long-term effects evinced by veterans posted to al Jubayl, Patrick Eddington calls the SCUD attacks on that port and airfield complex "the Gulf War's biological equivalent to Pearl Harbor." Saddam Hussein, the CIA researcher noted, "had successfully used a weapon of mass destruction against American forces and there was no response."

Before being relieved of his post as head of the Presidential fact-finding committee on Gulf War Illness, Dr. Jonathan Tucker had gathered enough evidence to strongly support such a conclusion. While blister agents such as mustard and lewisite, and nerve agents like sarin, display chronic and acute effects consistent with the Seabees, British personnel and other victims of the al Jubayl attacks, "only one known family of biochemical agents can cause many of the symptoms experienced by the affected troops," Tucker maintained, "Mycotoxins."

These naturally-occurring fungi can cause severe sickness – even death – in humans. When "weaponized" in warhead concentrations, the "dusty" aflatoxins and tricothecenes which form the twin mycotoxin families result in immediate symptoms distinctly dissimilar to sarin and mustard agents.

Tucker noticed that many survivors of the SCUD attacks on al Jubayl told of instant itching and burning on exposed skin. Within several hours, small blisters formed. The nausea, vomiting, diarrhea, fever and languor also reported by affected troops were all signs of low-level tricothecene exposure. Most telling was the tendency for the solvent the Iraqi Chemical Corps used to carry tricothecenes to evaporate, leaving a powdery residue on dusted surfaces. Tucker found the "yellow powder" some soldiers saw coating tents and vehicles the morning after the attack, "suggestive of a crude extract of Fusarium fungus, which contains a yellow pigment in addition to a mixture of potent tricothecene toxins."

Like an living ecology, an intact human body is resilient enough to break down the T-2 and DAS poisons present in tricothecenes. But the byproducts from this metabolic house-cleaning, such as HT-2, are themselves highly toxic, Tucker noted. In fact, HT-2 is about two thirds as toxic as the original T-2 found in SCUD warheads by UN inspectors after the war. Tests have also shown that T-2 and DAS can persist for weeks in fat and skin tissue. "Unfortunately," Tucker added, "little research has been done on the chronic effects of sublethal tricothecene exposures."

CHAPTER 18

MARKERS

By early 1996, researchers in a half-dozen laboratories were closing in on the causes of a disease that was by then afflicting at least 86,000 US and British Gulf War veterans. The Gulf War Veterans Association put the number of sick soldiers at nearly twice that official figure. Whichever number was chosen, if deformed infants, sick spouses and offspring were added to these totals, the resulting figure would add up to the biggest unreported medical emergency in US history.

But Washington and Whitehall faced massive credibility and liability problems that went beyond issuing PB/NAPPS to unsuspecting service personnel, sometimes over their objections. What about all those vaccines soldiers had been subjected to, on the "hurry up"?

In November, 1995, a Berkeley, California immunologist and microbiologist told Tucker's Presidential Advisory Committee on Gulf War Veterans Illnesses that the many vaccinations given to soldiers and support personnel before and after departing for the KTO weakened their immune systems, leaving them vulnerable to environmental poisons such as oil smoke, as well as to opportunistic infections.

Dr. Howard Urnovitz blasted DoD for giving multiple vaccinations in single sessions without first verifying the safety of a practice vaccine manufacturers warned against. The Leading Edge research group found that American GIs had been given simultaneous vaccines for cholera, polio, typhoid fever, meningitis, Pertussis, tetanus, diphtheria, yellow fever, hepatitis B and influenza. This literally dizzying brew was topped off with two experimental vaccines, cryptically referred to as "VAC-A1" and "VAC-A2" – as well as experimental vaccines for anthrax and botulism plague.

The Nicholsons also felt strongly that because so many veterans were showing up with Gulf War Illness who had been vaccinated but never sent to the Gulf, the mycoplasma incognitas they were seeing in nearly half of their Gulf War patients had been injected into the veins of US troops through contaminated anthrax vaccines given while they were still "stateside". At the very least, the microbiologists pointed out, multiple vaccinations would weaken immune systems, leaving soldiers more susceptible to later infections and more likely to incur severe side-effects.

As they told the US House of Representatives Committee on Government Reform and Oversight in late June, 1997: "deployed soldiers were given multiple inoculations of experimental vaccines in unproven immunization schemes, such as vaccines that were given all at once instead of within an appropriate schedule of inoculations. Multiple vaccinations given simultaneously can result in immunosuppression and leave an individual susceptible to opportunistic infections. Some of these experimental vaccines could also have been contaminated with small amounts of slow-growing microorganisms."

* * *

Besides Urnovitz's unsettling remarks, CNN headlined a new study by researchers at the University of Glasgow who had found a commonality linking British Gulf War veterans with seemingly inexplicable symptoms. Their report, published after peer review by the British Medical Association in its respected *Journal of Neurology, Neurosurgery and Psychiatry*, found dysfunctional nervous systems in each of 14 UK veterans tested. At least 700 other British Desert Storm veterans were reporting ailments similar to those afflicting American vets (though some sick British veterans believed their numbers to be twice as high). CNN also reported "high numbers of babies with birth defects being born to Gulf War vets and their spouses."

The Cable News Network's print service noted that French Troops who reported no signs of the Gulf War syndrome had not been immunized like their UK and US counterparts. CNN said that as far as was known, the Glasgow findings were the first to show a clinical explanation for GWI varied symptoms. Drs. Hu and Moss had been right in drawing the same conclusions regarding neurophysiological damage.

Despite these findings, the British Ministry of Defense continued to cling to the increasingly implausible suggestion that seriously sick UK veterans were simply suffering from Post-Traumatic Stress Syndrome. While no one was saying stress wasn't a factor, attributing biological infections, birth defects, nerve damage and transmissible diseases to "stress" pushes that escape clause into conjecture beyond belief. The MoD might just as well have laid the blame for GWI on PMS.

"Diagnoses biased on PTSD may be a gross over-simplification," the Nicholsons rebutted. "The variable incu-bation time of GWI, ranging from months to years after presumed exposure, the cyclic nature of the relapsing fevers and other signs and symptoms, and the types of signs and symptoms are con-sistent with diseases caused by combinations of biological and/or chemical or radiological agents."

The pioneering microbiologists suggested that the autoimmune syndrome variously characterized as GWI, CFS and FM "could be explained in many patients by exposure of veterans to various biological agents (chronic pathogenic infec-tions) in combination with chemical exposures and in veterans' family members to biological agents transported back home by the veterans."

Dr. Goran Jamal, the British neurophysiologist who led the Glasgow research team, emphasized that the underlying cause of

Gulf War Illness had yet to be determined. "Outside factors," such as exposure to pesticides and pollutants from burning oil wells, had all contributed to the mysterious malady affecting the neurological systems of tens of thousands of Gulf war veterans.

* * *

To add to the warmakers' woes, James Tuite was back in their face the day after the Glasgow story broke with more damning evidence of immune system problems among Gulf war veterans. Since leaving the senate, the indefatigable GWI investigator had formed the Gulf War Research Foundation. Now, here was Tuite on CNN saying that American troops given polio vaccines had failed to develop polio antibodies to the same extent as other members of the general population.

Tuite was referring to Howard Urnovitz. That PhD researcher had just finished presenting data to the Subcommittee on Human Resources and Intergovernmental Relations showing that US forces who showed an unexpectedly low antibody response to polio serotype 2 and serotype 3 had been deployed to the Gulf. Non-deployed military personnel exhibited the same antibody response as the general population.

"The poor antibody response to the polio boosters suggests that there is an underlying problem with the immune response of PGW military to a vaccine considered to be effective over the past four decades," Urnovitz told the Congressional committee earlier that day.

Dr. Marie Chow is Professor of Microbiology, Immunology and Pathology at the University of Arkansas for Medical Sciences, a renowned polio expert and consultant to Little Rock's Department of Veterans Affairs Medical Center. Chow believed that the GI's failure to develop an appropriate antibody response to the polio vaccine "suggests that factors perturbing these interactions may be inducing this unexpected outcome."

In plainer English, suggested Congressman Christopher Shays, one of these factors could be exposure to chemical warfare agents.

"This was the most toxic battlefield in the history of modern warfare," Tuite reminded the Congressional committee. "Studies since World War I show that individuals exposed to chemical agents and other related poisons have had symptoms similar to those of the Gulf War veterans."

Even worse, Tuite, added, US forces may have done it to themselves. Bound by its own fixed timetable, CENTCOM could not alter its tightly orchestrated aerial dismemberment of Iraq for vagaries of the wind.

"The incendiary weapons used to destroy Iraqi chemical munitions sites forced skyward vapors and toxic byproducts from chemical agents. Weather patterns moved them as fallout over US and coalition soldiers. As favorable conditions for evaporation developed, the heavier-than-air gases fell to the ground."

The former head of US Senate investigations into CBW exports to Iraq and health problems related to the Gulf War also pointed out that many of the hazardous chemicals detected by coalition chemical warfare experts are known to affect the central nervous and immune systems. The troublemaking Tuite further observed that other strong immuno-suppressants could be found in official reports of limited chemical and biological attacks, severe toxins released in large quantities by oil fires, "preventive" medicines and other exotic new "occupational hazards" of modern warfare. These contributing co-factors exacerbated the effects of detonated chemical ammo dump fallout.

The US defense department and the Department of Veterans Affairs had nothing to say about the polio vaccine or Glasgow studies. But their silence didn't matter. Though Moss had been sidelined, his pioneering work had not gone unnoticed by other researchers challenged by the puzzle of Gulf War Illness. Only a few weeks after the latest Shays hearings, researchers at Duke University and the University of Texas Southwest Medical Center independently reported finding an interaction between insecticides, insect repellents and the nerve agent pretreatment pill, PB.

On April 17, Duke University scientists working in collaboration with University of Texas Southwestern Medical Center researchers revealed that one factor in the neurological illnesses plaguing Gulf War veterans "may be the simultaneous exposure to multiple agents" ironically used to "protect the health of service personnel." These multiple organo-agents included Moss's top three chemical culprits: PB, DEET and permethrin.

Praising Moss as "a very fine scientist," Duke's head researcher Mohammed Abou-Donia pointed to the study's most ominous conclusion: at dosage levels where a single chemical was harmless, the combination of all three OPs resulted in an effect that "is very, very strong." So strong, in fact, that the synergistic combination of individually "harmless" dosages could be fatal.

"Our first task was to demonstrate the safety of each chemical when used individually," Abou-Donia said. "Even if a person was exposed to one chemical alone at three times the recommended dose, he or she would have remained healthy." Chickens exposed to two of the three OP chemicals exhibited signs strikingly similar to human sufferers of GWI: weight loss, diarrhea, shortness of breath, lassitude, stumbling, weak legs, a reluctance to walk and tremors. The chickens could fly better than humans, but not by much.

The combination of DEET, PB and permethrin produced chicken hell: total paralysis or death.

When the researchers analyzed central nervous system tissues they found that synergistic chemical exposure caused "enlarged axions and anonal degeneration." Nerve damage, in other words. The tests also suggested that the severity of symptoms depended on the ability of a cholinesterase-type "scavenger" enzyme called BuChE to scrub foreign chemicals like DEET and permethrin from the system.

There is just enough BuChE in the human bloodstream to neutralize DEET, PB or permethrin. But when two or three of those chemicals flood the bloodstream, the BuChE enzyme is overwhelmed. The resulting accumulation of OP chemicals then becomes toxic to the brain and nervous system.

PB proved to be an especially powerful inhibitor of BuChE. By binding to the scavenger enzyme, PB permitted more DEET and permethrin to roam unhindered through the central nervous pathways. Pharmacologist Abou-Donia found that after injecting rats with PB, DEET and permethrin, this OP overload weakened the brain's defenses, allowing PB to cross the "blood-brain barrier" protecting that organ from toxic harm. Once PB got into the brain, it performed as advertised, impairing cholinesterase and further damaging brain functions.

* * *

On May 27, Gary Lane picked up the trail for the Christian Broadcasting Network. A sick American veteran named Debbie Judd told the reporter on-air: "When I first got sick in Saudi, I thought, 'Well, once I get home and sleep in my own bed and, you know, get hot baths and eat right, then, you know, everything will be fine.' And it didn't. It's deteriorated. It's gotten worse through the years."

Nurse Judd had treated troops close to the Iraqi border. Today, chronic joint and muscle pain prevent her from keeping house, or a job. An unresponsive government had left her feeling bitter and betrayed. "I wouldn't recommend people trust their government," she told CBN listeners. "I don't want my children to join the military."

Dr. Howard Urnovitz also took to the CBN airways to announce that the antibiotic doxycycline was "basically reversing the symptoms" for some stricken veterans. Lane broke in to say that doxycycline had helped Judd "a bit."

Tom Hare is a doxy-believer. During the Gulf War, the 101st "Screaming Eagles" sergeant had been used to humping a hundred pound pack for 12 or 18 hours, sometimes traversing ten miles of blistering desert. He had also watched the Egyptians fire red star clusters, the CBW warning, a few miles from his position. After returning home, his wife Kristine noticed how odd he smelled when he sweated. Simple colds developed into sinus infections so strong they spread to his teeth. A rash across his upper thighs and buttocks would not go away. His gums bled. Intense pain in his bones left his knees feeling as if they were on fire.

In April, 1995, Hare's legs gave out at work and he was confined to a wheelchair. He started forgetting things. His moods swung giddily between coping and despair. Kristine had to dress him, and he couldn't even hold his baby girl.

Nothing seemed to help. When Kristine began showing the same disturbing symptoms as her husband, a physician named Dr. Louis McIntire decided to try very aggressive treatment for both patients by prescribing the antibiotic doxycycline. "The results of the treatment were quite dramatic." McIntire reported that both Tom and Kristine Hare showed immediate improvement.

Tom Hare's progress was remarkable. Within three weeks, his all-consuming pain had relented. Not long after that, his wheelchair went into storage and he took his first tentative steps. Though he is not cured, Hare credits doxycycline with giving him a new life.

Doxycyline's effectiveness in promoting "a good response" that sent 55 of 73 sick Gulf War veterans back to normal duty was described in the February 22, 1995, edition of the *Journal of the American Medical Association*. Despite successful treatments by the Nicholsons, Urnovitz and McIntire, JAMA raised doubts about the ability of any long term antibiotic therapy to maintain its effectiveness in the face of rapidly mutating microorganisms that eventually became resistant to those drugs.

Garth Nicholson reminded Gulf War veterans, "not every GWI patient has this problem or has chronic microorganism infections, but the vets with severe arthritis-like, or other auto-immune-like signs and symptoms are likely candidates for doxycycline treatment."

The question remained: Why were fit young soldiers contracting diseases which commonly strike older, less fit people whose immune defenses are no longer functioning at peak efficiency? Opportunistic infections including gram-positive cocci, microsporidium, candidiasis, Epstein Barr virus and cytomegalovirus were being diagnosed in some veterans. The Nicholsons felt strongly that other chronic infections, such as brucella and Q-fever were also contributing to his case of GWI. Both brucella and Q-fever were germ warfare weapons supplied by the US to Saddam's biowarfare labs before the Gulf War.

The biological component of GWI first described by Nancy and Garth Nicholson, was given fresh impetus in October, 1996, with the detection of genetic material in the blood of Persian Gulf War veterans. A Florida study led by microbiologist Howard Urnovitz found evidence of exposure to organophosphate chemical nerve agents, as well as epidemics caused by specific viral infections.

"We already know that the veterans appear to have immune anomalies that might put them at risk for common infections," Urnovitz told the press. "The results of this present study suggest that RNA can be isolated from the serum of Gulf

War veterans that appear to share some similarity to the enterovirus family. No similar RNA was found in the control civilian group."

HRV "enteroviruses" are among several hundred common viruses that use non-reproducing RNA rather than DNA for their genetic blueprint. Enteroviruses can give infected hosts colds or paralytic polio. Using new "gene amplification technology to look for unique RNA "bands," Urnovitz and his colleagues were able to identify the presence of microbial agents in serum samples taken from sick vets.

The results of the cellular search were especially provocative because 19 of 23 Gulf-deployed California veterans, 10 of 13 deployed Arkansas veterans, and 8 of 8 non-deployed Arkansas veterans showed up with nucleic acid viral markers belonging to the enterovirus family. Was some aspect of military service predisposing individuals to contracting a Persian Gulf War-related illness, even if they did not go to the Gulf? All eight non-deployed troopers were healthy. Some other co-factors specifically related to the Persian Gulf War must have been required to trigger actual illness.

Dr. Marie Chow was one of the Arkansas investigators. "While an actual virus has not been identified," Chow observed, "this is an important first step in trying to determine what contributions microorganisms may play in the development of PGWRI. We still have a significant way to go before we understand the complexity of this multifactorial disease. There are clearly many factors underlying these symptoms."

"Illness development actually requires a combination of several events," concurred Dr. Susan Guba. Assistant Professor of Medicine and Pathology at the University of Arkansas and the Little Rock Department of Veterans Affairs medical centers, and study coordinator for the Arkansas group, underlined the importance of the Urnovitz study. Because it identified one measurable factor associated with one potential viral "hit" responsible in part for GWI, Guba called for more research to identify other causal "hits" and their role in triggering the mystery illness.

Dr. Robert Garry, Professor of Microbiology at the Tulane University Medical School and an expert in discovering new human viruses and auto-immune neurologic diseases, also stressed the importance of Urnovitz's latest findings. "If a virus is found to be associated with this disease, significant resources need to be dedicated to learn whether these microbes are contributing to the illnesses of returning veterans and their families, as well as birth defects in their children after the war."

Urnovitz was certain that part of the GWI puzzle was viral in nature. The symptoms in the veterans he had studied appeared to be different than the acute symptoms of toxic chemical exposure. Their resemblance to epidemic fatigue syndromes pointed to a viral component. "This study strongly supports the concept that microbiological markers may be associated with this veteran population," Urnovitz concluded. The Chief Science Officer of his Calypte Biomedical lab hoped their findings would lead to the development of more precise diagnostic tools.

Dr. Jean Higashida, Assistant Clinical Professor of Medicine at the University of California-Davis, Chief of Rheumatology for the Department of Veterans Affairs in Northern California, and principal study coordinator for California veterans, was also "seeing many symptoms of chronic diseases that have always been considered to have some viral component to them." Higashida expressed hope that the microbe hunters would be able to isolate that virus so that an antiviral treatment could be initiated.

But it was Tuite who translated Urnovitz's RNA revelations into simple terms with not-so-simple implications for more than 100,000 sick vets. "The discovery of the activation of human endogenous retroviral (HERV) gene sequences in Gulf War veterans could be the keys," Tuite said, "to explaining the syndrome as it has actually been observed: the symptoms, the transmissibility primarily to family members, and the teratogenic (birth defect-causing) effects."

In the summer of 1996, Garth Nicholson and the Center for Disease Control proposed a joint research project to look for mycoplasma incognitus among more Desert Storm veterans and their families. The Pentagon had already refused to fund Dr. Hyman, a Louisiana physician who had found unexplained bacteria in the urine of Gulf War veterans. The Nicholson-CDC request was also rejected.

* * *

Whatever virulent whirlwind had blown back in the faces of coalition troops in a desert resounding to the explosions of SCUDs and allied bombing raids, Saddam's sadistic "cocktails" had definitely been augmented by germs injected directly into the arms of his opponents by their own governments. On Christmas Eve, 1996, readers of London's *Independent* newspaper received the unwelcome news that their own sons and daughters had been given secret injections to "protect" them against Saddam Hussein's known biological warfare agents: anthrax, Pertussis, bubonic plague and botulinum toxin.

Although members of Britain's parliament had been assured by Whitehall that all vaccinations had been fully disclosed, Defense correspondent Christopher Bellamy found five or six injections given by the Ministry of Defense that had yet to be acknowledged, let alone identified. These injections were never recorded on the medical documents of the soldiers and aircrews receiving them.

Just two weeks before Bellamy's bombshell, Britain's Armed Forces Minister Nicholas Soames told Parliament he was launching a multi-million dollar program to ferret out the cause behind the ailments which by then had affected more than 1,200

UK veterans. As Bellamy summarized for his readers: "It is widely believed that the various illnesses may have been caused by exposure to organophosphorous pesticides, by tablets taken as a precaution against chemical weapons, by the cocktail of injections against biological warfare agents given in a short period of time, or by a combination of these factors."

Labour Defense critic Dr. David Clarke was not impressed by "misinformation" being passed by the Defense ministry and other government spokesmen. "I find this appalling," he told reporters. "The Government must now come completely clean about what went on and ought to step up its efforts to find out what happened to these men and women. All drugs used in the Gulf ought to be declassified."

Shaun Ruslin, a 37 year old former medic who had served with 32 Field Ambulance, was by then too sick to work. Because he was a medic detailed to look after chemical and biological casualties at the Brit's Wadi al Batin field hospital, Ruslin received 24 injections. Most other British soldiers got about a dozen shots. In November, Ruslin was not reassured after receiving a letter from a Brigadier McDermott of the British Army medical directorate telling him that some of the injections he had been given were classified military secrets – and had never been recorded.

Rusling's lawyers ("solicitors" in England) contacted the RAF doctor initially tasked with looking into GWI for the British military. Before being transferred under protest from his incomplete investigations, Group Captain Bill Coker was never told about secret vaccines. Coker was also unaware that some British soldiers were made to give blood samples after being subjected to secret "biological warfare" injections. These non-consenting experimental lab humans were told their blood was being delivered to Porton Down, the British government's top secret chemical biological warfare lab similar to Fort Detrick in the USA, for analysis.

* * *

Years of official lies, deceptions and denial were finally being exposed by evidence that could not be refuted, hidden or ignored. The blood of American soldiers carried unmistakable medical "markers" whose DNA matching would point directly to criminal malfeasance – including deliberate toxic assaults and cover-ups, not only by Baghdad, but also by the Pentagon and Britain's Ministry of Defense as well.

At the same time Haley's chickens were coming home to roost, a lesson from Chaos Theory and a special computer program were picking patterns out of a constellation of baffling and seemingly conflicting symptoms. By using an algorithm developed to identify repeating iterations among apparently "chaotic" events, research scientists at UT Southwestern Medical Center discovered that some Gulf War veterans were suffering from several syndromes pointing to brain and nerve damage caused by wartime exposures to various synergistic combinations of low-level nerve agents and common pesticides.

Their findings appeared in three articles in the January 15, 1997, issue of the *Journal of the American Medical Association.* Each JAMA entry "solves a different piece of the puzzle that has baffled previous researchers of these mysterious illnesses," said Dr. Robert Haley, UT Southwestern's chief of epidemiology and the study's head investigator.

Ever since the war's end, debate had raged among medical doctors, researchers and sick veterans about whether the so-called "Gulf War Syndrome" really represented an identifiable syndrome. What did so many seemingly disparate symptoms have in common? After extensive studies and some fancy computer work, research scientists at UT Southwestern concluded that some Gulf War veterans were suffering from not one but three primary syndromes.

Each leg of this toxic triad points to brain and nerve damage caused by wartime exposure to combinations of low-level nerve agents and common pesticides. UT Southwestern's primary investigator, Dr. Robert Haley announced to the press that their findings "provide the first evidence of associations between symptoms in Gulf War veterans and exposures to chemicals, including chemical nerve agents."

That evidence had not been easily assimilated. After conducting exhaustive epidemiological and clinical studies on 249 Seabees from the 24th Naval Mobile Construction Battalion, the UT Southwestern team's top neurologists looked at each veteran individually – and became just as confused trying to pin down a single identifiable disease as military and Veterans Administration doctors had been before them. Nothing made sense. "Chronic Fatigue Syndrome" and the popular British government catch-all, "Post-Traumatic Stress Disorder" produced only a fuzzy frame around seemingly unrelated symptoms.

"No single test in an individual was abnormal enough to make a traditional diagnosis," Haley explained. But when the silicon-sleuths used Chaos Theory-derived algorithm to split each reported symptom into its individual components, their sophisticated math program was able to cross-match those components. As hard-to-discern patterns snapped into focus, the artificial intelligence picked out three distinctive patterns.

"The group comparisons showed a pattern of damage to a few nerve cells here and there throughout the nervous system – just what you would expect from chemical nerve damage. Without doubt," Haley added, "all three syndromes indicate damage to the brain, central, and peripheral nervous systems. Gulf War-related illnesses "are organic, not psychiatric or stress related."

One syndrome was found to be characterized by thought, memory and sleep problems. The second syndrome includes severe thinking difficulties, as well as confusion and imbalance.

The third shows sore joints and muscles, and tingling or numbness in the hands and feet.

Through a series of blind studies that hid 249 sick and healthy subjects from the researchers performing the tests, UT Southwestern scientists were able to trace the first syndrome to the use of flea and tick collars by insect-pestered soldiers in the Saudi desert. Those who wore the collars more often, or next to the skin rather than over their clothing, suffered more acute reactions.

The second syndrome matched reported CBW attacks on al Jubayl. Seabees who took their PB pills as ordered suffered even worse effects from an already severe syndrome.

The third and least severe syndrome came from government issue insect repellent, with a formulation of 75 percent DEET.

All three syndromes are variants of a rare disorder called organophosphate-induced delayed polyneuropathy. This OP-induced illness inhibits critically important cholinesterase. Flea-collars, insect repellent, pyridostigmine bromide and exposure to chemical warfare nerve agents were risk factors, the computer found, four to eight-times as prevalent among ill as healthy veterans.

Seabees who reported coming under an attack by chemical weapons at al Jubayl on the night of January 19 to 20, 1991, and who had experienced particularly severe side effects from the PB tablets they took, were five-times more likely to have at least one of the syndromes than other Seabees who had taken PB and ducked the SCUDs, or who had endured the missile attacks and skipped the PB. "This indicates a synergistic effect," Haley pointed out, between the nerve agent pill and the nerve agent itself.

The UT Southwestern conclusions contradicted presidential panel pronouncements that continued to insist there was no connection between GWI and chemical exposure in the Gulf. Only four days before, a presidential advisory committee claimed that the stress of overseas deployment and combat had played a major role in the soldiers' syndromes.

* * *

In theory, James Moss agreed. The PAC people had some strong science to back them up. "Stress will kill, and it will actually do nerve damage," Moss pointed out. Medical studies show that stress, and its handmaiden, depression, are among the most potent immune-suppressants. Stress triggers hormonal and other internal chemical changes that can leave people almost defenseless in the face of opportunistic infections or chemical attack. Fear is another kind of stress causing the same outcomes. Revulsion, horror, even nightmares trigger adverse chemical reactions throughout the body.

The only problem with the PAC's pat analysis, Moss saw, was that there was not enough combat-related stress among virtually unopposed US forces to prompt such strong reactions during the four brief days of a Desert Storm. The stress of deployment throughout Desert Shield, though often intense, was nowhere near the stress experienced by Vietnam-era grunts "walking point" during a 12-month "tour" of booby-trapped, ambush-prone jungle. Even then, Moss pointed out, even under constant threat from booby-traps and ambush, the only Vietnam vets to show symptoms resembling those from the Gulf War had also been exposed to a potent OP called Agent Orange.

But DEET might have added to the adrenaline overload of GIs deployed to Saudi Arabia. Turning his pesticide probe to mice, Moss had accumulated enough rough data to indicate that DEET might act like adrenaline in the human body. "We got synergisms from adrenaline on PB acting on immune system cells placed in a petri dish," he relates. No other co-factors were in sight.

Despite his ground-breaking work documenting hazards of the pyridostigmine bromide-pesticide combination, James Moss now says, "I'd be much more concerned about stress and PB than DEET and PB." The reason, he explains, is that more people in the Gulf were exposed to PB and stress than to PB and DEET. "If you have five chemicals and each potentiates the other – say many were exposed to PB and stress, fewer to DEET and permethrin – which ones are you suspicious about? It's gotta be first PB, then adrenaline."

Spikes of lingering adrenaline could have come from constant gas alarms, the *bang!* of exploding SCUDs, or even the caffeine-fueled stress of working 16 hour days to get urgent jobs done. "It's got nothing to do with things being in their heads," Moss explained. "Adrenaline's a chemical whether it's pumped out of your nervous system, or whether someone injects you with it. It's still a chemical that by itself would probably have less an effect than in combination with the pill. And since DoD knew there was a problem with stress and the pill, they should have known better."

DoD and MoD should also have known better than to keep insisting that Gulf War Syndrome was all in veterans' heads. That official lament was finally squelched for good by Dr. Jim Hom. After administering a series of psychological tests to the sick Seabees, the UT Southwestern neuropsychologist definitely ruled out Post-Traumatic Stress Disorder, combat stress, major depression, malingering and other psychological disorders as causes of Gulf War Illness.

As Dr. Robert Haley explained to Chronicillnet's moderator, "No one has ever suggested that brain damage can be caused by stress." The neural-damage genie was out of the bottle, Haley added, and could not be stuffed back in. "This is a physical illness that's manifested by brain damage and nerve damage, and it was caused by a combination of chemicals to which the veterans were exposed during the war."

Haley, whose long career with the CDC led him to investigate "much more obvious" Legionnaire's disease, toxic shock syndrome, and AIDS, called GWI "probably the most complicated new illness to appear in the last 25 or 30 years." After six years of study, he pointed out, no two researchers could even agree on what GWI meant, "or even if there was a disease." The syndrome's many symptoms are so ambiguous, so specific to each patient and group of patients, they resisted being grouped together. Nothing made sense until UT Southwestern came up with its computer-aided conclusions.

Haley hoped new screening tests could soon be developed to identify veterans with neurotoxic syndromes. Symptoms such as diarrhea, skin rashes and aching joints would be studied next, he said. Within the year, Haley thought doctors at VA hospitals, private hospitals and military clinics would have the tools necessary to "ID" populations with specific neurotoxic syndromes.

Chronicillnet asked Dr. Haley if his team were seeing any indication of "an infectious component" to the syndromes they were studying?

"No, we don't," Haley answered. "We looked pretty carefully for evidence of risk factors for infectious agents, and we did a lot of blood testing, and we were unable to find anything that looked infectious. That doesn't mean that there couldn't be an infectious agent; we just didn't find it. Others, I am sure, will continue looking, and we strongly encourage that."

A related question left unanswered by the UT Southwestern sleuths was the origin of similar symptoms experienced by the spouses and children of returning veterans. It was back to square one on that issue, Haley admitted. But now that a real illness had been found among GIs, it was going to be much easier to make a similar determination for their families.

The previous October, Donald Riegle had published the initial results of a study among 1,200 veterans showing that 78-percent of Gulf War veterans' spouses, one in four of their children born before the war and 65 percent born since, were showing symptoms of the devastating syndrome. A spokesman for the senator told the press that there could be no doubt that the Gulf War Syndrome "is transmissible and that it rules out some of the possible causes. It's not post-traumatic stress. It's got to be some kind of viral or bacterial infection. Our focus is on chemical or biological agents."

When asked if any known treatments could reverse the nerve damage showing up in sick personnel, Haley replied that medications and other therapies could lead to dramatic improvements in the veterans' debilitating symptoms. But "nerve damage, as you know, is permanent. There is nothing that will cure it."

That's what most of the medical community thought. But their near-consensus of doom did not account for a startling new therapy that was already achieving the "impossible" – growing new brain cells in primates with whom we humans share 99 percent of our genetic blueprint.

* * *

The real surprise at UT Southwestern was yet to come. At the end of their landmark study, the participating medical doctors declared that exposure to oil-well smoke, multiple vaccinations, depleted uranium munitions, burning jet fuel in tents and combat were only weakly associated with the Persian Gulf syndrome, or not at all.

Other researchers, as well as veterans supporting various GWI causation "camps," disputed these conclusions as fervently as they welcomed UT's first findings. Among the more informed critics was professor Siegwart Gunther, whose depleted uranium souvenir had caused such a stir among German authorities. Contact with DU, Gunther said, "results in the breakdown of the immune system. Other effects noticed, maybe many infectious diseases, with serious complications, are on the increase" in Iraq, as well as among returning veterans exposed to radioactive shell fragments and DU dust. "Herpes infections, Zoster infections and AIDS-like symptoms, all of them are possibly related to the breakdown of the immune system."

Even sharing space inside an Abrams tank with intact DU rounds risks a radioactive assault on the tank crews' immune systems. According to Darwin Taras, an Army expert on Depleted Uranium weapons, the 2/10ths of a millirem of gamma radiation given off every hour by onboard DU munitions would expose US tank crews to the equivalent of one chest X-ray every 20 to 30 hours. Were they expendable? Such dosages would never be permitted for civilians undergoing medical X-rays.

CHAPTER 19

BAD BLOOD

Was the Pentagon's panic over the near-certainty that the chemical and biological weaponry Washington had sold to Saddam would be used against its own troops limited to the desperate, fast-tracked approval of a dangerous experimental nerve drug called PB?

In the summer of 1997, Garth Nicholson learned of another drug hastily stockpiled by DoD as a shield against the bio-weapons and production equipment sent to Saddam under government license from US companies. "I know from several sources that the DoD put out emergency orders for doxycycline and ciprofloxacin a few weeks before the ground war started," Nicholson informed American veterans. "One of the generic pharmaceutical companies that contracted with DoD described delivering 18 million units of doxycycline to a USAF base for immediate shipment to Saudi just two weeks before the ground war. After the war soldiers described to me that antibiotics, such as doxycycline, were being buried in mass in the desert (with their shipment pallets)."

Nicholson found it "interesting" that the same antibiotics he and his wife had been recommending for mycoplasmal infections had been rushed to the Gulf in massive quantities just before the combined American assault on Kuwait and Iraq. "You can draw your own conclusions from this, but I feel strongly that the US knew exactly what we were facing in the Gulf War," Nicholson concluded. After all, he noted, the US, Europeans, Russians, Chinese and others had armed Iraqi forces with CBW weapons.

As a post-script, one of the USA's leading GWI researchers added that he had heard too many stories about "unconventional" NATO and US munitions turning up in Iraqi bunkers not to wonder if these shipments were the real reason behind Washington's increasingly implausible denials that chemical/biological weapons were ever used in the Gulf War.

While Gulf war watchers pondered these disturbing reports, another revelation rocked the research community. On August 25, 1997, *Insight* magazine reported that a synthetic chemical used in the experimental inoculations against HIV had been detected in the blood of languishing Gulf war-era soldiers.

Pentagon officials who had earlier proclaimed that no chemical weapons had been found on Persian Gulf battlefields and that fallout from Khamisiyah had injured no American soldiers now rushed forward to deny that the "investigational" HIV vaccine had been given to US armed forces personnel during that conflict. They might have had better luck peddling junked cars. No official medical agency could explain how a chemical compound called squalene had turned up in the blood tests of hundreds of vets – including those who had never left the continental USA. Squalene is an adjuvant that amplifies the effects of immunizations. It is not approved for human use except in certain US government-certified medical tests used to search for cures for diseases such as AIDS and herpes.

"Adding to the mystery," added Paul Rodriguez in the *Washington Times*, "is the inexplicable disappearance of as many as 700,000 service-related immunization records." Rodriguez's report came after a four-month investigation for the *Washington Times*, which also publishes *Insight* magazine.

Congressional oversight panels in the senate, as well as the House Veterans Affairs committee which had uncovered much of the Gulf War's dirtiest secrets, geared up for fresh scrutiny of the squalene scenario.

They could start with the National Institute of Health and the Walter Reed Army Medical Center. Rodriguez revealed that both government agencies were the only ones authorized to carry out human experimentation with experimental adjuvants. For more than a decade, the NIH and Walter Reed hospital had been testing adjuvant-boosted immunizations against the HIV virus.

Pamela Asa – the Tennessee immunologist working with Richard Shuster on his antibody assay studies – had first suggested the adjuvant angle to Gulf War Syndrome symptomology nearly two years before. In October, 1995, she had been shot down by Air Force Colonel Ed Koenigsberg, director of the Pentagon's Persian Gulf War Veterans' Illness Investigation Team. The PGIIT head told the presidential advisory panel investigating GWI that Dr. Asa's theory was "unfounded" because only non-experimental alum adjuvants had been injected into American troops. No secret immunizations were ever issued, Koenigsberg insisted.

In fact, at least two secret vaccinations – code-named "VAC-A1" and "VAC-A2" – had been given to Persian Gulf-bound US troops.

"We found soldiers who never left the United States but who got shots who are sick, and they have squalene in their systems," reported an independent lab scientist hired by *Insight*. "And we found people who served in the desert but were civilians who never got these shots who are not sick and do not have squalene."

With nearly three out of four Gulf War-vaccinated GIs testing positive for squalene antibodies, two questions with unsettling implications came immediately to mind: Who had given them the experimental immune booster? And if the squalene had not protected them from contracting Gulf War Illness, had it – like PB – actually made them sicker?

"I can't tell you why it's there, but there it is," a senior US government official told Rodriguez. "And I can tell you this, too: the sicker an individual, the higher the level of antibodies for this [squalene] stuff."

Another high-level defense department official who was also familiar with the blood tests provided another hint: "I'm not telling you that squalene is making these people sick, but I am telling you that the sick ones have it in them. It's probably whatever was used [mixed] with the squalene that's doing it, or in combination with the squalene. You find that, and you may be on to something."

* * *

Only the month before, congress had approved a five-year plan to slash veterans' programs by making the deepest incisions ever performed on that administration. Ostensibly done to "balance" the federal budget, Dave Autry pointed out in the American veteran's magazine *DAV* that "tens of billions of dollars" had been simultaneously made available for "new and expanded federal programs." An additional $85 billion in tax breaks – primarily for corporations and the wealthy – meant more than a $3 billion reduction in the VA's requested budget over five years at a rate more than twice as high as cuts to other federal departments and programs.

National Adjutant, Arthur Wilson declared that the "balanced budget agreement unfairly burdens veterans' programs and would severely hamper the VA's ability to provide top quality health care to those men and women who bear the deepest wounds and scars of war."

For fiscal 1998 alone, Autry advised, "funding for veterans' health care and other programs would be $400 million below the fiscal year 1997 appropriation." By 2002, when more than 100,000 Gulf War veterans (plus a high proportion of family members) would be facing even more dire predicaments from their degenerative illnesses, VA assistance will be cut by $750 million less than that agency had asked for.

Compensation for undiagnosed and still officially unrecognized wounds incurred either in the Gulf, or stateside during the military's mass inoculation programs and post-war cleanup of contaminated equipment, also meant that cost-of-living adjustments for disability compensation, pensions, and benefits to the survivors of deceased vets would also have to be "rounded down" to the next lowest category of payouts. Ungrateful legislators who had sent American soldiers to war were now assuring that those same veterans would lack the funds needed for the therapies necessary to arrest or at least cope with debilitating symptoms.

DAV's Executive Director David Gorman called on senators and representatives to "fend off the drastic cuts called for in the budget blueprint. These cuts would mean that hundreds of thousands of disabled and needy veterans would be denied health care. Veterans' hospitals and clinics would have to eliminate medical and nursing staff positions and cut back on health care services."

The VA said it hoped that private insurance carried by veterans would make up the short-fall. Veterans Administration officials were either unaware or unconcerned that Gulf war veterans were often finding it impossible to obtain medical insurance from private insurers who regarded them as poor health risks.

"Historically," Gorman noted, "the VA has needed an increase of almost $500 million a year just to pay for employee pay raises and rising costs of medical supplies and equipment. The appropriation level in the budget agreement leaves the VA at least $1 billion short of what it needs just to keep pace with inflation in fiscal year 1998."

As that gap translates into untold stress and suffering for veterans over the next five years, Gorman spoke for many when he said: "We did not risk our lives and health for America only to find that, in our day of need, the health care we have earned is threatened. I find it absolutely outrageous that the President and our elected representatives would even consider funding new programs before they have lived up to this nation's sacred obligation to veterans."

* * *

What of the suffering children living in a land of biblical antiquity? Six years after a war that left the health and sanitation of Iraq's major cities in ruins, the US was adamant that all of Saddam's weapons of mass destruction be located and eliminated before crippling sanctions could be lifted. In one of the first major speeches made by a representative of Iraq since the cessation of open hostilities, Mohammed Said al Sahaf addressed the 52nd session of the UN General Assembly in New York on October 2, 1997.

The UN had just announced plans for a major restructuring that would streamline its bloated bureaucracy and cut running costs substantially. "We believe that the reform process of the organization should not be limited to the management aspect, important as it is," said Iraq's Minister for Foreign Affairs in his opening remarks. "More importantly, there should be a common political will to redress the real and effective balance in the work of the organization and to prevent its machinery from being used for private political objectives and purposes of certain super powers. Above all, one should pay attention to the dangers inherent in one international pole breaking loose and trying to dominate the world."

In reiterating Saddam Hussein's years-old call for a "multi-polar" political landscape, Mohammed Said al Sahaf joined with Russia's President Yeltsin and China's Jiang Zemin in rejecting "hegemony by any state over world affairs."

In case his point wasn't pointed enough, Iraq's representative further stated that "The United Nations should not be controlled by the rich, although they are a small minority in the world." Underlining the UN Charter's mandate to ensure "the promotion of the economic and social advancement of all peoples," the Iraqi foreign minister said that his government "consider[s] it necessary to avoid marginalizing developing countries and denying them the chances and potential for economic and scientific development."

The people of Iraq continue to suffering gravely for a dictator's dreams of glory. In early June, 1997, a survey undertaken by Baghdad's health ministry and the United Nations Children's Fund (UNICEF) found that one in every four young Iraqi children was underweight for her or his age. Measurable malnutrition – as evidenced by abnormally low height-for-age had hit more than 27 per cent of all children under the age of five. After a child reaches two or three years of age, UNICEF warned, damage to the child's development is likely to be permanent.

Six years of UN sanctions so harsh even imported pencils remain banned lest they fall into the hands of an army already driving new tanks. Though Iraq's ruling elite continue to live in style, between 1987 and 1995, Iraq's annual budget for purchasing medicines had plummeted by more than 90 percent, from $450 million to just $22 million – or about a dollar per person. By December 7, 1995, diarrheal diseases had tripled. Some 576,000 Iraqi children had also died since the war's "end" as a direct result of sanctions imposed by the United Nations Security Council.

In May, 1996, CBS' *60 Minutes* reported on the effects of the US-led embargo on Iraq's children. Madeleine Albright, US ambassador to the United Nations at the time, was asked by CBS interviewer Lesley Stahl if a half million dead children – outnumbering even those killed at Hiroshima – was worth the price. Albright replied that it was.

Just five months later, UNICEF was begging for emergency financial assistance to assist 10 million children in Iraq suffering from hunger and disease. "The situation is disastrous for children. Many are living on the very margin of survival," said UNICEC representative Philippe Heffinck. "Around 4,500 children under the age of five are dying here every month from hunger and disease."

By March, 1977, UNICEF was reporting that the most threatened segment of Iraq's population were children under two years of age. The economic blockade continued to send prices for available commodities spiraling beyond the reach of families who had already sold off their most valued possessions to care for their children. The price of wheat flour in 1995 had risen to 11,667 times more than it had sold for in 1989.

Writing from Baghdad, Ibrahim J. Ibrahim reported in 1995 that scarce tires and spare parts had crippled public transport, forcing commuters to dig deep into their paychecks to pay the fares for rides that come infrequently "as they wait under a blistering sun." Worsening air pollution from a badly degraded environment and badly maintained vehicles, Ibrahim added, meant that "the number of people suffering from hay fever and other allergic illnesses is increasing at an alarming pace."

Once known as one of the cleanest cities in the Middle East, Baghdad's heavily bombed sewage system was operating at less than half its prewar capacity. Backed-up pipes, Ibrahim wrote, had "turned their gardens into a wasteland and their once-decent neighborhood into insect-breeding marshes." Even worse, strange plant diseases "have smitten entire areas of the country." Once stately date palms were drooping to the ground from diseases "researchers are still trying to define."

"For more than seven years, Iraq has been suffering under an unjust blockade the like of which has never been witnessed in human history. The comprehensive blockade imposed on Iraq is the most extensive and cruel boycott system ever imposed by the Security Council in its history. It covers and affects...every aspect of life. We are convinced, from our practical experience, that the insistence on the perpetuation of the blockade against Iraq is not connected to the fulfillment by Iraq of its obligations. It is rather a systematic plan to inflict severe damage on Iraq by putting an end to its development potential and destroying its economic infrastructure, to fulfill the selfish interests of an aggressive super power."

Iraq's environment had also suffered extensive damage, Mohammed Said continued, after the bombing "by the United States and some of its allies, which was aimed at power stations, sewage systems and factories, which we have not been able to rebuild fully because of the blockade."

Citing scientific studies by outside agencies that confirmed the use of banned weapons by the United States, the foreign minister said that depleted uranium munitions had "exposed vast tracts of Iraqi territory to contamination by deadly toxic materials. Numerous cases of hitherto unfamiliar illnesses have been recorded, such as congenital deformities in unborn children, bone deformities and many cases of leukemia among children."

Enough was enough, Mohammed Said declared, "Iraq has carried out what it was required to do under these resolutions...the truth is that Iraq no longer has any banned weapons, equipment, machinery or materials." Noting that "substantial advancement" had been made in the "common activity" of identifying and destroying unconventional weapons of mass destruction, Iraq's UN spokesman hoped that the imminent release of a new report by the UN investigating commission would mean "the beginning of the lifting of the blockade on Iraq."

In the meantime, the "oil-for-food-and-medicine" formula enacted by the UN to relieve human misery in Iraq was meeting only a small fraction of Iraq's needs, Mohammed Said remarked. In 1996, Iraq had been allowed to sell $4 billion dollars worth of oil. Half of those revenues were swallowed by war reparations, UN operations, aid to the Kurdish population and repairing Iraq's oil pipeline. Though never divided among the Iraqi people, the remaining income would have paid one US quarter to each person. "While the West can point to this gesture as a sign of its good will, in reality it is meant to continue its choke hold on Iraq," Dr. S. Amjad Hussain wrote in the Toledo *Blade*.

"This formula has experienced and continues to experience many major obstacles and difficulties, which the United States and Britain in particular try to impose with a view to hindering its proper and effective implementation, thereby contradicting the declared purpose of resolution 987," Iraq's foreign minister complained. "The conduct of the representatives of these two countries in the 661 Committee has led to the accumulation of rejected or suspended contracts on flimsy pretexts."

As a result, Mohammed Said al Sahaf continued, "This caused a huge gap in the smooth flow of approvals of such contracts and thus delayed the delivery and distribution of materials to the Iraqi people. Until now, over three months since the expiry of the implementation of the first period, Iraq has received only 25 percent of the medicine required and has not received any materials at all in the fields of agriculture, education, water, sewage and spare parts for electricity generating power stations."

Minister Mohammed Said finally resorted to reason, and the spirit of a people who would not be vanquished. "Iraq is an ancient country with a history extending 7,000 years," he told the UN assembly. "The Iraqi people who contributed immensely to human civilization will remain in charge of their own affairs, independent in their choice and able to overcome crises. While we stand at the threshold of the 21st century, we look forward to seeing the United Nations able to discharge its basic responsibilities to carry out its purposes embodied in the Charter."

By the time Mohammed Said al Sahaf sat down, another child had died in Iraq.

* * *

Would the sanctions finally be lifted? The month before al Sahaf's appeal, Iraq had handed a 639 page report on its biological weapons development to UN biological weapons expert John Spertzel at the Baghdad Ongoing Monitoring and Verification Center. "Now I will be able to say to the Security Council that all full, final and complete disclosures have been lodged," UN weapons chief, Richard Butler told Reuters news service. "What now remains is to proceed to verify the contents (of the declaration) so that we can empty all baskets of weapons as soon as possible."

Filing the bio-weapons report was an essential precondition for the lifting of UN trade sanctions imposed on Iraq for its invasion of Kuwait in August, 1990. Lifting the ban on Iraq's oil exports would reestablish that country's primary source of income – but only after all stocks of biological and chemical weapons, as well as production facilities, were crushed or burned. All of Iraq's long-range missiles would meet the same fate. Saddam Hussein's nuclear weapons program would also have to be dismantled – and strict weapons monitoring left in place – before the oil – and revenues – flowed again.

"We are getting very close to be able to account for the SCUD missiles that were imported by Iraq in the past," Butler told a special press briefing after the Iraqi foreign minister's speech. "Those missiles, which had numbered 819, were prohibited because their range exceeded 150 kilometers. Through the excavations, all of the launch vehicles and nearly all of the missiles had been accounted for, and only a very small gap remained – less than the fingers of one hand." A zero balance, said the UN weapons boss, "was close to being achieved."

Chemical VX weapons, which most Washington authorities were certain had never been developed by the Iraqi military before the Gulf War, had also been discovered and were being destroyed along with chemical weapons manufacturing facilities and the chemical precursors needed to make such weapons. Information Iraq had previously provided on its remaining CBW warheads "was not accurate," Butler noted. Further information and verification would have to be sought before sanctions could be relaxed or removed.

Four weeks later, with no sign of the embargo being eased, Baghdad's patience ran out. On October 29, 1997, Iraq ordered all US citizens serving on UN inspection teams to be out of the country within a week. The move followed a recommendation by Iraq's parliament that the country cease cooperating with UN personnel attempting to ensure that Iraq had identified and destroyed all weapons of mass destruction. Baghdad also wanted an immediate end to UN reconnaissance flights using US aircraft.

In a letter to the UN Security Council, Deputy Prime Minister of Iraq, Tariq Aziz stated that despite the progress made in the destruction of all the proscribed weapons and related factories, equipment and instruments – as well as the comprehensive and strict monitoring system in effect since 1994 – the Special Commission had not submitted a factual and objective report to the Council. As a result, said Aziz, economic sanctions against Iraq remained in place because of "the position of the United States and the roles of the American personnel and other personnel of the Special Commission who implement the American policy."

Iraq's ambassador to the United Nations, Nizar Hamdoon, hastened to explain that the Americans were being expelled because of "frustration" over continuing trade sanctions against Iraq. The decision, Hamdoon insisted, was not taken to provoke confrontation, but because of "the procrastination of the commission in doing its work."

Only the week before, Baghdad had incurred the wrath of the UN by blocking its weapons inspectors from entering a key site. Now that body reacted swiftly. A UN press release on the 30th condemned Iraq for attempting to "dictate terms" to the UN Special Commission charged with overseeing the destruction of that country's weapons of mass destruction. In demanding that a recalcitrant Iraq "cooperate fully, in accordance with the relevant resolutions and without conditions or restrictions," the UN Security Council warned that failure to immediately and fully comply would have "serious consequences."

On November 19, 1997, as US carrier aircraft loaded bombs for renewed strikes against Iraqi cities, about 200 protesters besieged the US Embassy in London, demanding an immediate end to the military threats by the US and Britain against Iraq. Protesters from Cambridge, Sussex, Birmingham and elsewhere in Britain included members of the British Parliament, trade unionists and representatives of community and religious organizations were in attendance.

A delegation of Iraqi children delivered a letter to the embassy addressed to Bill Clinton. The letter reminded the American president that only the Security Council of the United Nations can authorize the use of force under provisions of the UN Charter.

"No such use or threats of force have on this occasion been authorized by the Security Council, so that your Administration is clearly in breach of international law in adopting its present stance, and any attack on Iraq at this time would be quite simply a criminal act," the letter, written by the children's parents, pointed out. "On behalf of all in Britain who wish to see a relaxation of the present tension and danger in the Gulf region, we therefore urge you to desist from the dangerous military build-up and illegal threats of force against Iraq, so as to allow a resolution of the points at issue in the Gulf region to be negotiated by peaceful means."

* * *

Carol Picou was one of the first women to join front-line American troops in a wartime assault. Accompanying fast-moving armor into Iraq during Desert Storm, the combat nurse had been stunned by the violent lethality of depleted uranium cannon fire, which had never before been used in combat. Arriving within minutes of fierce attacks, the career Army nurse had never seen anything to compare with this smoking destruction. Even for modern warfare, she told RTV news service, "it just wasn't normal. To me it looked like we must have nuked them. The bodies were as black as can be and some of the bodies just melted."

Even the troops on the "safe" side of all that DU firepower had not fully appreciated the hazards that exotic weaponry posed to themselves. They had no clue that rapid-firing tank and aircraft cannons could create a radioactive battlefield within the few short minutes each engagement usually lasted. "No one," RTV's Parveez Syed pointed out, "told them they should avoid the smoldering wrecks of Iraqi vehicles or surrendering soldiers."

When incontinence, muscle weakness and memory loss followed Carol Picou back home, her suspicions turned from the PB pills she had been forced to take to the DU she had been exposed to on the battlegrounds of Iraq. The sick army nurse became the only Gulf War veteran "worked up" and diagnosed by Dr. Thomas Callender. The renowned occupational and environmental toxicologist was medical board-certified in five fields of medicine. The MD was also a PhD physicist who had served on the scientific teams sent into Chernobyl and India's Bhopal disasters.

When Carol and Tony Picou first met with Callender in 1992, the toxicologist had Carol admitted to hospital for a SPEC brain scan within three hours. The moving, "real time" pictures of her thalamus "message center" showed an abnormal blood flow to one side of Carol Picou's brain. After an intensive "QEEG", a medical computer was used to generate a "Qualitative" EEG, Callender determined that Carol Picou showed definite signs mirroring radiation exposure.

On September 10, 1994, Carol Picou's urine tests came back. She tested positive for low but persistent levels of uranium poisoning. When she was permanently retired in March, 1995, after 17 years of service, in the words of her husband, Carol Picou possessed "a clean decorated history." But she was very ill.

As a former US arms salesman, Tony Picou had seen Pentagon reports showing that DU creates a radioactive dust cloud that could travel downwind for 20 miles. "How many solders were in its path?" he wondered. "Let's face it, even the air was contaminated. My wife Carol breathed that air, and also dealt with injured Iraqi troops. Their clothes and gear all contaminated. Thousands of soldiers are sick."

Tony Picou began letting people know that he was sure the Pentagon was trying to block information on DU's hazards because "they realized that the depleted uranium penetrator is such an awesome weapon that they don't want to jeopardize its use in the next war."

As if to prove his point, unsubtle pressure was brought to bear on the Picous. Their second IRS audit in a row, "was just a nightmare," says Tony Picou. "You're guilty until proven innocent." All their checking accounts had to reconcile to zero-error for every month of 1993. When they moved to Lafayette to start the Mission Project, the government of Louisiana tried to collect back taxes from them – even though they had never lived there before. Had their number just happened to come up, Tony Picou wondered? Three years in a row?

While still living in San Antonio in 1994, the Picous had continued to raise sharp and embarrassing questions about the documented hazards of DU. The cover-up intensified. At that time, Carol Picou was flying up to Washington, DC every other month, testifying or attending meetings concerning the Persian Gulf War and the illnesses that had followed so many GIs home. The Picou's phone began ringing with anonymous warnings to "take a different route to the airport." In September of that year, the Picou's car was firebombed in their front yard.

But the Picous refused to back off from attempting to expose a cover-up that had grave implications not only for Gulf War veterans, but for communities around the USA that were suffering from DU exposure even more concentrated than the munitions expended in Iraq.

"This thing is bigger than any wartime era, bigger than the veterans being affected," Tony Picou observed from the Mission Project. "Communities at home have been fighting [DU and other radiation exposures] for 20 years." At the Jefferson Proving Grounds in Madison, Indiana, the Army acknowledged that "the low level radioactivity poses an environmental concern" after more than 125,000 pounds of Depleted Uranium penetrators had been test-fired. If nearby residents were drinking groundwater, their urine probably glowed in the dark.

Instead of abandoning her search for the truth, in May, 1997, Carol Picou became the first American soldier to return to the battlefields of Iraq. Accompanied by her husband, the army veteran was the subject of a TV documentary being filmed for the Arts & Entertainment network.

But a camera lens was not the only form of scrutiny. During a meeting that resembled an interrogation, stern-faced functionaries from the Hamadi "ministry of truth," a nuclear engineer heading Iraq's investigation into DU poisoning and "seven or nine generals" tried to determine if the couple sitting across from them were allies or spies. It turned out that the Picous were neither. They were tourists with an attitude, who wanted to revisit a region that had so dramatically changed Carol Picou's life.

One of the generals facing them had apparently been in charge of all tank divisions in southern Iraq during the war. He must have been an exemplary officer, both Picous thought, to have escaped the purges that swept many of Saddam's wartime commanders into shallow graves. When it was determined to everyone's satisfaction that the Picous were not CIA "plants," the atmosphere lightened considerably.

There was never any hostility towards them, for the rest of their two-week stay. "Even though we'd bombed the hell out of them and brought them back 50 years, they still look at us as somebody that can help," Tony Picou recalls.

One of their first visits was to a vast parade ground set in the center of the city. Baghdad's version of the "Trompe de l'Arch" featured crossed-swords forming hundred foot-high archways over each of the square's four entrances. Grand as it seemed, this gesture was not nearly as extravagant as its use of building materials. The eight towering swords, as well as the arms holding them, had been cast from melted down Iranian helmets.

'Lest there be any mistaking Saddam's sentiments, each sword-arm protruded from a massive mound of similar headgear no longer required by their previous owners. Even the speed bumps built into the parade ground were fashioned from Iranian helmets taken during that eight-year bloodletting. It was a step up from Pol Pot's decorative use of Cambodian skulls. But not a very big one.

Their hosts continued to show them the sights, without ever letting the Picous out of their sight. With so much poverty in evidence, both Picous were uneasy seeing Saddam's new palace – "blocks square" – going up in the center of the city. But this long after the war, it was hard to detect evidence of the allied aerial bombardment, Tony Picou related. An empty field had been a Coca-Cola factory. Government buildings destroyed during the war had been completely rebuilt.

Carefully worded UN sanctions which were preventing vital food and medicines from reaching Iraq's youngest residents had also permitted Saddam to replace his tanks and rebuild his shattered army into what *Jane's Intelligence Review* termed "an effective fighting force."

An aerial shooting gallery in 1991, the shell-pocked highway from Jordan had also been completely restored into a modern four-lane superhighway that whisked the Picous from Amman to Baghdad. But the highway heading south from Iraq's capital did not offer fast travel. In stark testimony to the sparks of rebellion still smoldering around Basra, soldiers armed with machine-guns stopped the Picou's party at barbed-wire check-points every 20 kilometers. What was their business? Where were they going?

They stopped at a town near Nasiriyah for breakfast. Unlucky Kut would soon be bombed by Iran, but this morning the closest warfare was taking place in Tony Picou's stomach. War-ruined waterworks had been convincingly translated from words on a page to 30 hours of doubled-over pain.

Unable to face food, Tony and his wife left their minders and made their way into a marketplace across the street. Stuffed with sellers and browsers and pungent exotic scents, the open-air market stretched for blocks. But there was something about the Picous, something more than the strangeness of foreigners in Kut or the sight of a woman on the arm of a man, that turned heads. "In 10 minutes," Tony Picou says, "we must have had 200 people following us."

Their escorts felt it, too. "The Iraqi officials and generals were dying for the peace spilling out of me and Carol," Tony Picou continues. One night at dinner, one of the Iraqi generals asked the serene American what it was that allowed him to have such peace. For Tony Picou, a deeply Christian man immersed in a land still vibrating with biblical meaning, the answer was simple. "Christian values," he told the general.

In Basra, the TV crew filmed Carol Picou speaking with an Iraqi colonel afflicted with symptoms that matched her own. "They were exact," Tony recalls. The Iraqi officer, who appeared not to have been briefed, was an "upright type of guy." As they talked, Iraqi parents kept coming up to Carol carrying comatose children in their arms. An interpreter explained that they wanted the Picous to take their child back to America for medical care – and a chance at a life with more promise than the bleak prospects of an embargoed Iraq.

Would they go back?

"In a minute," Tony Picou says. "For spiritual reasons." Though still sick from war-related injuries which saw her permanently retired in 1995 after 17 unblemished years in the Army, Carol Picou is feeling better. But she says the healing she's received has come from the Lord – not from the VA.

The Picous firmly believe that sick veterans would find more help by appealing to heaven instead of Washington. But Carol Picou continues to meet with combat veterans who were exposed to DU. Mike Flores' twin sons were each born with deformed arms – just like another child he knew who had been born around the same time to another veteran exposed to DU in the Gulf. "Deformed babies born in San Antonio in our support group of 125 veterans look like the babies born in Iraq," Carol observed.

Carol Picou's experiences during and after the war have made her a tenacious crusader in her search for the truth. "This is my life, trying to figure out what's wrong with me and try to figure out how to help myself, because I'm not getting any help from the (US) military doctors so I may as well keep researching to help myself get better and stronger," she told RTV.

But her husband and director of the MISSION Project is concerned that too many desperate and frustrated veterans are accepting the paltry financial benefits offered by a diagnosis of Post-Traumatic Stress Syndrome [PTSD]. In doing so, Picou warns, veterans going on record with PTSD are foreclosing on all future claims to compensation for much graver, war-related disorders.

Military Issues Surfacing In Our Nation is a non-profit educational service meant to alert veterans and active duty personnel on issues relating to family, career and health that are or soon will be showing up on GI radar screens. Like Moss and many other researchers, the MISSION Project's director feels that the answers to the GWI puzzle will be found at the molecular level. SPET scans for all sick veterans are crucial for proper diagnosis, Tony Picou points out. QEEGs, and PET scans – the next step above SPET – would be even better.

* * *

Would there ever be a resolution to the Gulf War Syndrome? The Pentagon's long-standing contention that the long-term symptoms exhibited by ailing Gulf War veterans were inconsistent with sarin exposure received remarkable confirmation thanks to the efforts of a religious cult half a world away.

On March 20, 1995, just after eight in the morning at the height of the Tokyo rush hour, well-dressed terrorists placed sarin-filled *o-bento* lunch boxes and soft-drink containers on the floors of five crowded subway cars on the Hibiya, Marunouchi and Chiyoda Lines. As the trains slid smoothly to a stop at their underground stations, the equally punctual terrorists punctured each container with umbrellas before exiting the trains.

The attack followed an incident in June the previous year, in which toxic sarin gas drifted over Matsumoto city in Nagano Prefecture. Seven people were killed and more than 200 injured. But the perpetrators were never found.

This time, the more concentrated subway strikes resulted in confusion, panic, widespread injuries – and more deaths. Within hours of the senseless attack, 11 commuters had been killed and more than 5,500 others injured.

Because the hardest hit subway station was near St. Luke's International Hospital, St. Luke's ended up treating the largest number of sarin victims. Some 641 injured Tokyo residents descended on that hospital's emergency reception area in the space of minutes. Though temporarily overwhelmed, staff who had trained for every disaster except nerve gas attack on rush-hour Tokyo subways responded with precision, decisiveness and initiative.

Confronted by mass symptoms of nausea and irritated eyes, doctors at St. Lukes immediately suspected OP exposure. But they had no indication at first that sarin was involved. Five victims with arrested hearts or lungs showed extremely low cholinesterase values. Two died. The other three went into convulsions and stopped breathing. Immediate CPR and quick injections of atropine and diazepam, followed by pralidoxime iodide (PAM), saved their lives. All three of these critically ill patients completely recovered from their physical symptoms and were released within six days.

Another 106 patients – including four pregnant women – were hospitalized with symptoms of mild to moderate sarin exposure. The remaining victims were released after six hours of observation.

Most of the injured showed initial symptoms – in varying severity – of darkened vision, headache, dyspnea, nausea, painful eyes, blurred vision, vomiting, coughing, muscle weakness and agitation. "Although these physical signs and symptoms disappeared within a few weeks, psychological problems associated with Post Traumatic stress disorder persisted longer," the doctors

~ 319 ~

noted. Almost one-quarter of the attending hospital staff also suffered deleterious health effects. But their symptoms quickly passed.

After discharge from the hospital, headache, eye problems and malaise were the most common and persistent symptoms. Some patients also experienced anxiety, fear, nightmares, insomnia, and irritability. "Almost 60% of victims suffered from PTSD that persisted longer than six months," the report noted. "Psychiatric consultation has been required for many victims."

Five released patients suffered such severe nightmares and insomnia they required psychiatric care. (Typical nightmares featured "big monsters" or "huge rocks falling on victims.") All four pregnant women subsequently gave birth to healthy babies without complication.

Gulf War veterans who understood that ChE is chemical shorthand for cholinesterase, were especially interested in findings that showed "about half of the patients showed decreased ChE levels a few hours after exposure. All severely ill patients showed markedly decreased ChE levels and 74% of admitted patients showed decreased ChE levels." The bigger the dose of PAM, the faster cholinesterase serum levels improved. "Other routine tests were within normal ranges. Electrocardiograms in admitted patients revealed no significant or specific abnormalities."

The study concluded – in bold type:

At present, there are no patients who show significant delayed side effects, including intermediate syndrome or rebounding symptoms, which have been seen in other OP intoxication cases. So, in acute phase of treatment, the most reliable predictor of outcome is the clinical status at 3 hours to 5 hours after the exposure including respiration, circulation, and consciousness level. Once the patient survives for a few hours, the prognosis is equally as good as that of unexposed people.

The evidence on sarin was in. Whether from direct attack or bombing fallout, exposure to low-levels of sarin during the Gulf War would not have been enough to cause the delayed, debilitating and chronic symptoms experienced by so many returning Gulf War troops. There was no question that multiple sarin exposures had taken place. But if sarin alone was not enough to cause such widespread nervous system degeneration, Baghdad, Whitehall and Washington suddenly stood indicted for supplying the missing ingredients that synergized sarin into such a disastrous syndrome.

Like the harried Tokyo commuters, soldiers with fully-functioning immune systems should have been able to shrug off sarin exposure within a few days or weeks. Unlike the stricken Japanese commuters, American and British military personnel had been severely immuno-suppressed by toxic cocktails administered by their own superiors. Experimental vaccines and non-approved adjuvant boosters administered simultaneously or in rapid succession, an "investigational" drug called PB with known severe side-effects, and an insecticide strong enough to discolor clothing and metal had "potentiated" Saddam's sarin into devastating secondary effects.

Stress, gallons of coffee and soft drinks (caffeine and sugar are powerful immune-suppressers), oil smoke, suspect drinking water, anxiety, fatigue, MREs (poor nutrition), heat, fatigue, strenuous exercise, tick-borne infections, broken sleep, lack of family contact – all had played additional and varying roles in suppressing Government Issue immune systems.

But there was more. Low level radiation exposure to DU rounds racked in American battle tanks – as well as varying rates of subsequent exposure to spent DU munitions and radioactive dust inhaled on the battlefield or inside blasted Iraqi tanks – also showed up in enough urine samples taken from returning veterans to indict the Pentagon on further charges of callous disregard for the safety of its own personnel. Whether high, low or "negligible," all radioactive depleted uranium exposures contributed to immune system suppression – and subsequent physical dysfunction.

So did electromagnetic radiation. In "The Zapping of America," EMR expert Paul Brodeur relates how exposure to toxic chemicals and electromagnetic and microwave radiation emitted by high-energy transmitters "may be joint factors in increasing the incidence of human cancer." When exposed to these alternating 60-hertz interferences, the growth rate of mutant cells "jumped by several hundred percent after 24 hours' exposure." This is a permanent acceleration, Brodeur noted in his July, 1978, *Genesis* article, which continues after stimulus on certain low frequencies is removed.

The tricothecenes supplied to Saddam's germ warfare scientists by the American Type Culture Collection company with Washington's blessing only added to the misery of their own countrywomen and men. The toxic fungal spores, which left a tell-tale yellow dusting in their wake, had caused immediate reactions among the victims of some SCUD attacks, as well as likely longer term effects.

Faced with this lengthy list of confirmed causal factors, there could be no doubt: British, Canadian, Anzac and American forces had been "done in" by the leaders they had followed – and trusted.

But none of these nasty weapons and counter-agents could explain how Gulf War Illness had spread from Persian Gulf veterans to such a high percentage of spouses and family members.

That mystery was solved when mycoplasma fermentans incognitas was positively identified in the semen and blood of sick spouses and veterans. Whether these mycoplasmas were the by-product of the auto-immune dysfunctions that are so characteristic of Gulf War Illness – or whether these cellular invaders were the cause – remain to be conclusively proven. But the fact that these infectious viruses had been under development for years as germ weapons by both the US and Iraq points to a fully-functional germ warfare agent delivered by warhead or vaccine.

The appearance of mycoplasma incognitas within an HIV-envelope in the cells of sick vets is also indicative of a genetically-modified germ warfare agent. Reports by some Gulf soldiers who had been told that their anthrax vaccines contained Recombinant DNA are similarly disturbing. Had the Pentagon taken advantage of a known chemical biological warfare environment to experiment with germ warfare agents on its own troops?

Many Americans veterans were beginning to think so. Even the perception of deliberate malfeasance by their superiors could severely damage the Pentagon's credibility, and future recruitment efforts, decades longer than any forthright dealing with their former soldiers' concerns.

CHAPTER 20

RX

Even if nerve damage from exposure to synergistic nerve agents like sarin, DEET and PB was considered to be permanent by the medical orthodoxy, some doctors felt that effective treatment of an illness that strikes at the cellular basis of human functioning must begin at the molecular level.

With one in four North Americans currently suffering from allergies, it seems obvious that the pesticide and chemical-laced foods we are eating, the poisoned air we are breathing and the unsafe tapwater we are drinking and washing in are making us increasingly allergic to 20th century technologies. Since allergies and related chemical sensitivities commonly exhibit symptoms of depression, fatigue, constant colds, irritability, dizziness, migraines, aggression, rashes and aching joints, it is crucial that all Americans – especially sick veterans – do everything possible to minimize their exposure to bad air, food and water.

The good news is that patients suffering from Multiple Chemical Sensitivity are being successfully treated with nutritional therapies. Noting the many similarities between GWI and MCS, some researchers now feel strongly that the same nutritional regime might prove helpful in rehabilitating very ill soldiers.

Garth Nicholson discovered that veterans suffering from Gulf War Illness are often deficient in vitamins B, C and E. Even more than an already deficient general population, they also lacked sufficient quantities of minerals such as magnesium, chromium, selenium and zinc needed for nerve, metabolic and brain functioning.

"Because the minerals can affect the absorption of certain antibiotics," Nicholson warned against taking mineral supplements at the same time as antibiotics. Antibiotics also destroy "friendly" stomach bacteria needed for digestion. Anyone taking antibiotics should also be eating natural yogurt and swallowing acidophillus tablets with every meal to refurbish lost bacterial allies.

Because GWI prevents proper nutrient absorption, Nicholson decided that high doses of vitamins would be needed to meet the cellular requirements of veterans already lacking in those vitamins. One of the world's foremost nutritional researchers backed up Nicholson's hunch. Dr. Michael Colgan, director of the Colgan Institute of Nutritional Science in San Diego, had collected enough solid medical research to make firm prescriptions for specific vitamin, mineral and "healthy foods" therapies. Though not specifically directed at Gulf War Illness, Colgan's *The New Nutrition* quickly became the single most important, and readable, medical book an ailing veteran could find.

Among the vitamins that directly address nerve functioning, Colgan points to vitamin B-5 as essential for the healthy functioning of the neurotransmitters that convey information from the brain to the nerve-muscle junctions. Vitamin B-12 is also important for nourishing red blood cells and repairing the intestinal track.

Among the top immune-boosters, Colgan's research found selenium and Coenzyme Q-10 to be extremely effective. Whey, he adds, has been found to improve weakened immune systems by as much as 500 percent.

Chemically damaged intestines cannot easily absorb vitamin B complex. If oral B-capsules don't seem effective, Garth Nicholson suggests that sick veterans hold sublingual tablets under the tongue or drink more readily absorbed liquid B-complex to transfer these potent vitamins into their bloodstreams.

But not all vitamins are created with equal integrity. When the world-renowned creator of the Epstein-Barr diagnostic kit subjected commonly available vitamin supplements to thorough lab tests, immunologist Dr. Myron Wentz found that "bargain" supplements were no bargains at all. After clinically evaluating 13 types of Vitamin C, Wentz found every one to be derived from inferior ingredients. When he fed popular, off-the-shelf vitamins and minerals to his cell cultures, the cells curled up and died. The microbiologist discovered that the nutrients he had picked at random were not being supplied in their proper proportions, or with the necessary "co-factor" activators needed to ensure full cellular absorption and benefit.

Wentz found that the hit-and-miss approach of buying different vitamins at random could also lead to an excess of some nutrients and deficiencies in others. Most brands of vitamins and minerals passed right through the body. His lab results also showed that most over-the-counter supplements contain stearic acid binders which prevent tablets from releasing minerals or completely dissolving in the body. Color coatings commonly contain aluminum, which has been linked to Alzheimer's.

Grape-seed extract proved to be one of the most powerful immune-boosters ever discovered. Garth Nicholson also favored grape-seed extract for helping to rebuild GWI-damaged immune systems. In addition, the GWI specialist also began recommending bioflavonids, Co-enzyme Q-10, beta-carotene, biotin, L-cysteine and L-tyrosine. Herbs such as ginseng, garlic, ginko-biloba, miso, shitake mushrooms, and echinacea are also among the top laboratory-proven immune-builders.

High-potency vitamins, herbs and chelated minerals like Dr. Wentz's, produced under "batch-by-batch" quality control and offered in the precise combinations and dosages needed to produce noticeable health improvements instead of expensive urine, could easily cost unemployed, suffering veterans up to $100 a month (multiplied for every sick family member).

While not directly addressing GWI patients, Wentz cautioned any poisoned person against popping handfuls of high-potency vitamins and minerals without checking with their personal physician first. The resulting rapid detoxification, he and other researchers noted, can overload sick bodies with poisons suddenly released from fatty tissues or other storage sites. In fact, Wentz warned purchasers of his high-powered supplements, symptoms among those suffering from super toxicity are likely to initially grow even worse as the body cleanses itself.

This helps flush the body of toxins while keeping the brain's electro-chemical "battery" fully hydrated. Most doctors recommended that anyone undergoing a drug and natural "detox" treatment should drink at least eight glasses of pure, unchlorinated water every day. If extreme discomfort occurs, Wentz and others suggested, daily dosages of supplements should be cut back. But these signs also indicate that the therapy is working, he added. Patients in such situations are advised to consult with their physicians and "stick with the program" if at all possible.

Jim Dearing favors vitamin supplementation and other natural remedies over prescription drugs. But herbal "energy boosters" may not be what the doctor ordered for sick veterans. This former US Air Force officer found that the Chinese herbal concoction Ma Huang gave him nightmares and anxiety. Another herbal product called Excel Energy, which he used to stimulate his metabolism while weight lifting, also makes him "nervous and jumpy," leading to angina and panic attacks.

Ask Carol Picou if repairing cells with herbs and nutritional supplements works. "What the VA was giving me was making me worse," she says. The synthetic form of thyroid the military doctors were prescribing was raising her blood pressure and making her even sicker. Last November, she made the decision to stop taking drugs. "I threw all my medicines into a pit. And I said, Lord you're either going to heal me now or bring me home."

He did bring her home...to Lafayette, Louisiana. "I'm better off without any medicine," Carol Picou says today. "I take all natural herbs now." In May, 1997, her thyroid's red blood count was checked..." and it's the first time I've been at the point eight level, which is the beginning of going towards hyper-thyroidism," and the beginning of recovery.

Once they recognize that they are suffering from Multiple Chemical Sensitivities, military personnel and family members "sensitized" by Gulf war-related exposures can also help themselves by avoiding re-exposure to chemicals that prevent weakened immune systems from recovering. Petroleum products and their derivatives, including pesticides, perfumes, fiberglass and the formaldehydes found in abundance in almost every office and home, should be kept as distant as possible. If you happen to be a sick Gulf war veteran, pumping your own gas is definitely not a good idea.

Chlorine exposure should also be avoided. Research has shown that anyone who is serious about making a complete recovery from Multiple Chemical Sensitivity should not drink, wash or bathe in chlorinated water, which is readily absorbed through the skin. Home filters capable of cleansing all household water supplies are available for a few hundred dollars.

Chlorine will make rashes and other skin problems associated with Gulf War Illness much worse. A civilian disabled for 14 years after being poisoned by non-Gulf War-related OP pesticides found that Hypericum and nutritional supplements helped relieve symptoms of neurological damage. Acute tenderness on the bottom of her feet was made manageable (though not cured), and feeling was restored to her hands using Hypericum and supplements. Other veterans state that pure Aloe has proven helpful in treating skin problems.

Proper diet is even more important than supplementation in helping people recover from auto-immune and related diseases. Caffeine, sugar, junk foods, fatty foods, MREs, and alcohol should also be avoided or strictly curtailed. These acid-forming foods suppress the immune system and promote allergic reactions.

Sharply increasing the daily intake of "organic" vegetables, fruits, fish and grains is a proven way to boost your immune defenses and improve overall health. Besides being free of OP-based pesticides which can severely depress already weakened immune systems among chemically-sensitized people, organic foods have been found to retain much more nutritional value than pesticide-weakened cuisine.

While the high cysteine content of whey is very beneficial for rebuilding immune systems, some grains and milk products, could make symptoms worse. Paul Shattock and Dawn Savery point to an excess of opioids in recommending that sick vets try diets that omit gluten and casein (found in milk products). While looking at autism, both British researchers found that proteins normally digested in the gut are broken down into amino acids. Intermediate compounds, known as peptides, are briefly formed during this process. These peptides produce various compounds from the milk-based casein protein and from the gluten found in wheat and other cereals. Few of these opioids exit the gut-wall into the bloodstream; even fewer find their way across the blood-brain barrier into the brain and central nervous system.

Those opioids that do cross the blood-brain barrier affect the transmission of chemical messengers to the nerves, usually by inhibiting their normal functioning. "Perception, cognition, emotions, mood and even motor activities would be affected by the presence of these compounds," the researchers stated. Chemical controls on anger and aggression, including searing speech, could also result from these disruptive opioids. "These abnormalities are clearly evident in the subjects with GWS with whom we have come into contact," Shattock and Savery informed British veterans.

The diarrhea and other bowel dysfunctions seen in Gulf War Illness victims tend to confirm the obstreperous opioid theory, they added. And "since opioids are intimately involved in the immune system, elevated levels of these compounds would have profound effects on this system and predispose to infections of all sorts."

This sounds bad enough. But if service personnel had been afflicted by increased opioids before being vaccinated, the increased permeability of their gut walls and blood-brain barrier occasioned by the opioids would ensure that, "The implementation of a severe active immunization program would, under these conditions, have very predictable and deeply unfortunate consequences."

About one-quarter of the general British population already has the opioid marker compound for increased membrane permeability. But the same marker was "either the largest or second largest component" in every soldier Shattock and Savery examined. The medical investigators believed that in individuals not already predisposed to opioid aggression, it most likely stemmed from the action of "organo-phosphorous compounds upon the normal metabolic processes." The pesticides used by British "environmental" units in the Gulf are OPs. So were the nerve weapons dispersed by SCUDs and fallout from British fighter-bombers.

Eliminating milk and wheat products from the diet of ill veterans could greatly alleviate their symptoms, Savery and Shattock suggested. Patients who tried this dietary approach were already showing "impressive improvements in many diverse ways, including speech and aggression control and bowel function."

What other treatments help? Garth Nicholson now recommends taking a 15 or 20 minute dry sauna at least three or five times a week and as often as twice a day. The idea, he says, is to eliminate chemicals without stressing an already stressed system. For the same reason, exercise should only be undertaken in moderation, though many ill veterans find it difficult even to climb a flight of stairs.

Ampligen also proved effective in some cases. An investigational drug not yet approved for sale in the United States, Ampligen is available in Canada under the Emergency Drug Release Program. A clinical study in Belgium found that almost 80 percent of Chronic Fatigue Syndrome patients treated with Ampligen returned to work or to school within six months after beginning the treatment.

As tens of thousands of Gulf war veterans learned, CFS has nothing to do with "feeling tired." Many people afflicted with this debilitating and terribly depressing illness report feeling tired after raising their arm. Taking three hours to do dishes or feeling exhausted after moving from one chair to another are other common symptoms of acute CFS attacks that can last for weeks or months or longer. All of the patients in the Belgian study had been bedridden with some of the extreme chronic fatigue symptoms experienced by ill Gulf war veterans for three to seven years prior to completing the Ampligen treatment and returning to active lives.

* * *

British researchers were also looking at Chronic Fatigue Syndrome in connection with possible cures for GWI. On June 29, 1997, the London *Sunday Times* reported that an immune-boosting drug that had proven useful in treating CFS sufferers could also be used to "reboot" the Th1 T-helper cells that had failed among British Gulf war wounded. Medical scientists at University College in London had produced a drug called SRL-172 that switches the Th1 defense system back on. Derived from a bacterial protein, SRL-172 is effective in treating allergies, lung cancer and TB. It is not being tested as a treatment for breast cancer – a malady which was also striking some female veterans.

When the University College researchers looked at CFS and GWI, they found that both syndromes had switched the immune system into a Th 2-only mode. But Th1 helper cells are necessary to provide immunity against infections and malignancy, the *Sunday Times* reported. "If the immune system is not working in the Th1 mode, which is believed to be the case in Gulf War Syndrome, the signals given off by the cells that are infected or undergoing malignant change are ignored and the disease or malignancy allowed to develop."

Since SRL-172 returns immune functioning to Th1, this British drug was thought to be effective in instances where fatigue was a primary symptom. SRL-172 encourages the body's own immune system to respond. This approach contrasts with chemotherapies which blast healthy cells along with invaders.

When SRL-172 nudges the immune system back into Th1 detection mode, immune system radar screens once again begin scanning for incoming infectious intruders. But it doesn't take oil smoke or chemical weapons fallout to drive the immune system toward TH 2; modern lives immersed in pollutants and stress can be enough to throw immune systems out of whack. Multiple vaccinations given simultaneously or in rapid succession to departing soldiers, said the British researchers, might have also depressed and altered the chemical balance in the immune system.

The profound depression reported by almost all GWI patients is also a marker for Th 2 disorders, they added.

Other British studies backed US findings by confirming that UK soldiers had been stricken by a potent combination of multiple vaccinations, including "experimental" plague vaccines and OP pesticides sprayed inside tents to rid them of flies.

But the British did not stop there. A sheep survey published in 1997 showed that low doses of pretreatment PB given to sheep about to be dipped in organic phosphate pesticides caused extensive muscular damage in strenuously exercised animals. Noting that the headaches, short-term memory loss, chronic fatigue, intestinal difficulties and chronic diarrhea reported by 150 sick UK Desert Storm Vets resembled the symptoms reported by hundreds of sheep farmers displaying similar adverse reactions to organic phosphate sheep dip, the study found that the organic pesticide was acting synergistically with the pyridostigmine to inhibit neurotransmitters in the peripheral nervous system, neuromuscular junctions, gastric and intestinal glands, and the brain. US veterans and their UK counterparts commented that they, too, had "strenuously exercised" during the Gulf war.

* * *

For Gulf war veterans suffering neurological damage from exposure to pesticides, PB and other chemical warfare agents, Michael Colgan came up with some excellent news in 1995. Noting that a decrease in neurotransmitters leads to a decrease in memory "storage" – and short term memory loss – the nutritional expert suggested that improving serotonin and acetylcholine levels would improve memory. Professors Eric Kandell and James Schwartz at the Center for Neurobiology at Columbia University found that serotonin levels can be boosted by a drug called zimelidine.

L-trypophan also forms serotinin in brain neurons. Commonly used throughout Japan and Europe, this essential amino acid is banned by the FDA, but may be obtained for "personal use" under special circumstances. Colgan recommends that l-trypophan be taken with bread or rice-cakes in order to help this amino acid's difficult journey across the blood-brain barrier.

Choline supplementation may also help restore nerve function, he added, but only if taken with pantothonic acid, proper diet, vitamin B-12, folic acids and thiamine. The bad news, he says, is that all of the above treatments "are useless if the neurons they are supposed to improve are already dead."

Every MD "knows" that carbamate-toasted brain neurons cannot be replaced.

But Dr. Fernando Nottebohm must not have gotten the word. Using intensive mental stimulation to exercise the "muscle" that is the brain – as well as intensive acetylcholine enhancement supplements – Nottebohm has been able to regenerate damaged brain cells and neural connections in test animals. He believes that similar treatments will work in humans. If so, it will be slow going. At least 10 months, and possibly as long as six years of treatment could be needed to accomplish the "impossible" feat of replacing damaged nerve cells.

Other European researchers have recently found that acetyl-l-carnitine helps protect the brain from further damage or deterioration. Scientists at the Life Extension Foundation in Florida also concur that acetyl-l-carnitine at dosages of 1,000 to 2,000 mg per day improves memory, prevents brain cell loss, boosts intelligence and helps restore normal acetylcholine metabolism. In fact, it is proving so effective, acetyl-l-carnitine is about to be banned by the FDA in favor of exclusive, high-cost distribution by the same pharmaceutical giants that developed chemical weapons in both world wars.

* * *

By the spring of 1997, the Pentagon finally appeared to be responding to an illness that had reached epidemic proportions among its current and former employees. In March of that year, the Veterans Administration announced that it was "committed to a thorough investigation of the health consequences of exposure to potential environmental hazards, including chemical warfare agents, during the Persian Gulf War." Seemingly ignoring the breakthroughs already announced by earlier studies, the VA promised that "carefully controlled scientific studies" would seek to answer the "key question" of why Gulf War veterans appeared to be sicker than healthy populations.

Many American veterans were not impressed. When it was learned that the Veterans Administration would be spending more than $3.6 million a year to conduct research among VA patients, some critics charged the studies were already flawed. Because many of those suffering from Gulf War Illness were not in VA hospitals, "representative sampling" could not be achieved. Would DoD really push for research that could very well find that agency liable for health care costing billions of dollars?

A health survey sent out in 1996 by the VA's Washington DC-based Environmental Epidemiology Service sought to expand its sample range by randomly selecting 15,000 Gulf War veterans and another 15,000 of "Gulf-era" veterans who were not deployed in the desert KTO. Everything would be tracked, the VA pledged: symptoms among veterans as well as their family members; exposures to vaccines, solvents, pesticides, oil well fire smoke, PB chemical warfare agents and others. Medical records that had not already mysteriously "disappeared" would also be checked, and some physical exams undertaken as well. Publication of the survey's initial findings was expected in mid-1998, with the final medical exams slated for release later that year.

Whatever happened, the results promised to be provocative. In Portland, the Oregon Center for Research on Occupational and Environmental Toxicology was using a $2.6 million federal grant to study the transmissibility of chronic GWI health problems. In Georgia, Dr. Charles Jackson, one of a growing number of Gulf War Illness specialists, examined medical publications dating back to 1947 and found studies demonstrating immune-system damage caused by chemical mustard gas agents mixed with oil.

But Jim Moss was still being shut out of more sensitive research. In late March, 1997, the frustrated PhD was turned down again by DoD. This time the Pentagon had just picked up a $27 million check from Washington to look into the most promising aspects of GWI research. Moss' application had scored "high" on its medical merits, and "low" on the "relevancy" of looking into how PB is potentiated by the synergistic effects of adrenaline (stress) and PB. No explanation was forthcoming as to why DoD had chosen not to turn to one of PB's leading researchers to look into a link shown by the deceased rats in the FDA's pre-Gulf War approval studies for PB.

"That's it," a demoralized Moss said in late October, 1997. "I'm sick of this crap. I'm still applying for jobs, I'm still consulting with lawyers and MDs on exposure cases. I can't keep doing that. It's not really my work."

Looking over the many battlefields of post-Gulf War struggles to pin down Gulf War Illness and receive recognition of responsibility on the part of governments and military commands, how far did Moss think sick veterans had come?

"I watch the tide go in and out on this," he replied. "There's so many skeins out there. The Danes who have problems took the pill but didn't get the shots. The French didn't have either one, the shots or the pill. The MoD's taking a real beating for mixing vaccines. They took different vaccines than we did and still got the same symptoms." He pauses, then continues with a caution aimed at various causation camps, "It's not simple."

Will we ever get to the bottom of a mystery that goes on and on? Moss thought so. "You've got to take it down to the molecule level to find out," he declared. "Or delay [meaningful investigation] for another five years. We talk molecules with DoD."

Was the Pentagon sincere in unraveling the GWI puzzle and helping the chronically ill veterans who had followed their directives to such a disastrous denouement? Or was DoD more serious about maintaining a cover-up that by now bore a remarkable resemblance to a DU-riddled tank? "If their intentions were good, if they wanted to find things out, they could – without even being friendly with me – attempt to find out where we're going," Moss replied. "I'm convinced they don't want to find out. No one from that crew has called me. So I think their motivation is to not find out."

* * *

The following month, the Department of Defense announced a "Specialized Care Program" for selected active duty military personnel, retired or discharged GIs, even civilians. Those veterans with "persistent disabling symptoms" who had completed earlier testing would be brought to the Walter Reed army hospital at the Pentagon's expense for three weeks of intensive treatment. During that period small groups of three to eight disabled veterans would receive state-of-the-art care for chronic multiple symptoms.

Those symptoms appeared to be consistent with auto-immune disease. To test that hypothesis, researcher Richard Shuster teamed up with auto-immune specialist Pamela Asa and other Memphis-based colleagues to apply to ailing veterans an antibody assay protocol developed by Dr. Bob Garry at the Tulane Medical School and published in Lancet in 1997.

Laboratory tests and physical examinations, as well as their response to various treatments, indicated the presence of immune dysfunction consistent with lupus, connective tissue disease, rheumatoid arthritis, Sjogren's syndrome, Reiter's syndrome, autoimmune hepatitis, auto-immune thyroid disease, multiple sclerosis, polmyositis, polyneuropathies and brain atrophy in the veterans studied. All patients tested positive for auto-immune disease. All, Garry reports, responded to appropriate treatment.

The Memphis-based team then located an adjuvant known to cause a similar syndrome of auto-immune indicators in vaccines used by the National Institute of Health, as well as in vaccines used by the National Institute of Health and DoD. NIH patients and GWI patients all showed similar antibody reactions. But GWI patients exposed to similar compounds sold under the same name but having a different molecular structure did not react. GWI patients who were never sent to the Persian Gulf, but were vaccinated, also reacted to the chosen adjuvant. Normal, healthy humans used as controls did not react.

It looked like the "investigational" vaccines administered to GIs during the Gulf conflict had interfered with their immune systems. But what exactly was going on at the cellular level? On May 7, Dr. Howard Urnovitz was back in the news. This time, the new head of the Berkeley-based Chronic Illness Research Foundation told his American Society for Microbiology colleagues that certain chromosomes detected in the blood of people stricken with a type of bone marrow cancer were also present in those patients suffering from multiple sclerosis, Parkinson's Disease, Lou Gehrig's disease (ALS), precancerous colon growth, prostate cancer, Hodgkin's disease, and illnesses related to service in the Persian Gulf War.

Urnovitz announced that 29 out of 32 bone-marrow cancer patients had this unique genetic marker circulating in their blood plasma. This marker, he added, was located on human chromosome number 22.

Chromosome number 22 has been identified as one of a hundred "fragile sites" in human DNA which are particularly prone to breakage. It is thought that "fragile sites" are targeted by viruses or other DNA-disrupting agents.

The study's co-author, Dr. Brian Durie, added that the remarkably consistent circulating genetic material could provide many "specific clues" regarding a "range of auto-immune and chronic diseases."

Dr. Alan Kramer, an internationally recognized cancer specialist at the University of California at San Francisco Medical Center, was also excited by Urnovitz's discovery. If further clinical studies confirmed the coded chromosome, it would be possible to diagnose early stages of cancer or GWI. Early detection of Gulf War Illness, perhaps in exposed family members, could lead to early treatment.

The detected genetic material matched a DNA chromosome called SINE. Able to jump in and out of chromosomes, this "jumping gene" is key to controlling cellular growth. If the cell's SINE "governor" goes out of control, cellular growth runs away and cancer can result. Durie further explained that if a link could be determined between genotoxic agents and SINE activation, cancers resulting from Agent Orange deployment in Vietnam, petrochemical and other toxic exposures could be diagnosed.

"The primary question now," said Urnovitz, "is whether SINE activation is also a central link to other cell dysfunctions that may lead to chronic illnesses in addition to cancer." The Berkeley researcher was referring to Gulf War Illness. His search for genetic markers had begun with blood samples taken from Gulf War veterans.

James Tuite was quick to note the implications of Urnovitz's latest findings. "We know from prior studies," the Gulf war investigator stated, "that many of the compounds to which the veterans were exposed interfere with DNA repair mechanisms, as well as the proteins and enzymes that regulate neuro-immune processes. We also know that the troops were exposed to nerve and blister warfare agents, as well as to other toxic compounds that by themselves or in combination have been shown to result in chronic illnesses and cancers."

Tuite was speaking as the director of the newly established Interdisciplinary Sciences department at the Chronic Illness Research Foundation. This non-profit Berkeley foundation seeks to study commonalities among all chronic diseases and disorders in order to provide more effective diagnosis and treatment. Its key goal, to catalog specific chromosome sites from which chronic illnesses originate, had just been given major impetus by Urnovitz's work.

Urnovitz himself hoped that the newly-identified molecular marker linking toxic exposure to damaged chromosomes could help solve the mystery of how anomalous genetic material found its way into the bloodstreams of Gulf war era soldiers. Cornell University associate professor of immunology, Dr.

Susanna Cunningham-Rundles, noted that the marker could also offer new insight into the role the immune system plays in either promoting or combating chronic diseases.

But for Dr. Roy Stevens, the real breakthrough was in looking at microbes as gene-poisoning agents capable of interacting with other genotoxic agents to trigger chronic illnesses.

* * *

The day after Urnovitz revealed his chromosome 22 marker, Gulf veteran Alvis Yonce appeared before the presidential Gulf War Illness advisory committee in Charleston, South Carolina. Yonce waved a binder filled with his medical records and doctors' comments attesting to his multiple immune system dysfunction, vertigo and other Gulf war-related ailments. The new multi-million dollar initiatives announced by the VA seemed to have passed Yonce and his fellow veterans by.

"We have been shoved from one place to another... and treated like trash," the former minister told the panel.

In January, 1997, six years after the "end" of the Persian Gulf War, the presidential panel had advised DoD to get moving in its GWI investigations and start informing its troops about health risks. Shifting uncomfortably in her chair, committee chairwoman Dr. Joyce Lashof told Yonce that "It's very clear we're going to have to be following up on a lot of issues."

But that follow-up would have to overcome a major foul-up. A month later, CNN's Jamie McIntyre reported that the Pentagon had just informed the US Congress that many more pages of chemical logs kept by front-line forces during the American assault on Kuwait had been "lost" than previously suggested. In fact, DoD declared, as many as 160 key pages had gone missing, perhaps eaten by an opportunistic computer virus.

Had anything really changed? As late as November 9, 1996, Reuter reported that President Clinton's Gulf war advisory panel had "found no evidence that nerve gas, biological weapons, pesticides, vaccines and drugs or smoke from burning oil wells are causing widespread illness among Gulf war veterans." This bit of disinformation was featured in the *Washington Post*.

The panel went on to explain that it was "highly unlikely" the intense aerial bombardment unleashed against Iraq could have spread nerve agents over the battle zone because coalition forces "hit only two of 11 Iraqi sites where chemical weapons were stored" and "only limited amounts of gas could have been released at either site." This fascinating conclusion was in sharp contrast to James Tuite's research, which had uncovered US military records documenting 23 separate air attacks on CBW sites in Iraq.

A month later, CNN reported that CENTCOM commander General Norman Schwarzkopf stated that he had never seen the logs or other reports of the chemical attacks passing through his command center. This was hard to buy from the overall commander of Desert Storm, especially since Schwarzkopf had often voiced his concerns over the likelihood of chemical attacks against his troops.

Nevertheless, in a follow-up interview with Katie Couric on the *Today Show*, Couric asked the general how he had come to believe that chemical weapons had nothing to do with the illnesses of so many soldiers. General Schwarzkopf replied with another folksy falsehood: "Well, really several things, Katie...But I think more importantly than anything else is the fact that never a single time I – we – were in the Gulf, did we ever have a confirmed report of any chemical weapons being used or being discovered, not one single time."

That was a mouthful, even for America's favorite unscrutinized war hero. Sick Gulf War veterans were becoming even more nauseous listening to Schwarzkopf's repeated denials of any chemical incidents during the Gulf War.

Perhaps the general in charge of Desert Shield and Desert Storm had been struck by the same ailment which seemed to have rendered a top US Marine officer completely blind to multiple entries in official USMC logbooks, cartons of FOX chemical analysis tapes and volumes of unit interviews. In May, 1997, the Marine Corp's chief of Chemical and Biological Warfare Agents Division, Lt. Col. Art Nalls, still insisted that "There is no substantive evidence to confirm or deny chemical presence" during the assault on Kuwait.

Two months later, on July 24, the Pentagon confirmed that nearly 100,000 US troops could have been exposed to trace amounts of nerve gas when chemical weapons were destroyed at the end of the Gulf war.

Was this the breakthrough admission more than a hundred thousand sick US veterans and families had been hoping for? Not quite. AP's Robert Burns reported that at the same time they made this admission, "officials have concluded that the low-level exposures to 98,900 troops over a three-day period in southern Iraq and northern Saudi Arabia probably are unrelated to mysterious maladies reported by some Gulf War veterans."

* * *

As Washington backpedaled rapidly toward a credibility cliff, Whitehall found itself swept far up a distinctly malodorous tributary without a proverbial propulsion device. A nearby splash on June 22, 1997, was the substantial, growing and ongoing tab for medical costs and veterans compensation rearing out of the depths like something with big teeth. Research scientists studying immunology at University College had just announced that they had solid "proof" that the combination of vaccinations forced on British troops and the insecticides sprayed in their tents could have caused many of the symptoms besetting those veterans. Their evidence was published in the heavyweight *Lancet* medical journal.

The MoD, which had steadfastly denied any single medical cause of the debilitating syndrome, promptly promised to "test" the UC findings. Hugh McMannes reported in the *Sunday Times* that if the findings checked out, claims by sick and disabled British vets "could force the Ministry of Defense into paying tens of millions of pounds in compensation".

There was more good news, at least for sick veterans. The study's principle investigators, Professor Graham Rook and Dr. Alimuddin Zumla, said their conclusions could soon lead to treatments for Gulf War Illness by allowing effective, targeted use of currently available drugs.

Rook told reporters that the effect of the vaccinations combined with insecticides had been devastating. The vaccine "cocktails," Rook reiterated, had suppressed the body's Th1 sector of the immune system, responsible for detecting and defending against viruses and cancers. Simultaneously, Th2 helper cells which usually react mildly against pollen and dust mites were made hypersensitive to airborne irritants by the immune-suppressing vaccines. This "double whammy" left many soldiers wide-open to common opportunistic diseases – even as their extreme allergic reactions further debilitated their immune defenses.

Rook also blamed increased Th2 reactions for "mood changes which we can attribute to the corresponding changes in their hormone and cytokine levels." This, he added, would account for "the extraordinary diversity of symptoms seen in the Gulf war veterans." Reporter McMannes pointed out that vaccines given to British and American troops for cholera, anthrax and bubonic plague were thought to cause the precise immune system changes described by Rook.

Terry Walker, the British vet who had watched his entire family sicken from symptoms that began after a SCUD attack on his position at al Jubayl, had a further thought on the whole Gulf War Illness mess: "By the time you toss in the DU, vaccines, smoke, etc., there may be as many as 30 combined causes! No wonder they too can't find a 'single' medical explanation!"

CHAPTER 21

"NO ALTERNATIVE TO PEACE"

On October 21, 1996, just after 10:00 in the morning, two curious Cubana Airlines pilots watched a single-engine airplane making repeated runs, "low and slow" over neatly squared farm fields in Matanzas province. The intruder, which was not of Cuban origin, was not a spy plane, but a US-registry spray plane. On the day it was reported over Cuba, the Model S2R had launched out of Patrick Air Force Base, just across the gulf in Florida.

Two months after the S2R sighting, Thrips plague suddenly broke out in potato plantations across Matanzas province. When the Cuban Ministry of Foreign Affairs formally complained to the American government, US authorities explained that the S2R pilot had used his "smoke generator" to assure positive visual contact with the Cubana airliner – a "first" in the annals of flight safety.

The Cubans learned that S2R aircraft are used by the US State Department to destroy cocaine crops. The crop duster carries two sprinkling systems, but no smoke generators.

On February 14, 1997, Cuba's Central Quarantine Laboratory confirmed that the Asian Thrips insect was exotic to Cuban territory until the moment of its discovery following the overflight. Thrips, which is easily spread by aerial means, reproduces every 15 to 21 days.

It was not the first bio-attack on this Caribbean country. In 1971, Cuba had hosted the first outbreak of African Swine Fever in the Western hemisphere. Half a million pigs had to be slaughtered after a container of Swine Fever was smuggled ashore near the US military enclave of "Gitmo" in Guantanamo Bay.

The Thrips insects quickly spread to corn, beans, squash, cucumbers and other Cuban crops. Overnight, the application of expensive and hazardous pesticides became necessary, thwarting Cuba's attempts to find new export markets by converting all of its croplands to organic farming. The pesticides have so far proven ineffective. Cuba has applied to the United Nations Food and Agriculture Organization for technical and financial assistance to fight the pest.

If a Cuban aircraft had dusted American wheat fields with a bioagent, the US government would have rightly regarded the incident as an act of war. But like so many of Washington's transgressions, the biological bullying of impoverished families went virtually unremarked by the American press.

* * *

Has the US warfare-entertainment establishment gone completely out of control? Gulf War veterans are calling White House complicity in the Gulf Bio-War an act of treason. As a full-page ad produced by the Gulf War Veterans association for the Washington newspaper explained: "If, during this time of war, the deliberate and willful withholding of vital information leads to the injury and death of America's military and civilian population, we contend that those withholding that information have thereby 'aided the enemy' and should be charged with neglect, murder and treason!"

It appears that the crime against "Trading With The Enemy" has been superseded by the imperatives of doing business. As late as 1992, anthrax spores could be purchased for just $35 from the American Type Culture Collection company. Any organization with an "official" letterhead could order deadly Junin virus. Saddam Hussein's military geneticists did not even have to pay for the cell cultures that would later be thrown in the faces of American sons and daughters. Germs and production facilities were provided by "agricultural subsidies," paid for by US taxpayers.

Even more astonishing, after the deliberate exposure of American military personnel to atomic radiation, CBW and Agent Orange, fresh crops of kids keep signing up at recruiting offices for fresh betrayals. Meanwhile, companies that had profited from the sale of weapons and weapons-making technology to Iraq go unpunished, perpetuating an arms racket now grown cynical and systemic enough to sacrifice its own constituents to profits made by arming enemies.

The leadership I had so deeply distrusted during the Vietnam war has not changed. If good officers do not question bad orders, the danger remains that their oath of fealty could be subverted to serve political expediency and the bottom line.

Already, almost without our realizing it, warmaking has become the world's biggest business. More than a decade after the dismantling of the Berlin Wall, the US military has transformed itself from a proud warrior elite to a major multinational whose managers control assets equal to half of all US manufacturing corporations combined. While Asian "Tigers" continue to cash in on the cresting wave of nearly three-billion "me-too" consumers, nearly 40 percent of America's industrial capacity remains tied up in military manufacturing. Seven out of every 10 dollars urgently required for environmental and social redress at home is being diverted to research and development of ever more exotic, and rapidly obsolescent, military hardware.

When peace is seen as a threat to profits, we are all in trouble. Today, the arming of tinpot tyrants and their frightened neighbors has become a priority for corporations bigger than nations, faceless entities that further profit by replacing the ever-more costly machines and munitions consumed in subduing each newly created threat.

Who's in charge here? Using "jobs" blackmail even as they rush to exploit Third World workers, and PAC payoffs to play politicians like puppets, "transnational" conglomerates are using the rubric of "globalization" to treat the world's blue collar citizens as serfs. Operating increasingly beyond the reach of public scrutiny, democratic process or suspended national laws, 200 corporations currently control more than a quarter of the planet's economic activity.

Not surprisingly, given the widespread resentment their policies engender, most of these transnationals make weapons. (At least one company has gone into the business of fighting proxy wars.) With combined sales bigger than the combined economies of all but 10 of the planet's 198 countries, these globe-girdling corporations carry nearly twice the economic clout of the poorest four-fifths of humanity – who do not yet have phones.

Isn't it time we reined-in transnational privateers plundering the planet for profit as if ecological bankruptcy does not affect us all? Isn't it time we examined the tales we are being sold by warfare-addicted corporations who own broadcast giants employing the most sophisticated media-mesmerization techniques ever devised?

Instead of questioning national values and priorities, corporate media manipulators have made it tantamount to treason to suggest that in a country whose military might is unrivaled by any wannabe warriors – and where one in eight children goes hungry while teachers hold bake sales to raise money for pencils and crayons – the expenditure of $800 million a day on arms may be proving counterproductive.

Are we chasing ghosts? A prudent policy of self-defense ought to begin not with the acquisition of more planet-threatening weapons, but in ending the arms proliferation that makes their repeated use mandatory. While it would be difficult to make a case against having a strong policing force as a last resort when all other avenues of reason and persuasion are exhausted, five decades of "overkill" have not made the world a safer place. We had better hurry up with a sane answer on how much national treasure devoted to killing is enough.

Even after the end of the Cold War, we waste vast resourcesh on this unproductive, unending addiction. The US Council for Economic Priorities calculates that every billion dollars spent on military purchases could employ 71,000 teachers. The US Employment Resource Association estimates that 16,000 permanent job opportunities are *lost* for each billion dollars spent on military procurement.

But much military bookkeeping remains hidden. The US Treasury Department continues to funnel nearly $100 million a day to such secret Pentagon projects as the very-much-alive Star Wars, and what *Wired* magazine describes as the National Security Agency's "key word" monitoring of domestic email and phone-calls. Spent largely without public knowledge or oversight, this backdoor, $36 billion a year "black budget" has already helped fund the 70 ton B-2 Stealth bomber, which glows on radars in the rain and would cost billions of dollars less if built of solid gold. Other projects like the USAF's powerful "ionospheric heater" in Alaska tinker with planetary weather patterns and low frequency brain waves with public funds, but without demur.

While we are busy defending ourselves to death, who is the enemy? Not even Tom Clancey could devise a workable scenario in which a revisionist Russian Old Guard could overcome national bankruptcy, lack of parts and paid personnel to revive high-maintenance missiles, fighters and accident-prone nuclear submarines now rusting in their pens.

* * *

We can no longer afford to be manipulated in such a callous and costly manner. Not when the armed "peace" funded by our taxes bears such a suspicious resemblance to war.

One nuclear war was bad enough. According to the father of the Soviet H-bomb, the detonation of more than 1,000 nuclear warheads among populations supposedly "at peace" with each other killed more than eight million people during the Cold War years. The UN reports that the sun-like ignition of 250 nuclear warheads in once-paradisiacal regions of the Pacific killed 150,000 islanders alone. Six islands disappeared from the face of the ocean.

We were conned. The "Red menace" that sparked multi-trillion dollar profits for weapons contractors – and the MADness of Mutually Assured Destruction for everyone else – never existed. As Gore Vidal points out, President Truman's first dire warnings of this new threat came "at a time when we had atomic weapons and the Russians did not." That enervated nation had just lost 28 million people before and during the Second World War.

In startling contrast, a triumphant USA had been energized by a conflict that had left humming production lines poised to deliver an unprecedented period of prosperity. Examining how the National Security Act of 1947 was used to establish military preeminence and create a "national security state" at home, Vidal notes that Bill NSC-68 "stipulated no negotiations with the Russians, and development of the hydrogen bomb." NSC-68 also called for the rapid build-up of conventional forces, a propaganda campaign to mobilize US society to combat the new "communist threat" – and hefty tax increases to pay for the emerging military state.

It was all a sham. U-2 overflights during the 1950s discovered the bomber and missile "gaps" to be in America's favor. But as late as his 1960 presidential campaign, John F. Kennedy continued to warn about a dangerous "missile gap." When Defense Secretary Robert McNamara stated publicly that the Soviets posed no threat, Kennedy privately rebuked him for telling the truth. McNamara apologized and promptly ordered a massive buildup of the US nuclear arsenal. Within a year, the Pentagon had 93 missiles aimed at the Soviet Union.

The Kremlin had less than three dozen atomic warheads targeted on the United States. "We simply didn't have enough raw material to go around," Nikita Khrushchev recounted in a memoir which explained why Russia could not build large numbers of nuclear weapons until the 1960s.

The threatened Soviet bear eventually acquired atomic claws, and a costly race was on. With both sides locked into rapidly escalating and mutually destructive paranoia, staying ahead in a suddenly very real game of "chicken" took precedence even over the safety of their respective citizenry. It's all there in *Scorched Earth*: how for more than four decades, the governments of both countries knowingly subjected their citizens to lethal doses of radioactivity in the name of "national defense."

The toxic legacy of those MAD decades will be with our descendants for thousands of years to come. Even the interim clean-up cost – diverted either from weapons manufacture or from life enhancing production and shrinking public service budgets – is huge. Decontaminating radioactive wastes at atomic weapons plants throughout the US and Former Soviet Union could easily top a trillion dollars.

In Washington state, where a 1997 explosion in an underground storage tank contaminated workers and the surrounding countryside with radioactive plutonium, the cost to decontaminate the Hanford nuclear reservation could run over $100 billion alone. Cleaning up the Savannah River nuclear bomb factory could take 50 years and cost another $25 billion.

Cancer rates are also going up sharply around the nuclear bomb-making factory at Rocky Flats, where plant fires have dusted Denver with the highest concentration of plutonium ever measured near an urban area – including Nagasaki in 1945. The "Mile High City" also faces a 26 square-mile underground plume of potent carcinogens migrating from a military test range located just 16 miles away. Dubbed "the most contaminated square mile on earth" by the US Army Corps of Engineers, the Rocky Mountain Arsenal produced nerve gas for three decades.

In the wake of inadequate clean-up technology, up to a dozen US nuclear warfare sites will have to be fenced off as "National Sacrifice Zones".

But the warmakers are just getting started. Among nations on the top of the world wealth pyramid, nuclear arms production is turning out smaller, more-likely-to-be-used, "enhanced" nuclear bombs. And "Gene Gap" paranoia is shoveling still more brainpower and cash into genetic weapons research in an effort eerily reminiscent of the 1950s atom bomb program.

* * *

American involvement with CBW actually began in the fall
of 1941, when US Secretary of War Henry Stimson was authorized
to develop a civilian agency "to take the lead on all aspects of
biological warfare." George Merck, founder of one of the
world's largest drug conglomerates, was a key member of the
panel advising President Roosevelt on BW. By the early 1990s, the
race to perfect more hideous forms of chemical-biological warfare
had outstripped all other military development in the USA, jumping from $15.1 million to $90 million in just five years.

By then, millions of people in the US, Africa, Haiti,
Europe and and the Caribbean had been stricken by a frightening
and fatal immune-system destroyer for which there remains no
known cure. Forget "green monkeys" who do not get AIDS even
when injected with HIV. The ever-dependable *US Congressional
Record* shows that the quest to develop HIV began not in African
rainforests but in a city in Maryland more than a decade before
the first outbreaks of AIDS.

In classified testimony presented during those 1970
Department of Defense Appropriation Hearings, a military doctor
expressed the hope that "within a period of five to 10 years it
would be possible to produce a synthetic biological agent, an
agent that does not naturally exist and for which no natural
immunity could have been acquired."

The US Army further testified that the unique, immune-
destroying virus could be developed at a total cost of $10 million.
House Appropriations Bill 15090 quickly approved funds to
produce "Immune-System Destroying Agents for Biological
Warfare."

Was this wise? Was it ethical? "It is a highly controversial
issue and there are many who believe such research should not be
undertaken," the appropriations committee admitted, "lest it lead
to yet another method of mass killing of large populations."

After this brief hand-wringing, US taxpayer-funded HIV
experimentation began in earnest. Aided by researchers at the
nearby, ironically-named National Institute of Health, army gen-
eticists at Fort Detrick sought to transfer "slow viruses" capable
of altering the immunologic response of T-lymphocyte cells in
sheep and cows into genetic envelopes capable of outwitting
human immune defenses.

The scientists succeeded. While the question of whether
the first widespread HIV outbreaks were the result of deliberate or
accidentally contaminated vaccines remains hotly debated, it is
well-documented that in 1977 the DoD-backed World Health
Organization inoculated more than 100 million black Africans
with an AIDS-laced smallpox vaccine. As Dr. Leonard Horowitz
so thoroughly documents in his chilling book, *Emerging Viruses,
Aids & Ebola*, one year later the Centers for Disease Control

injected more than 2,000 young white homosexual males with hepatitis B vaccine in New York City.

Soon after similar vaccination programs were initiated in San Francisco, Los Angeles, St. Louis and Chicago, the first cities to experience major outbreaks of AIDS were New York, San Francisco, Los Angeles, St. Louis and Chicago.

* * *

"Doing unto others before they do it to you" may be a smart way to conduct a war, but the doctrine of employing massive firepower to protect American troops is hard on non-combatants who have far outnumbered uniformed casualties in every war fought since 1936. People precariously balanced atop the planet's remaining resources would do well to remember that there are a lot more "others" than us. And that an aggrieved nation's recourse to vengeance can be concealed in a lunch pail.

While reshaping a military trained and equipped to prevail against aggressors foolish enough to challenge such evident superiority, we'd better start figuring out less drastic ways to resolve conflicts before they escalate into the kind of killing that threatens our species. The slaughter over oil in Kuwait and Iraq could be pale prelude to the looming struggle over water.

As the countdown continues toward a century of scarcity, threats to "natural security" are already redefining outmoded definitions of heavily armed national security. The real enemies at the gates – poverty, hunger, racism and suppression of the female in human nature and societies – cannot be countered by high-tech weaponry whose development and production continues to de-stabilize the economies and ecologies of the very nations they supposedly protect.

The president who warned us about the dangers of the military-industrial complex failed to anticipate the joining of entertainment technologies to that dangerous duo. But Eisenhower was wise enough to look beyond the bloodletting on Normandy Beach and declare: "There is no alternative to peace."

The commander in charge of the assault on Nazi-infested Europe had no wish to revisit those horrors. But the Gulf War veterans stricken by invisible weapons know that this new warfare has erased all front lines. A Canadian veteran and victim of the Gulf War calls germ weapons, "abhorrent." The very unpre-dictability of bioweapons, David Prestwich points out, "dissolves the them and us in armed conflict."

Is Prestwich angry? "I was in the military," he says. "I'd signed up, sworn an oath. You go where you're told." But like many other veterans from Victoria to Halifax, this former Canadian soldier wants to know: "How long is this going to go on?" The "troubling legacy" of a war that everyone lost has to be investigated, Prestwich insists. "There has to be some resolu-tion to all this."

* * *

One of the biggest hopes among ailing American, British, Canadian and Anzac veterans is that governments without shame or decency will drop their denials and acknowledge that something happened in the Gulf to fundamentally alter their personalities and their lives. With a loud enough public outcry, their stories could spur elected leaders to abolish weapons even more perverse than the atom bombs which have blighted this planet's health and serenity for the last 50 years.

President Clinton's April, 1997, ratification of an international Chemical Warfare Convention outlawing the production, shipment and use of chemical arms appears to be a major step forward. But that initiative was undermined by a senate stricture to continue the same "defensive" biochemical research originally used to justify this new arms race. While admitting that in bioweapons research, the chances of finding a "cure" against easily-modified germs are remote, the Department of Defense notes that in this area of research "the difference between offense and defense is purely a matter of intent." As the Gulf war demonstrated, there can be no biowar "defense" that does not harm the very DNA it is meant to protect.

We have come a long way from the US Civil Defense Administration's 1955 admonition to "Wash your hands" when under bio-attack. Experts now believe that the accidental or deliberate release of "hot agents" now being toyed with in BL-4 labs located in Suffield, Alberta; Toronto; Winnipeg; Fort Detrick, Maryland; Atlanta, Georgia; Porton Down, England; France's Pasteur Institute; the Tokyo Institute and Russia's Ivanofsky Institute is likely. Biolevel-4 laboratories handle viruses that are highly transmissible, and for which there is no known cure.

As this book goes to press, and the US once again prepares to attack Iraq over hidden bio-labs, there is no reason to believe that a tyrant as relentless, resourceful and risk-prone as Saddam Hussein has restricted germ warfare production within his own borders. Flying any flag of convenience, a nondescript "tramp" freighter berthed in any Indian Ocean backwater would do just as well as an apartment in New York city.

We'd better look sharp before that or a similar senario becomes real. We'd better pray to whatever gods we can summon that someone of conscience will spread the word before the germs. And we'd better move quickly on eradicating these shortcuts to Armageddon from the face of the Earth.

The bottom line is that this planet and its swarming peoples can no longer afford war. While we're thinking of more subtle ways to reach commonalities and resolve our differences, taxpayers everywhere must demand a choice in where their annual remittances are directed, as well as a full public accounting of every dollar, dinar and dinero spent on military research and procurement. Germ research must be brought under sole civilian

~ 344 ~

auspices, with independent oversight conducted into all bio-labs on a monthly basis.

The alarm is ringing. We had better not roll over and go back to sleep. We must not rest until we have regained control of a runaway genetic train. If secret police or propaganda prevail, and knowledge of our rulers' real agenda remains hidden, a dirty, secret, nearly forgotten war in the Gulf could become a dress rehearsal instead of the burial ground for the next germ warfare contest which could imperil us all.

CHAPTER 22

VOICES FROM THE STORM

The last to speak should be those who suffer and endure:

"Any idiot who wishes to play genetic god-hood and inflicts the kind of suffering, now being inflicted upon my son, his wife and children, should be neutered, stoned in public, beaten to death and their carcass thrown to the wolves or wild dogs. OK, does that tell you a little bit of the anger and anguish a father and grandfather feels? I hope so, because this Vet and father of Vets and grandfather of sweet young children, who are suffering of this man-made group of illnesses, is as ready to take arms, as he was when he did for his country. I'm beyond angry." – name withheld

"I don't want money. I want my life back. I want work with all of my faculties, without the pain, without the confusion, without the intrusion of health problems brought on as a result of my Gulf service." – Mike

"If you ask anyone if they feel any effects left over from the Gulf, no one would say no." – female veteran

"To any of you out there who is ill-don't give up-this is a bigger fight it's on our soil now!" – name withheld

"Everyone thinks the war was sanitary. Only 250 people died. Or at least 250 Americans. Besides, that war is long over. People don't like war. They don't like to look at it or their role in it, and they don't want to be reminded of it when they've got other things in their faces – like keeping their jobs, paying their bills and maybe getting laid. You had better wake up and learn about it because the Gulf War was a dress rehearsal for the next one." – name withheld

"We discussed primarily the trouble veterans were experiencing that I was aware of and they were receiving much of the same feedback. For instance active duty Sgt. Major's, Captain's and enlisted who were ill but afraid to come forward for fear of losing their careers. Distraught wives of veteran's calling on behalf of their husband who was about to lose his job because he could no longer perform his duties. Newlywed's concerned about the potential of birth defects and should they risk trying have a family.

"The mother of a gulf veteran who had died and wanting to know why her son died at 35 from liver and pancreatic cancer. Or the sister of a gulf vet who killed himself because of the chronic pain and the frustration he could no longer stand. "Can his wife and two little kids get compensated now that he is gone," she asks? – Jeffrey Ford Executive Director, National Gulf War Resource Center

"My wife has had three miscarriages since Desert Storm, Female problems that OBGYN Doctors and Specialist can't figure out or fix, and my daughter was conceived after Desert Storm and she is deaf. (My two children born before Desert Storm are fine!) Who do I talk to about this where do I go for help!!!!!!" – name withheld

"In my testimony, I will refer to many events, some recent, some historical. But all having a bearing on the state of mind of the institutions just mentioned. This mentality is one of denial, ignorance, and abuse of power given not as a right, but as a fig. The need to defend one's home and family is a basic one. However, when the responsibility of that defense is given over to another, there is a basic trust passed on which, once broken, may never mend. This broken trust is the real, basic reason we are here today." – Jim Brown, Director of Gulfwatch

"I also just learned from a GW vet that some units around Cement city were given Cipro and ordered to take it after it was thrown off the back of Humvees the day BEFORE the first SCUD attack in Cement City. Then several days later these same troops were ordered to turn in any remaining Cipro and were never given any other antibiotics. This particular vet is positive for the Mycoplasma fermentans. Other units in other places were never given doxycycline or Cipro throughout the war. Perhaps this was a crude 'Double-Blind' study? I wonder." – MD "Medicine Man" Larry G.

"Looking for info: Prymithin (mostly used in flea removal, lice and ticks on domestic animals i.e. flea collars, sprays) combined with Carbol or Sevins used in treating soldiers' clothing and around living quarters as an insect repellent."
– Mirleen

"Help, treated PTSD but still lost." –Richard

"It seems impossible to obtain an explanation from the Department of Defense that is consistent with the events as reported by the soldiers present...The Department of Defense steadfastly refuses to acknowledge this aspect of the problem. Their blanket denials are not credible. Recent American history provides grievous examples of official military cover ups and Defense Department mistakes...the poisoning of countless thousands of Vietnam Veterans by Agent Orange is just one compelling example.

"To my mind, there is no more serious crime than an official military cover up of facts that could prevent more effective diagnosis and treatment of sick US Veterans... Today, I will present additional evidence to show that despite repeated automatic denials by the Department of Defense, chemical weapons and chemical agents were present and found in the war zone...

"The evidence continues to grow that they will go to any length to deny the facts surrounding this subject...Will members of Congress and the soldiers have to uncover each and every exposure in order to determine the causes of these illnesses. and what can be best done to treat these sick, and often dying, Gulf war veterans?

"We cannot allow the US military establishment or our government to turn its back upon hundreds of thousands of Americans and their families who answered their country's call and who were almost certainly exposed to chemical or biological weapons agents during the Gulf war. And what of the risk of those same exposures in future wars? Is that why the department of defense is behaving in this manner – to hide their lack of ability to adequately protect our troops from these kinds of exposures in future wars?"– Senator Donald W. Riegle Jr.

"Still having some difficulty coping with the sights and sounds from the time over there."
– Rich

"I have a very good friend who married her husband after they both returned from Saudi. Last week there was a front page articles featuring her ailments attributed to the Gulf War." – Terry

"The laws are written as such that a country at war can kill as many people as is needed to end and win a war but you cannot march to Baghdad and hold Saddam Hussein accountable for his actions any more than you can hold the US and Soviet governments accountable for their part in supplying Iraq with the weapons of mass destruction during their eight year war with Iran that eventually were used against Kuwait and finally against your coalition force of better than 30 countries... The governments have been supplying each other with weapons of annihilation for years and the weapons are used for the purpose that they were designed for and you veterans were just another target... period." – James

"My fiance served in the Gulf and we both want a family but are apprehensive about ever starting one because of all the evidence of birth defects in Gulf War Vets. Please, if you have any information to ease our fears, e-mail me." – Kate

"Please, I'm in desperately in need of advice and support. I'm a MSG/E8 and would have twenty years active service in August, pending medical discharge. My medical board has returned, awarding me 40% disability (30% for depression and panic disorder and 10% for a back condition.)

"When notified of this award, I requested a formal hearing before the medical evaluation board with legal representation. My appointed lawyer contacted me (after I had left several messages on voice mail to please contact me) 2 days prior to my hearing. Her advice to me was that a formal hearing would not help my case. She seemed very knowledgeable about the board's reasoning for the awarded percentiles. She stated that, after listening to me, the 30% for depression and panic disorder was fair, as I could articulate my situation and had not been in the psych ward enough to justify a higher percentile and the 10% for my back problems and the other problems was because of the previous surgeries, that pain was rated at 0%, and incontinence did not and would not keep me from performing my military duties.

"I rescinded my request for a formal hearing not willing to subject myself to the emotional distress of presenting my case to the board, particularly since my appointed attorney was more interested in supporting the medical boards decisions, than listening to the circumstances which have brought me to this point.

"I have been hospitalized in the psych unit at XX Naval Hospital twice. The first time for three weeks due to depression, caused by discrimination and harassment within my immediate chain of command. The second time because of attempted suicide, after my command had ordered me back to duty, against my doctor's recommendations.

"On my second day after reporting to duty, because my choices were to either follow doctors recommendations or disobey a direct order to report to duty, a Major General 'happened' to find his way into the office in which I was performing my assigned duties of answering the telephone and taking messages, and while I was at the position of attention, began a tirade against me to include stating that "I was a drain on the army" and the "taxpayers" referring to my discharge proceedings and if "I was a civilian, with medical problems I would have been gone in 60 days."

"When I attempted to explain to him that I was ordered to duty against doctors recommendations, and asked him to look at my documents, he indicated that he didn't have the time. When I attempted to explain that the discharge proceedings were also evaluating damage to my back, resulting in incontinence, sciatica, atrophy of my legs--because of two back surgeries – the second one was performed because the first surgeon had operated on the wrong vertebrae – he continued to threaten me, and at one point looked at me and asked "what's wrong with you, you look like you are going to cry". Later that evening, was when I attempted suicide.

"I need some advice and help, feel like I have been used up and simply discarded. My shrink indicated to the medical board that my "industrial and social adaptability is severely hampered". The medical terminology for a basket case.

"I filed a complaint with the CID in November and that complaint has not been investigated – no response. I have a feeling it is buried at National Guard Bureau, because of the rank of the individuals involved. No one has had to answer for the sexual discrimination and harassment complaints, or why my command disregarded doctors recommendations, nor the "General's actions". In fact, the day after my suicide attempt, the chief of personnel told my doctors that I had "sought the General out and accosted him". I had informed the CID that I would volunteer to a polygraph test to support my statements as I realized that on several issues it was my word against someone else's.

"It seems, I'm losing everything – my career and have been forced into bankruptcy. I am 43 years old and losing everything I've worked for, I can no longer support my children and picture us living out of a car someplace and I haven't done anything wrong – my performance has always been exemplary and have learned that it means nothing – that one or two people within your chain of command can destroy you. Please send advice. Thank you." – woman vet

"Today is very hard for me! Yesterday was the anniversary of the birth of my only son. He passed away 5 days later! Sure, it has been 6 years. now, but that is the type of pain that never really goes away. No matter how hard you try! So it's hard for me to think of this day as a holiday! But I would like to wish each and every one of you well on this day! Enjoy your families and loved ones! And hold them dear in your heart! Not only this day, but everyday!" – woman vet

The Nuremberg Code is a 10-point declaration governing human experimentation, developed by the Allies after World War II in response to inhumane experiments conducted by Nazi scientists and physicians. The Code states that voluntary and informed consent is absolutely essential from all human subjects who participate in research, whether during war or peace. The Code states:

> The person involved should have the legal capacity to give consent; should be so situated as to be able to exercise free power of choice, without the intervention of any element of force, fraud, deceit, duress, overreaching, or other ulterior form of constraint or coercion; and should have suffic-ient knowledge and comprehension of the elements of the subject matter involved as to enable him to make an understanding and enlightened decision. This latter element requires that before the acceptance of an affirmative decision by the experimental subject, there should be made known to him the nature, duration, and purpose of the experiment; the method and means by which it is to be conducted; all inconveniences and hazards reasonable to be expected; and the effects upon his health and person which may possibly come from his participation in the experiments.

> "There is no provision in the Nuremberg Code that allows a country to waive informed consent for military personnel or veterans who serve as human subjects in experiments during wartime or in experiments that are conducted because of threat of war." – John D. Rockefeller IV, Chairman for the Committee on Veterans' Affairs United States Senate December 8, 1994

"Anyone interested in handcuffing themselves around the Pentagon to draw government and media attention to Desert Storm Syndrome/Gulf War Illness – please contact me." – name withheld

"I would like to know if any veterans that where over in the Gulf after the War for the clean up have any problems. I have had problems with my joints, memory and fatigue. I served with the 702nd Trans. We served all over the theater transporting all kinds of ammo are base camp was in KKMC. The VA has told me that there is nothing wrong with me, but I see myself getting worst as time goes on. If you can help me by answering my questions I would greatly appreciate it."
– John L.

"Am getting smoked over medical board."
– Mark

"My short-term memory loss is very real. My sons and wife are always ridiculing me for things I have done, or not done: things I have said or not said... One day I got in my car and headed for a neighboring town about 35 miles away...halfway there, I pulled over to the side of the road and began to cry. I had no idea where I was going...or why. I turned around and went home. I have missed meetings, failed to meet my wife or kids somewhere, because I simply forgot. I never used to be like that. I was a captain, I led hundreds of Marines during my career. I was a commanding officer of two units. There was nothing wrong with my memory prior to the Gulf War. I had a hell of a memory. Good enough to get me through a 4 year college in 3.5 years... I firmly believe that we vets are suffering from something that is affecting a part of our memory functions...what, I don't know. Please know that you are not alone...there are many of us like you today...if only I could remember some of their names..."
– name withheld

"Served in Dhahran KSA from Aug 90 thru Mar 91. Since returning I've been sick with headaches (daily), joint pain in the knees, lower back pain, reactive airway disease and a few minor problems. I've even passed some of my problems onto my one year son who had to have open heart surgery because of a large hole in his upper chamber (very uncommon) and now seizures. I was very proud in the job we all did over there I just wish I could be equally as proud of our government for taking care of us instead of spending more money to disclaim us." – Philip S.

"The military has released chemicals and biological agents through outdoor "open air" tests for over four decades. Some of these supposedly safe chemicals and biological agents, referred to as simulants, were also released over populated areas and cities. Although scientific evidence suggested that the tests may have caused illnesses to exposed citizens, the Army repeatedly claimed that these bacteria and chemicals were harmless until adverse health effects convinced them to change the stimulants used. The death of Edward J. Nevin was associated with the release of one simulant, Serratia marcescens, over San Francisco in 1950. A subsequent court trial revealed that on September 26 and 27, 1950, the Army sprayed Serratia marcescens from a boat off the coast of San Francisco.

"On September 29, patients at the Stanford University Hospital in San Francisco began appearing with Serratia marcescens infections. Although the judge denied the validity of the plaintiffs' claims that the exposures were related to the death of Mr. Nevin, the trial raised frightening questions about the selection of stimulants.

"Dugway Proving Ground has been a site for 'open air' testing of chemical and biological agents for decades. The purpose of the tests is to determine how the agents spread and survive, and their effect on people and the environment. In 1992, several military personnel from the Arizona National Guard experienced chemical burns during a summer training exercise at the Dugway Proving Grounds. According to two physicians, a daughter from one of the guardsmen also received chemical burns when she later handled her father's duffel bag.

"One of these doctors, Dr. Michael Vance, was contacted by military officials and encouraged to modify his written findings on the possible cause of the daughter's injury. He refused. According to scientists and doctors from the University of Utah, there is great concern over the potential health consequences not only for military personnel who work and train at Dugway, but also for civilians who live in a small town and on an Indian reservation near the Proving Grounds... the use of potentially harmful chemical and biological agents continues at Dugway even today." – John D. Rockefeller IV, Chairman for the Committee on Veterans' Affairs United States Senate

"I served with the 513th Transportation Company in Desert Storm. We delivered water, mail, and ammunition to the front lines, and I was fuel handler at Log Base Alpha. (I was sexually harassed, and my best friend was raped by someone in the chain of command). I have had a chronic cough since I have returned. It's been described as a 'smoker's cough.' I've never smoked in my life." – Linda

"Saw an excellent bumper sticker on my MSGs (a double vet – Vietnam/PGV) pickup truck. It said 'I love my country, but I don't trust my government'. Seems appropriate after our PGW health problems." – Steve

"When I read your letter I could have sworn that I had wrote it. I am suffering from exactly that same symptoms you are. There are days that I can barely function. I also am tired of being sick and tired. My wife can measure the lapses in my memory daily. I forget people I've just talked to in person and on the phone, My pin number to my ATM card which I use almost daily. I am reaching a breaking point. If you ever need anyone to talk to just write back and I will give you my phone number. God help us, The Government won't." – Rick H.

"I AM CURRENTLY INFECTED WITH THE GULF WAR SYNDROME. IT IS CONTAGIOUS I HAVE CONTRACTED IT FROM A WOMAN FRIEND AND

HAVE SEEN IT IN AT LEAST 20 PEOPLE. I HAVE STOPPED BEING IN CONTACT (CASUAL OR CLOSE CONTACT) WITH PEOPLE FOR FEAR OF GIVING IT TO OTHERS. I PROBABLY GAVE IT TO MY FAMILY AND FRIENDS AND KNOW 1ST HAND THAT IT IS CATCHABLE. ITS PROBABLY SOME KIND OF RETRO VIRUS ENGINEERED BY US OR THEM. BUT IT NONETHELESS IS A SERIOUS PROBLEM. I'VE LOST MOST OF MY MEMORY, HAVE SEVERE SKIN PROBLEMS, MY JOINTS ARE SHOT, MY BACK IS F--KED, ALONG WITH A MIRRIAD OF OTHER PROBLEMS; IE. FATIGUE, SERIOUS MIGRATING INFECTIONS. SEVEN DOCTORS HAVE SEEMED TO STONE-WALL THESE SYMPTOMS AND I CANNOT SEEM TO FIND HELP ON FINDING A DIAGNOSIS OR CURE."
– a civilian

"In April my husband and I gave birth to an infant with many serious birth defects. We lost her in April. The doctors tell me it was genetic, no explanations, nothing. We would love more children, but need to know if there is a connection with his time in the Gulf and these birth defects."
– Brenda

"To all of the men & women who served this country in the GW, I say thank you. I am deeply sorry that the US Government has lied to you, has not given you and your families the help you need to fight the GW illness, but I know that if we expose the lies, and those who have helped the lie to grow by lying about your exposure. Will someday pay the price to the GW Vets."
– name withheld

"I can barely recall but a few isolated moments of my tour in the Gulf. I have moments of clarity that more or less 'rush in' from time to time. I got another jolt to my memory problems this morning as I woke up. I looked at my phone to see I had a phone call last night at 10:30 P.M. Seeing who it was, I became concerned as I care for this person a lot and at 5:00 A.M this morning I called her to 'check the welfare' only to be reminded I had spoken to her for over 10 minutes the night before when the call came in. Having no recollection of this, I was embarrassed (still am) and now worried more for myself.

"It happens a lot these days. I forget something moments after I intend to remember it, forget to write it down, buy some tea at work, then do it again only to hear the cafeteria guy say 'man, you were just up here!' Forgetting was not 'me', is not 'me' at least not before my tour in the Gulf. Before – mind like a steel trap, names, places, messages, even their Date Time Groups, where the messages came from; regulations quoted verbatim, procedures, programs, plans, I even wrote annexes to warplans, but now....lost in a mist, my time in the Gulf even foggier and it seems, now, things are getting worse.

"Do you feel the frustration and extreme feeling of anger 'well' up inside you when it happens? Try to laugh it off and make cute little jokes about it so your peers don't think you're crazy? Struggle with the anxiety of desperately trying to recall even some of the simple things you are asked to reiterate or pass on? – Jim Dearing

"I was wondering. when did we declare war on Iran. Someone told me we never actually had a war, because congress never declared it. Could you clear that up for me please, if its no trouble."
– Doug C.

"In closing, I wish to say this: for the past five and a half years, I and other veterans have wanted one thing. Not money. We want for DoD and VA to honor the contract they made with the veterans, and to take care of them." – Jim Brown, Director of Gulfwatch

"Just another rule 23-D friendly-fire ill Gulf War era veteran wondering when the domestic war crime trials start?!!" – Christopher

"My only hope is to reach other vets and the public to let them know it is true and many of us are dying from this illness. I will not give up until we are recognized and taken care of by our government, who continues to blackball us on this endless journey." – name withheld

"...out of concern for my soon to be x-husband. I was wondering what were some of the symptoms of Gulf War Syndrome. Are any of the effects mental? My husband was based on the El Toro, Ca Marine Base...I don't exactly know how close he was to the area where sarin was released. He seems to have a lot of emotional problems, ones that I can't deal with but if there is some way I can help him, I would.

"We have one son he is now four years old. I got pregnant right after he returned from the war. My son doesn't have any side effects, but I had an extremely difficult pregnancy. I was in the hospital for over two months. None of the doctors knew what was wrong with me. My son had to be delivered while I was almost in my seventh month. My body just went absolutely haywire...I had high fevers, spots on my liver, I was emaciated. Can I tell you, I had never been sick before. My doctor told me I was just withering away and he didn't know why. Liver Biopsies, Brain Scans, at least four blood transfusions, heparin therapy, uterus biopsies, treatment for TB, still no clue.

"I remember wishing that I was just diagnosed with a fatal disease so I could just die. I was never formerly discharged from the hospital, I just walked out, me and my husband just walked out against the physician team wishes. I am glad I did that, I was finally able to hold my son and all my troubles just vanished. My mother swore it had something to do with my husband going to war, it looks like she might have been right, like she always is." – Virginia

"I lost a brother to the aftermath of this war and his name was James McCleary. My family and I want to know the truth." – Carla

"I was sick from back in 1991 after coming back. It is a shame that the government is treating us like this. If you suffer from your nerves, take your medication because this doesn't get better it gets worst – ask a Vietnam vet. They have help me a lot because they were treated worst than us." – Benjamin H.

"I was on the USS Barbey FF1088 during Desert Shield. After the war I was sent to Treasure Island, Ca for an advanced CBR/NBC course. Our instructors told us several times that there were 147 separate chemical/bio weapons attacks during the war. I believed then and I still believe that the instructors were telling the truth." – Art M.

"It's very scary knowing that because you picked up a [contaminated] mask that you might die from something you can't see." – Kevin

From the ruins of a country and a childhood that have been mostly ignored, Shaon Sabah composed a poem addressed to a:

"Blind, deaf and dumb world"

I sit and wait for the time to pass
For the world to wake up and open its eyes
I scream and shout at the top of my lungs
But my voice goes on unheard
I cry and weep until my eyes dry out
Until the emptiness fills my heart
With a bitter sadness impossible to describe

But the world is deaf and blind
And my voice and tears are blotted out
By the most ugliest sounds of all

The sound of weeping mothers
And starving children
Of horror and destruction
Of torture and suffering
Of a child crying out for help and salvation
Begging to be noticed and heard

And so I sit and watch the screen filled with blood and terror
While my heart grows with a vicious hatred
Impossible to scrape away

I see a woman holding a dead child in her arms
While the tears swim in her eyes

And the happiness in her heart fades away
Into eternal emptiness and despair

I see innocent people on the ground
Covered with a blanket of death
Their blood forming a red sea
Which would flow forever in their sleep

I see barefooted children on the streets
Searching for the truth
Wondering why they have been denied
Their childhood and rights

I see a tiny baby lying on his grave
A little creature in the wilderness
Who was born in the world that was falling apart
And died in its arms not knowing why and how

I see the remaining ruins of a building
That once stood beautiful and erect
And wonder why the world is blind
And still insists to pretend

The blood and suffering I see is real
But life still goes on
And I sit and watch the screen
While the leaders try to rule the world
And take away the only precious thing I possess
My family and friends

I hope and dream and the years go by
But still I'm lost and without a home
I laugh and talk and eat and drink
While inside I cry out for the one thing
That will make me whole

I am a stranger in an unknown land
An alien in a different world
A confused child in the body of a man

Where is the justice the West is on about?
Why are our children starving?
And why are my people been set aside to hurt and to die?
And why is the world so silent?

We have the right to be raised in our own Lands
Without a single threat
So go away and let us live our lives
Without suffering and fear

Take away all the money and all the riches
You have craved for
But don't you dare snatch a newborn
From its mother's womb
Or pluck a blooming flower from its roots

You have tried time and time again
To change the course of History
To abuse the Lands of civilization, wisdom and knowledge
But one thing you have struggled but failed to achieve
Is stab the American flag in its heart of hearts

I guarantee you that
One day we shall return
We will build and grow and learn
While you will be looking from outside
Tearing your hair apart from the crimes you have committed
That will place you down in History
As a coward and a fool

* * *

THE END

SELECTED REFERENCES

Gulf War Airpower Survey, Vol. 5; by Norman Friedman also "Desert Victory;" World Air Power Journal
www.webcom.com/~amraam/aaloss.htm
-AIRLOSS

"Pentagon Will Use Depleted Uranium for Making Armor Piercing Bullets" by Joseph Albright, Atlanta Journal Constitution March 12, 1978
-AJC

"Russia's Dirty Chemical Secret" by Cliff Kincaid, American Legion Magazine, February, 1995
-ALM

"Redistributes Processing of Undiagnosed Gulf Illness Claims" AOL News May 14, 1997
-AOL

"Metal Of Dishonor"; AP, Washington. May 6, 1997
-AP

"FDA Mulls Risky Gulf War Drug"; AP, May 9, 1997
-AP/2

Matthew Brown; Associated Press; March 18, 1997
-AP/3

"Marines: Chemicals Found in Kuwait"; by Bruce Smith; Associated Press; May 7, 1997
-AP/4 MINES

Associated Press; May 8, 1997
-AP/5

Greenpeace; Fifth Geneva Convention on the Protection of the Environment in the Time of Armed Conflict; London, June 3, 1991; William Arkin, Damian Durrant, and Marianne Cherni
-ARKIN

The BCCI Affair A Report to the Committee on Foreign Relations United States Senate by Senator John Kerry and Senator Hank Brown; December, 1992; 102nd Congress 2nd Session Senate; Print 102-140; www.fas.org/irp/congress/1992_rpt/bcci/index.html
-BCCI

Voices in the Storm BBC/FRONTLINE television series. Program 1-The Brink of War, Program 3-The Road to Basra, Program 4-Unfinished Business; WGBH Educational Foundation /; **www.wgbh.org; BBC Radio 5; www.bbc.co.uk/index/radio/radio5az.htm**
-BBC

"Bringing Home The War"; by William Thomas; Monday Magazine May 1, 1997
-BHTW

"US Policies Killing Children In Iraq"; by S. Amjad Hussain (Toledo, Ohio) The Blade June 14, 1997; The Wisdom Fund www.twf.org
-BLADE

And The Waters Turned To Blood; by Rodney Barker; Simon & Schuster 1997
-BLOOD

"Ecological decay – a serious side-effect of sanctions"; by Ibrahim J. Ibrahim; The Baghdad Observer September 26, 1995
-BO

Statement of Jim Brown, Gulfwatch Director before the Subcommittee on Human Resources and Intergovernmental Relations, House Committee on Government Reform and Oversight; December 11, 1996
-BROWN

"Russia Still Doing Secret Work on Chemical Arms"; by Will Englund; The Baltimore Sun, October 18, 1992
-BS

"Ex-Soviet Scientist Says Gorbachev's Regime Created New Nerve Gas In '91,"; by Will Englund; The Baltimore Sun; September 16, 1992.
-BS/2

"Bringing The War Home"; by William Thomas; Monday Magazine May 1-7, 1997
-BWH

AL-HAQIQA; Cairo, Feb. 10, 1991
-CAIRO

"Public Relationships: Hill & Knowlton, Robert Gray, and the CIA" by Johan Carlisle; Spring, 1993 issue of CAQ (Number44)
-CAQ

Veterans vs. the Pentagon; Christian Broadcasting Network; May 27, 1996
-CBN

Quantum Healing; by Depak Chopra; Bantam, 1990
-Chopra

ChronicIllnet: Jan, 1997; www.chronicillnet.org.
-CHRON

CDISS Bailrigg Memorandum 17, Center for Defense and International Security Studies; The Devil's Brews II. Weapons of Mass Destruction and International Security
-CDISS

"Scientist finds nerve damage in Gulf War vets"; CNN WORLD News; March 27, 1996
-CNN

"Iraq bans U.S. weapons inspectors"; October 29, 1997
-CNN/2

The New Nutrition; Dr. Michael Colgan; Apple Publishing 1995
-COLGAN

"All Services Face Anthrax Vac"; COMNAVSURFRESFOR
-COMNAV

Crusade: The Untold Story Of The Persian Gulf War by Rick Atkinson; 1993; excerpted by Jamal Munshi
-CRUSADE SEQUENCE

'Budget Plan Slashes Veterans' Programs"; by Dave Autry; DAV Magazine; July/August, 1997
-DAV

Chapter 1, Part 3 "Biological Warfare Defense, Types of Biological Agents Dissemination of Biological Agents Defensive Measures Iraq's Experience in the Use of Chemical Warfare Agents Gulf War Syndrome: The Case for Chemical/Biological Agent Exposure."
-DEFENSE/RIEGLE

"McPeak: Unclear If Air War Has Sapped Iraqi Will"; by Tony Capaccio; Defense Week, February 4, 1991
-DW

"Riegle Report"; May 25, 1994 U.S. Senate, Committee on Banking, Housing, and Urban Affairs, Washington, DC.
-DUAL

"Depleted Uranium, Durakovic, And The Children Of Chernobyl"
-DUDC

"USC Scientist Links Multiple Vaccinations of Military with Gulf War Syndrome"; Leading Edge Research; February 13, 1996
-EDGE

www.trufax.org

EMERGING VIRUSES: AIDS and Ebola; Leonard Horowitz; served on Harvard School of Dental Medicine faculty; Tetrahedron Publishing Group 1007
-EMERGE

Testimony of Jeffrey S. Ford; Executive Director, National Gulf War Resource Center before the U.S. House of Representatives Committee on Veterans Affairs Subcommittee on Health April 16, 1997
-FORD

"US Cyanide Shipped to Iraq Despite Warnings to CIA"; The Financial Times of London July 3, 1991
-FT

"Iraqi's Florida Plant Tied to Poison Gas: Export of Chemical Feared"; Financial Times of London Feb. 21, 1991
-FT/2

"Operation Desert Storm: The Army Not Adequately Prepared to Deal With Depleted Uranium Contamination"; GAO report, January, 1993
-GAO/1

"Never Reported Army Test could shed light on Persian Gulf Illnesses"; by Norm Brewer and John Hanchette; Apr. 4, 1997;Gannette News Service
-GANNETTE

GASSED IN THE GULF by Patrick Eddington; Insignia 1997
www.InsigniaUSA.com
-GSD

The London Gazette; August 27, 1993
-GAZETTE

"The Genie is Out of the Bottle"; by Neenyah Ostrom Jan. 9, 1997; **NONYN@aol.com**
-GENIE

"The New Crusaders"; by A. M. Amery; The Globe and Mail
-GLOBE/2

"Before War, Iraq Was 'Irresistible'"; The Guardian March 13, 1991
-GUARD

"Death and Indecency"; by Edward Pearce; The Guardian; November 3, 1991
-GUARD/2

The Guardian; November 3, 1991
-GUARD/3

"Biological Black Magic: Why Governments Are Covering-Up Gulf War Syndrome" by David Guyatt 1997
-GUYATT

July, 1995, DoD established GulfLINK; a web site on DefenseLINK, with info on Persian Gulf issues
www.fas.org/irp/gulf/cia
-GULFLNK

Mary Guzman; Americans for Truth
-GUZ

"Why Are We Stuck In The Sand?"; by Christopher Huchens Harpers; January, 1991
-HARPERS

"Defense Documents Support Claims of Gulf War Veterans" by Thomas D. Williams; The Hartford Courant May 29, 1995
-HART/1

The Hartford Courant; Feb. 8, 1995
-HART/2

It Doesn't Take A Hero by Peter Petre; Bantam Books, 1992
-HERO

A Higher Form of Killing: The Secret Story of Chemical and Biological Warfare Robert Harris and Jeremey Paxman. New York: Hill and Wang, 1982. 306 pages.
-HFK

"Why Were FOX Chemical Warnings Ignored?"; by Roger Young Insignia
-IGNORE

"Gulf troops given secret injections"; by Christopher Bellamy
The Independent; Dec. 24, 1996
-IND

Times of India, February 16, 1991
-INDIA

"The Cover-Up Of Gulf War Syndrome: A Question Of National
Integrity"; H. Lindsey Arison III
-INSIDE/ ARISON

IRAQ ACTION COALITION
www.leb.net/IAC/main.html

"The Massacre of Withdrawing Soldiers on 'The Highway of
Death'; by Joyce Chediac; The Commission of Inquiry for the
International War Crimes Tribunal, 1990
IWCT

"US Conspiracy to Initiate the War Against Iraq" by Brian
Becker
-IWCT/2

The Commission of Inquiry for the International War Crimes
Tribunal, 1990

"Final Judgment: International War Crimes Tribunal"; Ramsey
Clark May 9, 1991
-IWCT/3 RUNUP

Journal of the American Medical Association; August, 1991
-JAMA

Journal of the American Medical Association; February 22, 1995
-JAMA/2

Journal of the American Medical Association; January 15, 1997
-JAMA/3

The Journal of the National Cancer Institute; James Mathews; July,
1993
-JNCI

Journal of Occupational Medicine; June, 1994
-JOM

U.S. Demolition Operations At The Khamisiyah Ammunition
Storage Point by Bernard Rostker Special Assistant for Gulf War
Illnesses Department of Defense; Case Narratives April 14, 1997
www.gulflink.osd.mil/khamisiyah/n01_s05.htm
-KHAM

1st Marine Division, Task Force King; 1st Marine AAR Binder, Invasion chronology
-KING

Gulf War Syndrome Investigations In Kuwait; Oct. 14, 1994
Filename: 22010030.95a; DIA, Washington, DC
-KUWAIT

The Los Angeles Times; February 5, 1991
-LA

The Los Angeles Times; March 11, 1991
-LA/2

"DUranium Weapons Pass the Battlefield Test,"; H. van der Keur; The LAKA Foundation; Amsterdam June, 1994.
-LAKA

"USC Scientist Links Multiple Vaccinations of Military with Gulf War Syndrome"; Leading Edge research organization; February 13, 1996
-LE

"The Tiny Victims of Desert Storm"; LIFE Magazine; Nov. 1995
-LIFE

In Time of War; special edition – Heroes All; LIFE Magazine; March 11, 1991
-LIFE/2

Le Monde Diplomatique; April 1995
-LM

Letter to Dr. Bernard Rostker, Office of the Special Assistant to the Deputy Secretary of Defense for Gulf War Illnesses by Dan Fahey; March 31, 1997
-LTR/1

"The Gulf Crisis and a New World Order"; by Khaill Barhoun; The Middle East International; January 11, 1991
-MEI

"Why War?" by Joe Stork and Ann Leach; The Middle East Report; Nov-Dec. 1990
-MER

"From Rapid Deployment to Massive Deployment"; by Joe Stork and Martha Wenger; The Middle East Report; January/February, 1991
-MER/2

"Radioactive Ammo Lays Them to Waste"; by Gary Cohen; The Multinational Monitor; January/February, 1996
www.essential.org/monitor/monitor.html
-MM1

"A Poisoned Policy"; Lev Fedorov and Vil Mirzayanov; Moscow News weekly No. 39, 1992.
-MNW

"MoJo Wire"; US Army Special Operations Command Public Affairs Office, June 27th 1996
-MOJO

"Killing Our Own Again"; Military Toxics Project's Depleted Uranium Citizens' Network; Editor: Rebecca Solnit; January 16, 1996
-MTP

"Pentagon Poison: The Great Radioactive Ammo Cover-Up"; The Nation May 26, 1997
-NATION

"The Pentagon's Radioactive Bullet"; by Bill Mesler; The Nation 1996; **www.thenation.com/issue/961021/1021mesl.htm**
-NATION/2

Newsweek; January 21, 1991
-NEW

Newsweek; March 11, 1991
-NEW/2

"Satellite Photos Cast Doubt on US War Rationale"; Now magazine; March 20-27, 1991
-NOW

"Computer Projects Sarin's Scope"; by Patrick J. Sloyan; New York Newsday; September 27, 1996
-NYN

"Making the Desert Glow: U.S. Uranium Shells Used in the Gulf War May Be Killing Iraqi Children"; by Dr. Eric Hoskins; New York Times January 1, 1993
-NYT/1

New York Times; Aug.28, 1996
-NYT/2

New York Times; Jan. 31, 1989
-NYT/3

"Take this or die..."; by Tim Sebastion; Sept. 22,1996; The Observer
-OBS/1

"Gulf troops 'had too many anthrax jabs'"; by Peter Beaumont March 9, 1997; The Observer
-OBS/2

"Researcher says work's tie to war illness got him fired" by David Olinger; St. Petersburg Times January 11, 1997
-OL

"Gulf War Vets, Doxycycline and Miracles: The Story of Sgt. Tom Hare" by TJ Moriarty; OLNews@aol.com
-OLN

Organization for the Prohibition of Chemical Weapons briefing book, 1997; www.opcw.nl/chemhaz/detect.htm
-OPCW

"Radioactive Recycling, the Army Way"; by Edward Ericson Jr. Orlando Weekly
-OR

President's Advisory Committee of Gulf War Veterans' Illnesses – first chemical warfare meeting, Atlanta on April 16, 1996.
-PAC16

Presidential Advisory Committee On Gulf War Veterans' Illnesses Public Meeting July 9, 1996 Chicago, Illinois
-PAC9

Presidential Advisory Committee On Gulf War Veterans' Illnesses - Nicholsons' testify; January 12, 1996
-PACJAN

Presidential Advisory Committee On Gulf War Veterans' Illnesses July, 1996
-PACJULY

People; Commemorative Issue; Spring/Summer 1991
-PEOPLE

"A Report on the April 4, 1997 Meeting with the Pentagon's Persian Gulf Investigation Team Regarding Depleted Uranium Exposures in the Persian Gulf War" by Dan Fahey; April 16, 1997
-PGIT

DOD classified document #IIR 2 201 0243 92; Department of Intelligence; Alexandria, VA
-PIT

"Swords to Plowshares"; Dan Fahey; Military Toxics Project and June, 1994 AEPI report
-PLOW

CBW: The Poor Man's Atomic Bomb Neil C. Livingstone and Joseph D. Douglas Jr.; 1984 Northwest Veterans For Peace-sponsored
-POOR

First west coast medical conference on PGWS; Sept 9th-10th, 1996, Portland State University
-PORT

"US Used Radioactive Arms In Gulf War" by Francisco Lopez Rueda, Vietnam vet and coauthor of 1993 GAO report Uranium Battlefields Home and Abroad
-RUEDA LOPEZ

June 12, 1997, Reuter
-REUTER

"U.S. veterans want ban on depleted uranium weapons" Reuter May 6, 1997
-R/1

"Vets' Brain Scans Raise Questions"; Reuter April 9, 1997
-R/2

Reuter Sept. 7, 1997
-R/3

Riegle report; May 25, 1994
-RIEGLE CZECH IRAQI

www.gulfwar.org/report/r
BREACH EVAC

Gulf War Syndrome: The Case For Multiple Origin Mixed Chemical Biotoxin Warfare Related Disorders; Report to U.S. Senator Donald W. Riegle Jr., Oct., 1993
-RIEGLE/2 IRAQICBW CZECH

A Lecture By Captain Joyce Riley in Houston, Texas; Jan 15, 1996; **www.munshi.sonoma.edu/jamal/joyce.html**
-RILEY

IS MILITARY RESEARCH HAZARDOUS TO VETERANS' HEALTH? United States Senate; December 8, 1994, John D. Rockefeller, Chairman
-ROCKFLR ROCKY

Diagnosis And Treatment Strategies For Chronic Pyridostigmine Poisoning, In Gulf War Veterans by Lewis M Routledge Ph.D. Molecular Biologist; March 5, 1995
-ROUT

"Despite Fears Of Gulf War Germ Attacks, U.S. Unable To Develop Sensors" by Ed Offley; The Seattle Post-Intelligencer Mar 6, 1997
-SPI

"Inside The Shadow CIA"; by John Connolly; SPY Magazine Sept 1992 – Volume 6
-SPY

Shanti RTV; Parveez Syed; E-Mail INTERNET: **parveez@cr78ra1uk.win-uk.net**; August 27, 1997
-SHANTI

"Iraq gives UN bio-weapons statement"; South News; Nov. 1, 1997; s**outhmovement.alphalink.com.au**
-SOUTH

"The Stone Unturned"; by Dan Fahey 1996 **www.globaldialog.com/~kornkven/Stone1.htm**
-STONE

Scorched Earth: The Military's War Against The Environment; by William Thomas
-SCORCHED

With the Second Marine Division in Desert Shield/Desert Storm; History and Museums Division, Headquarters; US Marine Corps
-SECOND

Testimony during Senate Armed Services Subcommittee on Force Requirements and Personnel, 30 June, 1993
-SEN93 (SEN30)

"The Stone Unturned"; by Dan Fahey www.globaldialog.com/~kornkven/Stone1.htm
-STONE

United States Dual-Use Exports to Iraq and Their Impact on the Health of the Persian Gulf War Veterans; U.S. Senate, Hearing Before the Committee on Banking, Housing, and Urban Affairs, May 25, 1994
-SEN94 (RIEGLE) DUAL

"Gulf assault crimes: The ultimate bullet"; by Parveez Syed Shanti; RTV news agency London; August 27, 1997
-SHANTI

Subcommittee on Human Resources and Intergovernmental Relations chaired by Congressman Christopher Shays; March 28, 1997
-SHAYS

"Shay's Hearing"; PRNewswire; March 28, 1997
-SHAYS

"CIA Says It Failed to Give Data on Iraqi Arms"; by Philip Shenon; April 10, 1997
-SHEN

Son of the Morning Star, by Evan S. Connell; North Point Press, San Francisco 1984
-STAR

"Soviet Chemical Warfare Agents Novichok and Substance 33: Were They Used During the Persian Gulf War?"; by Howard T. Uhal
-SUB33

US intelligence memo, October, 1991; SU-22 SPRAY TANK
-SU22

"The War That Wounded The World"; William Thomas; Vancouver Sun
-SUN

Sunday Times, January 27, 1991
-SUNTIME

TASS; February 10, 1991
-TASS

London Telegraph; January 3, 1997
-TEL/1

"Questions raised in desert stay unanswered"; by Robert Fox London Telegraph; February 27, 1997
-TEL/2

London Telegraph; June 24, 1997
-TEL/3

"Howe says he misled House on Gulf victims"; by Jon Hibbs; London Telegraph; March 6, 1997
-TEL/4

"See you in court, Gulf veterans are told by Whitehall"; by David Wastell and Tom Baldwin; The London Telegraph; March 2, 1997
-TEL/5

"French Troops Hold Clue To Gulf War Illness"; by William Thomas; Environment News Service; June, 1997
-THOMAS

Time; March 4, 1991
-TIME

Time; March 18, 1991
-TIME/2

Time; February 25, 1991
-TIME/3

Time; January 28, 1991
-TIME/4

Time; February 4, 1991
-TIME/5

Time; December 10, 1990
-TIME/6

Time; March 11, 1991
-TIME/7

"Too Sensitive"; by William Thomas; Monday magazine Oct. 17, 1996
-TOO

"Treated Like Trash"; by Bruce Smith; Associated Press; May 8, 1997
-TRASH

"Was Saddam Set Up For The Kill?; by Linda Diebel; Toronto Star; March 10, 1991
-TS

"Attack Teaches Third World About US Might"; by Richard Gwyn; Toronto Star; February 24, 1991
-TS/2

"Was Gulf War Really The Mother Of All Deceptions?"; by Gerald Caplin; Toronto Star; March 3, 1991
-TS/3

Toronto Star; January 25, 1991
-TS/4

"Mycotoxins and Gulf War Illness: A Possible Link"; by Jonathan B. Tucker, Ph.D.
-TUCK

U.S. Chemical and Biological Exports to Iraq and Their Possible Impact on the Health Consequences of the Persian Gulf War U.S. Senate Committee on Banking, Housing, and Urban Affairs October 27, 1992; James J Tuite, III, Principal Investigator
-TUITE/92 EXPORTED

Selected Reports Of Direct Chemical Warfare Agent Deployment, Exposure, Or Limited Use During And After Operation Desert Storm for the Presidential Advisory Committee on Gulf War Veterans' Illnesses April 16, 1996; by James J. Tuite, III
-TUITE

"Report On The Fallout From The Destruction Of The Iraqi Chemical Research, Production And Storage Facilities Into Areas Occupied By US Military Personnel During The 1991 Persian Gulf War" by James J. Tuite, III 1966
-TUITE/2 FALLOUT

Classified DoD Intelligence. Report "United Nations Special Commission, Second CW Inspection 15-22 August 1991
-UNSCOM
see also GulfLINK www.gulflink.osd

"Research Team Identifies Genetic Material In Gulf War-Era Veterans" Calypte Biomedical press release; Tampa, FL, October 7, 1996
-URNOVITZ FLORIDA

"Illness Tied To Potent 'Cocktail'"; by Richard J. Newman U.S. News & World Report April 14, 1997
-USNWR

"UT Southwestern team traces Gulf War illnesses to chemicals"; UT Southwestern press release Jan, 1997; www.swmed.edu.
-UT

"VA Research On Persian Gulf Veterans' Health" Veterans Administration press release; April 10, 1997
-VA

Special hearing House Veterans' Affairs Committee, November 9,1993
-VAC

Certain Victory; Brigadier General Robert H. Scales; Office of the Chief of Staff, U.S. Army1993
-VICTORY

"The Vitamin Solution"; by William Thomas private; distribution to Gulf War vets
-VITS

Voices in the Wilderness, a campaign to end the UN/US sanctions against Iraq1460 W. Carmen Chicago, IL 60640
www.IAC/vitW.html May 15, 1997
-VIW

"How The US Avoided The Peace"; by Michael Emery; The Village Voice; March 5, 1991
-VV

"Who Lost Kuwait?"; by Murray Waas; The Village Voice; January 22, 1991
-VV/2

"The Myth of Surgical Bombing in the Gulf War"; by Paul Walker; Institute for Peace and International Security, Cambridge
-WALKER

"Based On A True Story"; by Ron Jones; Whole Earth Quarterly; Summer 1993
-WEQ

Washington Post; March 7, 1991
-WP

Washington Post; February 2, 1991
-WP/2

Winston-Salem Journal; Feb. 28, 1997
-WSJ

Washington Times; April 27, 1990
-WT

"Anti-AIDS mix found in Gulf Vets"; by Paul M. Rodriguez; The Washington Times; August 11, 1997
-WT/2

"The United States And The Iran-Iraq War"; by Stephen R. Shalom; Z magazine; Feb., 1990
-Z

"The 'Logic' of War"; by Noam Chomsky and Michael Albert; Z Magazine; Feb., 1991
-Z/2

"The Gulf Crisis"; by Noam Chomsky; Z Magazine; Jan., 1991
-Z/3

"The American Armada In The Gulf"; by Noam Chomsky; Z magazine; Jan., 1991
-Z/4

APPENDIX 1

Chapter References and End Notes

http://www.pbs.org/wgbh/pages/frontline/gulf/war/index.html

http://www.pbs.org/plwebcgi/fastweb?getdoc+pbsolbeta+all+5155+
0+wAAA+

PBS/BBC

1. THE GENERAL

the world's biggest PR firm – SECOND, PROG
The general knew he would have to wind up this war -HERO and IGNORED.
the US had continued to support the Shah of Iran for 25 years - RUNUP
world's "biggest and most aggressive" BW production facilities - CDISS, GULFLINK
tried and tested mustard gas -HFK, KW
Churchill – TEL/1
Haber's "A higher form of killing." -KW
a Washington-to-Baghdad link provided the Iraqi military with intelligence -GSD 174/281
The Iraqis were receiving bomb damage assessment satellite photos -GSD 174/279
Ishii -KW
shots "shriveled the body or caused great sores" -WEQ
Saddam provided his corps commanders autonomous "release authority"-GSD 10/10
Iraq conducted at least 10 major chemical warfare attacks -GSD 10/8
Iraq used "mixed agent" weapons against the Kurds – and Majnoon Island -TUCK/57
CBW bombs killed another four people in Birjinni -DEFENSE
the recapture of Iraq's al-Faw peninsula -GSD 10/9
the profligate use of artillery rounds filled with a sarin-mustard agent -GSD/UNSCOM
What really happened at Halabja? -DEFENSE
The general knew it was standard Iraqi war-fighting doctrine - GSD 10/11
some 50,000 Iranian soldiers had been killed by hideous weaponry -SCORCHED
Harken -BCCI
"we hold no opinion about..your border disagreement with Kuwait." -Z/3, VV, VV/2
Iraq's use of CBW during Iran-Iraq War -UNSCOM, DEFENSE

Iraq became the first nation in history to use nerve agents on the battlefield -CDISS
Iraq may have tested mixed agent tricothecene mycotoxins against Majnoon Island -IRAQ
some 50,000 Iranian soldiers had been killed by hideous weaponry -SCORCHED
"People do not like Kuwaitis," -TIME.4

2. FACE

Kuwait's royalty left everything behind -VV
King Hussein speaks to Saddam Hussein -VV
King Hussein speaks to Mubarak -VV
The "Iron Lady's" determination – would prove pivotal -VV
"America stands where it always has, against aggression" -Z/3
"Where were they?" asked Canada's Globe and Mail. -GLOBE/2
support for the US stand was muted in Jordan, Algeria, Yemen, and Tunisia -Z/3
Hawke's own Foreign Minister -Z/3
Saddam Hussein was already looking for a face-saving solution -Z/3
he would begin withdrawing his troops as the meeting began. -VV
The Arab League foreign ministers followed Egypt's lead and slammed Saddam. -TS
"Oh my God, the conspiracy is complete." -VV
Jordan's Hussein considered an Iraqi invasion of Saudi Arabia, preposterous. -TS
The king was then handed a sheaf of satellite photos, compliments of the CIA. -NOW
Iraq was following standard Soviet military doctrine -BRIT/TV
he would have kept on coming -VV
(Schwarzkopf briefs King Fahd) -BRIT/TV
the Saudis "pressed the panic button." -VV
landed in Saudi Arabia within 30 minutes of the Saudi-American meeting -TS
troops were halfway to their destination before the request came - TS/VV
the US president ordered 40,000 military personnel into Saudi Arabia -RUNUP
Colonel Schumacher- SENSORS
"aerosol generators" could be mounted on trucks or small boats -SENSORS minimum amount of sarin to activate M8A1 exceeded the threshold by 1,000 -SEN/92
the Iraqi leader proposed linking Iraq's immediate withdrawal from Kuwait -Z/3
Baghdad also wanted guaranteed access to the Gulf -IWCT/2
we don't see anything to indicate an Iraqi force in Kuwait -NOW
Thomas Friedman, New York Times -Z/3
a similar Iraqi offer was leaked to New York's Newsday -Z/3

Financial editor William Nelkirk of the Chicago Tribune explained to Americans -Z/3

Soviet satellite photos taken five weeks after the Iraqi invasion -NOW

Staff General Michael Dougan plans to "destroy the Iraqi civilian economy." -RUNUP

roads leading to Kuwait were drifted high with undisturbed sand. -NOW

two Marine divisions might have driven them back to Iraq -NOW

camels "dead as doornails" -email posting to GWVM

(Primakov's many meetings) -TIME

Saudi security forces were torturing hundreds of Yemeni "guest workers" -Z/3

"Give me the best-case and worst-case scenario." -IGNORE

an additional 200,000 American troops to "defend" Saudi Arabia -RUNUP

59 percent of Americans now favored intervention -TIME/6

Resolution 678 -TIME

Iraq offered to "scrap chemical and mass destruction weapons – REUTERS

shut down Iraq aircraft and armor – as well as its military industries – by summer -GLOBE

"the 20th Infantry Division has eight mustard and binary chemical rounds." -GSD 13/32

Saddam Hussein orders Iraqi II Corps, "prepare the chemical ammunition"-GSD 38/103

Schwarzkopf opened his Christmas package -PEOPLE

Manly's "NBC Material and Logistics" report -GSD 155/243

dusty agents can penetrate US CBW overgarments -GSD 156/244-GSD 133/221

"We had no way to defend against [dusty agent] and DoD knew it." -GSD/59

test firings of the new SCUD -UNSCOM, CDISS, GSD 12/211, GSD 12/22, GSD 12/23, GSD 12/25

David Prestwich – BWH

"a US war" -Z/3

Washington disclosed another Iraqi offer -Z/3

Mideast experts described the proposal as a "serious pre-negotiation position." -Z/3

All that is necessary to achieve Iraq's withdrawal from Kuwait -Z/3

the US president was reading Martin Gilbert's biography of Churchill at war -NEWS

Bush was still insisting he had the constitutional authority to attack Iraq -RUNUP

James Baker met Iraq's Tariq Aziz -BRIT/TV/NEWS

Muthanna State Establishment – and other Iraqi CBW plants -EXPORTED, UNSCOM/INSIDE/DUAL /IRAQICBW

chemical weapons removed from the Samarra -TUITE2

"Iraq has won the toss and elected to receive." -LIFE/2

Some aerial mustard bombs were also taken to al Taqqadum Air base -UNSCOM

some of the bombs and rockets were already leaking toxins -GSD 224/384/PACJULY

General Norman Schwarzkopf watched Aziz step to the hotel microphone.-BRIT/TV

Khaill Barhoun voiced what many Arabs were thinking -MEI

50 percent of Americans believed that control over oil is the "key reason" -Z/3

the Iraqi army transferred 2,160 sarin-tipped rockets from al Muthanna -BB, PACJULY, GSD 224/384

Steve Hudspeth was sickened by the experimental nerve agent - VACCINES

Neil Tetzlaff -ROCKY

Sgt. Tom Hare -ROKCY

Vil Mirzayanov, Novichok and 33 -NOVICHOK, EXPORTED

the Chemical Corps had an entire manual devoted to mycotoxin - EXPORTED, JAN19

"newcomer" weapons – which Moscow may have been presented to Iraq -ALM

Substance 33 could have been transported – while remaining undetectable -SUB33

"newcomer" weapons Moscow may have presented to Iraq in place of nuclear arms -ALM

Injuries from the "newcomer" were said to be practically incurable -MNW

a top Soviet CBW scientist says the USSR never sent Novichok to Iraq -SUB33

much weaker VX (Substance 33 was possibly 10 times stronger than VX gas) -BS/2

Iraq had CBW for mortars, artillery; bombs; FROG and SCUD warheads-IRAQICBW

Woolsey estimated Iraq possessed another 1,000 tons of chemical nerve agents -INSIDE

Salman Pak had provided Iraq with at least one ton of biological warfare agents -DUAL

development of the 950 kilometer-range al Abbas missile was dropped -DUAL

each al-Hussein missile could carry five gallons of sarin -IRAQI

25 Al Husseins filled with botulinum toxin, 10 anthrax 2 alfatoxin. -CDISS

al-Husseins were hidden in a tunnel, and near the Tigris -CDISS

Developing some of the world's first biological warheads -CDISS

Iraq put three different biological agents on bombs and missiles in four locations -CDISS

"Leave was suspended today for officers and men" -IraqiLT

Domino's declared that war was imminent. -TIME/4

3. ROCKETS

At least 71 million households tuned in worldwide. -TIME/4
a cruise missile motored past at eye level, turned the corner -TIME/4
F-15s and F-16s were forced to bomb through cloud cover from 20,000 feet -TIME/4
(7% smart); 70% of all bombs dropped missed their intended targets. -SCORCHED
at Ohio State University, 100 jubilant students marched through the campus -TIME./4
Sergeant Willie Hicks was fast asleep -SEN30, SEN93
chemical-nuclear facilities were also hit early in the air war -RIEGLE
Yevstafyev issued a national warning -CZECH
William Brady was jerked awake -EVAC
the special "detection paper" – OPCW
M256 kit. – Worldwide Chemical Detection Equipment Handbook
MiG downs F-18 – Desert Storm Coalition Fixed-Wing Aircraft Combat Attrition
"Alpha Bravo Six, we have a confirmed chemical agent." -RIEGLE
FROGs launched at the 644th -RIEGLE
"Not a fucking thing happened last night" -GSD 74/169
"and unleash "an unusual force." -RIEGLE
2,500 chemical rockets had been blown up by coalition bombing -PAC9
(The bombing of Muhammadiyat, Qabatiyah, Muthanna – all CBW air strikes) -INSIDE
Forward deployed field depots placed munitions in open-air squares -GSD 197
Muhammadiyat was situated 410 kilometers upwind from US troops at Rafa -2/5/6
the toxic plume was "not a likely hazard," CENTCOM killed the report -HART/1
minute traces of chem agent." – email, Jim Brown GULFWATCH
Michael Kingsbury had taken leave to visit Riyadh -4/3/14
over 30 at once -FALLOUT
Andy Ach complained the "sanitized news" gave no sense of casualties -TIME/4
boasted the most sophisticated NBC equipment in the Gulf. -GSD16
Dear Mom -INCIDENT, SEN30, TUITE2
As Jim Brown later described, the formula was simple – email, Jim Brown GULFWATCH
"Predictably, this has become/is going to be a problem." -GSD 75/175
"borderline life-threatening concentrations of the chemical agents"-CZECH
Mike Tidd was standing security in Tower 6-INCIDENT

a single toxic cloud moving south -USNEWS
Radio operators were later ordered to burn their log pages -TUCK
"Request immediate procurement and shipment" -GSD 134/222
Symm's unit was also told that they had heard a sonic boom – TUITE, SEN91, SEN93
Richard Turnbull
a British liaison officer near al Jubayl heard "a propeller driven aircraft" -GSD 75/172
CENTCOM reported "overhead at time traveling at high rate of speed." -TUCK,.GSD 264/432
I immediately thought we got gassed." -RIEGLE
three MiGs took off from Tallil Airfield -GulfLINK, SU22
the BW mission was apparently scrubbed. -TUCK,GulfLINK
"chemical bombs" were stored at Umm Qasr. -TUCK/ GulfLINK
designed to spray up to 2,000 litres of anthrax on a target -CDISS
Such symptoms were not indicative of red fuming nitric acid - GSD 262
two loud explosions split the sky directly over the Naval Air Station -GSD 75/164
Many saw a dense yellowish mist floating over the camp. -TUCK
four SCUDs impacted near Al Jubayl -SEN94, GSD 27/76
an enemy plane had been shot down over the desert -INCIDENT
Fred Willoughby was "hanging out" -TUITE, SEN 91
"Three or four had to be medevaced out." -GSD/1/16
Theodore Myers remembers an ear-splitting bang -email message December 25, 1996.
Larry Perry remembers being enveloped by a mist -INCIDENT
Larry Kay had fallen asleep – TUITE
CENTCOM never recorded the event -TUITE, SEN94
Two British M9 and CAM detections were reported -TUITE
the other two tests turned out positive for blister agent -TUITE, SEN 91
"Get me back to camp. Now!"-GSD7/1/17
such exchanges of MOPP gear were "an extremely rare occurrence -GSD 27/75
two British units "reporting positive H [mustard] readings" -GSD 75/171
there was a shortage of American MOPP-4 gear throughout the TO -TUCK
Nick Roberts noticed a thin yellow powder coating tents and vehicles -VAC
Patricia Browning was at the Khobar Towers. -5/1/15
(when members questioned) they were ordered not to discuss the incident -TUITE
(Moore's unit) ordered not to discuss the incident -INCIDENT
the radio in the bunker called for the decontamination teams to respond. -INCIDENT
Edwards was assigned to take out a 500 gallon water truck - INCIDENT

Iraq would be fighting back with "all the means and potential God has given us"-RIEGLE

Vallee put on his chemical gear on and sat down heavily. -INCIDENT

"We were discussing it anyway." -SEN30

4. "YOU WILL LOSE"

the Brits went to NBC Condition Black. -TUITE

"every chemical-agent monitoring device in the area was blasting the alarm," -TUITE

when the alarms go off it is for real -INCIDENT

standard UN practice for victims of chemical or biological attack -SCORCHED

beginning to suffer from extreme flu-like symptoms -TUCK

Czech chemical specialists reported tabun, soman and sulfur-mustard -GSD 75/173

Michael Adcock, a four-year high school football letterman -VAC

Brian Martin recorded that chemical alarms were going off almost every day -FALLOUT

Troy Albuck, a former anti-tank platoon leader with the 82nd Airborne -FALLOUT

Sergeant House never heard any alarms. -MINES

a trace quantity of tabun, soman and yperite -Sullivan

"No blood for oil!" -NEWS

Phoebe Jeter was watching a green radar scope -PEOPLE

6th French has detected 'light' traces if chem agents tabun and sarin." -GSD 157/247

Follow-up tests confirmed the presence of tabun and sarin. -GSD 75/173

people began heading over to the port's American Hospital -VETS/8/1/18

Allah Akbar. What a horrible thing to see." -Iraqi LT

"It was as if we had no adversary." -TIME/4

the RAF lost eight crewmen and six of their 36 Tornado fighter-bombers -TIME/5

coalition jets flying up to 3,000 sorties a day (22 lost) -TIME/5

took nearly five hours to fuel -TIME/4

"burn the ground under their feet" -NEWS

French assess incident to be result of bombing in as Salman -GSD 157/248

Morrow's numbness would persist for a week.. -INCIDENT

"I'd rather die than feel like this." -EVAC

Chris Alan Kornkven wasn't sure whether to believe his own eyes -IRAQ/TUITE

the surface winds in their area were blowing the wrong way -IRAQI/TUITE

According to Camp, the Saudi-based marines were told not to go to MOPP 4. -RIEGLE

Many became sick the following night -8/18

the Czechs reportedly detected an "unknown substance" -GSD 75/173

CENTOM ordered all units to "disregard any reports from the Czechs." -GSD 75/176

another Marine message was sent to the Albany facility -GSD 133

G-2 reported a "possible chem strike in the tri-border area." -GSD 158/255

to feed babies and stir into their coffee -PEOPLE

Iraqi troops had set alight storage tanks and oil wells at al Wafra -TIME/5

As he put his questions to Saddam Hussein, Arnett was careful - INSIDE

"suits manufactured by Camel Mfg....should not be used -GSD 134

101st Division Artillery reported NBC alarms going off. -GSD 158

The base was facing imminent biological attack from Iraq -OBS/1

sarin is nonflammable -MSD, GSD 32 /4/89

three other American units reported M8A1 alarms going off ..the fallout was undoubtedly coming from chemical warfare storage sites. -GSD 158/252

Corporal Jeffrey Brown and his companions heard a high-pitched whine. -PEOPLE

a ghost town abandoned by 20,000 fleeing residents -TIME/7

M8 alarms just two hours a day "due to battery shortage." -GSD 160/261

the Iraqi tanks and armored vehicles were in terrible shape. -TIME/7

NOAA satellite photos showed plumes extending into Saudi Arabia – GULF WX

(all Gulf War Weather) -GULF WX

"a little bit everywhere." -LIES

"Iraqi forces have been observed placing 55-gallon drums" - OCT 90, GSD 159/259

all 14 crew members were killed. -RIEGLE

This convoy was destroyed by F-6 fighter-bombers. -RIEGLE

multiple rocket launchers were deployed in the ar Rumaylah area. -GSD 213/365

two dozen decontamination sites spotted the KTO -GSD 12/27

"The worst case would be for our troops to get hung up on the wire" -TIME/7

a "Hail Mary" play -TIME/7

"somebody said, hey, what about the great big open flank over there?" -TIME/7

"The enemy is not worth shit." -IGNORE/HERO

General Franks was worried -IGNORE/HERO

"You cannot have VII Corps stopping for anything." IGNORE/HERO

the "Desert Rats" of Britain's famed First Armored Division
-TIME/7
Schwarzkopf – who was known to get angry enough to throw things -TIME/5

5. DOG SOLDIERS

bombing of Kirkuk, H-3, An Nasiriyah, K-2 Airfield, Qayyarah West, Taji and Al Qaim. CW stockpiles at Tikrit -INSIDE
US government officials confirmed the presence of radioactivity in Baghdad -WOUNDED
100 plant guards had been brought to the hospital after the air attack -TASS, CAIRO
Patricia Williams remembers a late afternoon explosion in the desert -10/1/19
napalm-dispensing US Marine Harriers
-SCORCHED/author's interview with pilots
attack jets were doused with ozone-destroying Halon fire-retardents -SCORCHED
"26 soldiers were condemned to death" -Iraqi LT
Darren Siegle was told by Iraqi POWs of "many chemical mines" -GSD 42/119
its insensitivity to 'alien' cultures, its appalling jingoism."
-INDIA
"I think our leaders have wrongly attacked the peaceful people of Iraq." -TIME/5
"We heard them give the release order" -IRAQI
the only shots Prestwich had heard were rifles being "cleared" into a sandbox -BWH
transferring 6,000 155 mm mustard rounds from a bunker at an Nasiriyah -PAC9
The leaking rounds were buried and camouflaged with canvas
-PAC9
anthrax found in hundreds of dead sheep and camels outside al Jubayl -SCORCHED.
the US Army's only active psychological operations unit -MOJO
CARC can have neurotoxological effects -VACCINES 12 hour days in poorly ventilated enclosures – initially with no respirators
- 1993 report by Dr. William Johnson, formerly of the Eisenhower Army Medical Center
"The 17,000 US Marines on board the assault ships never went ashore." -TIME/7

6. HIGHWAY TO HELL

"we were already inside Iraq days before the war began." - Jeffrey Ford, email
a nearby M-60 tank opened fire on a possible Iraqi armored troop carrier – "Battle Assessment Documentation of the 6th Marine Regiment, Operations Desert Storm"

A second FOX vehicle confirmed the initial report. -RIEGLE

British troops were also reporting chemical mines -BREACH, RIEGLE< GANNET

250 "Ababil" missiles -UNSCOM

Sixth Marines detected chemical agents in Lane Red 1 -SEN94, SIXTH

Marines crossed the departure line carrying their masks in plastic bags -GSD

once-lethal contents had been degraded after baking for months - GSD 42/117

Sergeant Michael Bradford rode the fifth armored vehicle through the breach -TRASH

Marine Air Group 26 reported another nerve agent detection 1st Battalion 7th Marine Command Chronology; Tiger Brigade Command Chronology.

"Flash" message: "IZ III Corps preparing chemicals." -GSD 183/299

a unit of self-propelled Iraqi artillery to fire chemicals -GSD 110/197

a nerve agent detection by the Marines 26th Air Group 1st Battalion 7th Marine Command Chronology/Also Tiger Brigade Command Chronology

a lingering mustard agent strong enough to blister the exposed arms -GSD 32 /94

Al Stenner heard the casualties being reported over the command net -GSD 40/108

King Khalid Military City had been hit by anthrax -GUYATT

on February 25, Task Force Ripper detected gas – 1/7 Marines Command Chronology.

another Ripper artillery unit also reported a chemical detection - 1st Marine Division After Action Review, 117 Marines Command Chronology.

This detection was confirmed by a FOX -1st Marine Division After Action Review.

another FOX found lewisite -Tiger Brigade Command Chronology.

Ripper detected gas at grid coordinate 756862. -1/7 Marines Command Chronology

At 1735, another Task Force Ripper artillery unit reported a chemical detection. -1st Marine Division After Action Review, 117 Marines Command Chronology.

Marine Major General Michael Myatt had to use a flashlight to read his map. -TIME/7

lst Division had already destroyed another 50 or 60 Soviet-built T-72s -TIME/7

an Iraqi POW warned of a chemical minefield
-Tiger Brigade Command Chronology

a FOX picked up more lewisite
-Tiger Brigade Command Chronology

"Maybe a cloud of agent had blown through" -GSD 41/110

the RASCAAL was a good gadget -GSD 153/237

"It put the fear of God into us." -GSD 42/117EP

Marine Staff Sergeant George Grass was driving the first FOX. – TUITE2, SHAYS

Bobby Harris reported from the Iraq border -HART/1

"complete with a Corps-level C3 vehicle." -GSD 207

had just been calibrated by General Dynamics Land Systems the previous day -TUITE

they were running out of things to shoot at. -TIME/7

Cottrell ordered Grass to return to Ripper Main -SEN93

The area around the missile was flagged with chemical warning tape. -GSD 55/148

"I was told to forward the tape up the chain of command," -GSD

the ever-vigilant Czechs again detected sarin -SEN92

"Gas, gas, gas!" -INCIDENTS, SEN93

Robert Maison's men went to MOPP-4 for two hours -SEN93

a company of 11th Marines had detected blister agents using two separate M-256 tests -1st Marine Division After Action Review

not all 11th Marines donned protective gear -GSD 122

others were crushed by tanks trying desperately to flee – author's observations

At 1045, Task Force Shepherd detected more mustard gas – Tiger Z Brigade Command Chronology.

An hour later. Task Force Ripper reported detecting gas -1/7 Marines Command Chronology and 1st Marine Division After Action Review.

a FOX with the 8th Marines also detected gas. -8th Marines Command Chronology.

Task Force Ripper was ordered to reposition units -GSD 123/211

1/11 Marines detected gas near the burning, shell-pocked Kuwait International Airport -1st Marine Division After-Action Review.

"3/23rd under NBC attack"-Battle Assessment Documentation, 6th Marine Regiment

3/1 1 Marines was logged at 1735.- 1st Marine Division Maneuver Chronology.

"captured chem munitions" -GSD 184/300

"EPWs stated Coalition forces were going to get hit by chemicals." -GSD 110/198

the typed notes never mentioned the EPWs' reports -GSD 110

Each rocket was filled with 18 kilograms of nerve agents mixed at a 2:1 -PAC9

Ripper once again relocated "to get out of an area contaminated with chemical weapons."

-1st Marine Division After-Action Review

they reportedly moved 1,100 chemical rockets into an open storage area -GSD 224, 5/385

9. OBJECTIVE GOLD

Craddock directed his armored battalion toward a canal north of the highway -VICTORY

rounds detonate harmlessly against the Abrams' depleted uranium hide -MM/1

American "tankers" feared "friendly fire" more than the enemy- 1962 GAO report, MM/1

(DU's) first combat trials -LOPEZ

1,400 blackened, burnt-out Iraqi vehicles would attest to the effectiveness of DU -DUDC

bulk destruction may have international implications." -FORD

combat engineer Dwayne Mowrer identified DU hits -BULLETS

"It leaves a nice round hole, almost like someone had welded it out," -OR

Uranium can cause lung cancer, bone cancer and kidney disease - BULLETS

US tanks and aircraft fired close to one-million large and small caliber DU rounds -PGIT

Containing about .2 % U-235, as well as potent U-238 isotopes - ORLANDO, JNCI

Depleted Uranium penetrator rounds are as toxic as lead -LOPEZ

the aluminum covering was stripped away and its energy converted to heat -VACCINES

70% of the shell into an aerosol of fine uranium particles and radioactive gas -PLOW

Five other Abrams tanks were contaminated during on-board fires -MTP

35 American soldiers were killed; 72 others wounded by DU - MTP, JOM

six American Abrams tanks and 15 APCs would be hit by "friendly fire." -MTP

their own DU munitions "cooking off" after being struck by Hellfire missiles – LOPEZ

"a field of burning Iraqi tanks." -BULLETS

Robert Sanders' tank was hit by his own forces -MM/1

25 American GIs later helped prepare DU-contaminated tanks for shipment – BULLETS

apparently buried in a radioactive waste disposal site -BULLETS

"it's just a little dirt" Jeff Ford -GVWM

"The lindane is a very, very fine powder, much finer than talc" - GWVM

Tony Newcomb remembers "the gross smell of the laundry when it came back" -GWVM

Reservists with the 371st were deployed to decontaminate buses - VACCINES/124

Iraqi enemy prisoners of war suffered skin rashes, sores, nausea - EXPOSED, INCIDENT hundreds of thousands of other GI's scrambled into disabled Iraqi vehicles. -survey by Vic Sylvester and the Operation Desert Shield/Desert Storm Association shows that four out of five U.S. soldiers entered destroyed Iraqi vehicles, many of them DU-contaminated, MTP,

also: 82 percent had entered captured enemy vehicles-BULLET

Not one of the soldiers veteran Dan Fahey spoke with "donned a respirator" -MTP

Corporal Santos suffered chemical injuries.-GSD 43/120

Khamisiyah was reached and secured on March 1 – 2/505

or hung fragments of DU rounds around their necks -BULLETS

David Allen Fisher was cautiously going from bunker to bunker, hunting Iraqis -TUITE

"caused by exposure to liquid mustard chemical warfare agent." -GSD 48/133

Bob Wages commanded the FOX vehicle called in to check – PAC16, GSD 192/316

the FOX operator would win a Bronze Star -TUITE

the leaking crates "made you choke" -TUITE

"I saw alot of frigin' Iraqi decon kits opened and scattered about the ground" -GWVM

Tom Hare remembers the sky opening up and pouring black rain -TUITE

No other area that my FOX vehicle checked was designed like that" -GSD 209/344

The rounds were clearly marked with Jordanian stamps. -GSD 41/111

Jordan had played a key role in funneling arms from the US to Iraq -GSD/185

precision mass spectrometer readout indicated the presence of HD -TUITE

The inserts of white phosphorous rounds could be changed with little difficulty -GSD 180

their real interest lay in verifying specific lot numbers – TUITE, GSD 180/290

"downplaying the environmental risks posed by depleted uranium contamination" -LTR/1

a large number of locals and animals inside sector GOLD – Unit 1SG interviews July 1996

"blisters 1/2" to 1" on his upper arm... co-ink-o-dink, yes? -Jim Brown GULFWATCH

Bashaw drove past bunkers cordoned off by contamination marking tape -GSD 108/190

(Trew) at Tallil -GSD 108/191

the yellow bands indicated a blister agent fill. -GSD 108/192

some of their vehicles sported M8A1 chemical alarms mounted on their fenders -37th EN Bn Operations Log

the battalion's NBC officer used an M256 kit to check some of the bunkers for chemical agents – unit interview with EOD NCO, June 1996.

Two bunkers – 98 and 99 – were wired with demolition charges and blown in place to test demolition techniques -37th EN Bn Operations Log

The secondary explosions would continue for 24 hours -Unit NCO interview, Jan. 1997

10. KHAMISIYAH

"These are safe to destroy." – Interviews with 37th EN Bn Commander June 1996.

A faulty time-fuse spared Bunker 92 -37th EN Bn Operations Log

the flag on a nearby hummer pointing southeast directly toward US positions -FORD

Some soldiers went to MOPP-4 status. -XVIII Corps Desert Shield Chronology

others only donned their masks -EOD NCO interview, October, 1996.

EOD teams performed several M256 tests -Fort Leavenworth Press conference video

Bravo Company's commanding officer and another NBC specialist registered negative readings -Interview of NCO and commander, June 1996

munitions detonated around Tallil and Jalibah – XVIII Corps SITREP, March 5, 1991

The idea was to implode the bunkers -Fort Leavenworth Press conference video, "a jeep with chem ammo and documents." -GSD 46/127

One of the Iraqi Army's biggest chemical weapons storage sites -GSD 46/129

"all destruction of ammunition stocks in country of Kuwait is to stop." -GSD 184/304

The engineers spent this time rehearsing the big blast and inventorying -307th EN Bn Operations Summary, and 60th EOD Incident Journal

crates containing more than 1,000 Katyusha rockets -Interviews with BN S-3, October 1996 and 307th Liaison Officer, January, 1997

his FOX sounded the alarm for lewisite. -GSD 182/295

a highly centralized and secretive Joint Staff -GSD /183

"It was a matter of not deploying chemical weapons" -WP, TUITE

"The shells were not marked, they were not special." -PAC9

A noncom was ordered to destroy all 13 stacks of rockets - NCO interview, July, 1996

approximately 859 rockets were detonated – along with 60 remaining bunkers – Leavenworth Press conference video, interviews with the headquarters and EOD NCOs, Sept. and Oct., 1996.

The wind was blowing almost due south -NYN, CIA the Engineers completed their mission and drove south
-60th EOD Incident Journal
the contingent continued driving south for four hours
- Operations Log, 37th EN Bn
The silent plume drifted over elements of seven US Army divisions -NYN
The sarin may have passed over parts of the British 1st Infantry, (and Saudi) – NYN
Jabar – BRIT/TV
they held fire, returned to base and departed their leader's employ -GulfLINK
a chemical mine-filling depot -CENTCOM log
more than 400 revetted bunkers – XVIII Corps CTOC Journal Sheet, March 12, 1991
found plans for the earlier intended chemical attack -GSD/122
Many official unit logs were destroyed prior to returning to CONUS. -GSD/160
"many chemical incident reports were destroyed" -GSD 160/262
"pernicious careerism of the officer corps had not been purged at all." -GSD/161
"Nerve agent antidotes present an unnecessary health and safety hazard" – HART/1
these detonated munitions were also dispersed on the wind.- Leavenworth Press conference video.
for Saudi Arabia and long-awaited rides home – 307th EN Bn Desert Storm Narrative
their reconnaissance had yielded negative results – VII Corps Tactical Chemical Spot Report, March 28, 1991
a large explosion in the vicinity of Tallil – unit history file
six bunkers required additional detonations – Leavenworth press conference video
Iraqis working in those same BCW plants had become ill -HART/1
Watkinson walked up to the tank and tested the brown colored vapor -TUITE2
US troops took part in the cleanup without protective gear - BULLETS
3,000 US troops stationed at the base took part in the cleanup -OR
Depleted Uranium rounds had long been linked to subsequent cancers, birth defects -OR
Kuwaiti civilians within a radius of 25 miles of the huge DU blaze were also dusted -MTP
Wiping the sample on two types of detector paper -TUITE
Captain Johnson ordered yet another mass spectrometer test - TUITE2
Further analysis indicated traces of phosgene -GSD 49/135
21 separate, positive tests for mustard gas and phosgene
The tapes have since disappeared -TUITE
(eight) Army medals -TUITE/2
he could have died within minutes -TUITE/2

Military Chemical and Biological Agents -TUITE
mustard agent and nitric acid have no tracing "peaks" in common -TUITE2
desert camouflage uniforms with no rank or distinguishing patches -GSD 49/140
About 1,000 captured tanks...washed and prepped in Dhahran - Wayne Clingman, GWVM
Wayne Clingman was in charge of a "pit crew" cleaning Iraqi military vehicles -GVWM
UN disarmament inspectors had by now inspected 18 chemical sites -HART/1
red-flagged for White House, CIA and State Department attention – NYT/2
UNSCOM. inspectors also found more than 46,000 CW-filled munitions -INSIDE
Besides cataloging some 5,000 tons of stockpiled chemical agents -DUAL
25 other al Husseins had been deployed tipped with botulinum toxin -GSD 12/27
"This is really lethal stuff." -PAC9
"no reports of anybody experiencing those effects at the time." - BB
"the effects of repeated exposures are cumulative" -SEN92
three non-lethal viruses developed by the Iraqis -TUCK58
they can have a significant impact many weeks after the initial attack -CDISS

11-12. KC, ECOWAR

blackening buildings as far away as Riyadh
all other references: SCORCHED EARTH, chapter 13
OV-10 crash Gulf War Airpower Survey, Vol. 5 by Norman Friedman and Desert Victory; World Air Power Journal.

12. WHEN JANEY CAME MARCHING HOME

Many women veterans also suffer from vaginal yeast infections - DEFENSE
114 said they were sick with illnesses stemming from the war - NYT/3
Seabees who served at al Jubayl have developed lymphatic cancers -TUCK
hundreds of Gulf vets had been summarily discharged – LIFE
"Shouldn't they have the same criteria?" -GWVM
85 percent of the members of that special unit -FALLOUT
in May, 1993, Brady suffered a heart attack. -EVAC
John Stewart tried treating his physical decline with "self-denial" -VETS

Treiber is still bothered by occasional swelling in his right shoulder -WSJ

Dwayne Mowrer didn't worry when a truck loaded with DU rounds exploded -BULLETS

Another vet from the 144th National Guard -PGIT, BULLETS

Turnbull has been forced to give up diving -TEL/2

Erika Lundholm is the sick sister of a vet. -CBN

a startling 65 percent reported birth defects -LIFE

55 infants born to four Mississippi National Guard units -SCORCHED

just received the connex boxes from in-country -GVWM

His wife suffers from nearly all of the same symptoms -MINES

civilian personnel assigned to Army depots -VACCINES

Girl Guides and Scouts could be exposed to dangerous chemicals -TEL/3

Charlene Davis is still plagued by the recurring rashes -GWVM

12. PARTING SHOTS

pyridostigmine bromide may cause damage to neuro-muscular junctions -ROCKY

US researchers knew very little about non-lethal exposure -ROCKY

PB was administered to 28,000 other servicewomen -INSIDE

463,000 US troops the Pentagon estimates who took PB -INSIDE

defense department's Study Report 8740 -May 6,1994 Senate VA Affairs hearing

Lyster Army Hospital -INSIDE

pyridostigmine bromide was never tested on women -INSIDE

making females especially vulnerable -ROCKY

Air Force pilots had crashed-landed in hospitals with serious side effects -LIFE

Craig Crane was one air crewman -ROCKY

if they are used after exposure to nerve agent -ROCKY

their ability to increase acetylcholine activity amplifies previous poisoning -ROCKY

PB also binds to and inhibits the enzyme -ROCKY

PB is considered to be a potent nerve agent by itself -VACCINES

a test of their response to the experimental drug while exercising -ROUT

"War is stressful, even if you are the supply clerk." -GWVM

It only works in combination with other drugs, such as atropine -INSIDE

pyridostigmine is unable to enter and protect the brain -ROCKY

DoD elected to stay with the lower, ineffective dose of atropine -ROCKY

Carol Picou -VACCINES, ROCKY

"informed consent" -ROCKY

soldiers bound for the Persian Gulf not told of the risks – AP/2 half of the 41,650 members of the XVIII Airborne Corps who were issued PB -JAMA

"If I'm going to feel like this I might as well be dead" -VACCINES

product license number 4537/0003 -GAZETTE

1,500 former UK servicemen and women said they were sick -TEL/2

British units purchased local pesticides and began spraying -TEL/2

Mottram, was at that time still handling "new, and very distressing cases." -TEL/2

as many as 17 different live viral and killed bacterial vaccines -SHAYS

responded to a Senate survey -LIFE

a capsule confiscated from a German Army Officer in 1918 -COMNAV

six doses of vaccine must administered over a year and a half -COMNAV

botulism vaccine was produced by the Michigan Department of Health -ROCKY

the thin Gaulic line soon spread across a third of Iraq. -TIME/7

expressed concern about the existing supply of anthrax vaccine -ROCKY

150,000 US military personnel who were eventually inoculated with the anthrax -ROCKY

up to five doses of anthrax – in barely three weeks. -OBS/2

Pertussis adjuvant to enhance the effect of the hastily given anthrax vaccine -ROCKY

"five or six" secret vaccinations -OBS/2

the botulism vaccine was not licensed -VACCINES(116)

Centers for Disease Control considered halting distribution of botulism vaccine -ROCKY

dosages too low and too late to protect them against an Iraqi plague attack -ROCKY

DoD officials reiterated that at least verbal information would be provided -ROCKY

prescription only plague vaccine – "Directions for use" leaflet, number 14-7600-000

the directions warned of "accentuated side-effects" – "Directions for use" leaflet

The British military eventually injected 8,000 soldiers -VACCINES

Dr. Howard Urnovitz, a Berkeley, California immunologist and microbiologist -EDGE

US personnel were reportedly given simultaneous vaccines -EDGE

"No physician would recommend you subject yourself to a live virus vaccine." -ROCKY

"The question that must be answered immediately" -SHAYS

failed to mount a proper antibody response to polio serotype 3 -SHAYS

13. SUFFER THE CHILDREN

"flames rising up from the city" -WALKER
reporter Evelyn Leopold – GUARD/3
"people like the living dead" -SCORCHED
"they have eradicated all their feelings and have no joy." - GUARD/3
veterans with decades of war experience -GUARD/3

"smart" bombs, one in four missed their intended targets - WALKER
dumb "iron bombs" fared far worse -WALKER
phosphorous fire bombs and napalm were also used -WALKER
heavy bombers could obliterate a "box" more than half-a-mile wide -SCORCHED
"...carpet bombing is not my favorite expression." -DW
There were no civilians left in this city of 800,000 -WP/2
"bomb craters the size of football fields" -LA
Raw sewage submerged the streets of Basra, and poured into Baghdad's rivers -SE
had left Iraq in "a near apocalyptic" condition – WCT
At least 21 power generating plants and hydroelectric dams were attacked -SCORCHED
One meal per day, without protein, was the norm -GUARD/3
war's "end" was followed by the catastrophic failure of Iraq's harvests -SCORCHED
typhoid, brucellosis, hepatitis, gastroenteritis, meningitis, hepatitis, polio and cholera were endemic. Rates of rare cancers and birth defects were also rising sharply. -INCIDENT/SE
Preventable diseases like polio and measles surged -GUARD/3
"the struggle against him falls upon innocent heads." -GUARD/2
Hoskins and his team found -GUARD/3
"If you bust the water supply and sewage plants...cholera is what you get. -GUARD/2
By 1993, typhoid, gastroenteritis and cholera were still endemic across Iraq -SCORCHED
one projectile emitted more radiation in five hours than is allowed per year -BULLETS
Meningitis, hepatitis, malaria and polio rates were also up sharply - SCORCHED
marsh Arabs -SCORCHED
landed shells with a thud – "not the usual explosion," -DEFENSE
350 or 800 tons of DU fragments still littered Gulf War battlefields -LAKA, PLOW
(more than 600,000 pounds of DU) -PGIT
the poisons found saturating the Texas soil could migrate -MTP
"They're just children." -LOPEZ
frightening increases in child leukemia and aplastic anemia - MM/1

Health ministry officials warned that the frightening figures were low -LOPEZ

1995 Iraqi news reports cited health statistics -HART/1

("toys") One little girl who collected 12 of the projectiles died of leukemia. -BULLETS

fled to Jordan after a "chemical cloud" enveloped streets -interviews by the author

cyanide, organochlorines, dioxins and heavy metals had all been released -SCORCHED

everybody in the room is getting irradiated -LOPEZ

health officials were reporting alarming increases in rare and unknown diseases -MTP

Dr. al Harbi -HOME

four American citizens risked a dozen years in prison -VTW

15 to 20 percent of the populations of Kuwait and Jordan currently suffer from GWI.

-Nancy and Garth Nicholson survey, as presented to the author

14. SEE NO EVIL

Dr. Gunnar Heuser proposed a universal protocol -SEQUENCE

Albert Donnay totaled the costs – GWVM

John Deutch became intimately involved with the cover-up."
-GSD 257

special sampling units (controlled by Schwarzkopf, Powell and the JCS) -GSD 155/241

his career is in jeopardy. -TUITE

special units were responsible for the transport of chemical agents -GSD 45

all BCCI references – 1990 House Banking Committee investigation records

oil revenue kickbacks paid to Saddam, and shared by Bush. - Spotlight Aug. 19, 1991

on the average of $25 billion per year, which he shared with Bush. -Interview with the author

The Financial Times of London, reported "U.S. Cyanide Shipped to Iraq -FT

"I don't think Barbouti is dead," – interview with author

The Chicago Federal District Court heard case 90C6863
- Sherman Skolnick interview

the firm which had made gas for death camps had also shipped chemical to Iraq -GUARD

American firms also played a major role in helping develop Saad 16 -GUARD

investigation carried out in southern Iraq from October 22 to November 2 -GSD 196/327

crippling ailments were the result of "very fine sand," "lack of recreation," -INSIDE

Despite the alteration of a key document dealing with shipments - DUAL all invoices of germ shipments from the USA to Baghdad - EXPORTED

"less than $60.00." -GUYATT

biological warfare program was the most advanced in the Arab world -DUAL

"skin sensitization, chronic lung impairment, cough," -DUAL

Czech Minister of Defense made public the detection of sarin - BANKING

the company received "direct encouragement" from the US Commerce Department -FT/2

Lummus Crest of Bloomfield, NJ, also worked on the PC2 project near Baghdad -WT

Alcolac International sold the thiodiglycol used as a SCUD rocket propellant -NYT/4

Having assessed the Czech detections as "valid," -GSD 17/40

defense department officials began ordering armed forces personnel not to testify -DUAL

Gulf War vets were told the Iraqis couldn't initiate chemical attacks -DUAL

she was told "it would get lost." -TUITE

they had observed "hundreds of records from the Gulf War being destroyed." -GUYATT

satellite imagery shows the fallout plume moving southeast - HEARINGS

Guy Smith knew what to do when the public smelled a rat - INSIDE

stamped with multiple and conflicting declassification dates -GSD 85

"no information that chemical or biological weapons were used" -DUAL, TUITE

"misled medical research efforts for a period of nearly one year." -TUITE

15. RIEGLE'S REVELATIONS

16. MELTDOWN

Lawrence Livermore gas mask tests -Brian Andresen, Ph.D., Jackie Stilwell, M.S., Patrick Grant, Ph.D., Jeff Haas, M.S., Richard Whipple, B.A., and Armando Arcaraz, M.S., "Preliminary Results of Gas Masks and Exposure-Monitoring Equipment Associated with Desert Storm: Chemical and Biological Analyses of First Samples Sent," Forensic Science Center, J Division/NAI Directorate, Lawrence Livermore National Laboratory, June, 1994

The veterans intimidation program was being run out of Prociv's office. -GSD 164/265

"a deliberately misleading document." -DUAL

the Santa Cruz city council passed a resolution calling for a ban on blood -AP Nov. 1994

"Veterans' service medical records are difficult to find." -ROCKY

"We need to try to get control of this situation." -GSD/45

"Dr. Germs" was hand-picked to protect Iraq's bio-warfare capability. -JAN 19

"the VA is not even testing these people for exposure to chemical warfare" -GSD

"Many veterans' disability claims are being turned down," -HART/1

Captain Johnson was immediately reassigned to Korea. -GSD 117

100 specific reports to a Senate Select Committee Intelligence meeting -GSD 106

"chemical-nuclear war is morally allowable." -LM

"the CIA does not plan a comprehensive review of DoD information" -GSD 115

there was now "considerable doubt" over his previous assurances -TEL/4

"a complete departure from normal Agency practice," -GSD 117/206

(General Franks) "never showed up for a single meeting." -GSD 124

their ailments matched those exposed to chemical and biological weapons -HART/1

"public relations and damage control campaign" -GSD 124

6,526 US Persian Gulf War dead – Dept. of Veterans Affairs press release July 1, 1995

"I was horrified by his condition – and amazed by his courage and strength." -LIFE Managing Editor, Daniel Okrent, "Tiny Victims Notes."

'reckless disregard.' -LIFE

"How many people would want to join the Army?" -GSD 170

"The symptoms they reported were strikingly consistent" -TUCK

"The Iraqis had an entire manual dedicated to fungal mycotoxins." -GSD 263/430

"Tucker's integrity had cost him his job," -GSD 167

"The PAC was nothing more than an exercise in damage control." -GSD 258

They wanted "to make sure that I didn't take any of the files" December 24, 1996 PHILIP SHENON

interview with Brian Martin for an intelligence analyst to make the connection – [86]

UNSCOM had found chemical weapons at Khamisiyah -[89].

damage to filled chemical warfare munitions at only two facilities -GSD 14/370

"it now appears that one of these destroyed bunkers contained chemical weapons,"-[90].

young Scouts and Guides could be exposed to hazardous chemicals -TEL/3

Institute of Medicine concluded that no scientific evidence has been found -HART/2

"US troops were not exposed to chemical agents" -GSD 229/395 not one member of the PAC staff or panel challenged Copeland's assertions," -GSD 230

"the destruction of 43 bunkers," -TUITE, FORD

more than 5,000 troops may have been exposed at Khamisiyah -SHAYS

the number of US troops exposed from Khamisiyah was increased to 20,867. -INSIDE

"unnecessary exposure of many individuals could have occurred." -AP, Dec. 1996

Schwarzkopf had seen at least 55 NBC incident reports -GUYATT

"does not indicate any confirmed use of chemical warfare agents" -GUYATT

A lawsuit filed on January 16, 1997 by Patrick and Robin Eddington -author's interview

the city of Nashville alone had 36 claim handlers for sick desert war veterans. -GWVM

1,500 sick British veterans – Independent Newspaper, London. Dec. 24, 1996

17. THE COCKROACH CONNECTION

mysterious maladies affecting more than 80,000 returning Gulf War veterans. -WWW

a little white pill taken by more than a quarter-million US, British and Anzac forces. -OL,

permethrin was used by perhaps five percent of US forces there. -LIFE

James Moss and his boss -OL

"get hit with nerve gas and you wind up with 100% of your cholinesterase tied up."
-GWVM posting, March 23, 1997

"If you synergize PB with adrenaline" -interview with the author

Organophosphate-derived pesticides and nerve gas act just like myashthenia gravis in jamming these gateways open. -DEFENSE

"Any distinction between the effects of PB, sarin, or OP pesticides is artificial." -GWVM posting, March 23, 1997

Seawright "should not offer him guidance" -OL

used in combination with PB, DEET became almost seven times more toxic -ROCKY

Some tests showed a 10-fold increase in toxicity. -INSIDE

"All these delayed effects could just as likely come from PB" – interview with author

PB, permethrin "increased the toxicity of the repellent DEET to some degree." -OL

"the Dept. of Agriculture was not very happy about your coming here to testify." -OL

the dysfunctions are usually neuropsychological, and include memory loss. -DEFENSE

almost every other symptom lumped under "Gulf War Illness" can be neuropsychological -DEFENSE

some of that neuro-damage is irreversible. -DEFENSE
low levels of sarin caused chronic brain and nerve damage in animals -UT
the feline and her human family were "positive" for Mycoplasma Incognitas. -RILEY
Mycoplasma incognitas tested by Saddam Hussein's CBW researchers. -UNSCOM
we usually find that almost every family member has the same infection." -GWVM posting
"only if the correct antibiotics in the correct doses are used" - GWVM posting
mycoplasma incognitas can be transmitted through repeated casual contact -DEFENSE
the mycoplasma incognitas had been packed in an HIV cellular "envelope" -RILEY
gram-positive cocci, microsporidium were also being diagnosed -TUITE
The results showed something called mycoplasma incognitas in the blood leukocytes. -The New York Native, by Neenyah Ostrom, October 11,1993
Nicholson lost four teeth and had a jawbone infection that required removal of one bone, and part of another. Interview with the author
vaccines were at the top of their list. -Interview with the author
The Nicholsons began having encouraging results -GWVM posting
the unusual HIV gene suggested a weapon. -Interview with the author
"As long as your immune system is all right it will not affect you," -GWVM posting
mycoplasma incognitas had been packed in an HIV cellular "envelope" -GWVM posting
Hamden's statement – Statement To Presidential Advisory Committee – May 1, 1996
International Gulf War Illness Coalition www.dnet.net/~pkawaja/
spate of crashes listed – Reuter, Sept. 17, 1997
"the Gulf War's biological equivalent to Pearl Harbor." - GSD 263
"only one known family of biochemical agents can cause many of the symptoms" -TUCK
Tucker found the "yellow powder" suggestive -TUCK
"little research has been done on the chronic effects of tricothecene exposures." -TUCK
when they were paired, Rueda noted, "the potency rose by 160 to 1600 times" -interview with the author
vaccinations weakened their immune systems and made them vulnerable -Leading Edge Feb. 13, 1996
simultaneous vaccines... "VAC-A1" and "VAC-A2" - Leading Edge Feb. 13, 1996

had failed to develop antibodies to the polio vaccine -CNN
one set of such factors could be exposure to chemical warfare agents. -SHAYS
"Shay's Hearing" PR Newswire March 28, 1997
more than 3,900 US Marine volunteers had been injected
- Journal of Infectious Diseases Dec., 1976
the University of Maryland was also testing these germ warfare mycoplasmas on civilians – "Army said University of Maryland to do Germ Studies" Baltimore Sun, April 1, 1977
the University of Glasgow had found a commonality -CNN
Non-deployed military personnel exhibited the same antibody response as the general population. -CNN
factors perturbing these interactions may be inducing this unexpected outcome." -CNN
"forced skyward vapors and toxic by-products from chemical agents." -CNN
OP weakened the brain, allowing PB to cross the "blood-brain barrier" -USNWR
Hare credits doxycycline with giving him a new life. -BETTER
JAMA raised doubts -BETTER
Joy Chavez warned veterans not to treat chemical exposures – GWVM posting
the detection of genetic material in the blood of Persian Gulf War veterans. -FLORIDA
RNA can be isolated from the serum of Gulf War veterans - FLORIDA
microbes are contributing to the illnesses of returning vets and their families -FLORIDA
"seeing chronic diseases that have some viral component to them." -FLORIDA
"an important first step" -FLORIDA
"Illness development actually requires a combination of several events," -FLORIDA
"The discovery of the activation of (HERV) could be the keys," - TUITE
Garth Nicholson and the Centers for Disease Control proposed a joint project -GWVM posting Aug. 1, 1996 (Dannie Wolf)

18. MARKERS

veterans and exposures to chemicals, including chemical nerve agents." -UT
The artificial intelligence spotted three distinctive syndromes. -UT
a rare condition called organophosphate-induced delayed polyneuropathy. -UT
just what you would expect from chemical nerve damage. -UT
Post-Traumatic Stress Disorder, combat stress had been eliminated -UT
"This indicates a synergistic effect" -UT
the three syndromes -GENIE

"I'd be much more concerned about stress and PB than DEET and PB." -OL

"DoD should have known better." – interview with the author

Nicholson found that veterans are often deficient in vitamins B, C and E -GWVM posting

minerals...needed for nerve, metabolic and brain functioning - VITS

Contact with DU "results in the breakdown of the immune system" -GWVM posting

"He was charged with illegally 'releasing ionizing radiation'." -New York Times, Jan. 1, 1993

Most brands of vitamins and minerals passed right through the body. -VITS

GW casualties – are cautioned against popping handfuls of high-potency vitamins -VITS

help themselves by avoiding re-exposure to certain chemical -VITS

2/10ths of a millirem of gamma radiation given off every hour -AJC

"It's got to be some kind of viral or bacterial infection." -Reuter, Oct 21, 1996

"Communities have been fighting for 20 years." – interview with the author

Army acknowledged that "the low level radioactivity poses an environmental concern" – Draft Environmental Impact Statement, April 1991, U.S. Army, titled "Closure of Jefferson Proving Grounds in Indiana and Realignment to Yuma Proving Ground, AZ." Also, Indiana Department of Environmental Management, report to the Governor. U.S. Army Jefferson Proving Ground evaluation. April 20th, 1988.

Caffeine, sugar, junk foods, fatty foods, MREs, and alcohol should also be avoided -VITS

Nicholson also recommends taking a 15 or 20 minute dry sauna -GWVM posting

Hypericum helped repair her damaged nerves. -GWVM posting

"These abnormalities are clearly evident in the subjects with GWS -GWVM posting

A sheep survey published in 1997 -GWVM posting

the VA promised that "carefully controlled scientific studies" -VA

Oregon Center for Research and Dr. Jackson -PORTLAND

"And guess what...it came back positive!" -GWVM posting

Wentz – USANA promotional material and taped interviews

Chlorine exposure should also be avoided. – TOO SENS

"That's it," Moss told his US veterans audience -GWVM posting

DoD announced a "Specialized Care Program" for selected military personnel – Suzanne Des Marais Clinical Coordinator 202-782-6563   Fax: 202-782-3539 The Gulf War Health Center at the Walter Reed Army Medical Center in Washington, DC. Bldg. 2, WD 64, 6900 Georgia Avenue NW, Washington, DC 20307

Douglas S Schrum **dschrum@erols.com**
Tuite was speaking as the director of the Interdisciplinary Sciences department – ChronicIllnet: "**http://www.chronicillnet.org/**".
"It's very clear we're going to have to be following up a lot of issues." -AP May 8, 1997
"There is no evidence to confirm or deny chemical presence" -AP May 8, 1997
"the pill was not, has never been and would never be approved" -Email to the author
GWI patients who were never sent to the Persian Gulf – but were vaccinated – GWVM posting
"there may be as many as 30 combined causes!" -GWVM posting
their husbands' semen "burned like ammonia" -HOME
"possibly resulting in enhanced polyamine synthesis" -TUITE
James Tuite had uncovered 23 separate air attacks on CBW sites. -JIM'S
many more pages of chemical logs had been "lost" -CNN, Feb. 27, 1997
he had never seen the logs or other reports of the chemical attacks -CNN, Dec. 6, 1996
the Pentagon confirmed that nearly 100,000 US troops could have been exposed – CNN, July 24, 1997
"probably are unrelated to mysterious maladies reported by some Gulf War veterans." -AP July 23, 1997
treatment. Based on this doctrine, a chemical warfare agent attack might carry a variety of nerve agents, vesicant and blood agents, blister agents, and biotoxins. -RIEGLE

19. TREATMENT

Garth Nicholson treatment – email, author's interview, statement to Congress July, 1997
Dr. Colgan recommendations – The New Nutrition by Dr. Michael Colgan, Apple Publishing, 1995
Dr. Myron Wentz discoveries – USANA video, literature
brain studies and neuron repair – New Nutrition

20. BAD BLOOD

a synthetic chemical used in the experimental inoculations against HIV -ROD
DoD put out emergency orders for doxycycline -GWVM posting
the vaccines had been laced the experimental adjuvant squalene or mf59 – interview with the author
Deaths related to diarrheal diseases have tripled; 28 percent of Iraqi children are stunted in growth. – "Legacy Of The Last War: Half A Million Children Die In Iraq" by Rebecca Toledo Worker's World December 7, 1995

June 3, 1997 By Waiel Faleh a new palace in the middle of Baghdad -Tony Picou, Mission Project

even imports of pencils are banned -"Ecological decay – a serious side-effect of sanctions" by Ibrahim J. Ibrahim, The Baghdad Observer September 26, 1995

"Since the end of the U.S. war against Iraq in 1991, some 576,000 children have died -"Legacy Of The Last War: Half A Million Children Die In Iraq" by Rebecca Toledo December 7, 1995 IAC

Iraq's annual budget for purchasing medicines -UNICEF press release Oct. 5, 1996

Albright replied that it was. -"US Policies Killing Children In Iraq" by S. Amjad Hussain June 14, 1997 Toledo, Ohio, The Blade, the Wisdom Fund www.twf.org

"Around 4,500 children under the age of five are dying here every month from hunger and disease."
-Oct. 5, 1996 Xinhua News Agency

the price of wheat flour in 1995 was 11,667 times more than it had sold for in 1989.
- UNICEF press release Oct. 5, 1996

Iraq had handed a 639 page report on its biological weapons – Reuter Sept. 7, 1997

By the time he sat down, another child had died in Iraq. -Hussain, The Blade

"Mr. Butler can give us his opinion, Dejammet said. '"But that's only his opinion."
-South News Nov. 1, 1997
(www.sma.org)

"Sarin Poisoning on Tokyo Subway"
-The Southern Medical Journal, June 1997
Sadayoshi Ohbu, Akira Yamashina, Nobukatsu Takasu, Tatsuo Yamaguchi, Tetsuo Murai, Kanzoh Nakano, Yukio Matsui, Ryuzo Mikami, Kenji Sakurai, and Shigeaki Hinohara

Gulf soldiers had told that their anthrax vaccines contained Recombinant DNA – The New York Native, Neenyah Ostrom, February 26,1996

"If anything it has increased due to the no treatment policy of the VA," -interview with the author

21. VOICES FROM THE STORM

All quotes courtesy of the GWVM network.

Shaon Sabah's poem to a "Blind, deaf and dumb world" courtesy of RTV news service

all other references, Scorched Earth
"Corporations rule as governments cower and flee" by Maude Barlow Victoria Times-Colonist, Nov 6, 1996
Stimson was authorized to "take the lead on all aspects of biological warfare." -EMERGE
"lest it lead to yet another method of mass killing "-etimes@teleport.com
He warned "of the possibilities of worldwide spread of infectious disease." -EMERGE

APPENDIX II

INVOICES of Bio-Warfare Agents Shipped from the USA to Baghdad with White House Approval.

INVOICES (EXPORTED)

Date: February 8, 1985 Sent To: Iraq Atomic Energy Agency Materials Shipped: Ustilago nuda (Jensen) Rostrup

Date: February 22, 1985 Sent To: Ministry of Higher Education Materials Shipped: Histoplasma capsulatum var. farciminosum (ATCC 32136) Class III pathogen

Date: July 11, 1985 Sent To: Middle and Near East Regional A Material Shipped: Histoplasma capsulatum var. farciminosum (ATCC 32136) Class III pathogen

Date: May 2, 1986 Sent To: Ministry of Higher Education Materials Shipped:

1. Bacillus Anthracis Cohn (ATCC 10) Batch # 08-20-82 (2 each) Class III pathogen

2. Bacillus Subtilis (Ehrenberg) Cohn (ATCC 82) Batch # 06-20-84 (2 each)

3. Clostridium botulinum Type A (ATCC 3502) Batch # 07-07-81 (3 each) Class III pathogen

4. Clostridium perfringens (Weillon and Zuber) Hauduroy, et al (ATCC 3624) Batch # 10-85SV (2 each)

5. Bacillus subtilis (ATCC 6051) Batch # 12-06-84 (2 each)

6. Francisella tularensis var. tularensis Olsufiev (ATCC 6223) Batch # 05-14-79 (2 each) Avirulent, suitable for preparations of diagnotic antigens

7. Clostridium tetani (ATCC 9441) Batch # 03-84 (3 each) Highly toxigenic

8. Clostridium botulinum Type E (ATCC 9564) Batch # 03-02-79 (2 each) Class III pathogen

9. Clostridium tetani (ATCC 10779) Batch # 04-24-84S (3 each)

~ 407 ~

10. Clostridium perfringens (ATCC 12916) Batch #08-14-80 (2 each) Agglutinating type 2

11. Clostridium perfringens (ATCC 13124) Batch #07-84SV (3 each) Type A, alpha-toxigenic, produces lecithinase C.J. Appl.

12. Bacillus Anthracis (ATCC 14185) Batch #01-14-80 (3 each) G.G. Wright (Fort Detrick) V770-NP1-R. Bovine Anthrax Class III pathogen

13. Bacillus Anthracis (ATCC 14578) Batch #01-06-78 (2 each) Class III pathogen

14. Bacillus megaterium (ATCC 14581) Batch #04-18-85 (2 each)

15. Bacillus megaterium (ATCC 14945) Batch #06-21-81 (2 each)

16. Clostridium botulinum Type E (ATCC 17855) Batch # 06-21-71 Class III pathogen

17. Bacillus megaterium (ATCC 19213) Batch #3-84 (2 each)

18. Clostridium botulinum Type A (ATCC 19397) Batch # 08-18-81 (2 each) Class III pathogen

19. Brucella abortus Biotype 3 (ATCC 23450) Batch # 08-02-84 (3 each) Class III pathogen

20. Brucella abortus Biotype 9 (ATCC 23455) Batch # 02-05-68 (3 each) Class III pathogen

21. Brucella melitensis Biotype 1 (ATCC 23456) Batch # 03-08-78 (2 each) Class III pathogen

22. Brucella melitensis Biotype 3 (ATCC 23458) Batch # 01-29-68 (2 each) Class III pathogen

23. Clostribium botulinum Type A (ATCC 25763) Batch # 8-83 (2 each) Class III pathogen

24. Clostridium botulinum Type F (ATCC 35415) Batch # 02-02-84 (2 each) Class III pathogen

Date: August 31, 1987 Sent To: State Company for Drug Industries Materials Shipped:

1. Saccharomyces cerevesiae (ATCC 2601) Batch # 08-28-08 (1 each)

2. Salmonella choleraesuis subsp. choleraesuis Serotype typhi (ATCC 6539) Batch # 06-86S (1 each)

3. Bacillus subtillus (ATCC 6633) Batch # 10-85 (2 each)

4. Klebsiella pneumoniae subsp. pneumoniae (ATCC 10031) Batch # 08-13-80 (1 each)

5. Escherichia coli (ATCC 10536) Batch # 04-09-80 (1 each)

6. Bacillus cereus (11778) Batch #05-85SV (2 each)

7. Staphylococcus epidermidis (ATCC 12228) Batch # 11-86s (1 each)

8. Bacillus pumilus (ATCC 14884) Batch # 09-08-80 (2 each)

Date: July 11, 1988 Sent To: Iraq Atomic Energy Commission Materials Shipped:

1. Escherichia coli (ATCC 11303) Batch # 04-875 Phase host

2. Cauliflower Mosaic Caulimovirus (ATCC 45031) Batch # 06-14-85 Plant Virus

3. Plasmid in Agrobacterium Tumefaciens (ATCC 37349) (Ti plasmid for co-cultivation with plant integration vectors in E. Coli) Batch # 05-28-85

Date: April 26, 1988 Sent To:: Iraq Atomic Energy Commission Materials Shipped:

1. Hulambda4x-8, clone: human hypoxanthine phosphor-ibosyltransferase (HPRT) Chromosome(s): X q26.1 (ATCC 57236) Phage vector Suggest host: E coli

2. Hulambda14-8, clone: human hypoxanthine phosphor-ibosyltransferase (HPRT) Chromosome(s): X q26.1 (ATCC 57240) Phage vector Suggested host: E coli

3. Hulambda15, clone: human hypoxanthine phosphor-ibosyltransferase (HPRT) Chromosome(s): X q26.1 (ATCC 57242) Phage vector Suggested host: E. coli

Date: August 31, 1987 Sent To: Iraq Atomic Energy Commission Materials Shipped:

1. Escherichia coli (ATCC 23846) Batch # 07-29-83 (1 each)

2. Escherichia coli (ATCC 33694) Batch # 05-87 (1 each)

Date: September 29, 1988 Sent To: Ministry of Trade Materials Shipped:

1. Bacillus anthracis (ATCC 240) Batch #05-14-63 (3 each) Class III pathogen

2. Bacillus anthracis (ATCC 938) Batch #1963 (3 each) Class III pathogen

3. Clostridium perfringens (ATCC 3629) Batch #10-23-85 (3 each)

4. Clostridium perfringens (ATCC 8009) Batch #03-30-84 (3 each)

5. Bacillus anthracis (ATCC 8705) Batch #06-27-62 (3 each) Class III pathogen

6. Brucella abortus (ATCC 9014) Batch #05-11-66 (3 each) Class III pathogen

7. Clostridium perfringens (ATCC 10388) Batch #06-01-73 (3 each)

8. Bacillus anthracis (ATCC 11966) Batch #05-05-70 (3 each) Class III pathogen

9. Clostridium botulinum Type A Batch # 07-86 (3 each) Class III pathogen

10. Bacillus cereus (ATCC 33018) Batch # 04-83 (3 each)

11. Bacillus ceres (ATCC 33019) Batch # 03-88 (3 each)

Date: January 31, 1989 Sent To: Iraq Atomic Energy Commission Materials Shipped:

1. PHPT31, clone: human hypoxanthine phosphoribosyltransferase (HPRT) Chromosome(s): X q26.1 (ATCC 57057)

2. Plambda500, clone: human hypoxanthine phosphoribosyltransferase pseudogene (HPRT) Chromosome(s): 5 p14-p13 (ATCC 57212)

Date: January 17, 1989 Sent To: Iraq Atomic Energy Commission Materials Shipped:

1. Hulambda4x-8, clone: human hypoxanthine phosphoribosyl-transferase (HPRT) Chromosomes(s): X q26.1 (ATCC 57237) Phage vector; Suggested host: E. coli
2. Hulambda14, clone: human hypoxanthine phosphoribosyl-transferase (HPRT) Chromosome(s): X q26.1 (ATCC 57540), Cloned from human lymphoblast, Phase vector Suggested host: E. coli

3. Hulambda15, clone: human hypoxanthine phosphoribosyl-transferase (HPRT) Chromosome(s): X q26.1 (ATCC 57241) Phage vector; Suggested host: E. coli

Additionally, the Centers for Disease Control has compiled a listing of biological materials shipped to Iraq prior to the Gulf War. The listing covers the period from October 1, 1984 (when the CDC began keeping records) through October 13, 1993. The following materials with biological warfare significance were shipped to Iraq during this period.

Date: November 28, 1989 Sent To: University of Basrah, College of Science, Department of Biology Materials Shipped:

1. Enterococcus faecalis

2. Enterococcus faecium

3. Enterococcus avium

4. Enterococcus raffinosus

5. Enteroccus gallinarium

6. Enterococcus durans

7. Enteroccus hirae

8. Streptococcus bovis (etiologic)

Date: April 21, 1986 Sent To: Officers City Al-Muthanna, Quartret 710, Street 13, Close 69, House 28/I, Baghdad, Iraq Materials Shipped:

1. 1 vial botulinum toxoid (non-infectious)

Date: March 10, 1986 Sent To: Officers City Al-Muthanna, Quartret 710, Street 13, Close 69 House 28/I, Baghdad, Iraq Materials Shipped:

1. 1 vial botulinum toxoid #A2 (non-infectious)

Date: June 25, 1985 Sent To: University of Baghdad, College of Medicine, Department of Microbiology Materials Shipped:

1. 3 years cultures (etiologic) Candida sp.

Date: May 21, 1985 Sent To: Basrah, Iraq Materials Shipped:

1. Lyophilized arbovirus seed (etiologic)

2. West Nile Fever Virus

Date: April 26, 1985 Sent To: Minister of Health, Ministry of Health, Baghdad, Iraq Materials Shipped:

1. 8 vials antigen and antisera (r. rickettsii and r. typhi) to diagnose rickettsial infections (non-infectious)

APPENDIX III

Vesicants and Blood Agents

Lewisite – A vesicant toxic agent, industrial lewisite is a dark brown liquid with a strong smell. Lewisite is a contact poison with practically no period of latent effect. Lewisite vapors cause irritation to the eyes and upper respiratory tract. According to the Centers for Disease Control, lewisite would cause stinging and burning. Its smell, generally characterized as the strong smell of geraniums, could be confused with the smell of ammonia (the reaction to which is regulated by pain fibers rather than smell). Iraqi stores of lewisite were not located after the war according to the Department of Defense.

Cyanogen Chloride – The French first suggested the use of cyanogen chloride as a toxic agent. U.S. analysts have reported that it is capable of penetrating gas mask filters. Partially soluble in water, it dissolves well in organic solvents. It is absorbed easily into porous materials; its military state is a gas. Cyanogen chloride is a quick acting toxic agent. Upon contact with the eyes or respiratory organs, it injures immediately. Lethal exposures result in loss of consciousness, convulsions and paralysis.

Hydrogen Cyanide – A colorless liquid smelling of bitter almonds, hydrogen cyanide is a very strong, quick acting poison. Hydrogen cyanide affects unprotected humans through the respiratory organs and during the ingestion of contaminated food and water. It inhibits the enzymes which regulate the intra-cell oxidant-restorative process. As a result, the cells of the nervous system, especially those affecting breathing are injured, which in turn leads to quick death. An important feature of hydrogen cyanide is the absence of a period of latent effect. The military state of hydrogen cyanide is a gas. The toxic and physiologic properties of hydrogen cyanide permit it to be used effectively in munitions – predominantly in rocket launched artillery. Death occurs after intoxication due to paralysis of the heart. Non-lethal doses do not cause intoxication.

Blister Agents – According to the material safety data sheet (MSDS) for sulfur mustard gas (HD) prepared by the U.S. Army Chemical Research, Development and Engineering Center, Aberdeen Proving Ground, Maryland, "Chronic exposure to HD can cause skin sensitization, chronic lung impairment, cough, shortness of breath, chest pain, and cancer of the mouth, throat, respiratory tract, skin, and leukemia. It may also cause birth defects.

The U.S. Army Chemical and Biological Defense Command lists the current detector sensitivity threshold for the M256A1 kits, a commonly used piece of chemical agent detection equipment in the Gulf War, as 2.0 mg/m3. According to the Material Data Safety Sheets for sulfur mustard, total weight average exposures of greater than .003mg/m3 over an 8 hr. period requires the use of protective equipment. Therefore, the detection kit would not detect the agent until the amount of agent present exceeded the safety threshold by a factor of over 660. The M8A1 automatic alarms do not detect blister agent.

Mustard Gas – This is a colorless, oily liquid which dissolves poorly in water, but relatively well in organic solvents, petroleum, lubricant products, and other toxic agents. The injurious effect of mustard gas is associated with its ability to inhibit many enzyme systems of the body. This, in turn, prevents the intra-cell exchange of chemicals and leads to necrosis of the tissue. Death is associated mainly with necrosis of the tissue of the central nervous system. Mustard gas has a period of latent effect (the first signs of injury appear after 2-12 hours), but does not act cumulatively. It does not have any known antidotes. In military use it can come in gas, aerosol, and droplet form. It therefore acts through inhalation, cutaneously, perorally and directly through the blood stream. The toxic and physico-chemical properties of mustard gas allow it to be used in all types of munitions.

Related Chemical Agent Information

Committee staff has learned that Iraq may have acquired any one of a number of the Soviet binary novachok ("newcomer") series of chemical warfare agent compounds or information relevant to the development of those compounds. This series of chemical warfare agents reportedly contains both lethal and debilitating agents. According to a confidential Committee source, if the Iraqis had obtained samples of these compounds they could be easily analyzed and produced with readily available materials. Several of these compounds are described as agents that even in microdoses can have long lasting effects.

These agents are described as inducing myosis, vomiting, memory loss, involuntary motions and internal organ dysfunction. Many of these materials are also described as having mutagenic effects. These materials are, according to the source, stored in the lipids (body fats) and have no known antidotes. In addition, according to the Committee source, the Soviets were believed to have conducted research in a number of dioxin-based chemical warfare agents, and on at least one agent that could be used to contaminate drinking water supplies. Committee staff is conducting further inquiries to determine if Iraq may have had access to any of these compounds.

Biotoxins -Biotoxins are natural poisons, chiefly of cellular structure. A distinction is made between exotoxins which are given off by an organism while it is alive, and endotoxins which are given off after a cell's death. The exotoxins cause the injurious effects of biological weapons, but endotoxins guarantee the effects of chemical weapons and do not cause the widespread disease outbreaks associated with biological warfare. Some examples of biotoxins include botulinus toxin and staphylococcic enterotoxin.

APPENDIX IV

Biological Warfare Capability

According to the U.N., the Iraqi biological warfare program was initiated in mid-1986 at Salman Pak. UNSCOM inspectors discovered evidence of research into certain biological agents including botulinus toxin and anthrax – as well as organisms responsible for gas gangrene, tetanus and brucellosis, components of a biological weapons program which was not defensive in nature. In four years of work prior to the war, only 10 papers were published. These research programs focused on Iraqi efforts to isolate the most pathogenic spores. They also did research on the aerosolization and on the environmental survivability of some of these biological materials according to the United Nations.

While the Department of Defense maintains that the Iraqi military did not weaponize its biological warfare program, UNSCOM is less certain, reporting that their degree of confidence that weaponization did not occur is low. In fact, readily high performance agricultural aerosol generators could easily be converted to both decontaminate areas in which chemicals are used and to aerosolize biological and chemical warfare agents.

Other ways in which biological materials could have been weaponized include the use of Iraqi 250 and 500 lb bombs, aerial rockets, unmanned aerial vehicles, FAW ground-to-ground missiles, helicopters and Iraqi aircraft. The Committee has received several reports of Iraqi helicopters penetrating Saudi airspace during the war by flying at low levels through the wadis and of Iraqi aircraft penetrating the area over the northern Persian Gulf.

According to UNSCOM, indications that suggested that the program was offensive in nature include:

> * No declared links between the BW defense program and medical corps research.

> * No links between aerosolization research and research on defensive filters.

The United Nations said that the Biological Inspection was initiated on August 8, 1991 at Salman Pak. The inspection was delayed because of the need to extensively immunize the members of the inspection team. The Salman Pak facility was razed one week prior to the arrival of the inspection team.

The United States is aware of the Iraqi potential for using biological weapons. The employment of biological agents in a "cocktail" mix with chemical warfare agents is consistent with Soviet military doctrine. It is clear that biological weapons are much more difficult than chemical weapons to detect and defend against. Some of the symptoms experienced by veterans suffering from Persian Gulf Syndrome are consistent with biological warfare agent use. Verification will require sophisticated medical diagnosis, which to date has not been publicly undertaken.

The question of whether U.S. forces were attacked with a biological agent is problematic. According to Chemical/Biological Program: A Department of Defense Perspective, "it has been recognized that our biological defense program was inadequate. Credible analysis indicated that optimal employment of biological agents could result in a significantly large hazard area." It further cites a memo from the Chairman of the Joint Chiefs of Staff to the SECDEF (Secretary of Defense) noting: "inadequate ability to counter BW (biological warfare) attack/BW defense is a priority requirement. The inadequacy of the current biological defense and detection program was also supported by Deputy Secretary of Defense John Deutch in an unclassified May 6, 1994 address delivered at a Department of Defense sponsored counter-proliferation conference at the Los Alamos National Laboratory. According to Deputy Secretary Deutch, the United States has "no biological detection capability deployed with any forces, anywhere."

Novel BW agents created by altering DNA plasmids and vectors are specifically intended to avoid detection. As noted below, several shipments of biological materials that might have been used to carry out such a program were licensed for export from the United States to the Iraq Atomic Energy Commission. In such a program, common intestinal flora such as e. coli could be altered to produce viral, bacterial, or other toxins and would be difficult to treat. If Iraq was successful in developing such agents, diagnosis will continue to elude physicians testing for traditional illnesses. Novel BW agents would certainly elude biological detection devices. There is evidence, based on the nature of the materials imported, that this type of research was being conducted. Since the Iraqi government managed to dismantle much of its biological warfare program prior to the UNSCOM inspections, we can only speculate on how advanced this program might have been.

It has been suggested that if these problems the veterans are experiencing are Gulf War related, then we should be seeing even more serious problems among the Iraqis. Since beginning this investigation we have learned that many Iraqi enemy prisoners of war (EPW) suffered skin rashes, sores, nausea, vomiting, coughing and other medical problems while they were being detained in Saudi Arabia. Many members of units who had close contact with these individuals are now reporting to the Committee symptoms consistent with those being suffered by other Gulf War veterans. In addition, Iraq has claimed a dramatic rise in reported cases of communicable diseases since the end of the Gulf War including typhoid, brucellosis, hepatitis and cholera.

Further, reports of Gulf War illnesses being reported are no longer limited to veterans of the Gulf War. Others reporting manifestation of these symptoms include:

> * Department of Defense civilians who served in the Persian Gulf War.

> * Department of Defense civilians working at the Anniston (AL) Army Depot and the Sharpsite (CA) Army Depot decontaminating equipment which was returned from the Persian Gulf.

> * Spouses, particularly the spouses of male veterans, are reporting the following symptoms: chronic or recurring vaginal yeast infections, menstrual irregularities (excessive bleeding and severe cramping), rashes, fatigue, joint and muscle pain, and memory loss.

> * Children born to veterans prior to the Gulf War. In many cases both male and female children born prior to the war have experienced symptoms similar to those of the veterans and their spouses.

> * Children born following the Gulf war. Some reports have been published which suggest a high rate of miscarriages in the families of Gulf War veterans. Further, several reports have surfaced which suggest that there has been a high rate of physical abnormalities in children born to Gulf War veterans since the war.

APPENDIX V

U.S. Exports of Biological Materials to Iraq

The Senate Committee on Banking, Housing, and Urban Affairs has oversight responsibility for the Export Administration Act. Pursuant to the Act, Committee staff contacted the U.S. Department of Commerce and requested information on the export of biological materials during the years prior to the Gulf War. After receiving this information, we contacted a principal supplier of these materials to determine what, if any, materials were exported to Iraq which might have contributed to an offensive or defensive biological warfare program. Records available from the supplier for the period from 1985 until the present show that during this time, pathogenic (meaning "disease producing"), toxigenic (meaning "poisonous"), and other biological research materials were exported to Iraq pursuant to application and licensing by the U.S. Department of Commerce. Records prior to 1985 were not available, according to the supplier.

These exported biological materials were not attenuated or weakened and were capable of reproduction. According to the Department of Defense's own Report to Congress on the Conduct of the Persian Gulf War, released in April, 1992: "By the time of the invasion of Kuwait, Iraq had developed biological weapons. It's advanced and aggressive biological warfare program was the most advanced in the Arab world... The program probably began late in the 1970s and concentrated on the development of two agents, botulinum toxin and anthrax bacteria.. Large scale production of these agents began in 1989 at four facilities in Baghdad. Delivery means for biological agents ranged from simple aerial bombs and artillery rockets to surface-to-surface missiles."

Included in the approved sales are the following biological materials (which have been considered by various nations for use in war), with their associated disease symptoms:

Bacillus Anthracis: anthrax is a disease producing bacteria identified by the Department of Defense in The Conduct of the Persian Gulf War: Final Report to Congress, as being a major component in the Iraqi biological warfare program.

Anthrax is an often fatal infectious disease due to ingestion of spores. It begins abruptly with high fever, difficulty in breathing, and chest pain. The disease eventually results in septicemia (blood poisoning), and the mortality is high. Once septicemia is ad-

~ 419 ~

vanced, antibiotic therapy may prove useless, probably because the exotoxins remain, despite the death of the bacteria.

Clostridium Botulinum: A bacterial source of botulinum toxin, which causes vomiting, constipation, thirst, general weakness, headache, fever, dizziness, double vision, dilation of the pupils and paralysis of the muscles involving swallowing. It is often fatal.

Histoplasma Capsulatum: causes a disease basically resembling tuberculosis that may cause pneumonia, enlargement of the liver and spleen, anemia, an influenza like illness and an acute inflammatory skin disease marked by tender red nodules, usually on the shins. Reactivated infection usually involves the lungs, the brain, spinal membranes, heart, peritoneum, and the adrenals.

Brucella Melitensis: a bacteria which can cause chronic fatigue, loss of appetite, profuse sweating when at rest, pain in joints and muscles, insomnia, nausea, and damage to major organs.

Clostridium Perfringens: a highly toxic bacteria which causes gas gangrene. The bacteria produce toxins that move along muscle bundles in the body killing cells and producing necrotic tissue that is then favorable for further growth of the bacteria itself. Eventually, these toxins and bacteria enter the bloodstream and cause a systemic illness.

In addition, several shipments of Escherichia Coli (E. Coli) and genetic materials, as well as human and bacterial DNA, were shipped directly to the Iraq Atomic Energy Commission.

The following is a detailed listing of biological materials, provided by the American Type Culture Collection, which were exported to agencies of the government of Iraq pursuant to the issuance of an export licensed by the U.S. Commerce Department:

INVOICES

Date: February 8, 1985 Sent To: Iraq Atomic Energy Agency Materials Shipped: Ustilago nuda (Jensen) Rostrup

Date: February 22, 1985 Sent To: Ministry of Higher Education Materials Shipped: Histoplasma capsulatum var. farciminosum (ATCC 32136) Class III pathogen

Date: July 11, 1985 Sent To: Middle and Near East Regional A Material Shipped: Histoplasma capsulatum var. farciminosum (ATCC 32136) Class III pathogen

Date: May 2, 1986 Sent To: Ministry of Higher Education Materials Shipped:

1. Bacillus Anthracis Cohn (ATCC 10) Batch #08-20-82 (2 each) Class III athogen

2. Bacillus Subtilis (Ehrenberg) Cohn (ATCC 82) Batch #06-20-84 (2 each)

3. Clostridium botulinum Type A (ATCC 3502) Batch #07-07-81 (3 each) Class III pathogen

4. Clostridium perfringens (Weillon and Zuber) Hauduroy, et al (ATCC 3624) Batch #10-85SV (2 each)

5. Bacillus subtilis (ATCC 6051) Batch #12-06-84 (2 each)

6. Francisella tularensis var. tularensis Olsufiev (ATCC 6223) Batch #05-14-79 (2 each) Avirulent, suitable for preparations of diagnostic antigens

7. Clostridium tetani (ATCC 9441) Batch #03-84 (3 each) Highly toxigenic

8. Clostridium botulinum Type E (ATCC 9564) Batch #03-02-79 (2 each) Class III pathogen

9. Clostridium tetani (ATCC 10779) Batch #04-24-84S (3 each)

10. Clostridium perfringens (ATCC 12916) Batch #08-14-80 (2 each) Agglutinating type 2

11. Clostridium perfringens (ATCC 13124) Batch #07-84SV (3 each) Type A, alpha-toxigenic, produces lecithinase C.J. Appl.

12. Bacillus Anthracis (ATCC 14185) Batch #01-14-80 (3 each) G.G. Wright (Fort Detrick) V770-NP1-R. Bovine Anthrax Class III pathogen

13. Bacillus Anthracis (ATCC 14578) Batch #01-06-78 (2 each) Class III pathogen

14. Bacillus megaterium (ATCC 14581) Batch #04-18-85 (2 each)

15. Bacillus megaterium (ATCC 14945) Batch #06-21-81 (2 each)

16. Clostridium botulinum Type E (ATCC 17855) Batch # 06-21-71 Class III pathogen

17. Bacillus megaterium (ATCC 19213) Batch #3-84 (2 each)

18. Clostridium botulinum Type A (ATCC 19397) Batch #08-18-81 (2 each) Class III pathogen

19. Brucella abortus Biotype 3 (ATCC 23450) Batch #08-02-84 (3 each) Class III pathogen

20. Brucella abortus Biotype 9 (ATCC 23455) Batch #02-05-68 (3 each) Class III pathogen

21. Brucella melitensis Biotype 1 (ATCC 23456) Batch #03-08-78 (2 each) Class III pathogen

22. Brucella melitensis Biotype 3 (ATCC 23458) Batch #01-29-68 (2 each) Class III pathogen

23. Clostribium botulinum Type A (ATCC 25763) Batch #8-83 (2 each) Class III pathogen

24. Clostridium botulinum Type F (ATCC 35415) Batch #02-02-84 (2 each) Class III pathogen

Date: August 31, 1987 Sent To: State Company for Drug Industries Materials Shipped:

1. Saccharomyces cerevesiae (ATCC 2601) Batch #08-28-08 (1 each)

2. Salmonella choleraesuis subsp. choleraesuis Serotype typhi (ATCC 6539) Batch #06-86S (1 each)

3. Bacillus subtillus (ATCC 6633) Batch #10-85 (2 each)

4. Klebsiella pneumoniae subsp. pneumoniae (ATCC 10031) Batch #08-13-80 (1 each)

5. Escherichia coli (ATCC 10536) Batch # 04-09-80 (1 each)

6. Bacillus cereus (11778) Batch #05-85SV (2 each)

7. Staphylococcus epidermidis (ATCC 12228) Batch #11-86s (1 each)

8. Bacillus pumilus (ATCC 14884) Batch # 09-08-80 (2 each)

Date: July 11, 1988 Sent To: Iraq Atomic Energy Commission Materials Shipped:

1. Escherichia coli (ATCC 11303) Batch #04-875 Phase host

2. Cauliflower Mosaic Caulimovirus (ATCC 45031) Batch #06-14-85 Plant Virus

3. Plasmid in Agrobacterium Tumefaciens (ATCC 37349) (Ti plasmid for co-cultivation with plant integration vectors in E. Coli) Batch #05-28-85

Date: April 26, 1988 Sent To: Iraq Atomic Energy Commission Materials Shipped:

1. Hulambda4x-8, clone: human hypoxanthine phosphoribosyl-transferase (HPRT) Chromosome(s): X q26.1 (ATCC 57236) Phage vector Suggest host: E coli

2. Hulambda14-8, clone: human hypoxanthine phosphoribosyl-transferase (HPRT) Chromosome(s): X q26.1 (ATCC 57240) Phage vector Suggested host: E coli

3. Hulambda15, clone: human hypoxanthine phosphoribosyl-transferase (HPRT) -Chromosome(s): X q26.1 (ATCC 57242) Phage vector Suggested host: E. coli

Date: August 31, 1987 Sent To: Iraq Atomic Energy Commission Materials Shipped:

1. Escherichia coli (ATCC 23846) Batch #07-29-83 (1 each)

2. Escherichia coli (ATCC 33694) Batch #05-87 (1 each)

Date: September 29, 1988 Sent To: Ministry of Trade Materials Shipped:

1. Bacillus anthracis (ATCC 240) Batch #05-14-63 (3 each) Class III pathogen

2. Bacillus anthracis (ATCC 938) Batch #1963 (3 each) Class III pathogen

3. Clostridium perfringens (ATCC 3629) Batch #10-23-85 (3 each)

4. Clostridium perfringens (ATCC 8009) Batch #03-30-84 (3 each)

5. Bacillus anthracis (ATCC 8705) Batch #06-27-62 (3 each) Class III pathogen

6. Brucella abortus (ATCC 9014) Batch #05-11-66 (3 each) Class III pathogen

7. Clostridium perfringens (ATCC 10388) Batch #06-01-73 (3 each)

8. Bacillus anthracis (ATCC 11966) Batch #05-05-70 (3 each) Class III pathogen

9. Clostridium botulinum Type A Batch #07-86 (3 each) Class III pathogen

10. Bacillus cereus (ATCC 33018) Batch #04-83 (3 each)

11. Bacillus ceres (ATCC 33019) Batch #03-88 (3 each)

Date: January 31, 1989 Sent To: Iraq Atomic Energy Commission Materials Shipped:

1. PHPT31, clone: human hypoxanthine phosphoribosyl-transferase (HPRT) Chromosome(s): X q26.1 (ATCC 57057)

2. Plambda500, clone: human hypoxanthine phosphoribosyl-transferase pseudogene (HPRT) Chromosome(s): 5 p14-p13 (ATCC 57212)

Date: January 17, 1989 Sent To: Iraq Atomic Energy Commission Materials Shipped:

1. Hulambda4x-8, clone: human hypoxanthine phosphoribosyl-transferase (HPRT) Chromosomes(s): X q26.1 (ATCC 57237) Phage vector; Suggested host: E. coli

2. Hulambda14, clone: human hypoxanthine phosphoribosyl-transferase (HPRT) Chromosome(s): X q26.1 (ATCC 57540), Cloned from human lymphoblast, Phase vector Suggested host: E. coli

3. Hulambda15, clone: human hypoxanthine phosphoribosyl-transferase (HPRT) Chromosome(s): X q26.1 (ATCC 57241) Phage vector; Suggested host: E. coli

Additionally, the Centers for Disease Control has compiled a listing of biological materials shipped to Iraq prior to the Gulf War. The listing covers the period from October 1, 1984 (when the CDC began keeping records) through October 13, 1993. The following materials with biological warfare significance were shipped to Iraq during this period.

Date: November 28, 1989 Sent To: University of Basrah, College of Science, Department of Biology Materials Shipped:

1. Enterococcus faecalis

2. Enterococcus faecium

3. Enterococcus avium

4. Enterococcus raffinosus

5. Enteroccus gallinarium

6. Enterococcus durans

7. Enteroccus hirae

8. Streptococcus bovis (etiologic)

Date: April 21, 1986 Sent To: Officers City Al-Muthanna, Quartret 710, Street 13, Close 69, House 28/I, Baghdad, Iraq Materials Shipped:

1. 1 vial botulinum toxoid (non-infectious)

Date: March 10, 1986 Sent To: Officers City Al-Muthanna, Quartret 710, Street 13, Close 69 House 28/I, Baghdad, Iraq Materials Shipped:

1. 1 vial botulinum toxoid #A2 (non-infectious)

Date: June 25, 1985 Sent To: University of Baghdad, College of Medicine, Department of Microbiology Materials Shipped:

1. 3 years cultures (etiologic) Candida sp.

Date: May 21, 1985 Sent To: Basrah, Iraq Materials Shipped:

1. Lyophilized arbovirus seed (etiologic)

2. West Nile Fever Virus

Date: April 26, 1985 Sent To: Minister of Health, Ministry of Health, Baghdad, Iraq Materials Shipped:

1. 8 vials antigen and antisera (r. rickettsii and r. typhi) to diagnose rickettsial infections (non-infectious)

APPENDIX VI

UNSCOM Biological Warfare Inspections

UNSCOM inspections uncovered evidence that the government of Iraq was conducting research on pathogen enhancement on the following biological warfare related materials:

o bacillus anthracis o clostridium botulinum
o clostridium perfringens o brucella abortis
o brucella melentensis o francisella tularensis
o clostridium tetani

In addition, the UNSCOM inspections revealed that biological warfare related simulant research was being conducted on the following materials:

o bacillus subtillus o bacillus ceres o bacillus megatillus

UNSCOM reported to Committee staff that a biological warfare inspection (BW3) was conducted at the Iraq Atomic Energy Commission in 1993. This suggests that the Iraqi government may have been experimenting with the materials cited above (E. Coli and rDNA) in an effort to create genetically altered micro-organisms (novel biological warfare agents).

The Centers for Disease Control has compiled a listing of biological materials shipped to Iraq prior to the Gulf War. The listing covers the period from October 1, 1984 (when the CDC began keeping records) through October 13, 1993. The following materials with biological warfare significance were shipped to Iraq during this period.

Date: November 28, 1989 Sent To: University of Basrah, College of Science, Department of Biology Materials Shipped:

1. Enterococcus faecalis

2. Enterococcus faecium

3. Enterococcus avium

4. Enterococcus raffinosus

5. Enteroccus gallinarium

6. Enterococcus durans

7. Enteroccus hirae

8. Streptococcus bovis (etiologic)

Date: April 21, 1986 Sent To: Officers City Al-Muthanna, Quartret 710, Street 13, Close 69, House 28/I, Baghdad, Iraq Materials Shipped:

1. 1 vial botulinum toxoid (non-infectious)

Date: March 10, 1986 Sent To: Officers City Al-Muthanna, Quartret 710, Street 13, Close 69 House 28/I, Baghdad, Iraq Materials Shipped:

1. 1 vial botulinum toxoid #A2 (non-infectious)

Date: June 25, 1985 Sent To: University of Baghdad, College of Medicine, Department of Microbiology Materials Shipped:

1. 3 years cultures (etiologic) Candida sp.

Date: May 21, 1985 Sent To: Basrah, Iraq Materials Shipped:

1. Lyophilized arbovirus seed (etiologic)

2. West Nile Fever Virus

Date: April 26, 1985 Sent To: Minister of Health, Ministry of Health, Baghdad, Iraq Materials Shipped:

1. 8 vials antigen and antisera (r. rickettsii and r. typhi) to diagnose rickettsial infections (non-infectious)

APPENDIX VII

Vietnam vets won $180 million damages Agent Orange dioxins against DOW, Monsanto and other US corporations.

On October 27, 1992, the Committee on Banking, Housing and Urban Affairs held hearings that revealed that the United States had exported chemical, biological, nuclear, and missile-system equipment to Iraq that was converted to military use in Iraq's chemical, biological, and nuclear weapons program. Many of these weapons – weapons that the U.S. and other countries provided critical materials for – were used against US during the war. – TUITE

On February 9, 1994, Chairman Donald W. Riegle, Jr. disclosed on the U.S. Senate floor that the U.S. government actually licensed the export of deadly microorganisms to Iraq. It was later learned that these microorganisms exported by the United States were identical to those the United Nations inspectors found and recovered from the Iraqi biological warfare program. – TUITE

Germ warfare was used on our troops – using biologicals that were made in the United States of America. It was made in Houston, Texas and Boca Raton, Florida. It was passed through the Centers for Disease Control (CDC) and through companies such as American Type Culture Collection (ATCC) in Maryland. It was passed to Saddam Hussein – sold to Saddam Hussein, as late as 1989. Just prior to the war. Drs. Garth and Nancy Nicholson revealed that a Houston company was involved in the manufacture of a biological weapon that was sold to Iraq and was used on American soldiers in the Gulf War. Riegle found out that we had been exporting these biological substances through ATCC. This information is known to every Senator that was in office in 1994. – RILEY

United States companies shipped Saddam Hussein 1,500 gallons of Anthrax. Out of 39 tons of biological warfare agents imported by Iraq from the United States, each ton could have produced ten tons of biological warfare material. – RILEY

Items for the SCUD missiles that were given to Saddam Hussein were made in Connecticut and in Pittsburgh. The Media Bypass article continues, "Because Iraq defaulted on payment for the biological agents received from U.S. companies, American taxpayers ended up stuck with the bill for weapons that were later used against coalition forces." – RILEY

Peter Kawaja

Peter Kawaja operated under a government code name. The reason he did this is that he found out that biological agents were being made in the United States, and he was aware of the fact that it was essentially treason, and that it was wrong, and he went to the CIA, FBI and U.S. Customs and told them that this was going on. He told them that "they are making biological agents in Boca Raton, Florida, and that they are being used for germ warfare." The government then said to him to let them know everything he found out, and they wanted to stay on top of it. – RILEY

Peter was a security systems person that was hired to do security contracts. In doing so, he was able to see what was happening at this plant, called P.I.T, the Product Ingredient Technology plant. This plant was a project of Dr. Barbouti, who is from Houston. His son still lives in Houston. Dr. Barbouti had been involved in the (illegal) sales of arms to Iraq, had originally built the biological warfare plant in Libya, had come to the United States and had cloned the Libyan plant in Boca Raton, Florida. They said they were making a cherry flavoring there. That was the cover story. Well, he got a letter after he signed the contract to do the security arrangement. In the letter, PIT stated that "we forgot to tell you that we need a cyanide detection system." – RILEY

Saddam's plan was to give them a long-term illness that they would bring back to their families. What better way to give a country a disease than to give it to the military, who move all over the country. This cyanide that was to be made in Boca Raton was for Prussian Blue, which is a hydrogen cyanide derivative, and the purpose for its manufacture was that it was placed in the SCUD rockets with the biochemical substances. When the missile blew up, the Prussian Blue would deteriorate the materials of which the gas masks were made, especially the filters. So, even if they did put their protective gear on, it wouldn't work. All the time, they thought the chemical suits were protecting them. Again, this Prussian Blue was made by a company in the United States. - RILEY

When Peter Kawaja continued to get this information and found out about all of this, he then did something the government did not expect him to do. He wire tapped all the telephones at the PIT plant. He wire tapped all the phones at the corporate living quarters of the International Headquarters of IBI International (Ishan Barbouti International). When he wiretapped all of these phones, he heard Congressmen, officials in the Bush administration, high-level world officials, and he found out that he had been had – that this was a joint venture with the United States government. – RILEY

Now, they realized that he had tapped the phone lines, and they served him with a "War Powers Act Subpoena" – the first one ever issued since World War II. It takes an Executive Order from the President to issue this. They came to his business with armed guards and took all his recordings, documents – everything. This is significant. He was not served with the affidavit of the search warrant to go along with it, all of this evidence remains at the Department of Justice and it is being held under "national security" until "the investigation" is "complete." – RILEY

On January 17, 1991, the British press: "Boca Plant begins trail to Washington." You see, what Peter Kawaja did is that he sent a FedEx letter to the NSA telling them terrorists were in the United States making biological weapons, and he wanted President Bush to know. That is when they came and took his documents.
- RILEY

Here are more British headlines, "Congress Probes Linking Gates to Arms Deal" and "Barbouti Acted in Accord with U.S. Plan Toward Iraq" and "Gates and Secord Linked to Iraqi Pipeline". Down here, in the Financial Times of London, July 3, 1991, there is an article "U.S. Cyanide Shipped to Iraq Despite Warnings to CIA", and "Iraqi's Florida Plant Tied to Poison Gas: Export of Chemical Feared". Ishan Barbouti, by the way, died one week before the war began. He is buried under eight feet of cement, "for religious purposes", in London. – RILEY

This is a lawsuit that Peter Kawaja has filed in the Southern District Court of Florida. He is charging war crimes against the Bush administration. He has filed a lawsuit against 100 federal agents. He has accused them of war crimes, concealment, conspiracy, corruption, aiding and abetting, fraud, obstruction of justice, tampering with a witness, and more. – RILEY

It has been in the system for two years now, and he has kept it there. He is saying that they attempted to conceal U.S. Government dealings with terrorists and terrorist nations – the same terrorists the Bush administration had publicly declared war against. – RILEY

Under item "I" in this lawsuit, it reads, "to conceal from the American public, and from American forces, and their families, who were knowingly placed in harm's way, that the same terrorist nations the Bush administration had declared war against, had acquired new weapons of mass destruction from the United States, which American forces could not defend against." When he filed this lawsuit against the U.S. Government, they didn't come back and deny anything. They simply said "we deserve immunity, because we are the United States Government." – RILEY

"I got involved with a project called "Product Ingredient Technology" in Boca Raton, Florida. I was also involved throughout the United States with IBI (Ishan Barbouti International), the builder of Pharma 150, the chemical and biological weapons complex in Rabta, Libya. From my investigation, I found a lot of things that were not legitimate, and I ran. I was green about a lot of these things upon going in. I went to the CIA and FBI, and operated for the U.S. government under a code name, because they said these people were international terrorists and that they were going to prosecute them. However, they did not count on me bugging telephone lines, buildings, and certain other locations throughout the United States. I intercepted the Commodity Credit Corporation, the Banca Nazionale del Lavorro (CCC-BNL), the letters of credit of the BNL, which came from Switzerland, as well as a lot of other communications regarding the Gulf War that was to come. I recorded calls going to and coming from Baghdad, to and from the United States and London, CIA, FBI, FBI counter-intelligence, U.S. Customs, certain politicians and numerous other individuals. This is my information. It is not second-hand."
-KAWAJA

"What I found at the PIT plant was very heinous. I found that a strain of hydrogen cyanide called Prussian Blue was being tested on gas mask filters more than 1 year prior to the Persian Gulf War. This information was known to the President of the United States, George Bush. It was arranged through Trevor Armbrister, a CIA asset and a Senior Editor of Reader's Digest, to fly me to the steps of the White House. Time does not permit me to tell my story, but the information that I want to get out to the American people is that the Gulf War illnesses are actually communicable diseases. The microbes will live almost indefinitely, but for a minimum of seven years. It's on the gas masks, the clothing, the weapons – any of the materials brought back from the Gulf War. I have reports from several different states where civilians that bought some of the clothing, went home and wore them, and now the entire family is in wheel chairs; there have been some deaths as a result of this." -KAWAJA

We do know that the U.S. licensed the export of genetic materials capable of being used to create these types of genetically-altered biological warfare agents to the Iraqi Atomic Energy Commission – an Iraqi governmental agency that conducted biological warfare-related research – prior to the war. One method of creating these genetically altered microorganisms is by exposing them to radiation. The U.S. also licensed the export of several species of brucella to Iraqi governmental agencies.(76) Both Q-fever and Brucellosis are also endemic to the region. -TUITE

* * *

In 1986, the Iraqi government paid nearly 30,000 West German marks to purchase samples of four tricothecene mycotoxins from Sigma-Chemie in Munich, a subsidiary of a St. Louis-based company that manufactures specialty biochemicals for research institutions.

On May 2 of that year, three sets of Clostridium Botulinum Type A – Batch # 07-07-81 – were shipped to Baghdad. On this same day, two-dozen batches of disease-causing bacteriums and plagues – including Anthrax – were also shipped to government-controlled laboratories in Iraq. The anthrax shipment was signed off by G.G. Wright at Fort Detrick.

A particularly nasty bacteria, Clostridium Botulinum causes vomiting, constipation, thirst, general weakness, headache, fever, dizziness, double vision, dilation of the pupils and paralysis of the muscles involving swallowing – often until death.

Its bacterial cousin, Histoplasma Capsulatum, causes a disease resembling tuberculosis. It also causes pneumonia, swelling of the liver and spleen, anemia, a flu-like illness and an acute inflammatory skin disease marked by tender red nodules. Records of the government-run American Type Culture Collection only go back to 1985, when records begin showing government-approved shipments of Histoplasma Capsulatum to the Iraqi Ministry of Higher Education.

Brucella Melitensis is another toxic bacteria. Its symptoms are strikingly familiar to hundreds of thousands of suffering Gulf War vets and their families: chronic fatigue, loss of appetite, profuse sweating when at rest, pain in joints and muscles, insomnia, nausea, and damage to major organs. Clostridium Perfringens, a highly toxic bacteria which causes gas gangrene, was also shipped from US firms to Iraq on at least a dozen occasions between February 8, 1985 to Nov, 28, 1989. This muscle-eating bacteria rots the body from the inside-out. In addition to these deadly and debilitating bacteriums, several shipments of Escherichia Coli (E. Coli) and genetic materials, as well as human and bacterial DNA, were shipped directly to the Iraq Atomic Energy Commission.

These were not a few, freak shipments but part of a deliberate transfer of germ warfare "biologicals" to Saddam Hussein. Between early February, 1985 to late November, 1989 at least 72 shipments of germ warfare materials were made by the US government and its regulated companies to Iraq. West Nile Fever Virus, candida, rickets, Streptococcus.

Even more worrying – and diabolical – were the e-coli shipments, such as the Escherichia coli – Batch # 04-875 – sent to the Iraq Atomic Energy Commission on July 11, 1988.
From: U.S. Chemical and Biological Exports to Iraq and Their Possible Impact on the Health Consequences of the Persian Gulf War Committee Staff Report No. 3: "Chemical Warfare Agent Identification, Chemical Injuries, and Other Findings"; U.S. Senate Committee on Banking, Housing, and Urban Affairs; James J Tuite, III, Principal Investigator; October 27, 1992

SOURCE: "Riegle Report" May 25, 1994 U.S. Senate, Committee on Banking, Housing, and Urban Affairs, Washington, DC.

APPENDIX VIII

Acronyms used in this and related Gulf War books

ASP...Ammunition Storage Point
ANZAC...Australia, New Zealand
Bn...Battalion (Army unit)
CAM...Chemical Agent Monitor
C-3...Commad, Control, communications
CENTCOM..Central Command
CIA...Central Intelligence Agency
Co...Company (Army unit)
CONUS...Continental United States
CSG...Corps Support Group
CSM...Command Sergeant Major
DECON...Decontamination
DIA...Defense Intelligence Agency
Div...Division
DoD...Department of Defense (U.S.)
Du...Depleated uranium
DVA, VA, ...Department of Veterans Affairs
EOD...Explosive Ordnance Disposal
Fwd...Forward
GB...Nerve agent (sarin)
GF...Nerve agent (cyclosarin)
Gulfwatch.....International Veteran's Information/Support Network
Hq...Headquarters
KTO...Kuwaiti Theater of Operations
mm...millimeter
MOD...(British) Ministry of Defense
MOPP...................................Mission Oriented Protective Posture
MSR...Military Supply Route
NBC.................................Nuclear, Biological, and Chemical
NCO...Non-Commissioned Officer
NSA.....................................National Security Agency
NW...northwest
PGIIT...........................Persian Gulf Illnesses Investigation Team
SE...southeast
SITREP...Situation Report
SW...southwest
UN...United Nations
UNSCOM...........................United Nations Special Commission
VIW.................... Voices in the Wilderness – a campaign to end
                          UN/US sanctions

Resource Guide

Earthpulse Press
P. O. Box 201393
Anchorage, Alaska 99520 USA

24 Hours a Day
VISA or Master Card Accepted
Voice Mail Ordering: (888) 690-1277
Fax: (907)696-1277
http://www.earthpulse.com

1. **Earthpulse Flashpoints** is a Microbook series edited by Dr. Nick Begich. Microbooks cover four major areas: government, frontier health sciences, earth science, and new technologies. The goal of the publication is to get hard-to-find information into the hands of individuals on their road to self empowerment and self discovery. For six issues send $24.95 in the U.S. and $30.95 internationally.

2. **Angels Don't Play this HAARP: Advances in Tesla Technology** is a book about non-lethal weapons, mind control, weather warfare and the government's plan to control the environment or maybe even destroy it in the name of national defense. The book is $17.95 Air Mail in the U.S. or $19.95 internationally.

3. **The Coming Energy Revolution** was written by Jeane Manning. The book is about some of the more interesting new energy systems just on the horizon which could revolutionize the production and uses of energy. The book is $15.95 Air Mail in the U.S. or $17.95 internationally.

4. **Eco War** is an award winning video dicumentary produced by William Thomas. It contains exclusive footage of the Gulf fires and oil spills, which aired on CNN and the CBC. Fully narrated with original sound track (26 Minutes). $34.95 in the USand internationally.

5. **The New Nutrition: Medicine for the Next Millennium** by Dr. Michael Colgan is an internationally acclaimed research scientist and best selling author. This book is one of the best books on nutrition available. It is highly recommended for anyone seeking to optimize their health.The book is $17.95 Air Mail in the U.S. or $19.95 internationally.

6. **Natural Earth: The English Standard Reference on Herbal Substances, Volume I: The Herbal Cernter of Healing** by Gary Lockhart is the first in a five part set. This set is the best collection of materials on herbal substances ever assembled in the English language. The book is an 8.5" X 11" format with 288 information packed illustrated pages.The book is $32.95 Air Mail in the U.S. or $35.95 internationally.

* * *

A free catalog of all of our products and publications is available on request.